THE REAL GUIDE

SAN FRANCISCO

AND

THE BAY AREA

G000019893

REAL GUIDE CREDITS

Series Editor: Mark Ellingham
Editorial: Martin Dunford, John Fisher, Jack Holland, Jonathan Buckley,
  Greg Ward, Richard Trillo
US Text Editor: Ellen Sarewitz
Production: Susanne Hillen, Kate Berens
Typesetting: Gail Jammy, Andy Hilliard
Series Design: Andrew Oliver

Many people have been involved in the production of this book, none more so than Martin Dunford, without whose drive and commitment it might never have happened. Thanks also to Matthew Yeomans, for information from the US. Individually, the authors would like to thank:

Deborah thanks to Brett Bennett for his help with research, Debora Matsumoto at Chronicle Books, my tireless families, the Bosleys and the Burtons, for their support, Saly, Irvin and Kayla for fun days out, Toni Ring (and baby) and Paul Derek Gidley for their mercy missions to California, but most of all to Rick "007" Olson and Lebro Turchetti for being themselves.
Jamie thanks to everyone who has helped fill the pages of this book, especially Ramiro Morán, Adrian Sington, Joe Gouig, Karen DeCasas, Blake Riley, Alison Gold, Wayman and Lili, David, Laura and Elliot, Marcia Beales, and dozens of others who've pointed out things along the way. Congratulations to John and Pam, and love to Catherine, Brando, and Judah.

The publishers and authors have done their best to ensure the accuracy and currency of all the information in
San Francisco: The Real Guide; however, they can accept no responsibility for any loss, injury, or
inconvenience sustained by any traveler as a result of information or advice contained in the guide.

Published in the United States and Canada by
Prentice Hall Press
A division of Simon & Schuster Inc.
15 Columbus Circle
New York, NY 10023

Prentice Hall Press and colophons are registered trademarks of Simon & Schuster Inc.

Typeset in Linotron Univers and Century Old Style.
Printed in the United States by R.R. Donnelley & Sons.

Illustrations in Part One and Part Three by Ed Briant.
Basics illustration by Tommy Yamaha. Contexts illustration by Christina Brimage.

Library of Congress Cataloging-in-Publication Data
Bosley, Deborah.
The real guide. San Francisco and the Bay Area / Deborah Bosley and Jamie Jensen.
304p. cm—(The Real Guides)
Includes index.
ISBN 0-13-770744-4 : $11.95
1. San Francisco Bay Area (Calif.)—Description and travel—Guide-books. 2. San Francisco (Calif.)—Description—Guide-books.
I. Jensen, Jamie. II. Titlle. III. Series.
F868.S156B67 1990
917.9404'53—dc20
90-48391 CIP

THE REAL GUIDE

SAN FRANCISCO
AND
THE BAY AREA

Written and researched by

DEBORAH BOSLEY and JAMIE JENSEN

with additional contributions by
BRETT M. BENNETT

Edited by
MARTIN DUNFORD

PRENTICE
HALL
PRESS

NEW YORK LONDON TORONTO SYDNEY TOKYO SINGAPORE

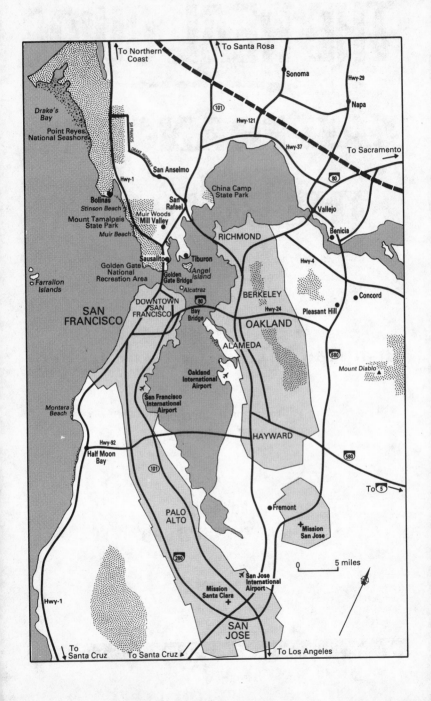

CONTENTS

The Bay Area is so beautiful, I hesitate to preach about heaven while I'm here.

Billy Graham

INTRODUCTION

America's favorite city sits at the edge of the Western World, a location which lends even greater romantic currency to its legend. Arguably the most beautiful, self-proclaimed the most liberal city in the country, and with more platitudes heaped upon it than any other, **San Francisco** is in serious danger of being clichéd to death. But despite being the cosy favorite of the tourist boards, with legions of foreign visitors riding high on the chronically sick dollar—a billion of which go into its coffers every year—it has changed remarkably little over the years, and remains a surprisingly small, almost provincial city, booming throughout the Eighties but still clinging to a few remnants of its radical past.

San Francisco's days as a center of dissent are, however, pretty much over, and apart from a progressive caucus in the gay community, it is a rather complacent and self-satisfied place nowadays, dominated by bumper-sticker-style politics that does little to address the city's undeniable—and growing—problems: drug use and violence are on the increase, and the level of homelessness in the city is a disgrace. Indeed, San Franciscans enjoy a rarified kind of mutual appreciation, priding themselves in being the cultured counterpart to their philistine cousins in LA, the last bastion of civilization on America's self-obsessed western fringe, and less concerned with money and less riddled with status than the inhabitants of the southern part of the state. It's a narcissism that's rooted in the sheer physical aspect of the place. The city is incredibly beautiful in parts, and with its switchback hills and rows of wooden Victorian houses, unique; it is also a compact, approachable place, one of the few American cities where you can comfortably do without a car; the majority of buildings are on a human scale, the neighborhoods inviting and secure, and open space very much in evidence. This is also emphatically not the California of monotonous blue skies and slothful warmth: flanked on three sides by water, the city is regularly invigorated by the fresh winds that sweep across the peninsula, and even during the summer temperatures rarely exceed the seventies—and they can drop much lower when heavy fogs muscle in on the city and the area as a whole.

The City

The best way to get a grip on what makes San Francisco special is to walk. The city's many hills don't always make this easy, but they're useful for orientation, and give a good insight into San Francisco's class distinctions: as a general rule, geographical elevation is a good indicator of wealth—the higher you live on one of the city's forty-odd hills, the better off you are. Commercial square-footage is surprisingly small and is in any case mostly confined to the downtown area. Armed with a good map you could plow through much of the city center in a day, although it's better to dawdle, unbound by itineraries: the most interesting districts, certainly, merit at least half a day each just for hanging around.

The most concentrated area of the city, and where you're likely to find yourself doing much of your initial exploring, is the three square miles of contradictions that comprise **downtown**. Situated on the north side of **Market Street**, the city's main artery, its streets are lined with high-class stores and fancy hotels that sit somewhat strangely between the poor, rather sleazy districts to the west and the exaggerated skyscrapers of the **Financial District** to the east. Walk another block and you enter the more chaotic enclave of **Chinatown**, above which sits the otherworldly wealth of San Francisco's most famous peak, **Nob Hill**, from which the whole of downtown can be easily surveyed. Far from homogenized, San Francisco shocks you every time you turn a corner; changes are abrupt and often unannounced. **Civic Center**, for example, a little way west of downtown, is San Francisco's municipal and arts nucleus and site of the city's more grandiose architecture, plonked somewhat awkwardly between the surrounding slums. Across the other side of Market Street, the **SoMa** (South of Market) neighborhood is one of the city's main club and bar focuses—desolate during the daylight hours, neon-lit and buzzing by night.

Another hodgepodge, the northern tip of San Francisco's peninsula begins with the old Italian enclave of **North Beach**, just north of downtown, a popular neighborhood which despite gentrification still harbors a vaguely bohemian population—a hangover from the days when the major Beat figures lived here. It's a good place for eating and drinking, with some of the city's best bars and restaurants. Farther north, the hideous kitsch of **Fisherman's Wharf** is (unjustifiably) the city's number-one tourist magnet, thronged by crowds jostling to cruise the bay, visit Alcatraz, and buy cheap souvenirs and overpriced food. While by no means essential viewing, it does give access to a lengthy bay-front promenade which takes you past exclusive, lofty neighborhoods like **Pacific Heights** before leading into the vast expanse of cypress-lined avenues and windswept bluffs of the **Presidio**—a massive, largely inactive army base, ideal for long secluded walks and ocean-gazing across the orange spires of the **Golden Gate Bridge**. Beyond the bridge lie some of San Francisco's most enthralling stretches of coastline, including the city's only **beaches**.

Outside the center, the city is not surprisingly more residential, made up of a patchwork of small and self-sufficient neighborhoods largely defined by their distinct social and ethnic characteristics. In one part of town you'll find yourself combing bars and restaurants in the vigorously Latin, non-stop **Mission** district; a short bus ride from here lies the comparative tranquility of **Golden Gate Park**—San Francisco's gargantuan urban oasis with a collection of fine art museums, flower gardens, and some convincingly bucolic open spaces. In between, the mix is no less varied: the **Castro** has long been San Francisco's primary gay district, an affluent, gentrified neighborhood that, despite the sobering effects of AIDS, still boasts an energetic bar scene and plenty of good eating options. For voyeuristic strolling, the **Haight-Ashbury** is no less rewarding. Formerly the nucleus of San Francisco's 1960s counterculture, it maintains an air of radicalism manifest in its left-wing bookstores, some tastefully tacky café society, and a smattering of residents still flying a slightly limp freak flag.

The Bay Area

While San Francisco proper occupies only 48 hilly square miles at the tip of a slender peninsula, the metropolitan area sprawls out far beyond these narrow confines, east and north across the two impressively engineered bridges that span the chilly waters of its exquisite natural harbor. This, together with the peninsula suburbs south of the city, is the **Bay Area**, a spread of small towns and scenic areas that is often overlooked in the scramble to savor the attractions of the city. There's no doubt about the supporting role these places play in relation to San Francisco—always "The City"—but each has a distinctive character and contributes to the range of people and landscapes that makes the Bay Area one of the country's most desirable places to live or visit.

The biggest, and, in many senses, the most interesting part of the surrounding region is the **East Bay**. Joined to the city by the monumental Bay Bridge, it is principally made up of the twin cities of Oakland and Berkeley—the former an industrial, slightly depressed area that has some of the best nightlife options in northern California, the latter essentially a university town which achieved international notoriety in the Sixties for its anti-war (and anti-government) demonstrations. While not quite such a hotbed of militant activity these days, it harbors a self-consciously progressive population and some of the landmark restaurants that spawned California Cuisine. The weather is generally much sunnier and warmer than in the city, and the area as a whole is easy to reach by way of the space-age *BART* trains that race under the bay.

Across the city's other, more famous—and better loved—bridge, the Golden Gate, lies **Marin County**, a region that's in complete contrast to the East Bay. By far the wealthiest of the Bay Area counties (indeed among the richest in the entire country), Marin divides into two distinct sections: the magnificent shoreline around **Point Reyes National Seashore** and the redwoods of **Muir Woods** to the west, and the swanky bay-front resorts of **Tiburon** and **Sausalito** in the eastern part, separated by a range of 2500-foot peaks. The leafy landscape and rugged coastline make it the perfect place to head for camping, hiking, or cycling, and set it apart from the rest of the Bay Area in its sheer physical majesty.

The same cannot be said of the **Peninsula**, home to some of San Francisco's oldest and most upscale suburbs, which reach down along the bay into a monotonous, seemingly endless suburban sprawl around **San Jose**. As home to the multi-billion-dollar computer industry, known to the world as "Silicon Valley," there's little left of the agriculture that predominated here as recently as twenty years ago. Thankfully, some excellent **beaches** remain—clean and sandy, surprisingly uncrowded, and with a couple of youth hostels in old lighthouses overlooking the Pacific.

Finally, you should check out the two valleys collectively known as the **Wine Country**, at the top of the bay an hour north of San Francisco. **Napa Valley**, the largest (and, in terms of wine production, most important) area, is home to some of California's most prestigious wineries, and whether you come for a day or a weekend, it provides an excellent opportunity to sample your way around its vineyards or soak in natural hot springs. Its neighbor,

Sonoma Valley, contains more informal, family-run wineries. Not as busy as Napa, it's great for cycling your way along the winding roads that snake through rolling green hills and stopping off to try the odd vintage.

Climate and When to Go

San Francisco's **climate** is among the most stable in the world, with a daytime temperature that rarely ventures more than 5°F either side of a median 60°F. However, the city's position surrounded by water means that it's often damp and can feel much colder, particularly in **summer** when heavy fog rolls in through the Golden Gate, smothering the city in gloom. This isn't to say it's never sunny, just that San Francisco doesn't conform to the California ideal of endless summer. **Winters** bring most of the city's rainfall, sometimes in torrential storms. Almost everywhere else in the **Bay Area** is warmer than San Francisco, especially in summer when the **East Bay** cities are basking in sunshine, and the **Wine Country** and other inland valleys are baking hot and dry.

As for **when to go**, if you want to avoid the crowds try not to come in summer, although even then most of the tourist congestion is confined to a few of the most popular parts of the city, and is rarely a turn-off. The best times to visit are late May and June, when the hills are greenest and covered with wild flowers, or in October, when you can be fairly sure of good weather, and space in the hotels and restaurants.

AVERAGE TEMPERATURE (°F) AND RAINFALL												
	Jan	Feb	Mar	Apr	May	Jun	Jul	Aug	Sep	Oct	Nov	Dec
Maximum temperature	55	59	61	62	63	66	65	65	69	68	63	57
Minimum temperature	45	47	48	49	51	52	53	53	55	54	51	47
Rainfall (inches)	4.7	3.8	3.1	1.5	0.7	0.1	0	0	0.3	1.0	2.5	4.4

PART ONE

THE

BASICS

GETTING THERE

Getting to San Francisco isn't a problem, as the Bay Area is well serviced by air, rail and road networks. All the main airlines operate daily scheduled flights into San Francisco from across the US, and there are daily flights from Toronto and Vancouver as well. Flying remains the most expensive way to travel; taking a train comes a slow second. Traveling by bus is the cheapest way, but again is slow—much less comfortable than either train or plane.

BY AIR

Beside the main **San Francisco International Airport** (known as SFO), there are two other Bay Area airports which may be useful, particularly **Oakland International** (OAK)—across the bay but easily accessible. The third Bay Area airport, **San Jose Municipal** (SJO), forty miles south, is a bit out of the way but has good connections with the western US, LA especially. Both airports are well served by US domestic carriers like *United*, *Continental*, *US Air*, and *America West*. Transport details for the various airports are given

under "Points of Arrival" in Part Two, and in Chapters Nine and Ten in Part Three.

The price of **flights** to San Francisco is fairly consistent whichever airline you fly with, but varies a great deal depending on when you buy your ticket. The cheapest tickets you can get (advertised by some airlines as *Supersaver* fares) must be reserved at least two weeks prior to departure (three weeks in Canada), and must include at least one Saturday night at your destination. *Continental* and *TWA* both offer round-trip fares from New York for $405, and from Chicago for $421; flying from Toronto with *American Airlines* costs $389 round trip, and with *Delta* a round-trip from Vancouver is $215. With all tickets the cheapest time to fly is during the week—prices can rise considerably at weekends. The same flight booked only a week before departure can cost over $100 more; if the booking is left any later you may have to pay double what you would have two weeks before. There are no advantages to be gained by delaying booking your flight as the age of standby bargains is now long gone. At certain times of the year, however, mainly holidays, airlines offer special cut-price deals where real savings can be made. It's worth noting that one-way tickets usually work out far more expensive than round trips, as they're based on regular bus fares.

BY TRAIN

If you have the time (and money) and are looking to take in some of the other states on your way to San Francisco, then a train journey could be the answer. *Amtrak* (☎800/USA-RAIL) connects all major US cities and the cars are clean, comfortable, and rarely crowded. It services Oakland on four main routes, from where there is a bus connection to take you on to San Francisco, though if you're traveling from the Southwest you may have to change at Los Angeles. You might

---

MAJOR AIRLINE NUMBERS

Air Canada ☎1-800/776 3000
American Airlines ☎1-800/433 7300
America West ☎1-800/247 5692
Canadian Pacific ☎1-800/426 7000
Continental ☎1-800/525 0280

Delta ☎1-800/221 1212
Pan Am ☎1-800/687 2600
TWA ☎1-800/21 2000
United Airlines ☎1-800/241 6522
US Air ☎1-800/428 4322

find it easier to get off at Richmond, which is connected to the city by *BART*. All routes from the Northeast go via Chicago, and there is one direct train from Chicago via Denver and Salt Lake City to Oakland. Fares aren't cheap, New York to San Francisco costing over $300 round trip, but the further ahead you buy your ticket, the cheaper it will be. *Amtrak* also offers a limited period "all aboard fare", with reduced rates.

For the purposes of fare calculation the country is divided into three zones. At present round-trip travel within one zone is $189, within two zones $269, and in all three zones $309. From the East to the West coast takes three days, which includes two stopovers, and you can choose the route you want to take there and back. *Amtrak* also runs a very cost-effective rail pass system, valid for unlimited travel over a period of 45 days. **The National Rail Pass** ($299) can be used on all US trains; the **Western Regional Rail Pass** ($239) covers everywhere west of Chicago and New Orleans (there is also a Far Western Rail Pass once you get out there). For full details of the National Rail Pass phone in New York ☎212/736-4545; elsewhere consult the phone book or dial ☎800/872-7245. *VIA Rail Canada* (☎204/949-1830) also sometimes has special offers for travelers out of Quebec or Ontario to the West Coast; give them a call for the latest details.

BY BUS

Bus travel is the most time-consuming and uncomfortable way to travel to the West Coast, and, because of recent financial squeezes by the major coast-to-coast operators, is no longer the bargain it once was. Having said that, a bus trip remains the cheapest way to cross the country— taking *Greyhound* or *Trailways* from New York to San Francisco will cost you only $68 if you buy

your ticket thirty days in advance. The price rises steadily the closer it gets to your departure, up to $144.60 if you pay and leave the same day. Check with local offices for details.

Green Tortoise (☎415/821-0803) offer a more comfortable and scenic ride across the country in the summer months, and more expensive too. Their coast-to-coast "Summer Route" costs $279 and takes ten days, visiting the Great Lakes, the Badlands of South Dakota, the Rocky Mountains, Las Vegas, and LA, before reaching San Francisco. There are beds on the buses, and you contribute to a food fund for communal cooking. Other summer routes are offered, but in winter the San Francisco-based company restricts itself to West Coast trips to Mexico and Seattle.

BY CAR

For many travelers, it's the prospect of a "road trip" that inspires the journey to San Francisco. If you don't have a car then consider a **driveaway**, where you drive someone else's car across the country for them. You normally have to be over 21 and are given ten to twelve days to deliver the car (in one piece) to the correct destination. You must leave $100 deposit, and all you have to pay for is the gas (after a complimentary first tank). Naturally, this method of transportation depends heavily on availability. Many driveaway agents are listed in the Yellow Pages or, failing that, check the classified sections of the local papers.

Though it's not really necessary if you're planning to stay in San Francisco itself, **renting a car** is the usual story of phoning your local branch of one of the majors (*Avis, Hertz, Budget, Thrifty*, etc.), of which *Thrifty* tends to be the cheapest. Most companies have offices at destination airports, and addresses and phone numbers are comprehensively documented in the Yellow

---

BRANCHES OF GREEN TORTOISE IN THE USA AND CANADA

Main Office: P.O. Box 24459, San Francisco, CA 94124; ☎415/285-1441.

Seat Reservation Numbers:

Vancouver: ☎604/732-5153	Santa Cruz: ☎408/462-6437
Seattle: ☎206/324-7433	Santa Barbara: ☎805/669-1884
Portland: ☎503/224-0310	Los Angeles: ☎213/392-1990
Eugene: ☎503/937-3603	New York: ☎212/431-3348
San Francisco: ☎415/821-0803	Boston: ☎617/265-8533

From other points outside California: ☎800/227-4766

Pages. Also worth considering are **Fly-drive deals**, which give cut-rate (and sometimes free) car rental when buying an air ticket. They usually work out cheaper than renting on the spot and are especially good value if you intend to do a lot of driving. Though you can rarely get a deal if you're flying on a cheap ticket, competition between carriers and tour operators makes it worthwhile to phone them before approaching any car rental firm directly. Fly-drive deals can bring the cost of a week's car rental down considerably, and 1000 free miles or even unlimited mileage are often part of the package. See "Getting Around" in Part Two for more on renting cars and driving.

PACKAGES

Many operators run all-inclusive **packages** combining plane tickets and hotel accommodation with (for example) sightseeing, wining and dining, or excursions to tourist sites. Even if the "package" aspect doesn't thrill you to pieces, these deals can still be more convenient and sometimes even more economical than arranging the same thing yourself, providing you don't mind losing a little flexibility. With such a vast range of these packages available, it's impossible to give an overview—major travel agents will have brochures detailing what's on offer.

CUSTOMS: A NOTE FOR CANADIANS

No passport or visa is required for Canadians visiting the US, though be aware that if you cross in your own car, trunks and passenger compartments are subject to spot searches by US Customs personnel. This sort of surveillance is likely to decrease as remaining tariff barriers fall over the next few years. Free entry or not, Canadians are still legally barred from seeking gainful employment in the States (see "Staying On", later in this section).

HEALTH AND INSURANCE

If you need a doctor, look in the Yellow Pages under "Clinics" or "Physicians & Surgeons." If you have an accident, emergency medical services will get to you quickly, and charge you later, like anywhere else. For emergencies or ambulances, the number you should dial is ☎911 (or whatever variant may be on the information plate of the pay phone).

Your **health insurance** should cover you for any charges or costs; if you don't have any you can get adequate coverage either from a travel agent's insurance plan or from specialist travel insurance companies such as *The Travelers*. If you are unable to use a phone or if the practitioner requires payment up front, save all the **paperwork** to support a claim for subsequent reimbursal. Remember also that time limits may apply when making claims after the fact, so promptness in contacting your insurer is highly advisable.

However, few, if any, of the above plans will cover you against theft while traveling, particularly in a city such as San Francisco. **Renter's or homeowner's insurance** can compensate for this, as most policies will cover you for up to $500 in losses while on the road. If you have anything stolen, report it to the nearest police station and make a note of the precinct number. You'll be issued with a reference number to pass on to your insurance company, instead of the full statement usually required. Don't worry unnecessarily; these details should be enough to get your agent started.

A final word about health: one of the most serious health problems affecting the West Coast is, of course, **AIDS**. Although the comparatively high number of HIV-positive cases has led to a more informed and open attitude to the virus than is the case in many other parts of the US, it still can't be stressed strongly enough that sex without condoms is wildly irresponsible.

HOSPITAL EMERGENCY DEPARTMENTS OPEN AT ALL TIMES

San Francisco General Hospital, 1001 Potrero Ave., near 22nd St. in the Mission (☎821-8111).

University of California Medical Center, Parnassas Ave. at Third Ave. in the Sunset District (☎476-1037).

Mount Zion Hospital, 1600 Divisadero St. at Post St., Western Addition (☎885-7520).

Pacific Medical Center, 2333 Buchanan St. at Washington St., near LaFayette Park in Pacific Heights (☎923-3333).

MONEY AND BANKS

TRAVELERS' CHECKS

The best way to carry your money is in travelers' checks. The most widely recognized are *American Express* and *Visa*. The advantage of using the better-known checks is that they can be cashed in more places—shops, restaurants, and gas stations (don't be put off by "no checks" signs in windows; this only refers to personal checks). Order mostly $10 and $20 denominations (although lately the $10 ones seem to be an endangered species); you won't make many friends in stores where you pay for a five-dollar purchase with a fifty-dollar check.

CREDIT AND AUTOTELLER CARDS

If you have a **Visa**, **Mastercard**, **Diners**, or **American Express** card you really *shouldn't* leave home without it. Almost all stores, most restaurants, and many services will take some kind of plastic. In addition, hotels and car rental companies will ask for a card either to establish your credit-worthiness, or as security, or both. And some people, even in these dark days for credit buying, still get funny about cash.

With *Mastercard* or *Visa* it is also possible to **withdraw cash** at any bank displaying relevant stickers; or with the correct card and a PIN (Personal Identification Number) you can use an automatic teller. *American Express* and *Diners Club* cards, on the other hand, cannot generally be used to withdraw cash, but if you can find a *Citibank* branch and belong to *Diners Club*, you can cash personal checks. An *American Express* card will get you cash or enable you to buy travelers' checks at any *American Express* office (check the Yellow Pages) or, using your PIN number you can operate the travelers' check dispensers at most major airports. For Canadians, most credit cards issued by hometown banks will generally be honored in the US.

Thanks to relaxation in interstate banking restrictions, holders of **ATM** (automatic teller machines) cards from out of state may discover that their cards work in the ATMs of certain West Coast banks. For example *Chase Manhattan* cards are compatible with *Security Pacific* machines. Before you leave home, check with your bank to see if any such affiliations exist with West Coast institutions; not only is this method of financing you trip safer, but at only about a dollar per transaction it's more economical as well.

BANKS

West Coast **banking hours** are generally 10am–3pm Monday to Thursday and 10am–5pm on Fridays. Most major banks—*Bank of America, Citibank, Security Pacific, Wells Fargo*—will change travelers' checks for their face value, although a few are known to charge for this; be sure to ask first.

EMERGENCIES

If you're flat broke and at a loss for what to do, don't give up hope: there are several alternatives before committing suicide.
● Wire money from home to a San Francisco bank. This requires an understanding friend or

Phone Hotlines for Lost Credit/ATM Cards and Travelers' Checks

American Express cards: ☎800/528-2121
American Express checks: ☎800/968-8300
Diners Club: ☎800/525-9150
Visa checks: ☎800/227-6811

relative, and a wait of a day or two for the funds to clear.
● Sell some blood. Check the Yellow Pages for agencies and hospitals; you can get $12 for a pint.
● Approach the nearest Salvation Army branch or city shelter for accommodation and a frugal meal.

INFORMATION AND MAPS

For advance information on San Francisco, apply by mail to the **California Office of Tourism**, 1121 L Street, Suite 103, Sacramento, CA 95814 (☎916/322-1396), or for more specific information, the **San Francisco Convention and Visitors' Bureau**, 201 Third Street, Suite 900, San Francisco CA 94103 (☎974-6900). They publish a handy eighty-page *San Francisco Book*, and a very useful map, both of which they'll send to you for free.

You can get a similar level of advance help—maps, brochures, accommodation lists, etc—on the Bay Area towns and regions from the relevant visitors' bureaus; their addresses are listed in the appropriate chapters of Part Three.

TOURIST OFFICES

Once in the Bay Area, there are a number of offices which dispense brochures and information, though these can vary from indispensable to absolutely useless. Among the former is the main **San Francisco Visitor Information Center**, in Hallidie Plaza, on the concourse of the Powell Street *BART/Muni* station (Mon–Fri 9am–5:30pm, Sat 9am–3pm, Sun 10am–2pm; ☎974-6900). They have free maps of the city and the Bay Area, and can help with accommodation and travel information. The center also makes a good landmark for getting your bearings as it's centrally located at the hub of city transportation systems.

All the various **Bay Area regions** also have at least one main source of information, usually some kind of visitors' bureau, and almost every town will have at least an office operated by the very business-oriented local **Chamber of Commerce**. Where useful we've listed them under "Information" in the appropriate sections of Part Three.

MAPS

Most of the tourist offices we've mentioned can supply you with good **maps**, either for free or for a small charge, and, supplemented with our own, these should be enough for general sightseeing and touring purposes. The best of the commercially available alternatives are the easy-to-read city plans published by *Rand-McNally* (available in advance from 150 East 52nd Street, New York, NY 10022; ☎212/758-7488), which have especially detailed sections on downtown, showing important buildings—very handy for keeping your bearings. They also publish maps of Oakland and the East Bay, San Jose and the Peninsula, and Marin County. *American Auto Association* members can get information and maps from the office situated in San Francisco at 150 Van Ness Avenue (☎565-2012), near the Civic Center, and at other locations all over the Bay Area.

For something more detailed, say for **hiking** purposes, you should wait till you're in San Francisco. Ranger stations in parks and wilderness areas all sell good-quality local hiking maps for $1–2, and camping shops generally have a good selection. Most bookstores will have a range of local trail guides, the best of which we've listed under "Books" in *Contexts*.

COMMUNICATIONS: PHONES AND MAIL

Public telephones invariably work and can be found everywhere. The minimum cost of a **local call** from a public phone is 20¢ for the first few minutes, plus a further amount if you talk for a long time; the operator—or a synthesized voice—will come on the line and ask you for the money. Detailed rates are listed at the front of the **White Pages**.

Many government agencies, car-rental companies, hotels, and other services have a **toll-free number**: at a public phone simply dial the number direct, always prefixed with ☎800.

POSTAL SERVICES

Post offices are usually open Monday–Friday 9am–5pm and Saturday 9am–1pm. They're the best places to buy **stamps** and send mail that you want to arrive quickly—though stamps are also available from vending machines on the walls outside, and there are **mail boxes** on many street corners. If you want to send—or receive—anything **general delivery**, have it addressed to:

Your Name
General Delivery
San Francisco, CA94101
USA

TELEPHONES

San Francisco **telephones** are run by *Pacific Telephone (Bell System)*—or *PacBell*—and linked to the nationwide *AT&T* network. The **area code** is ☎415. All San Francisco and most Bay Area phone numbers are within this area code and we have in general omitted it from our listings; where they are not—in outlying Bay Area regions like the Wine Country (☎707) and San Jose (☎408)— we've listed the relevant code.

USEFUL NUMBERS

Emergencies ☎911. Ask to be connected with the appropriate emergency service: fire, police, or ambulance.

Local directory information ☎411
Long-distance directory information ☎1 (Area Code)/555-1212

Toll-free directory inquiries ☎1-800/555-1212.
Operator ☎0

Letters so addressed can be picked up at the San Francisco Main Post Office (Mon–Fri 9am–5:30pm, Sat 9am–1pm; ☎550-6500) at 228 Harrison Street, South of Market, but will only be held for thirty days before being returned to sender, so make sure there's a return address on the envelope. If you're receiving mail at someone else's address, it should include "c/o" and the regular occupant's name; otherwise it too is likely to be returned.

Rules on sending **packages** are very rigid: you must use special containers bought from post offices and sealed according to their instructions. Packages are sent surface mail unless air mail is specified and, not surprisingly, costs increase the farther the destination and the heavier the package. To send anything out of the country, you'll need a **customs declaration form**, available from a post office.

To send a **telegram** (sometimes known as a wire) go to a *Western Union* office (listed in the Yellow Pages). If you have a credit card, you can phone and dictate your message. **International telegrams** are slightly cheaper than the cheapest international phone call. For domestic telegrams ask for a **mailgram**, which will be delivered to any address in the country the following morning.

MAIN SAN FRANCISCO AND BAY AREA POST OFFICES

228 Harrison St. (☎550-6500). Zip code 94101.

Chinatown, 867 Stockton St. (☎956-3566). Zip code 94108.

North Beach, 1640 Stockton St. (☎956-3581). Zip code 94133.

Marina, 3225 Fillmore St. (☎563-4673). Zip code 94123.

Oakland Main, 1675 7th St. (☎874-8200). Zip code 94607.

Berkeley Main, 2000 Allston Way (☎845-1100). Zip code 94704.

THE MEDIA

San Francisco is a bit of a media backwater compared to Los Angeles or New York City, but what it lacks in high-power status it makes up for with in-depth coverage of local news and features. The provincialism of its daily newspapers—about half the stories in the main *San Francisco Chronicle* are straight reprints from other papers—is a continual source of embarrassment, but there are dozens of free weekly newspapers, focusing in on the city or parts of the Bay Area, that are informative and entertaining. San Francisco's television is no different from the rest of the US, and its radio stations are excellent, offering an amazing range of music—the best of which is commercial-free, 24 hours a day.

NEWSPAPERS

San Francisco's major **daily newspapers** are the *San Francisco Chronicle* (35¢) in the morning, and in the afternoon, the re-vamped *San Francisco Examiner* (25¢), which is making great efforts to capture the liberal market with in-depth reporting, and, in the case of Hunter S. Thompson, controversial columnists. On Sundays the two papers combine into a very large edition ($1), most of which can be discarded apart from the very useful "Datebook" (also called the "Pink Pages") which gives detailed listings of arts, clubs, films, and events. Perhaps the best daily paper for straight coverage of local, national, and international events is the *San Jose Mercury-News* (25¢), based in the Silicon Valley but available all over the Bay Area.

There's also an abundance of **free publications**, led by the *San Francisco Bay Guardian*, which has 100 pages of lively reporting and invaluable listings every week. Other San Francisco freesheets to look out for (cafés and record stores are likely places) include the *SF Weekly* and the lesbian, gay, and bisexual-oriented *Bay Times*, which has tons of listings and the best personal ads.

For listings of what's on in lively Oakland and Berkeley, and yet more voyeuristically interesting personal ads, the weekly *East Bay Express* is unsurpassed, while the Berkeley-based *Poetry Flash* has details of poetry readings, workshops, and other literary events. If you're interested in more active pursuits, the monthly *City Sports* has rundowns of upcoming running and cycling and similar events in the whole Bay Area. There are dozens more locally-based newspapers throughout the Bay Area, the best of which are listed in the "Information" sections of the relevant chapters.

TV

San Francisco **TV** is pretty much the standard network sit-com and talk-show barrage you get all over the country, with frequent interruptions for hard-sell commercials. Game shows fill up most of the morning schedule; around lunchtime you can take your pick of any of a dozen daily soap operas. Slightly better are the **cable networks**, which you'll have access to in most hotels—the around-the-clock news of *CNN*, or *MTV*'s non-stop circuit of mainstream pop videos.

SAN FRANCISCO TV

2 KTVU NBC	9 KQED PBS
4 KRON CBS	5 KPIX CBS
7 KGO ABC	

RADIO

Bay Area **radio**, in contrast, is probably the best in the US, with some eighty stations catering to just about every conceivable taste. Best are those on the **FM** band, which is broadcast in stereo, and includes a dozen non-commercial stations—most affiliated with a college or university. In the main the programming on these stations is anarchically varied, from in-depth current affairs discussions to mind-boggling industrial thrash. The far left end of the radio dial (88–92 FM) is set aside for such stations; scan through a few until you find something you like.

SAN FRANCISCO RADIO

KSFO 560 AM Oldies music and Bay Area sporting events.

KCBS 740 AM News, talk-shows, and excellent commentaries.

KGO 810AM News, and the most intense talk-shows.

KNEW 910 AM Country and western music.

KQED 88.5 FM Classical music, talk, community affairs.

KPOO 89.5 FM Community-based radio—blues, reggae, soul.

KUSF90.3 FM Excellent college station with rock, news, and off-beat issues.

KALX 90.7 FM Voted best US college station most years for its blend of anything-but-mainstream rock and reggae, though the UC Berkeley-based signal rarely makes it across the bay.

KCSM 91.1 FM Diverse but consistently high-quality programming, especially good for late-night jazz.

KJAZ 92.8 FM Mellow, laid-back style, good jazz.

KPFA 94.1 FM Long-running, listener-supported station known for its in-depth investigative reporting as well as arts programs.

KSAN 94.5 Modern country and western music.

KKHI 95.7 FM Classical music.

KRQR 97.3 FM Album rock.

KBLX 102.9 FM "The Quiet Storm": Soul, jazz, and lots of house.

KFOG 104.5 FM Best of the rock stations with lots of oldies and the best of newies.

KMEL 106.1 Soul, house. Very funky.

KSOL 107.1 FM Dance music, with a good line in the latest rap.

FOOD AND DRINK

It's not too much of an exaggeration to say that in San Francisco and the Bay Area you can eat whatever you want, whenever you want. Whether it's for basic daily sustenance or for a special social occasion, San Franciscans dine out far more than most other Americans: though the swarms of tourists inflate the figures, per capita locals spend an average of $2000 a year in restaurants and bars (the highest in the country), enough to support the mass of restaurants, fast-fooderies, and coffee shops that lines every main street.

Things are further improved by California being one of the most agriculturally rich—and health-conscious—parts of the country. Junk food is as common here as anywhere else, but the state also produces its own range of highly nutritious goodies: apples, dates, grapes, kiwi fruit, melons, oranges, peaches are everywhere, joined by abundant fish and seafood from the Pacific and high-quality meat and dairy products, all finding their way into Bay Area kitchens. You'll rarely find anything that's not fresh, be it a bagel or a spinach-in-Mornay-sauce croissant (California's mix'n'match food concoctions can be as anarchic as its architecture), and even fast food won't necessarily be rubbish.

BREAKFAST

For the price—on average $3–5—breakfast is the best-value and most filling meal of the day. Go to a **diner**, or, slightly smarter, a **café** or **coffee shop**, all of which serve breakfast until at least 11am (though diners sometimes offer it all day). The breakfasts themselves are pretty much what you'd find all over America—though you may be offered San Francisco's specialty—white, dense, and tangy **sourdough bread**. A concession to California's love of light food is the option of **fruit**—typically apple, banana, orange, pineapple, or strawberry, wonderfully styled and served on their own or with pancakes, though costing as much as a three-course breakfast.

LUNCH, FAST FOOD, AND SODA

Most San Francisco workers take their **lunch-break** between noon and 2:30pm, and during these hours you should look for the low-cost **set menus** on offer—generally excellent value. Chinese restaurants, for example, frequently have rice and noodles or dim sum feasts for $4–6, and many Japanese restaurants give you a chance to eat sushi much more cheaply ($7–10) than usual. Mexican restaurants are exceptionally well-priced all the time, and you can get a good-sized lunch in one for $4–5.

As you'd expect, there's also **pizza**, available from familiar chains like *Pizza Hut* and *Pizzaland* —all dependable and with broadly the same range; count on paying $5–7 for a basic two-person pizza. If it's a warm day and you can't face hot food, look for a **deli** (see below) that has a salad bar, where you can help yourself for $2. Consider also the West Coast's favorite healthy fast food: **frozen yoghurt**, sold in most places by the tub for $1.50.

For **quick snacks**, you'll find many **delis** do ready-cooked meals for $3–5, as well as a range of **sandwiches** that can be meals in themselves, filled with a custom-built combination of meat, cheese, seafood, pasta, and salad. **Bagels**, also, are everywhere: thick, chewy rolls with a hole in the middle, filled with anything you fancy. Be a little wary of the grungier **Mexican fast-food** stands if you're buying meat, although they're generally filling and very cheap. There are chains, too, like *El Pollo Loco* and *Taco Bell*, which sell swift tacos and burritos for around $3. And of course the inevitable **burger chains**—*Wendy's*, *Burger King*, and *McDonalds*—are as ubiquitous here as anywhere in the US. Less familiar ones include *Jack-in-the-Box*—a drive-through takeout where you place your order by talking to a plastic clown (and with a recently updated menu including croissants and shrimp salads).

Finally, just about any of these places will serve **soda**. Each brand is available in caffeine-free and sugar-free varieties; there's even, in reaction to this, a new brand, *Jolt*, which promises "all the sugar and twice the caffeine." Most places also offer a range of **mineral waters**: *Calistoga* is the main local brand, from the eponymous small town in the Wine Country (see Chapter Twelve), and is available in a variety of natural fruit flavors.

FREE EATS AND BRUNCH

Some **bars**, particularly in downtown San Francisco, are used as much by diners as drinkers, who turn up in droves to fill up on the free **hors d'oeuvres** laid out between 5 and 7pm Monday to Friday—an attempt to nab the commuting classes before they head off to the suburbs. For the price of a drink you can stuff yourself silly on nachos, seafood, or pasta, though bear in mind it will help to look like an office worker; look like a bag lady and you won't get in.

Brunch is another deal worth looking out for, indulged in at weekends (though Sunday is more usual) between 11am and 2pm. For a set price ($8 or more) you get a light meal and a variety of complimentary cocktails or champagne—perfect for serious daytime boozing, though rarely great value for money.

RESTAURANTS

Even if it often seems swamped by the more fashionable regional and ethnic cuisines, traditional American cooking can be found all over the Bay Area. However, it's **California Cuisine**, geared toward health and aesthetics, that's raved about by foodies—and rightly so, especially in Berkeley, its acknowledged birthplace and a not-to-be-missed gourmet ghetto. Basically a development of French *nouvelle cuisine*, utilizing the wide mix of fresh, locally available ingredients, California Cuisine is based on physiological efficiency—eating only what you need to and what your body can process. Vegetables are harvested just before maturity and steamed to preserve a high concentration of vitamins, a strong flavor, and to look better on the plate; seafood comes from oyster farms and the catches of small-time fishermen; and what little meat there is tends to be from animals reared on organic farms. The result is small but beautifully-presented portions, and high, high prices—not unusually $50 a head for a full dinner with wine; the minimum you'll need for a sample is $15, which will buy a substantial portion. To whet your appetite, hors d'oeuvres include things like mussels in jalapeño and sesame vinaigrette, snails in puff pastry with mushroom puree, and, among entrees, roasted goat's cheese salad with walnuts, swordfish with herb butter, and tuna with cactus ratatouille.

Of other American regional cooking, it's **Cajun** that's currently in vogue. Also known as "Creole," it originated in Louisiana as a way of saving money by cooking up leftovers. It's centered on black beans, rice, and seafood, and is always highly spiced. There are a few relatively inexpensive places to find it (charging around $8), but its current cachet has pushed prices up, and in most places it's not really a budget option.

Although nominally ethnic, **Mexican** food is so common it often seems like (and historically is) an indigenous cuisine. What's more, day or night, it's the cheapest type of food to eat: even a full dinner with a few drinks will rarely be over $10 anywhere except in the most upmarket establishment. San Francisco's Mexican food—found all over the city, but especially in the Mission District—is different from what you'd find in Mexico, making more use of fresh vegetables and fruit, but the essentials are the same. Salsa, a spicy (sometimes very spicy) tomato, onion, and coriander sauce, is the key ingredient, backed by lots of rice and pinto beans, often served refried (ie boiled, mashed, and fried in bacon fat), with a **tortilla**—a thin cornmeal dough pancake that comes in several ways. You can eat it as an accompaniment to your entrees; soft and wrapped around the food—a **burrito**; folded, fried, and filled—a **taco**; filled, rolled, and baked in a sauce—an **enchilada**; or baked flat and covered with a stack of food, known as a **tostada**. Another, less starchy option is the **chile relleno**, a green pepper stuffed with cheese, dipped in egg batter, and fried. **El Salvadorean** and **Peruvian** food is often available in Mexican eateries, with the emphasis on seafood, as in the delicious Peruvian dish *ceviche*, which consists of chunks of raw fish marinated in lime juice, onion, and coriander.

GLOSSARY OF ETHNIC FOOD TERMS

MEXICAN

Arroz	Rice, usually prepared in tomato sauce	*Mariscos*	Seafood
Burritos	Folded tortillas stuffed with refried beans or beef, and grated cheese	*Menudo*	Soup made from a cow's stomach, said to be a cure for hangovers
Chiles Rellenos	Green chillies stuffed with cheese and fried in egg batter	*Nachos*	Tortilla chips topped with melted cheese
Enchiladas	Soft tortillas filled with meat and cheese or chilli and baked	*Salsa*	Chillies, tomato, onion, and cilantro, served in varying degrees of spiciness
Fajitas	Like tacos but a soft flour tortilla stuffed with shrimp, chicken, or beef.	*Tacos*	Folded, fried tortillas, stuffed with chicken, beef, or (occasionally) beef brains
Frijoles	Refried beans, ie mashed, fried beans	*Tamales*	Cornmeal dough with meat and chilli, wrapped in a corn husk and baked
Guacamole	A thick sauce made from avocado, garlic, onion, and chilli, used as a topping	*Tortillas*	Cornmeal dough pancakes used in most dishes
Margarita	*The* cocktail to drink in a Mexican restaurant, made with tequila, triple sec, lime juice, and limes, and blended with ice to make slush. Served with or without salt.	*Tostada*	Fried, flat tortillas, smothered with meat and vegetables
		Quesadilla	Folded soft tortilla containing melted cheese

ITALIAN

Cacciatore	"Hunter's style"—cooked with tomatoes, mushrooms, herbs, and wine	**Pasta**	
		Cannelloni	Large pasta tubes, stuffed with ground meat and tomato and baked
Calzone	Pizza folded in half so the topping is inside	*Cappelleti*	"Little hats" stuffed with chicken, cheese and egg
Alla carbonara	Sauce made with bacon and egg	*Cappelli d'angeli*	"Angel's hair," very fine pasta strands
Alla Veneziana	Cooked with onions and white wine	*Fettucini*	Flat ribbons of pasta
Alfredo	Tossed with cream, butter, and cheese	*Fusilli*	Pasta spiral
		Gnocchi	Pasta and tomato dumplings
Al forno	Cooked in the oven	*Linguine*	Flat pasta noodles, like tagliatelle
Posillipo	Tomato cooked with garlic, Neapolitan style	*Manicotti*	Squares stuffed with cheese; ravioli are the same only with meat
Puttanesca	Literally "whore style," cooked with tomato, garlic, olives, capers, and anchovies	*Tortellini*	Rings of pasta stuffed with either spiced meat or cheese
		Vermicelli	Very thin spaghetti
Zabaglione	Dessert of whipped egg yolks, sugar, and marsala	*Ziti*	Small tubes of pasta, often baked with tomato sauce

JAPANESE

California roll	Mild tasting sushi with a slice of quocado	*Sake*	Strong rice wine, drunk hot
		Sashimi	Thinly sliced raw fish eaten with soy sauce or *Wasabi*
Gyoza	Meat and vegetable dumplings		
Karagei	Fried chicken	*Sushi*	Raw fish wrapped up in rice in seaweed (see next page)
Larmen	Noodles in spicy broth		
Negimayaki	Sliced beef with scallions	*Tempura*	Seafood and vegetables deep-fried in batter
Okonomi	Literally "as you like it," usually used with regard to sushi when choosing the topping	*Tonkatsu*	Deep-fried pork with rice
		Wasabi	Hot green horseradish sauce

JAPANESE (CONTINUED)

Sushi/sashimi

Anago	Sea eel	Nigiri	Rice topped with fish
Ebi	Shrimp	Tai	Red snapper
Ikura	Salmon roe	Tekka(maki)	Tuna with rice rolled in
Kappa(muki)	Cucumber with rice and		seaweed (nori)
	seaweed	Toro	Extra meaty part of the tuna
Maguro	Tuna	Chirashi	Mixed fish on rice

CHINESE

Cantonese	**Szechan/Hunan**		**Dim Sum (Cantonese)**	
Chow	Ch'ao	Stir-fried	Bao, bau	Bun
Doufu	Tofu	Bean curd	Cha Shew Bao	Steamed roll filled with sweet
Fun, fon	Fan	Rice		cubes of roast pork
Gai, gee	Chi	Chicken	Chow fun	Fried rice noodles
Har, ha	Hsia Jen	Shrimp	Chow mai fu	Rice vermicelli
Hew	Shao	Roasted	Har Kow	Shrimp dumplings
Jyuyuk	Jou	Pork	Jook	Congee, or rice gruel
Ngow yuk	Niu Jou	Beef	Kow, gow	Dumplings
Opp	Ya	Duck	Lo Mein	Mixed noodles
Ow	Cha	Deep-fried	Mai fun	Thin noodles
Yu	Yu	Fish	Tang mein	Soup noodles
			Wontons	Thin-skinned dumpling filled with
				fish or meat

Other ethnic cuisines are plentiful too. **Chinese** food is everywhere, and can often be as cheap as Mexican; **Japanese** is more expensive and more fashionable—sushi is worshipped by some Californians; **Italian** food is popular but can be expensive once you leave the simple pastas and explore the exotic pizzas or the specialist Italian regional cooking that's fast catching on in the city. **French** food, too, is widely available, though always pricey, the cuisine of social climbers and power-lunchers. **Thai**, **Korean**, and **Indonesian** food is similarly in vogue, though usually cheaper. **Indian** restaurants, on the other hand, are thin on the ground and often very expensive—although as this spicy cuisine catches on the situation is gradually changing for the better, with a sprinkling of moderately-priced outlets, particularly in West Berkeley.

We've **listed restaurants** by cuisine in Chapter Seven. Whatever and wherever you eat, service will always be enthusiastic and excellent, mainly because the staff depend on **tips** for the bulk of their earnings. You should always top up the bill by 15–20 percent; not to tip at all is frowned upon. Many (not all) restaurants accept **payment** in the form of credit/charge cards: if you use one a space will be left to fill in the appropri-ate tip; travelers' checks are also widely accepted, so long as you have some form of identification.

DRINKING

San Francisco is the consummate boozing town, with a huge range of **bars** and **cocktail lounges** that are fun to spend an evening in even if you don't plan to get legless; indeed, the city's water-ing holes are one of its best attributes. They're generally pretty true to their popular image: long dimly-lit counters with a few customers perched on stools before a bartender-cum-guru, and tables and booths for those who don't want to join in the drunken bar-side debates.

To **buy and consume alcohol** in California you need to be at least 21 years old, and could well be asked for an ID even if you look much older. **Licensing laws and drinking hours** are, however, among the most liberal in the country (though laws on drinking and driving are not): alco-hol can be bought and drunk any time between 6am and 2am, seven days a week; and besides, bars, nightclubs, and restaurants nearly always have a liquor license. More cheaply, you can buy beer, wine, or spirits easily in supermarkets, many delis, and, of course, liquor stores.

The usual brands of **beer** such as *Budweiser*, *Miller*, and *Schlitz* are found everywhere. As an alternative, the San Francisco-based *Anchor Brewery* cooks up the tasty, medium-bodied *Anchor Steam* beer and the richer-flavored, creamy *Liberty Ale*, both available by the bottle in most bars and cafés and on tap at better establishments. There are also dozens of micro-breweries popping up all over the West Coast, and any good liquor store should stock a range. Another recent development is the so-called **"brew-pubs,"** serving a range of generally good beers brewed on the premises. Many locals simply stick to **imported** beers, best of which are the Mexican brands *Bohemia*, *Corona*, *Dos Equis*, *Superior*, and *Tecate*. Expect to fork out $1 for a glass of draft beer, $2–3 for a bottle of imported beer. See Chapter Seven for a rundown on **specific places** to drink.

Although nationally known, **wines** such as *Gallo* and *Paul Masson* are held in low regard on the West Coast, and produced in plants resembling oil refineries. Most people drink the produce of California's innumerable smaller wineries—invariably good, with the best of the lot in the nearby Napa and Sonoma valleys, made from French-strain grapes and predominantly dry.

Wines are categorized by grape-type rather than place of origin: *Cabernet Sauvignon* is probably the most popular, a light and easily-drunk red; also widespread are the heavier reds—*Burgundy*, *Merlot*, and *Pinot Noir*. Among the whites, *Chardonnay*, the grape champagne is made from, is very dry and flavorful, and generally preferred to *Sauvignon Blanc* or *Fumé Blanc*, though these have their devotees. The most unusual is the strongly flavored *Zinfandel*, which comes as white, red, or rosé.

You can learn a lot about California wine by taking a **winery tour**, most including free tastings, a number of which we've detailed in Chapter Twelve. Or, before leaving home, write to the *Wine Institute*, 165 Post Street, San Francisco, CA 94108, for their informative booklet and winery directory. The best lesson of all, of course, is simply to buy the stuff. It's fairly inexpensive: a glass of wine in a bar or restaurant costs about $1.50, a bottle $5–8. Buying from a supermarket is cheaper still—just $3–6 a bottle. If you do visit the wineries, it's worth remembering that their prices are no lower than you'd pay in a store, although you won't always be able to find the smaller wineries' product elsewhere.

POLICE AND THIEVES

No one could pretend that San Francisco is trouble-free, though by and large the worst areas for crime are also the most unusual places for tourists to visit, so you're unlikely to have to deal with any of the threatening environments of some other cities. Most of the violent crime that does occur is drugs-related and generally concentrated in deprived areas like Hunter's Point, on San Francisco's southeast waterfront, or West Oakland. By being careful, you're unlikely to have problems even in these places, though you may well feel distinctly uncomfortable.

STREET CRIME

The biggest problem for most travelers is the threat of **mugging**. It's impossible to give hard and fast rules about what to do if you're confronted by a mugger. Whether to run, scream, or fight depends on the situation—but most locals would just hand over their money.

Of course, the best thing is simply to **avoid being mugged**, and there are a few basic rules worth remembering in order to make it more unlikely: *don't* flash money around; don't peer at your map (or this book) at every street corner, thereby announcing you're a lost stranger; even if you're terrified or drunk (or both), *don't* appear so; *avoid* dark streets, especially ones you can't see the end of; and in the early hours stick to the roadside edge of the sidewalk so it's easier to run into the road to attract attention.

If **the worst happens** and your assailant is toting a gun or a knife, try to stay calm: remember that he (for this is generally a male pursuit) is probably scared too. Keep still, don't make any sudden movements—and hand over your money. When he's gone you'll be shocked, but try to find a cab to take you to the nearest police station, or **phone ☎911**, and the police will send an officer to the scene, who'll take you to the nearest station. Here, report the theft and get a reference number on the report to claim insurance (see

"Health and Insurance" above) and travelers' check refunds. For **more help**, ring the local *Travelers Aid* (☎781-6738) for sympathy and practical advice. For advice specifically for women in case of mugging or attack, phone the Rape Crisis Line (☎647-7273).

STOLEN CHECKS

Needless to say, having bags snatched that contain travel documents can be a big headache,

and one common problem is **lost or stolen travelers' checks**. You should keep a record of the numbers of your checks separately from the actual checks, and if you lose them, ring the issuing company on their toll-free number. They'll ask you for the check numbers, the place you bought them, when and how you lost them, and whether it's been reported to the police. All being well, you should get the missing checks reissued within a couple of days—and perhaps an emergency advance to tide you over.

MAIN SAN FRANCISCO AND BAY AREA POLICE STATIONS

San Francisco Police Department, 850 Bryant St., SoMa (☎553-1373).

Central Station, 766 Vallejo St., North Beach (☎553-1532).

Mission Station, 1420 Valencia St., Mission District (☎553-1544).

Northern Station, 841 Ellis St., Western Addition (☎553-1563).

Golden Gate Park Station, Stanyan and Waller Sts. (☎553-1061).

Potrero Station, 2300 Third St., Hunter's Point (☎553-1021).

Richmond Station, 461 Sixth Ave. (☎553-1385).

Oakland Police Department, 455 Seventh St. (☎874-8218).

Berkeley Police Department, 2171 McKinley Ave. (☎644-6743).

LOST OR STOLEN TRAVELERS' CHECKS

American Express ☎1-800/968-8300
Diners Club ☎1-800/968-8300

Thomas Cook ☎1-800/223-7373
Visa ☎1-800/227-6811

FESTIVALS AND HOLIDAYS

Someone is always celebrating something in San Francisco, and while many of these are uniquely local affairs, most have their

roots in the ethnic or national holidays of other countries, highlighting the region's diverse background. Street fairs and block parties take place all over the city throughout the summer months, and at the bigger events, like the Chinese New Year parade in February or Gay Freedom Day in June, it can seem as if the entire city is joining in.

FESTIVALS

The first big event in San Francisco's festival season is the **Chinese New Year** celebration, usually at the end of January or early in February, depending on the Chinese calendar. A week of low-key activities in and around Chinatown culminates in the Golden Dragon Parade, in which hundreds of people march through the downtown area leading a 75-foot-long dragon. To find out more, contact the *Chinatown Chamber of Commerce*, 730 Sacramento Street (☎982-3000).

A month later, on March 17, the whole city dresses up in emerald hues to celebrate **St Patrick's Day**, which is marked by excessive consumption of green-tinted beer and by a lengthy parade through downtown San Francisco.

Other celebrations continue the international flavor, starting with late April's low-key **Cherry Blossom Festival** in Japantown and picking up steam around the **Cinco de Mayo**, celebrating the Mexican victory at the battle of Puebla with a 48-hour party in the Mission over the weekend nearest to May 5.

June is the biggest party month, with the boisterous, music- and fun-filled **Festival on the Lake** on Oakland's Lake Merritt, followed by numerous San Francisco **street fairs**—the **North Beach Fair** and the **Haight Street Fair** to name two of the biggest—and the lively **Carnaval** happenings in the Mission. The month's main event is the **Lesbian and Gay Freedom Day Parade**, held on the last Sunday in June, when crowds of up to a quarter of a million pack Market Street for the city's biggest parade and party. The bands and dancers converge on City Hall afterward for a giant block party, with outdoor discos, live bands, and numerous craft and food stalls.

Apart from the **4th of July** fireworks at Crissy Field in the Presidio, for the rest of the year the streets are comparatively quiet, except of course for the city's predominantly gay areas—the **Polk Street Fair** at the end of July, for example, which brings out the black leather brigades. Many of these celebrants resurface for the end-of-summer **Castro Street Fair**, early in October, and at the end of the month when there's one last burst of pre-winter activity on **Halloween** (October 31). Locals dress up and strut their stuff, promenading from bar to bar. Halloween also provides the basis for one of the Bay Area's most unexpected events, the **Pumpkin Festival** in Half Moon Bay, when local farmers open their fields to jack-o'-lantern hunters, and host a range of pumpkin-based cooking and eating competitions.

PUBLIC HOLIDAYS

Banks and offices, and many but not all shops, will be closed for the full day on the following **public holidays**: New Year's Day; Martin Luther King's Birthday (January 15); Presidents' Day (third Monday in February); Easter Monday; Memorial Day (last Monday in May); Independence Day (July 4); Labor Day (first Monday in September); Columbus Day (second Monday in October); Veteran's Day (November 11); Thanksgiving (fourth Thursday in November); and Christmas Day (December 25).

SPORTS AND OUTDOOR ACTIVITIES

With such a mild climate and wide range of landscapes to choose from, it's not surprising that so many San Franciscans spend so much time outdoors. The fitness many locals exude is not the cosmetic "body-beautiful" kind that California, especially LA, is renowned for. Rather, people here just seem to lead more healthy lives. However, for all the outdoorsy windsurfers and hikers, there are an equal number of armchair sports fans who watch avidly but would collapse if forced to take part.

SPECTATOR SPORTS

In the Bay Area, where professional teams often top the national leagues, sports-fans' dedication can verge on the obsessive. Just as fanatical are the followers of the various local university teams, and the rivalry between the University of California at Berkeley and Stanford University,

Palo Alto, in any sport—football, basketball, and baseball, even swimming—is at least as intense as that between Harvard and Yale.

Tickets for the big games sell out well in advance, though it's generally possible to take in a game just by showing up on the day, and it needn't cost all that much: a seat in the sun-drenched bleachers to watch the *Oakland Athletics* goes for around $5, with seats closer in topping the scale at around $12. However, if you have your heart set on watching Joe Montana lead the fabulous *San Francisco 49ers*, be prepared to fork out as much as $100 for a good seat, since games generally sell out—though you sometimes get a ticket for around $25. The baseball season runs from April to October, football from September to January, and basketball from October to April. Tickets for almost all Bay Area sports events are available through *Ticketron* (☎392-7496)

BASEBALL

In the 1990 season, the best team in the US professional league were the *Oakland Athletics (A's)*, who've topped their division three years running. In 1989, they defeated the San Francisco *Giants* in the World Series, despite a week-long delay caused by the October earthquake. The *A's* play at the Oakland Coliseum (☎638-0500), the *Giants* at Candlestick Park south of the city (☎467-8000).

AMERICAN FOOTBALL

Last year, and for most of the last decade, the best team in the NFL were the *San Francisco 49ers*, three-time Super Bowl champions, who play at Candlestick Park (☎468-2249). Their one-time Bay Area rivals, the *Oakland Raiders*, moved to Los Angeles some years ago (inspiring locals to call them the Traitors) but have been on the verge of returning ever since. The latest rumors have them back in Oakland by 1992.

BASKETBALL

The most exciting team is the *Los Angeles Lakers*, who play their games in front of a crowd of celebrities (actor Jack Nicholson, for example, has a front court seat season ticket). Unfortunately, their Bay Area counterparts, the Golden State *Warriors*, who play at Oakland Arena (☎638-6000), aren't so good, but many of the local college teams are worth a look. **Tickets** cost $10–30 for professional games, $4–10 at college level.

CYCLING

Cycling is quickly becoming the most popular sporting pastime in San Francisco, and almost every evening or weekend on the more popular cycle routes, bikes may well outnumber motorists on the road. There are many fine circuits in the East Bay and Marin County, and a fine tour, riding the crest of the coastal mountains from the city south down the Peninsula, looking out over the bay and the Pacific. The Wine Country is another good place for a lengthy tour. We've detailed possibilities throughout the guide.

The biggest boom has been the rise of **mountain biking**, which is said to have been invented on the broad slopes of Mount Tamalpais in Marin County, across the Golden Gate. If you don't want the bother of bringing your own, you can rent touring bikes and cruise around for about $15 a day; mountain bikes are available from about

$25; we've given addresses in "Getting Around the City" and throughout Part Three. For further information on Bay Area cycling, contact the *Bicycle Advisory Committe*, 3313 Grand Avenue, Oakland 94610 (☎452-1221).

The rise in popularity of cycling has been at the expense of the Bay Area's previous obsession, **jogging**, though you'll still see people running around Golden Gate Park and the Marina Green—the two most popular jogging circuits. This slight paling of interest hasn't affected one distinctly San Franciscan institution, late May's **Bay-to-Breakers Race**, in which throngs of costumed joggers—waiters carrying wine glasses, giant centipedes, and the like—follow a dozen world-class runners from the Embarcadero seven and a half miles across the city to Ocean Beach. If you're tempted to join in, phone ☎777-2424 for details. Another, much more serious race happens in June, when the annual **Dipsea** race takes place in Marin County, with several hundred runners racing across the mountains from Mill Valley to Stinson Beach.

Surfing, probably the best-known West Coast pastime, is more of a Southern California phenomenon, thanks largely to the fairly chilly water off the San Francisco coast. However, you'll see wet-suited enthusiasts getting radical off most Bay Area **beaches**, particularly **Stinson Beach** in northern Marin County. For plain sunning, there are a number of other fine beaches along the Peninsula south of San Francisco—**Gray Whale Cove** and **San Gregorio** to name just two—and a couple of gems within the city itself: **Baker Beach** and **China Beach**, both just west of the Golden Gate Bridge. **Windsurfing** is another popular activity, especially around the Berkeley Marina, where you can also rent **sailboats** from the *Cal Sailing Club* (☎527-7245) and cruise around the bay. A more relaxing place to sail, or just paddle around, is Oakland's Lake Merritt (☎444-3807). All details, as ever, are in the relevant parts of the guide.

OTHER OUTDOOR ACTIVITIES

Besides the above, there's a whole range of considerably less athletic things to do in the great outdoors. If you're into gambling, you might fancy a day out at one of the two Bay Area **horseracing** tracks: *Golden Gate Fields* in Albany in the East Bay (☎526-3020), and *Bay Meadows*, south of San Francisco down the Peninsula (☎547-7223). If you prefer **riding** them yourself, *Chabot Stables*, above East Oakland (☎569-4428), and *Miwok Livery* (☎383-8048) in Marin County both hire out animals for trail-riding in fine locations. They charge around $30 for a three-hour ride.

One truly exceptional outdoor adventure the Bay Area offers is **whale-watching**, following herds of mighty California gray whales on the annual migration, generally December to April, from Alaska to the Sea of Cortez. You can usually spot them from headlands (Point Reyes is one of the best), but to really get a sense of their size and might, you have to join them on the seas. The best local operator of boat trips is the non-profit *Oceanic Society*, Building E, Fort Mason Center (☎441-1104), which offers all-day trips out to the

Farallon Islands, where even if it's not the right time of year for gray whales you'll see thousands of seabirds, including pelicans, cormorants, and rarer creatures, and may possibly spy the world's largest mammal, the glorious blue whale.

Another possibility for wildlife-watchers (especially good for those prone to sea-sickness) happens around the same time as the whale migration—during the mating season of the massive and grotesquely beautiful **northern elephant seals**. These two-ton creatures spend most of January and February at Año Nuevo State Reserve, down the coast thirty miles south of San Francisco, the trunk-nosed males battling it out for the right to make babies—see Chapter Ten for details.

GAY AND LESBIAN SAN FRANCISCO

San Francisco's reputation as a city for gay celebration is not new. It could even be outdated. It is undoubtedly still the gay capital of the world, but despite a high profile, the gay scene hasn't had much to celebrate in the last few years and there's been a definite move from the outrageous to the mainstream. It's unlikely that even AIDS will wipe out the increasing number of gay activists in public office, but it has made them more conservative in approach, if not in policy. The exuberant energy that went into the posturing and parading of the 1970s has taken on a much more sober, down-to-business attitude, and these days you'll find more political activists organizing conferences than drag queens throwing parties. Things have changed.

From its beginnings as a Gold Rush town, when scores of men unaccompanied by their womenfolk came to San Francisco, an exclusively male culture has, not surprisingly, thrived. More significantly, the 1940s saw a big increase in the gay population, when a military purge of homosexual soldiers resulted in several thousand—who were serving in the South Pacific—being booted out at San Francisco; unable to return home to the stigma and shame of their expulsion, many stayed. Since that time gays have been coming here to make their homes away from the prejudice and isolation of the rest of America, much of which still hasn't changed a great deal—23

states still outlaw homosexuality, with penalties ranging from a $200 fine in Texas to twenty years' imprisonment in Georgia. It's still America's most liberal city for gay men *and* women, who, it's true to say, can genuinely enjoy their sexualities openly and without fear here. However, the moral backlash caused by AIDS has inevitably awakened prejudice in San Francisco as it has everywhere. The basic principles of tolerance and support endure, though, and have even in some senses been reinforced.

Certainly, in the age of AIDS, San Francisco's gay scene is a different way of life altogether. The Seventies were notorious for the bar and bathhouse culture and the busy and often anonymous promiscuity which went with it, but this toned down abruptly when AIDS first became a problem in the latter part of the decade. This wasn't a foregone conclusion by any means. Many men saw the closure of the bathhouses as an infringement on their civil liberties—an action rooted in homophobia—and the belief that AIDS is germ warfare by the US government is an albeit dwindling rumor that has yet to die. Nowadays, however, the gay community has become a much more politicized grouping than it once was, directing its energies toward fundraising and programs for AIDS patients. Some groups have gone farther still and mushroomed into the field of political lobbying to maintain gay rights against the encroaching Republican Administration, who at best were slow to make the treatment of AIDS a

CONTACTS AND RESOURCES

AIDS Hotline (☎863-2437). 24-hour information and counseling.

Bay Area Bi-Sexual Network, 2404 California St. (☎5654-2226). Referral service for support groups, social connections, and counseling.

Dignity, 133 Golden Gate Ave (☎584-1714). Catholic worship and services.

Gay Cocaine Counseling Service (☎800/2622463).

Gay Legal Referral Services, Box 1983 SF (☎621-3900). Inquiries regarding legal problems and legal representation.

Lesbian/Gay Switchboard (☎841-6224). 24-hour counseling and advice. Contacts and activities referral service.

Gay Men's Group, 450 Stanyan St. (☎750-5661). Support group and advice on places to go, contacts, etc.

Gay Men's Therapy Center (☎673-1160). How to cope with AIDS issues and fears, grief counseling, etc.

Gay Therapy Center, 3393 Market St. (☎558-8828). Counseling and help with coming out.

SF AIDS Foundation, 25 Van Ness Ave (☎864-4376). Referral service providing advice, testing, support groups.

Shanti Project, 525 Howard St. (☎777-1162). AIDS support group that offers care of PWA's, advice, testing, and counseling.

SOL (Slightly Older Lesbians), Pacific Center, 2712 Telegraph Ave., Berkeley 94705 (☎841-6224). A gathering-place and referral service for women over thirty.

Woman to Woman (☎939-6626). Confidential introductions.

priority, and at worst have bowed to pressure from religious fundamentalists within their ranks, some of whom have called for the quarantine of AIDS and ARC victims. One of the biggest issues is the campaign to pass legislation to give bereaved lovers the same rights as those enjoyed by heterosexual couples.

Socially, San Francisco's gay scene has also mellowed, though in what is an increasingly conservative climate in the city generally, gay parties, parades, and street fairs still swing better than most. Like any well-organized section of society, the gay scene definitely has its social season, and if you're here in June, you'll coincide with the Gay and Lesbian Film Festival, Gay Pride Week, the Gay Freedom Day Parade, and any number of conferences. Come October, the street fairs are in full swing and Halloween still sees some of the most outrageous carrying-on.

The 1980s have also seen the flowering of a **lesbian** culture to rival the male 1970s upsurge, and while there still isn't anything like the number of women's bars and clubs that exist for men, they are catching up quickly. As with gay male haunts, we've detailed the best ones in Chapters Seven and Eight.

NEIGHBORHOODS AND PUBLICATIONS

Traditionally, the area for gay men has been the **Castro**, together with a few bars and clubs in the

SoMa area—although gay life these days is much less ghettoized and there are bars and clubs all over town. Rent boys and pimps prowl **Polk Street**, not the safest area at 2am but hardly a danger zone if you use common sense. Lesbian interests are more concentrated in the East Bay than the city, although women's activities thrive in the **Mission**.

New clubs and groups spring up all the time, and you should keep an ear to the ground as well as referring to the many free gay publications available: *The Sentinel, Coming Up, The Bay Area Reporter*, and *Gay Times* all give listings of events, services, clubs, and bars in the city and Bay Area. Women should also keep an eye out in bookshops for *On Our Backs* and *Bad Attitude*, two magazines that often have useful pointers to lesbian organizations in town. Also useful for both men and women is *The Gay Book*, a telephone-cum-resource book that's available in gay bookstores. For a complete gay guide, you might try *Bob Damron's Address Book* (PO Box 11270, San Francisco, CA 94101; ☎777-0113), again available from gay bookstores, which has complete listings of gay accommodation, bars, clubs, and shops in California.

> The best of San Francisco's **gay and lesbian bars and clubs** are detailed under the relevant sections of Chapters Seven and Eight.

WOMEN'S SAN FRANCISCO

The flip side of San Francisco's gay revolution has in some women's circles led to a separatist culture, and women's resources and services are sometimes lumped together under the lesbian category. While this may be no bad thing, it can be hard to tell which organizations exist irrespective of sexuality. Don't let this stop you from checking out anything that sounds interesting, especially with regard to the bars and clubs listed in the Gay and Lesbian sections of Chapters Seven and Eight. Nobody is going to refuse you either entry or help if you're not a lesbian—support is given to anybody who needs it. Similarly women's health care is very well provided for in San Francisco and there are numerous clinics you can go to for routine gynaecological and contraceptive services: payment is on a sliding scale according to income, but even if you're flat broke, you won't be refused treatment.

CONTACTS AND RESOURCES

Bay Area Resource Center, 318 Leavenworth St (☎474-2400). Services, information, and clothing.

Metropolitan Community Church, 150 Eureka St. (☎863-8843). A "women's spirit group" is held here each Wednesday at 7:30pm.

Radical Women, 523A Valencia St. (☎864-1278). Socialist feminist organization dedicated to building women's leadership and achieving full equality. Meetings held on the second and fourth Tuesday of each month.

Rape Crisis Line (☎647-7273). 24-hour switchboard.

Women's Building, 3543 18th St. (☎431-1180). Central stop in the Mission for women's art and political events. A very good place to get information also—the women who staff the building are happy to deal with the most obscure of inquiries. Don't be afraid to ask.

Women's Health Center No.1, 3850 17th St. (☎558-3908). Free contraception, AIDS testing, pregnancy testing, and a well-women's clinic.

Women's Needs Center, 1825 Haight St. (☎221-7371). Low-cost health care and referral service.

Women's Yellow Pages, 270 Napoleon St. (☎821-1357). Call for a copy of this invaluable directory, with everything from where to stay to where to get your legs waxed.

STAYING ON

The West Coast sun may have gotten to you; you may be a Canadian wanting to live out the rest of his or her days watching the Great Gretzky do the same in LA; or perhaps the micro-breweries of Washington have stolen away your taste buds (or your taste for Bud); whatever the reason, you suddenly have a yearning to stay around San Francisco and the Bay Area for a while. The following are a few basic suggestions to help you do this, and if you are a Canadian, represent the limits of what you can do without the all-important Social Security number (without which you can't legally work at all).

FINDING WORK

Since the government recently introduced fines of up to $10,000 for illegal employees, employers have become understandably choosy about whom they hire. If you are legit, there are always the usual casual jobs—catering, restaurant, and bar work—but if you're without a **Social Security number** even these jobs have tightened up. Try for **unskilled work** like cleaning or construction and you stand a better chance—also the bottom end of catering, dishwashers, and such. **Agricultural work** is always available on Californian farms during harvest, but often entails working miles away from major centers and is wearying "stoop" (continually bending over) labor; the apple-picking season in Washington and Oregon is another good bet. The

best way to find farm work is to check with the nearest university, which will have notice boards detailing what's available. There are usually no problems with papers in this kind of work— simply because you won't be asked for them— and if you can stick it out the pay is often good and comes with some basic kind of board and accommodation. Finally **babysitting** and **house-cleaning** are feasible, if not very well-paid options. Check the notices in supermarkets, drugstores, local papers, and again, universities. As with anything it's **who** you know that counts; the more contacts you've got, the better chance you have of finding somebody to put some work your way. Don't be afraid to ask around; the West Coast responds to an enterprising spirit.

For Canadians there is always the option of making up a Social Security number or borrowing somebody else's, but this means borrowing their identity too—it's too tricky to bother with really, as well as highly illegal. In an effort to get around the recent stringency more and more people are opting for **marriages of convenience**, usually on the basis of some kind of payment to the person willing to marry you. While such marriages are common, they're no guarantee of a **Green Card** (that cherished document that declares you legally entitled to work and reside in the US). Indeed the authorities treat all marriages involving foreigners with suspicion, and will interview you rigorously; should they suspect that your marriage is not on the up and up, you qualify for immediate deportation.

FINDING A PLACE TO STAY

West Coast **apartment hunting** is not the nightmare it is in, say, New York: accommodation is plentiful and not always expensive, although the absence of housing associations and co-ops means that there is very little really cheap accommodation anywhere except in very isolated country areas, or, as mentioned above, as part of a crop-picking job. Accommodation is almost always rented unfurnished so you'll have to buy furniture; in general, expect to pay $600 a month for a studio or one-bedroom apartment, $900 per month for two to three bedrooms. Most landlords will expect one month's rent as a deposit, plus one month in advance. Utilities such as electricity and gas are all charged monthly.

There is no statewide organization for accommodation so you'll have to check out the options in each place. By far the best way to find somewhere is to ask around—often short-term rentals come up via word of mouth. Otherwise rooms for rent are often advertised in the windows of houses and local papers have "Apartments for Rent" sections. To find a place, scour the *San Francisco Chronicle*, or, more usefully, the many free papers such as the *Bay Guardian* or the *East Bay Express*—and, for women, *Bay Area Women's News*. **Housing agencies** do exist, but unfortunately require two weeks' rent as a finding fee.

DIRECTORY

AIRLINES *American Airlines*, 433 California St. (☎498-4434); *Continental Airlines*, 433 California St. (☎397-8818); *Delta Airlines*, 433 California St. (☎552-5700); *Pan Am*, 721 Market St. (☎221-1111); *TWA*, 605 Market St. (☎864-5731); *United Airlines*, 433 California St. (☎397-2100).

AIRPORT TAX $15, but always included in the price of your ticket.

BABY-SITTING *Bay Area Babysitting Agency* (☎991-7474).

CHILDREN Traveling with kids in San Francisco is more or less problem-free: restaurants are well-used to them, and hotels don't usually charge extra. However, the city is still very much a place for adults—more so than, say, LA, where Disneyland and Universal Studios are major attractions—and there aren't many things to occupy young ones. Of the few places that exist, the *Exploratorium* in the Marina District is excellent, as is the *Steinhart Aquarium* in Golden Gate Park; and the *Lawrence Hall of Science* in Berkeley will captivate any young mind. For more organized distractions, try the *Great America* amusement park in San Jose, or the animal-themed *Marine World/Africa USA* in Vallejo, accessible by transbay ferry. See the relevant chapters of the guide for full details of these and other attractions.

DISABLED VISITORS Steep hills aside, the Bay Area is generally considered to be one of the most barrier-free cities around, and physically challenged travelers are well catered for. Most public buildings have been modified for disabled access, all *BART* stations are wheelchair accessible, and most buses have lowering platforms for wheelchairs—and, usually, understanding drivers. In San Francisco, the *Mayor's Council on Disabilities* puts out an annual guide for disabled visitors; write to them c/o Box 1595, San Francisco CA, or phone (☎554-6141). The *Center for Independent Living*, 2539 Telegraph Avenue in Berkeley (☎841-4776), has long been one of the most effective disabled people's organizations in the world; they have a variety of counseling services and are generally a useful resource.

DRUGS Possession of under an ounce of the widely-consumed marijuana is a non-criminal offense in California, and the worst you'll get is a $200 fine. Being caught with more than an ounce, however, means facing a criminal charge for dealing, and a possible prison sentence. Other drugs are, of course, completely illegal and it's a much more serious offense if you're caught with any. Of the most widespread, crack and PCP ("angel dust") are confined to ghetto areas and the only contact you'll have with them will be if an addict tries to rob or kill you (statistically improbable). Ordinary cocaine, by contrast, is still the drug of the rich, though the sharp decrease in its street price means it's much more prevalent than it was. The fad for designer drugs such as Ecstasy, with which the Bay Area became associated for a while, has largely faded.

DRUG AND SUICIDE HOTLINE ☎752-3400.

EMERGENCIES Dial ☎911 for police, fire, or ambulance services.

GRATEFUL DEAD HOTLINE ☎457-6388. Join the Deadheads and find out about upcoming gigs and other essential Dead facts.

ID Should be carried at all times. Two pieces should diffuse any suspicion, one of which should have a photo: driver's license and credit card(s) are your best bets.

LEGAL ADVICE *Lawyer Referral Service* (☎764-1616).

PHARMACY *Walgreen*, 498 Castro Street (☎861-6276), is open 24 hours every day.

POISONINGS *Poison Control Center* (☎476-6600).

SMOKING A much-frowned-upon activity in San Francisco: all movie theaters and theaters are non-smoking, restaurants are divided into non-smoking and smoking sections, and smoking is universally forbidden on public transit and in elevators.

TAX In San Francisco and the Bay Area sales tax is 7.5 percent, plus a 0.5 percent "earthquake" tax. Hotel tax will add 5–11 percent on to your bill.

TICKETS For music, theater, sports, and camping reservations, use a charge-by-phone agency: *Ticketron* (☎392-7469), *BASS* (☎762-2277), or *MISTIX* (☎800/442-7275). For half-price theater tickets, try the *STBS* booth on the Stockton Street side of Union Square (☎433-7827).

TIME The West Coast runs on Pacific Standard Time (PST), three hours behind the East Coast. Daylight Saving Time is implemented from the last Sunday in April to the last Sunday in October.

TRAVEL AGENTS *Council Travel*, 312 Sutter St., San Francisco (☎421-3473); 2511 Channing Way, Berkeley (☎848-8604). *STA Travel*, 166 Geary St., Suite 702, San Francisco (☎391-8407).

VENEREAL DISEASE HOTLINE ☎495-6463.

PART TWO

THE
CITY

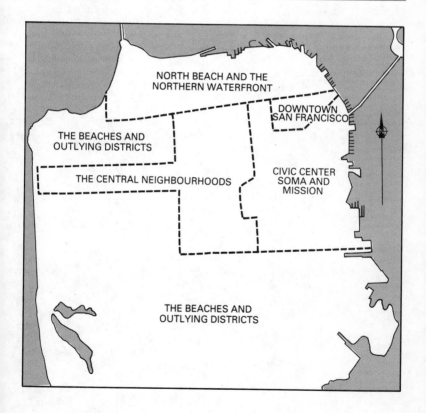

NORTH BEACH AND THE
NORTHERN WATERFRONT

DOWNTOWN
SAN FRANCISCO

THE BEACHES AND
OUTLYING DISTRICTS

THE CENTRAL NEIGHBOURHOODS

CIVIC CENTER
SOMA AND
MISSION

THE BEACHES AND
OUTLYING DISTRICTS

POINTS OF ARRIVAL

THE AIRPORTS

All international and most domestic flights arrive at **San Francisco International Airport** (SFO), about fifteen miles south of the city. There are several ways of getting into town from here, each of which is clearly marked from the baggage reclaim areas. Cheapest is the half-hourly San Mateo County Transit (*SamTrans*) **buses** ($1.75), which leave from the lower level of the airport to downtown San Francisco—either take the #7F express, which takes around forty minutes to get downtown, or the slower #7B, which stops everywhere and takes over an hour. Bear in mind, though, that you're only allowed as much luggage as you can carry on your lap. The San Francisco **Airporter** bus ($4) picks up from outside each baggage claim area every fifteen minutes and travels to the downtown terminal on Ellis and Taylor Street in about forty minutes. If you can spend a little more, the blue **Supershuttle** and the **Yellow Airport Shuttle** are much quicker: they pick up every five minutes from outside the baggage claim area and will take you and other passengers to any city center destination for around $10 a head. Be ruthless, though—competition for these is fierce and lines nonexistent.

Taxis from the airport cost $25–30 (plus tip) for any downtown location, more for East Bay and Marin County, and are only worth considering if you can fill one. If you're planning to drive, there's the usual clutch of **car rental** agencies at the airport. All of them operate shuttle buses that circle the top departure level of the airport road, and will take you to their depot free of charge (see "Getting Around" for details).

A number of domestic airlines (*America West* and *Continental* are two) fly into **Oakland International Airport** (OAK; see Chapter Nine for details), across the bay. This airport is actually closer to downtown San Francisco than SFO, and efficiently connected with the city by the $1 AirBART shuttle bus from the Coliseum *BART* station. The third Bay Area airport, **San Jose Municipal** (SJO), also serves domestic arrivals, but is only worth considering if flights into the other two are booked up (see Chapter Ten for more).

BUSES, TRAINS, AND DRIVING

The San Francisco **Greyhound** terminal (☎433-1500) is on Seventh Street just south of Market Street, near the Civic Center. **Green Tortoise** buses (☎285-2441) disembark behind the Transbay bus terminal on First and Natoma streets, also south of Market, near the Embarcadero *BART* station. **Amtrak** trains stop across the bay in Richmond, where you can transfer easily to *BART*, and continue to Oakland, from where a shuttle bus will take you across the Bay Bridge to the Transbay Terminal.

The main route **by car** from the east is I-80, which runs via Sacramento all the way from Chicago. The main north–south route through California, I-5, passes by fifty miles east, and is linked to the Bay Area by I-580. US-101 and Hwy-1, the more scenic north–south routes, pass right through downtown San Francisco.

ORIENTATION: LAYOUT AND TOPOGRAPHY

Surrounded on three sides by water, the land mass of San Francisco is scrunched up into the four dozen steep hills that give the city its beautiful setting. This fact was not taken into account when the city was laid out in the traditional grid pattern, and so streets (San Francisco has few thoroughfares that merit a grander name) climb straight up and then plummet down the other side. The hills—Nob Hill, Russian Hill, and Telegraph Hill, to name only the best known—are so steep that sidewalks often turn into stairways, and their hulks provide distinct borders between sections of the city.

Downtown San Francisco, where most of the city's interest lies, is very compact, crowded into the northeastern corner of the peninsula between the hills and the bay; its towering skyscrapers, like the Transamerica Pyramid, are clearly visible from almost anywhere in the city. San Francisco's main commercial street, **Market Street**, cuts diagonally across the foot of the downtown grid, a generally flat stretch but eventually climbing up to Twin Peaks, the city's main protrusion before the skyscrapers went up in the 1960s. **Van Ness Avenue** (also known as US-101) is the main north–south artery and pretty much marks the

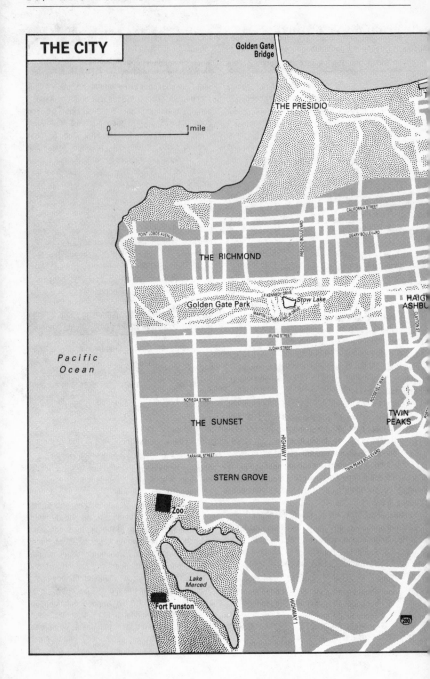

THE CITY

Golden Gate
Bridge

THE PRESIDIO

0   1mile

POINT LOBOS AVENUE

CALIFORNIA STREET

GEARY BOULEVARD

PARK PRESIDIO BLVD

THE RICHMOND

HAIGHT
ASHBU

J.F. KENNEDY DRIVE

Golden Gate Park   Stow Lake

MARTIN LUTHER KING JR DR

CLAYTON ST

IRVING STREET

JUDAH STREET

Pacific
Ocean

NOREGA STREET

TWIN
PEAKS

THE SUNSET

HIGHWAY 1

PORTOLA DRIVE

TARAVAL STREET

TWIN PEAKS BOULEVARD

STERN GROVE

Zoo

Lake
Merced

Fort Funston

HIGHWAY 1

290

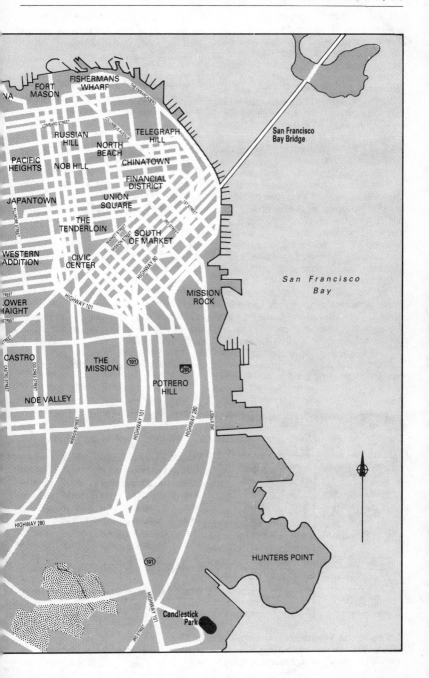

western extent of the downtown area. **Geary Street**, which becomes Geary Boulevard west of Van Ness, is a major east–west corridor, running from downtown Union Square five miles west to the Pacific shore. **Lombard Street** serves a similar purpose, linking the downtown area with the Golden Gate Bridge and lined by motels and 1950s-style drive-in diners. The only major stretch of **freeway** in San Francisco, I-80, slices through the southeast quarter of the city joining the Bay Bridge with the Peninsula; the rest of the limited freeway network was rendered unsafe by the 1989 earthquake and may be torn down.

If you have your own set of wheels, you can orient yourself—and see some of the best of San Francisco—by way of the **49-Mile Drive**, a route laid out around the city taking in the most important scenic and historic points in about half a day. Marked by blue and white seagull signs, it circuits the Civic Center, Japantown, Union Square, Chinatown, Nob Hill, North Beach, and Telegraph Hill, before skirting Fisherman's Wharf and the Marina and Palace of Fine Arts—after which it passes the southern approach to the Golden Gate Bridge and winds through the Presidio. From here it sweeps along the ocean past the zoo and doubles back through Golden Gate Park, vaulting over Twin Peaks and dipping down to Mission Dolores and back to the waterfront for a drive by the Bay Bridge, Ferry Building, and Financial District. Maps of the entire route are available (free) from the Visitor Information Center on Market Street.

ADDRESSES

When pinpointing an **address** verbally, to a cab driver or when giving directions, San Franciscans always give the cross street rather than the number (eg Valencia and 18th), and you'd do well to follow their example. However, you may see numbered addresses written down (in this guide for example), in which case there is a formula for working out where it is on the city's very long thoroughfares. All streets work on blocks of 100 from their downtown source, which on north–south streets is Market Street, on east–west streets it is either Market Street, or, above here, the Embarcadero. For example, 950 Powell Street is on the tenth block of Powell north of Market; 1450 Post Street is on the fifteenth block of Post west of Market; 220 Castro Street is on the third block of Castro south of Market. Unlike many American cities, most streets have names rather than numbers, the only grid of numbered streets being that radiating into the docks area south of Market. Farther out from downtown, in the Richmond and Sunset, the avenues all have their origin at the foot of the Presidio and travel south in increasing blocks of 100.

GETTING AROUND THE CITY

Getting around San Francisco is simple. In spite of the literally breathtaking hills, the city center is small enough to make walking a feasible way to see the sights and get the feel of things. In addition, the excellent public transit system is cheap, efficient, and easy to use, both in the city and the more urbanized parts of the surrounding Bay Area—though to go any farther afield you'd do well to rent a car. Cycling, and—outside the city center—mountain biking, is a good option, too, though you'll need stout legs to tackle the many steep hills of San Francisco.

MUNI

The city's public transit is run by the **San Francisco Municipal Railroad**, or *Muni* (☎673-6864), and made up of a comprehensive network of **buses**, **trolley buses**, and **cable cars**, which run up and over the city's hills, and underground

USEFUL BUS ROUTES

#38 from Geary St. via Civic Center, west to to the ocean along Geary Blvd.

#5 From the Transbay Terminal, west along the north side of Golden Gate Park to the ocean.

#7 From the Ferry Terminal (Market St.) along Haight St. to the ocean.

#24 From Castro St. north along Divisadero St. to Pacific Heights and Marina.

#37 From Market St. to Twin Peaks.

#30 From the CalTrain depot in SoMa, north to Fisherman's Wharf via North Beach and the Financial District.

#22 From the Mission along Fillmore St. north to Pacific Heights.

#15 From 3rd St. (SoMa) to Pier 39, Fisherman's Wharf, via the Financial District and North Beach.

#20 (Golden Gate Transit) From Civic Center to the Golden Gate Bridge.

MUNI TRAIN LINES

Muni N-JUDAH LINE From downtown west to Ocean Beach, via the Haight.

Muni J-CHURCH LINE From downtown to Mission and East Castro.

Muni L-TARAVAL LINE From downtown west to the zoo and Ocean Beach.

Muni K-INGLESIDE LINE From downtown to Balboa Park.

Muni M-OCEAN VIEW From downtown west to Ocean Beach.

CABLE CAR ROUTES

Powell–Hyde: from Powell St. along Hyde through Russian Hill to Fisherman's Wharf.

Powell–Mason: From Powell St. along Mason via Chinatown and North Beach to Fisherman's Wharf.

California St.: From the foot of California St. in the Financial District through Nob Hill to Polk St.

trains—which become **streetcars** when they emerge from the downtown metro system to branch off and serve the suburbs. On buses and trains there's a flat **fare** of 85¢, $2 on cable cars; with each ticket you buy, ask for a **free transfer**—good for another two rides on a train or bus, and a fifty-percent reduction on the cable car fare if used within ninety minutes. With trains, you must purchase tickets to get through the barriers before descending to the platforms; on the buses, correct change is required on boarding.

A **24-hour pass**, costing $6, or a **three-day pass**, costing $10, can be bought from most Market Street *Muni* stations and are good on all *Muni* services. If you're staying more than a week or so and need to rely heavily on public transit, get a **Fast Pass**, which costs $28 and is valid for unlimited travel on the *Muni* system and *BART* stations (see below) within the city limits for a full calendar month. Fast Passes are available from most *Muni* and *BART* stations, supermarkets, and newspaper stores.

Muni trains run **throughout the night** on a limited service, except those on the M-Ocean View line, which stop around midnight; buses, too, run all night—though, again, services are greatly reduced. For **more information** pick up a *Muni* map ($1.50) from the Visitor Information Center or bookshops, though it's unlikely that you'll need to be familiar with more than a few of the major bus routes, the most important of which are listed below. See also the route map overleaf, which details all major bus and *Muni* lines.

OTHER PUBLIC TRANSIT SERVICES

There are a number of **other public transit networks** running into the city, though these are most useful for the rest of the Bay Area. Along Market Street in downtown San Francisco, *Muni* shares the station concourses with *BART*, the Bay Area Rapid Transit system, linking major points in San Francisco with the East Bay and outer suburbs. The **CalTrain** commuter railroad (Depot at 4th and Townsend streets, South of Market) links San Francisco with points along the Peninsula south to San Jose. **Golden Gate Ferry** boats leave from the Ferry Building on the Embarcadero, crossing the bay past Alcatraz to Marin County. For more details see the "Getting Around" sections of the various Bay Area chapters, Nine to Twelve.

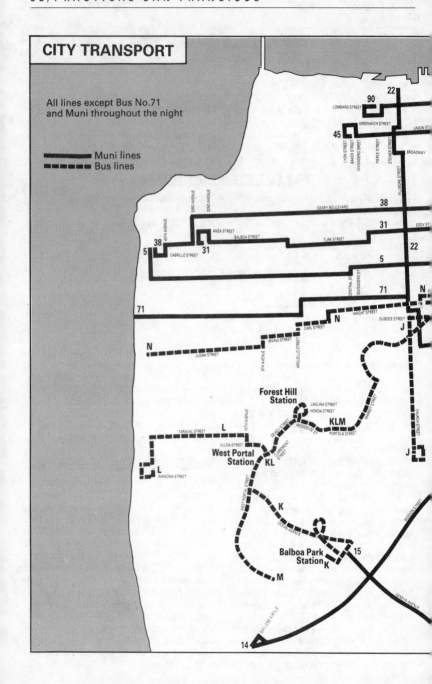

CITY TRANSPORT

All lines except Bus No.71
and Muni throughout the night

━━━━━ Muni lines
▬ ▬ ▬ ▬ Bus lines

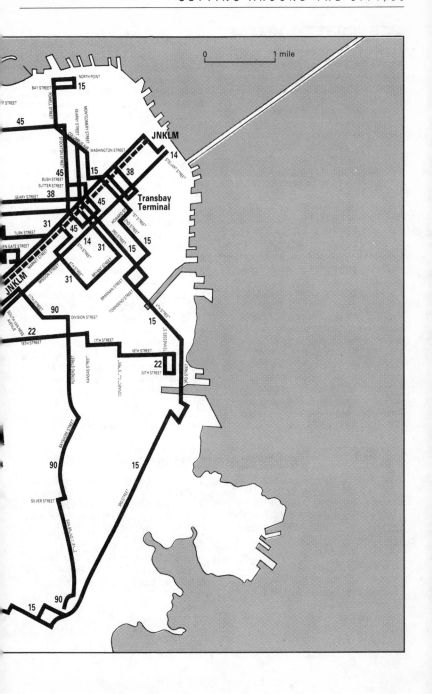

DRIVING: TAXIS AND CARS

Taxis—as in most cities, normally colored yellow—don't cruise the streets in San Francisco the way they do in some cities. If you want one and you're not in a busy part of town or near a big hotel you'll probably have to telephone: try *Veterans* (☎552-1300) or *Yellowcab* (☎626-2345). Fares work out at approximately $3 for the first mile, $1.50 a mile thereafter.

You don't need a **car** to get around San Francisco, but if you're staying some way out from the center, it can make life easier—especially if you want to see something of the Bay Area while you're here. Under-25s may encounter problems if trying to **rent a car** and will probably get lumbered with a higher than normal insurance premium; those under 21 will find it impossible. Car rental companies will also expect you to have a credit card; if you don't have one they may let you leave a hefty **deposit** (at least $200) but don't count on it.

Often the cheapest way to **rent a car** is either to take a fly-drive deal (see *Basics*, "Getting There") or book **in advance** with a major agent like *Avis*, *Budget*, *Hertz*, or *Thrifty*—all of which have offices around the country. You don't have to pay until you pick up the car, but make sure you get written confirmation of the quoted price and take it with you when you get the car.

Once you have a vehicle, you'll find **gas** (US: gasoline) is amazingly cheap at just $1 a gallon, $1:25 for **unleaded** gas, which most cars use. Most rental cars have automatic transmission,

power-assisted brakes, and power-assisted steering, and use unleaded gas. If you're unfamiliar with these features, take a chug around the block to get used to them.

As for **local laws**, front-seat passengers must always wear seat belts. **State Highways** and **US Highways** run through the city—though in San Francisco and the more built-up parts of the Bay Area most roads are better known by their local name. Hwy-1, for instance, is known as 19th Avenue. The speed limit in the city and other built-up areas is 30–35mph; otherwise it's a maximum of 55mph. There are no **spot fines**, but if given a ticket for **speeding** reckon on being fined at least $75.

Other than these, there are no special rules to **driving** in the city beyond contending with its often very steep gradients—remember to turn the wheel toward the curb when parking on hills. Bear in mind that **DWI—"Driving While Intoxicated"**—laws are very strict, and that all opened containers of alcohol in the vehicle are deemed illegal. If a police officer smells alcohol on your breath, he/she is entitled to administer a breath, saliva, or urine test—and you can be fined up to $200 if you fail—or in extreme (or repeat) cases, imprison you for thirty days.

It can be maddeningly difficult to find a place to leave the car, but don't lose your cool: **no parking** regulations are strictly enforced, and traffic wardens will ticket you in a matter of seconds—which at an average of $20 a ticket can get expensive; worse, they'll sometimes tow your car away. There are a number of **parking lots** in the South

---

CAR RENTAL COMPANIES

Besides the big international **car-rental companies**, all of which have outlets at the airport, there are a number of other, more local companies worth looking into. Several are listed below, but its always worth checking with the bigger companies first—they can afford to cut their rates and special offers (especially on compact and economy models) come up all the time. Bear in mind, though, that **insurance** is extra, and can add a hefty amount onto the daily rate.

Alamo, 687 Folsom St. (☎882-9440). Good daily rates, from as little as $21.95 per day.

Avis, 675 Post St. (☎885-5011). Good week-long deals from $115 with unlimited mileage.

Continental, 404 O'Farrell St. (☎441-1771). $22.95 per day.

Dollar, 333 Taylor St. (☎673-2137). $26.95 per day.

Enterprise, 1133 Van Ness Ave. (☎441-3369).

Small cars available from $23 per day.

Hertz, 433 Mason St. (☎771-2200). Good weekly deals with unlimited mileage from $145.

Reliable, 349 Mason St. (☎928-4414). $22 per day.

Rent-a-Wreck, 555 Ellis St. (☎776-8700). For just $20 a day you may find yourself an old Cadillac or Thunderbird to pose around in.

Thrifty, 435 Taylor St. (☎673-6674). $29.95 per

of Market industrial area that charge $5 a day; more central garages charge that much per hour. Of these, the best deals are to be had in the parking lots under Union Square downtown, under Portsmouth Square in Chinatown, and at Ghirardelli Square near Fisherman's Wharf.

If you **break down** in a rented car, there'll be an emergency number pinned to the dashboard. Otherwise you should sit tight and wait for a member of the Highway Patrol, who cruise by regularly.

CYCLING

In general, **cycling** is a cheap and healthy method of getting around San Francisco and the Bay Area, some parts of which have cycle lanes; local buses are often equipped to carry bikes strapped to the outside. In **country areas**, there's much scenic, and largely level, land, especially around the Wine Country. Bikes can be **rented** for $8–15 a day, $45–70 a week, from outlets usually found close to beaches, university campuses, or simply in areas which are good for cycling. City rental shops are listed below, those elsewhere in the appropriate sections of the guide; the local visitors' center will also have details.

BIKE AND SCOOTER RENTAL

California Scooter, 640 Stanyan St. (☎751-4100). Scooters for around $45 a day.
Park Cyclery, 1865 Haight St. (☎221-3777). Touring bikes for $18 a day, mountain bikes $25 a day, weekly rates from $75.

ORGANISED TOURS

If you've just arrived, you may want to orient yourself by taking an **organized tour**. *Gray line Tours* (☎558-9400) will whip you around the city in three fairly tedious hours, stopping at Twin Peaks and Cliff House, for around $25 a head. Skip it unless you're really pushed for time and want to get a general idea of the city's layout with minimal effort.

Excruciatingly expensive but spectacular **aerial tours** of the city and Bay Area in light aircraft are available from several operators, the cheapest of which is *Airship Industries Skycruise* (☎568-4101), which offers one-hour airship cruises for $150. Much cheaper are *Commodore Helicopters* (☎332-4482), which hover over the city for around $70 per hour, with longer tours up and down the coastline available for considerably larger sums. You might prefer one of the more leisurely two-hour **bay cruises** operated by the *Blue & Gold Fleet* (☎781-7877) from piers 39 and 40—though at $17 a throw these don't come cheap either, and in any case everything may be shrouded in fog.

For **tours of the Wine Country and other parts of the Bay Area**, see the relevant chapters in *Part Three*.

WALKING TOURS

There are some excellent personalized **walking tours** available in San Francisco. The better ones usually have no more than five to a group and can often be an informative and efficient way of getting to know a particular area of town. The Visitor Information Center will be able to give you a full list, but among those you might like to try are:

A.M. Walks, 1433 Clay St. (☎928-5965). If you can stand the early start (7am or 9am) you can take advantage of the cheapest downtown walking tour available. For only $10 San Francisco author John McCarroll will take you around Union Square, Chinatown, and the Financial District on a two-and-a-half-hour witty, anecdotal trek.

Café Walks (☎751-4286). Detailed walking tours of the Haight-Ashbury, a Mansion tour of Pacific Heights, and best of all a tour of North Beach and Russian Hill are available for $18 each. Tours last two to three hours and include a light lunch.

Cruisin' the Castro, 375 Lexington St. (☎550-8110). The Supreme Champion of the walking tour circuit in San Francisco, Trevor Hailey, a resident of San Francisco's gay community for fifteen years, takes you on a fascinating tour of this small area. Her knowledge includes everything from politics to the best parties, and she embellishes her three-and-a-half-hour tour with funny stories. $25 per person includes breakfast. Worth every cent.

Friends of Recreation and Parks, MacLaren Lodge, Stanyan and Fell Sts. (☎221-1311). Explore Golden Gate Park with trained guides who point out the flora, fauna, and history of the park. $15.

Helen's Walk Tour (☎524-4544). Helen Rendon, a four-feet-ten-inch dynamo, leads you around the murals of the Mission with her personal brand of commentary and historical perspective. $20 per person includes a stop for coffee and pastries.

San Francisco Art Tours (☎832-2421). Two-hour tours of either the downtown galleries or

(much better) the alternative art spaces South of Market. Traces the history of San Francisco's artistic community and discusses local artists. $15 per person.

San Francisco Discovery Walks, 1200 Taylor St. (☎673-2894). Four different tours highlighting major architectural sights. $15–20.

ACCOMMODATION

San Francisco isn't short on accommodation. Visitors are its number one business, and even during the busier months failure to phone ahead needn't result in getting stuck for a place to stay, though it's a good idea to make advance reservations in late summer and fall. However, it is a major expense, with prices running at a minimum $10 for the cheapest dormitory bed, $30 a night for the most basic hotel or motel room—$70 for anything fairly decent. The city's stock of bed and breakfast inns, starting at around $30 a night, often offers better value. Camping isn't really an option in San Francisco itself, but is one of the best ways to experience the untrammeled natural beauty of the surrounding Bay Area; it's also sometimes free, though campgrounds with hot showers or other facilities charge $8–12 a night.

We've listed the various city options below; for **specific accommodation possibilities in the Bay Area**, see the relevant chapters in Part Three. In all cases bear in mind that all quoted room rates are subject to an **eleven-percent room tax**. If you do have trouble finding a place, call either **Central Reservations of Hotel Group of America** (☎775-4600) on Market Street at Mason, or **Golden Gate Lodging Reservations** at 1030 Franklin Street (☎771-

6915), both of which, for a small fee, will find you a room from around $40 for a single, $50 a double. If all else fails and you've got a car, **motels** are legion along the highways and bigger roads throughout the Bay Area, at a fairly standard rate of $30–40 a night.

HOSTELS AND YMCAS

At the bottom end of the price scale, there are a number of **hostels** in both the city and the Bay Area in general, some in very beautiful settings. Beds in dormitories go for around $10 on average, and many hostels also offer cut-rate single and double rooms, too.

There's really little else you can expect from a hostel apart from a clean safe bed and somewhere to lock your valuables. Some are livelier and more liberal than others, though those with curfews can generally be described as the safest—for women traveling alone they can often be good places to feel secure and meet other people. The hostels vary between the unofficial private places, where things will in general be more relaxed, and the official AYH hostels, which will be better equipped but normally have some kind of curfew. There are a dozen or so AYH hostels in the Bay Area, charging around $10 on average for a dormitory bed—easily the cheapest option under a roof. There're also the **YMCAs** – cheap hotels for young people really, not offering dormitory accommodation but single and double rooms for $20–30 and good facilities including gyms and swimming pools, and sometimes a cheap cafeteria.

Particularly if you're traveling in high season, it's advisable to reserve **ahead** in writing, enclosing a deposit, or by sending an *IYHF Advance Booking Voucher*, available free from any international youth hostel office or specialist travel agent (though first check that the hostel you're after accepts them—a few don't). Beds reserved in this way will be held until 9pm. Some hostels will allow you to use a **sleeping bag**, though officially they should (and many do) insist on a **sheet sleeping bag**. You can buy these, or they can be rented at the hostel. The maximum stay at each hostel is technically three days, though this is again a rule which is often ignored if there's space. Few hostels provide meals but most have **cooking** facilities, and there's almost always a curfew some time between 10pm and midnight; alcohol, smoking, and drugs are banned.

European Guest House, 763 Minna St. (☎861-6634). Dormitory-style accommodation with communal kitchen. No curfew; safe locker facilities. $9 per night per person.

Globe Hostel, 10 Hallam Place (☎431-0540). Funky, lively hostel with music room, sauna, and no curfews. From $12 per person, per night.

International Network Cotel, 1906 Mission St. (☎864-3629). Shared dormitory-style accommodation, with some private rooms available, in this upmarket crash-pad with kitchen facilities. $10 per person per night. Private rooms $25–30.

San Francisco International Hostel, Building 240, Fort Mason (☎771-7277). On the waterfront between the Golden Gate Bridge and Fisherman's Wharf. Annoying 11pm curfew, but one of the most comfortable hostels around. $9 per person Nov–April; $9.50 May–Oct.

YMCA Central Branch, 220 Golden Gate Ave., two blocks from the Civic Center (☎885-0460). Well-equipped and centrally located YMCA. Singles $22, doubles $32. Facilities include a gym, swimming pool, squash courts, and sauna.

Youth Hostel Central, 116 Turk St. (☎346-7835). Bit of a flop house but only $8 per person. Private rooms available. $15 a single and $20 for a double.

HOTELS AND MOTELS

San Francisco **hotels and motels** have a good reputation for comfort and cleanliness, and there's often little to choose between the two. Hotels tend to be more centrally situated than motels, which are more often located along the main arteries leading out of town—Lombard St. is one; indeed they are perhaps a better option if you're driving: San Francisco is a notoriously difficult city to park in, and most have free parking facilities. Motels are perhaps, on average, slightly cheaper. Whichever you decide to stay at, you can

expect a fairly uniform standard of comfort—double rooms with bathroom, TV, and phone—and on the whole you won't get a greatly better deal by paying, say, $50 instead of $30. Over $50, the room and its fittings simply get bigger and more luxurious. Paying over $100 brings you into the decadent realms of the en suite jacuzzi ....

Hotels in the slightly seedy areas south of Market and the Tenderloin start at around $25 a night or $100 a week, though don't expect a private bath or even toilet for that amount. In the glitzier areas around Union Square and Nob Hill it's hard to find a place for under $100 a night. Very few hotels or motels bother to compete with the ubiquitous diners and offer **breakfast**, although there's a trend toward providing free coffee (from paper cups) and sticky buns on a self-service basis from the lobby).

Wherever you stay, you'll be expected to **pay in advance**, at least for the first night and perhaps for further nights, too, particularly if it's high season and the hotel's expecting to be busy. Payment can be in cash or in US dollar travelers' checks, though it's more common to give your credit card number and sign for everything when you leave. **Reservations** are held until 5pm or 6pm unless you've told the hotel you'll be arriving late. Bear in mind the most upscale establishments have all manner of services which may appear to be free but for which you will be expected to **tip** in a style commensurate with the hotel's status—ie *big*.

We've listed hotels and motels together by neighborhood rather than price, with a separate section detailing the city's most luxurious places. In general, none of our recommendations will cost much more than $80 a night, and very few clock in at much under $30. We've also included a section on hotels near the airport, though, because downtown San Francisco is so close (about 20min in a taxi or car), you'll only need to use one of these if you're arriving late at night and are bound for a farther-flung destination. In all cases close to the airport, expect the standard international comforts and facilities of the big chain hotels.

AIRPORT HOTELS

Best Western Grosvenor Hotel, 380 South Airport Blvd. (☎873-3200). Large comfortable hotel with pool, health club, and free shuttle service to the airport. Rooms from $69 per night.

Best Western Lighthouse Hotel, 105 Rockaway Beach Ave., Pacifica (☎355-6300). Far enough away from the airport to ensure you get a good night's sleep, but with a free shuttle service so you don't miss your plane. Rooms from $75 a night.

La Quinta Inn, 20 Airport Blvd. (☎583-2223). Overnight laundry service and a pool make this a comfortable stopover. Free shuttle service to the airport. Rooms from $65.

Radisson Inn San Francisco Airport, 275 South Airport Blvd. (☎873-3550). Great facilities include restaurant, pool, jacuzzi, live music, and a free shuttle to the airport. Rooms from $85 per night.

Super 8 Lodge, 111 Mitchell Ave., South San Francisco (☎877-0770). Plain, motel-style accommodation with free laundry service, breakfast, and airport shuttle. Rooms from $53.

DOWNTOWN

Beverly Plaza Hotel, 342 Grant Ave. (☎781-3566). Clean if uninspiring rooms whose main reccommendation is their location in Chinatown. Doubles from $75.

Hotel Mark Twain, 345 Taylor St. (☎673-2332). Elegantly decorated colonial-style hotel in the middle of the Theater District. Doubles from $79.

Gates Hotel, 140 Ellis St. (☎781-0430). Super-cheap downtown location with double rooms from $35.

Geary Hotel, 610 Geary St. (☎673-9221). Affordable, no frills Theater District hotel with rooms from $36 per night.

Grant Plaza Hotel, 465 Grant Ave. (☎434-3883). Newly renovated hotel with clean rooms in the middle of Chinatown. Doubles $40.

Lotus Hotel, 580 O'Farrell St. (☎885-8008). Sophisticated, European-style hotel with reasonable rates. Rooms from $45 per night.

THE NORTHERN WATERFRONT

Bel Aire Travelodge, 3201 Steiner St. (☎921-5162). Cheapest of the large motel chains, with rooms available from $50 per night.

Holiday Inn, 1300 Columbus Ave. (☎771-9000). Reliable if dull chain motel with large clean rooms with TV and phone. Doubles $130.

Howard Johnson's Motor Lodge, 580 Beach St. (☎775-3800). Modern, standard motel with rates from $80 per night.

Manor Motel Friendship Inn, 2358 Lombard St. (☎922-2010). Simple, budget accommodation with rooms from $40 per night.

The Mansion, 2220 Sacramento St. (☎929-9444). Up in the fancy reaches of Pacific Heights, this Victorian mansion sits on the hill and charges $90 for a double, which considering the luxury you're swaddled in, isn't bad.

Marina Motel, 2576 Lombard St. (☎921-9406). Cheapest of the motels around here, with rooms going for under $30 per night.

San Remo Hotel, 2237 Mason St. (☎776-8688). Very basic—you'll have to share a bathroom—but for this part of town it's the cheapest you're going to find. Rooms from $30 per night.

The Wharf Inn, 2601 Mason St. (☎673-7411). Comfortable, family-style hotel with free parking. Doubles for around $80.

Van Ness Motel, 2850 Van Ness Ave. (☎776-3220). Large rooms with TVs within walking distance of Fisherman's Wharf. Doubles $50–60.

CIVIC CENTER, SOMA, THE MISSION

The Argyle Suite Hotel, 146 McAllister St. (call collect ☎552-7076). Nothing remarkable about this place, but it's clean, comfortable and safe. $75 a double.

Bay Bridge Motel, 966 Harrison St. (☎397-0657). Basic and somewhat noisy but perfectly placed for late nights in SoMa's clubland. Doubles $60.

Dolores Park Inn, 3641 17th St. (☎621-0482). Tiny but elegant pension-style hotel in the Mission. Doubles from $35.

Embassy Motor Hotel, 610 Polk St. (☎673-1404). Bland but neat hotel close to Civic Center with doubles from $40–48.

Friendship Inn, 860 Eddy St. (☎474-4374). Slightly dodgy location, but good rates with rooms starting from $36 per night.

Golden City Inn, 1554 Howard St. (☎431-9376). Best of the South of Market hotels, far from a flop-house and smack in the middle of the SoMa nightlife scene. Unbelievably good value with doubles for $23–28.

Hyde Plaza Hotel, 835 Hyde St (☎885-2987). Reasonable, no frills Tenderloin hotel with rooms from $25 per night.

San Francisco Central Travelodge, 1707 Market St. (☎621-6775). Dependable chain motel with rooms from around $50 per night.

Travelodge Downtown, 790 Ellis St. (☎775-7612). Same as the above but in a slightly seedier location.

UN Plaza Hotel, 7th and Market St. (☎626-4600). Good location just opposite the Civic Center. Glitzy lobby and large, comfortable rooms. Doubles from $55.

THE CENTRAL NEIGHBORHOODS

Beck's Motor Lodge, 2222 Market St. (☎621-8212). Good Castro location, with large, clean rooms and rates from $50 per night that includes morning coffee. See also "Gay Men's Accommodation," below.

Best Western Kyoto, 1800 Sutter St. (☎921-4000). Immaculate hotel in Japantown with steambaths. Doubles around $80.

Metro Hotel, 319 Divisadero St. (☎861-5364). Homely, clean, and cheap with doubles from $35.

Queen Ann Hotel, 1590 Sutter St. (☎441-2828). Pricey but with full amenities including valet service and free afternoon tea and sherry. Rooms from $95 per night.

THE BEACHES AND OUTLYING DISTRICTS

Ocean Park Motel, 2690 46th Ave. (☎566-7020). A fair way from downtown (15min by car) this is nonetheless a great Art Deco hotel opposite the zoo and the beach. Doubles $40–60.

Oceanview Motel, 4340 Judah St. (☎661-2300). Good access for the park and zoo and right on the *Muni* N Judah line. Rooms from $35 per night.

Sunset Motel, 821 Taraval St. (☎681-3306). One of San Francisco's finest little motels—clean, friendly, and safe with rooms from $45 per night.

LUXURY HOTELS

Fairmont Hotel, 950 Mason St. (☎772-5000). Most famous of San Francisco's top-notch hotels, the Fairmont is an excessively decorated palace with seven restaurants, ten lounges, and fantastic views from the rooms. Rooms go for $145–250 per night.

Huntington Hotel, 1075 California St. (☎474-5400). Understated and quietly elegant compared to its Nob Hill compatriots, this is the hotel for the wealthy who don't need to flash it about. Its bars are neither rooftop nor revolving, but instead opt for simple dark wood furnishings, a piano player, and a very intimate atmosphere. The free limousine service makes it a must if you're going for the full luxury treatment. Rooms cost $160–210.

Mandarin Oriental San Francisco, 222 Sansome Street (☎885-0999). You'll need silly amounts of money if you want to stay in what are reputedly San Francisco's most luxurious hotel rooms. Amenities include valet, concierge, and 24hr room service. Rooms cost $230–450 a night.

Portman Hotel, 500 Post St. (☎771-8600). This place caused a big stink when it went up two years ago, and if you prefer your luxury hotels on the classical side, you'll hate it. If slabs of granite and sparse furnishings are what you're into, however, it might just be for you. Rooms from $175 to $325 per night.

San Francisco Marriot, 777 Market St. (☎777-2799). Most people reckon it's the biggest blight on San Francisco's cityscape to date, but there's a surreal quality to this giant mirrored building that looms up like a huge jukebox on the skyline. Rooms cost $200–350.

St Francis, 335 Powell St. (☎397-7000). Truly grand hotel with a sumptuous lobby, five restaurants, an elegant bar, and disappointingly plain rooms. Its reputation far outstrips the reality of a stay here, but as long as you don't mind the throngs of tourists who pour in to gape at the lobby, you'll be happy. Rooms from $145 to $235.

BED AND BREAKFAST

Bed and breakfast on the West Coast (and in the Bay Area particularly) is often a luxury, and can be a more intimate alternative to a mid-range hotel or motel—even the mattresses have to conform to a standard of comfort far higher than those in hotels, and the largest of establishments will have no more than ten rooms, without TV and phone but often with plentiful flowers, stuffed cushions, and an almost over-contrived homey atmosphere. Other places may just be a couple of furnished rooms in someone's home, or an entire apartment where you won't even see your host, bookable through a number of B&B agencies.

While always including a huge and wholesome breakfast (five courses is not unheard of), prices vary greatly: anything from $30 to $200 depending on location and season; most fall between $45 and $75 per night for a double, a little more for a whole apartment. Bear in mind, too, that most get booked up well in advance.

B&B AGENCIES

Bed and Breakfast International, 1181-B Solano Avenue, Albany CA 94706 (☎525-4569).

Bed and Breakfast San Francisco, Box 349, San Francisco, CA 94101 (☎931-3083).

DOWNTOWN

Adelaide Inn, 5 Isadora Duncan Court, between Geary and Post (☎441-2261). Small hotel with shared bathroom facilities. Doubles from $38.

Alexander Inn, 415 O'Farrell St. (☎928-6800). Great location, just off Union Square. Doubles $39–49.

Ansonia Hotel, 711 Post St. (☎673–2670). A charming inn, three blocks from Union Square and cheap to boot with breakfast and dinner included in the price. Rooms from $35.

Beresford Arms Hotel, 701 Post St. (☎673-2600). Luxury B&B in the heart of town, well worth the few dollars more. Doubles $75.

Cornell Hotel, 715 Bush St. (☎421-3154). Pleasant Nob Hill/Union Square location with basic, clean rooms. Doubles $45–50.

David's, on Theater Row, Geary St. near Taylor (☎771-1600). Not the cheapest place in town, but a great location above San Francisco's largest and best Jewish delicatessen, in the heart of the Theater District. Rooms $69 for one or two people and all you can eat from the deli in the morning.

Pensione International, 875 Post St. (☎775-3344). Small standard rooms with shared bathrooms. $30 a double.

THE NORTHERN WATERFRONT

The Art Center Bed and Breakfast, 1902 Filbert St. (☎567-1526). Home away from home, mainly for painters who come to sit in the grounds and attend the classes given by the owners of this quirky little inn. Apartments or suites from $65 to $120.

Edward II, 3155 Scott St. (☎921-9776). Large and comfortable inn-style accommodation with free wine and breakfast. Doubles from $60.

Marina Inn, 3110 Octavia St. (☎928-1000). Comfortable, homey set-up with rooms from $55 a night.

Washington Square Inn, 1660 Stockton St. (☎981-4220). Bang on North Beach's lovely main square with rooms from $65.

CIVIC CENTER, SOMA, THE MISSION

Albion House, 135 Gough St. (☎621-0896). Small B&B above a fine restaurant. Rooms from $65 a night.

Amsterdam Hotel, 749 Taylor St. (☎673-3277). Midway between Union Square and City Hall, this is one of the cheaper B&Bs with rooms from $42.

Inn at the Opera, 333 Fulton St. (☎863-8400). Deluxe B&B with laundry service. Rooms from $105 per night.

Pensione San Francisco, 1668 Market St. (☎864-1271). A good base near the Civic Center, with doubles from $40.

THE CENTRAL NEIGHBORHOODS

Alamo Square Inn, 719 Scott St. (☎922-2055). A beautifully restored old Victorian building, this place isn't cheap, but for handsome dwellings with fireplaces and a jacuzzi, it could be worth the investment for some. Rooms $70–200.

Grove Inn, 890 Grove St. (☎929-0780). Nothing fancy, but good value and a fine location. Rooms from $35 per night.

The Red Victorian Bed and Breakfast, 1665 Haight St. (☎864-1978). Bang in the middle of the Haight Ashbury, a lively B&B with art gallery and rooms with transcendental themes, courtesy of owner Sami Sunchild. A real relic of the Sixties and worth a visit for the free wine evenings. Rooms $45–70.

Stanyan Park Hotel, 750 Stanyan St. (☎751-1000). Gorgeous small Victorian hotel in a great setting across from Golden Gate Park, with friendly staff and free continental breakfast. Doubles for around $80.

GAY ACCOMMODATION

There are, of course, a number of places in San Francisco either sympathetic to—or specifically catering to—**gay travelers**. Most are inevitably geared toward men: although it's unlikely that lesbians would be excluded, they may be outnumbered and should refer to "Women's Accommodation," below, for more suitable alternatives. Information, up-to-date recommendations and referrals are available from the **International Gay Travel Association**, based in Key West, Florida, which has a lot of resources at its fingertips and can book ahead for you. You can call toll-free on ☎1-800/448-8550.

GAY MEN'S ACCOMMODATION

Beck's Motor Lodge, 2222 Market St. (☎621-8212). Motel close to the Castro. Rooms from $50.

Casa Loma Hotel, 600 Fillmore St. (☎552-7100). Mid-sized, friendly hotel with sauna, jacuzzi, sundeck, and lively bar. Singles $30, doubles $38.

Gough Hayes Hotel, 417 Gough St. (☎431-9131). Informal favorite in San Francisco, no private toilets but 24hr sauna and sundeck. Singles from $25, doubles from $29.

Inn on Castro, 321 Castro St. (☎861-0321). A long-standing favorite with visiting gays, this luxury bed and breakfast doesn't come cheap, but is worth it for the large rooms and good breakfasts. About two minutes' walk from the Castro. Singles $85, doubles $95.

Leland Hotel, 1315 Polk St. (☎441-5141). Attractively decorated Russian Hill hotel with singles from $40 and doubles from $68.

Queen Anne Hotel, 1590 Sutter St. (☎262-2663). Very much a gay hotel with overdone decor, full valet service, and complimentary afternoon tea and sherry. Rooms $95 and up.

San Francisco Apartments, 224 Douglass St. (☎861-3220). Well-maintained, upscale accommodation for long-term travelers who need more of a home base. $95 per night, $550 per week.

24 Henry, 24 Henry St. (☎864-5686). Intimate guesthouse in a quiet street just off the heart of the Castro. Singles from $40, doubles $55 and up.

Twin Peaks Hotel, 2160 Market St. (☎621-9467). Set in the hills above, this is a quieter and prettier location not far from the Castro, even if the rooms are small and short on luxury. Singles $25, doubles $30.

WOMEN'S ACCOMMODATION

Bock's Bed & Breakfast, 1448 Willard St. A basic, secure, and friendly hotel for women. Rooms from $35.

The Langtry, 637 Steiner St. (☎863-0538). Each room in this nineteenth-century mansion is dedicated to a famous woman in history. Hot tub, sundeck, views of the city. Fabulous but not cheap with rooms at $75–200 per night.

Women's Hotel, 642 Jones St. (☎775-1711). Comfortable, secure building that is sadly situated in the unpleasant Tenderloin district. Weekly rates only: singles $100 per week, doubles $120. A good deal for two women traveling together.

CAMPING

Though camping isn't really an alternative in San Francisco, it's a very real possibility in the rest of the Bay Area. We've listed all the likely alternatives, ranging from the primitive (a flat piece of ground that may or may not have running water) to others which are more like open-air hotels, with shops, restaurants, and washing facilities. Naturally enough, prices vary according to the facilities, ranging from nothing at all for the most basic plots, up to $12 a night for something comparatively luxurious.

Fully half the land in the Bay Area is in the public domain, and, if you're backpacking, you can **camp rough** in the **wilderness areas** pretty much anywhere you want.

You must, however, always get a **Wilderness Permit** first (either free or $1) from the nearest park rangers' office.

CHAPTER ONE

DOWNTOWN SAN FRANCISCO

an Francisco spreads fairly evenly over most of its 49 square miles, but the greatest concentration of activity is jammed into its oldest and easternmost plot, between the waterfront and the hills that rise steeply to the west. It's difficult to draw clear borders, and the parameters shift according to who you ask, but most of what the locals call **downtown** is contained within a square mile clustered around the northern side of **Market Street**—San Francisco's main commercial and traffic drag, which bisects the northeastern corner of the peninsula. In keeping with its quirky development as a city, downtown San Francisco is a real mixed bag, conforming to no overall image: one block may be thronged with multinational banks and the suited young executives who work in them, another home to Chinese markets and sidewalk evangelists; turn the next corner and you'll find upscale department stores, private clubs, and all the hallmarks of an affluent city.

The nearest thing to a center is **Union Square**, San Francisco's largest and liveliest urban space, populated in equal degree by high-style shoppers, eager street musicians, and out-of-it tramps and beggars. It's the city's main hotel and shopping district, and, as the point where the city's major transport lines cross, makes a logical base for exploring the downtown area. From Union Square you can hop on a cable car up the steep incline of **Nob Hill** to check out the grand mansions of old San Francisco's monied elite, or wander around the bottom of the hill through the **Financial District**, land of San Francisco's only real skyscrapers. Leading off of this, the most recently developed part of town is also the oldest—**Jackson Square** and the historic **Barbary Coast**, nestling inconspicuously in the shadows of the modern city, and for the moment at least giving hardly any hint of its past importance beyond the heavily spruced-up **Embarcadero** next door. On the opposite side of the city center, and worlds away from the glitz and glamor, sits **Chinatown**, a dense and bustling warren of tacky shops and tasty restaurants that's home to the second largest Chinese community outside Asia.

As with most of central San Francisco, **walking** is the best way of seeing all this, perhaps catching the cable car up to Nob Hill on to points farther afield. It's possible, if exhausting, to cover the entire downtown area in a day—it's not a particularly large area. But unless you're on the tightest of schedules you'll get much more out of downtown (and indeed all of) San Francisco just mooching around.

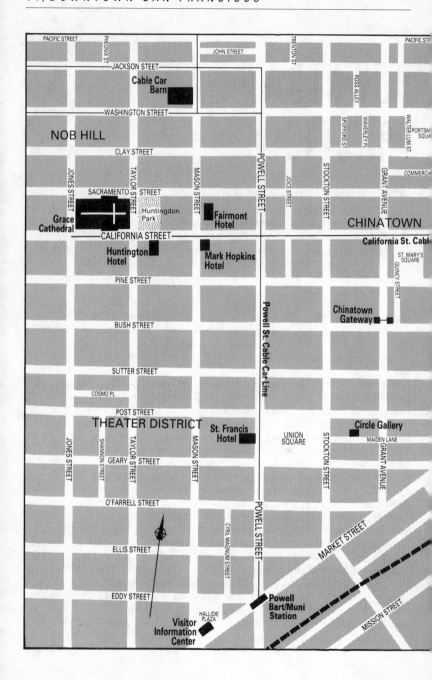

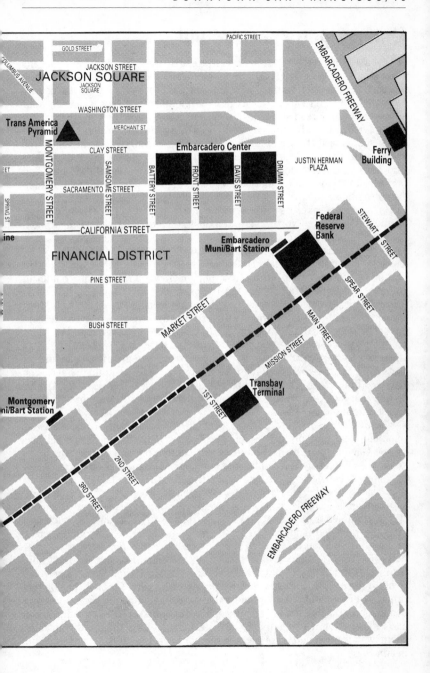

Union Square and Around

It probably isn't at the top of the list of places to see in San Francisco, but the area around **UNION SQUARE** is home to most of the city's hotels, and a few of its more noteworthy bars and restaurants. As a result it's usually thronged with tourists and locals in equal numbers. During the lunch hour office workers spread out with a picnic to watch the street musicians and street performers who congregate here. The square is also the heart of the city's shopping district: limousines are bumper-to-bumper on the surrounding streets—Powell, Geary, Post, and Stockton—and the well-heeled cruise in and out of exclusive department stores, in sharp contrast to the bums and winos from the nearby Tenderloin, who sprawl across the open space's green patches, hoping to do a brisk trade panhandling from passing shoppers.

Union Square takes its name from the mass meetings held here on the eve of the Civil War by Northerners demonstrating their loyalty to the Union. The modern-day square also sees its fair share of protests, and, given its strategic commercial and transit location, a well-organized demonstration can usually draw traffic to a halt. Drably landscaped and mostly paved, its main feature is the **Dewey Monument**, a pigeon-crowded Corinthian column in the center, topped by a miniature statue of winged Victory put up in 1904 to mark Admiral Dewey's naval successes in the Spanish-American War. More recently, in 1975, Union Square saw some raw action when Sarah Jane Moore, a member of the Manson family, attempted to assassinate President Gerald Ford outside the exclusive **St Francis Hotel** on Powell Street, facing the square—a regular temporary home to visiting dignitaries, changing its flags to honor the country of its more important guests. Nothing so flash for Queen Elizabeth II, who had to be put up at the tacky **Sir Francis Drake Hotel**, one block up Powell, when the Britannia broke down during a West Coast tour in the late 1970s.

The *St Francis* was used as the location of Francis Ford Coppola's most paranoid (and possibly best) film, *The Conversation*, in which surveillance expert Gene Hackman spied on lovers strolling in the square from his hotel room. The hotel played a similar role in many of **Dashiell Hammett**'s detective stories, as well as in his own life. In the 1920s Hammett worked there as an operative for the Pinkerton detective agency, investigating the notorious rape and murder case against the silent movie comedian Fatty Arbuckle. When Hammett later came to write *The Maltese Falcon* and other classic tales, he modeled many of the locations on the *St Francis*, though there's nothing in the hotel that makes anything of the connection. One of surprisingly few ventures that does capitalize on the Hammett link is the **Union Square Hotel**, a block toward Market Street at 114 Powell Street, where he wrote some of *The Thin Man* series. There's a bar called *Dashiell's* just off the ornate Art-Deco lobby. A more authentic locale, and a better place to absorb some appropriately hard-boiled atmosphere, is **John's Grill** down the street at 63 Ellis Street. It's been there since 1908 and looks it, though the upstairs room, with walls covered in Hammett memorabilia, is a little too museum-like in atmosphere.

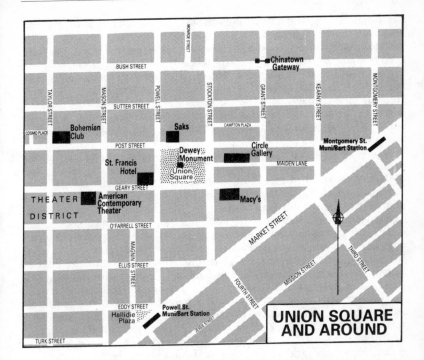

UNION SQUARE
AND AROUND

The sort of shady characters that inhabited Hammett's fictional world would today be more at home west of Union Square, along Geary Street in what's optimistically called the **THEATER DISTRICT**. As in New York's Time Square, the Theater District of San Francisco shares space with less rarefied entertainments, namely porn and prostitution, that spill over from the neighboring Tenderloin near the Civic Center (see Chapter Three), and in fact the legitimate theater scene here is small and not very highly rated. The flagship *American Conservatory Theater* playhouse at 415 Geary Street has been closed since the 1989 earthquake, and even though it continues to put on performances at other venues around the city, it's no compensation for the loss of the city's best theatrical space. In any case, San Francisco has always been much better at the extremes—at the cutting edge of avant-garde performance, or in high-powered opera productions—than it has at mimicking Broadway. Music, theater, and dance options are covered in the "Nightlife" section of Chapter Six.

Also part of this district, just north of the Square along Post and Sutter, are the least visible downtown landmarks—some fourteen private clubs hidden away behind discreet facades. Money isn't the only criterion for membership to these highly esteemed institutions, though being *somebody* usually is. Most notorious is the **Bohemian Club** at Post and Taylor. Better known for its *Bohemian Grove* retreat at the Russian River, where ex-presidents and corporate giants get together for masonic rituals and schoolboy pranks, the San Francisco chapter is housed in a Lewis Hobart Moderne-style building that includes a large theater, as well as more predictable amenities like a bar and good restaurant. Organized in the late 1800s by newspapermen and artists, it evolved into a businessmen's club with an arty slant (during its golden age, the club's members included Frank Norris, Ambrose Bierce, and Jack London), though these days the membership—all male—includes some of America's biggest political and business movers and shakers. A bronze cornerstone bears an owl (the club's emblem) and the motto "Weaving Spiders Come Not Here."

Union Square's claim to fame as **shopping** heaven is supported by the presence of large department stores like *Macy's*, *Saks Fifth Avenue*, and *Neiman Marcus*—the latter worth a look for its marvelous stained glass rotunda, preserved from the old *City of Paris* store which stood on the site until Phillip Johnson did a uninspired job of designing the new store in 1982. The unlikely named *Gump's*, at 250 Post Street, just off the square, specializes in Oriental fabrics and Art-Nouveau objects, and is world-renowned for its museum-worthy collection of jade figures. Elsewhere on this block you'll find the likes of *Gucci*, *Tiffany*, and *Cartier*, though the most attractive place to window-shop is undoubtedly **Maiden Lane**, a chic little urban walkway that leads out of the square half a block south. Before the 1906 earthquake and fire this was supposedly one of the city's roughest areas, where prostitutes solicited openly and homicides averaged around ten a month. Legend has it that women sat behind open windows and the gentlemen could lean through and have a feel for 10¢; an inside visit cost anywhere between 25¢ and a dollar. Nowadays, aside from some prohibitively expensive boutiques, its main feature is San Francisco's only Frank Lloyd Wright building, the expensive little **Circle Gallery** at no. 140—a try-out for the Guggenheim in New York. Inside, a gently curving ramp rises toward the skylighted ceiling, taking you past some of the city's most expensive artwork, while in the cases on the lower floor fine china and crystal command equally high prices.

If you're moving on from Union Square, **cable cars** run along the Powell Street side of Union Square but are usually too packed to board. If you want to ride one up to Nob Hill—or on to the waterfront—try squeezing on a block or so up the hill, or line up with everybody else at the Market Street start, near the **Visitor Information Center**. Better still, wander east into the looming forest of steel and glass towers that forms the city's Financial District.

ACCOMMODATION Hotels *Beverly Plaza Hotel, Hotel Mark Twain, Gates Hotel, Geary Hotel, Grant Plaza Hotel, Lotus Hotel, Portman Hotel, San Francisco Marriot, St Francis;* **Bed & Breakfast** *Adelaide Inn, Alexander Inn, Ansonia Hotel, Beresford Arms Hotel, Cornell Hotel, David's.*

BARS *Edinburgh Castle, Dashiell's, Redwood Room, Starlight Roof.*

RESTAURANTS American *David's Delicatessen, John's Grill, Original Joe's, Trader Vic's;* **Chinese, Thai, and Indonesian** *China Moon Cafe, Indonesian Restaurant, Jing Wah;* **Japanese and Korean** *Benkay.*

The Financial District

The **FINANCIAL DISTRICT** is San Francisco's most highly charged neighborhood—and the city's phenomenal recent development is never more apparent than in these few square blocks, which have some 38 million square feet of office space packed into them. Scattered between the banks and insurance companies are the copy centers and computer boutiques which serve the offices above, with an occasional restaurant of note—jam-packed at lunchtime but otherwise deserted. Sharp-suited workers clog the streets in well-mannered rush-hour droves, racing between the Montgomery *BART/Muni* station on Market Street and their offices. There's not a great deal to come here for if you're not a high-finance wheeler-dealer, or a fan of opulent commercial architecture, but as financial quarters go, San Francisco's is not unattractive. The area is small and merits a stroll at least, even if it's just on the way to somewhere else; it's entirely deserted at the weekend, save for rubbernecks. It contains a virtually comprehensive library of architectural styles and periods, from Palladian piles to post-modern redoubts, though the old-style banking halls have been overshadowed since the frenetic building boom of the 1970s, when they became flanked by newer, taller structures of corporate power. To avert the wholesale demolition of the area for more profitable towers, the city is nowadays directing new development to the south of Market Street.

Montgomery Street has been San Francisco's financial center since the Gold Rush, when it formed the young town's waterfront. To capture the trade of arriving prospectors, canny merchants built long wharves from their Montgomery Street warehouses across the mud flats which stretched out into the bay. Since then the shoreline has been filled in and built on: many of the cross streets—Commercial, Clay and Washington—were simply constructed on top of the old docks, and today's steel and glass towers conceal the remains of over 100 wooden vessels abandoned here in the haste to get to the mines. Nowadays tagged "the Wall Street of the West," Montgomery Street is still the main artery of the Financial District, but the contrast between generations is a stark one: the Ionic columns and robust stone details of the 1922 **Security Pacific Bank**, on the corner of Montgomery and California, are thoroughly overpowered by the ominous hulk of the former **Bank of America** headquarters tower across the street. Though not the tallest, this broad-shouldered monolith of dark red granite is surely the biggest thing on the San Francisco skyline, in the early 1970s challenging the city not only with its size but also with the startling contrast of its hue—San Francisco used to be known as "a city of white." Ironically, the bank founded here in 1904 was forced to sell off the otherwise characterless tower in the early 1980s as a result of its over-zealous lending to developing countries. On the California Street side of the tower is a small plaza with a sleek granite sculpture grandly entitled "Transcendence," though San Franciscans who know better have dubbed it "The Banker's Heart."

The other widely hated Financial District monster is **101 California Street** between Front and Davis, a graceless structure—the biggest of Phillip

Johnson's creations in the city and probably the least successful product of his post-modern dotage. It's a 48-story serrated glass and granite cylinder which rests, in all its bulk, upon a wedge and plaza. The lobby aspires to greenhouse status and has been rudely shoved between the tower's spindly legs. The plants trapped inside cry out for sunshine in the land of high-rise shadows and are removed regularly for therapeutic purposes. The people who work here are less fortunate.

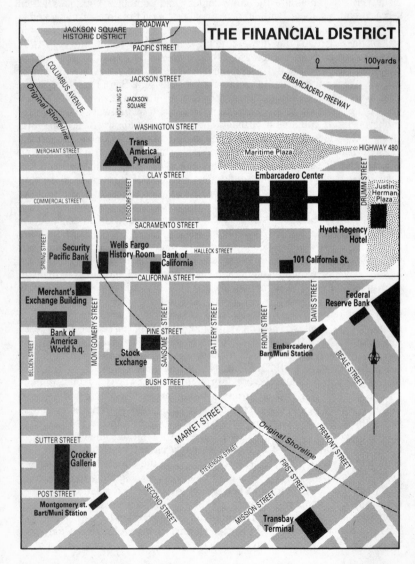

THE FINANCIAL DISTRICT

0   100yards

Surprisingly, there's some fine **art** tucked away in hidden corners of the district. Several blocks north, the **Merchants' Exchange Building** at 465 California St., has a series of nineteenth-century marine paintings by Irish painter William Coulter. At the entrance of its **Grain Exchange Hall** are four huge columns, beyond which the six vast oil canvases depict the history of San Francisco as a seaport. This room was the original center of commercial life in the city, monitoring the comings and goings of every Pacific Coast ship. It was also the place where shippers, warehousemen, and traders would gather to do their bidding.

To get a better sense of San Francisco's historic importance as the financial center of the West, there are a handful of places worth a quick look. The old **Stock Exchange** building at 310 Pine Street is sadly closed to the public nowadays, but it's an impressive structure from the outside—not the original, but a 1930s Art-Deco monument fronted by musclebound figures. The **Wells Fargo History Room**, 420 Montgomery Street (Mon–Fri 10am–5pm; free), details the origins of San Francisco's banking and financial boom with exhibits from the days of the Gold Rush. Mining equipment, gold nuggets, photographs, and even an old stagecoach show the far-from-slick roots of San Francisco's big money. The **Museum of the Money of the American West**, in the Bank of California at 400 California Street (Mon–Thurs 10:30am–3pm; free), offers a similar fare of gold nuggets and the like, and for a more hands-on grasp of the dynamics of modern finance, you should try the Economics Gallery in the **Federal Reserve Bank** (see below).

If negotiating the charging throngs down on the street is too much, you can always just gaze down on them from the rooftop garden of the **Crocker Galleria** at 1 Montgomery Street. Skip the three floors of expensive boutiques and opt for a lunchbox with the office workers.

The Transamerica Pyramid

The **Transamerica Pyramid** is San Francisco's most distinctive landmark, indisputably the most memorable signature of the city's skyline and serving as a useful dividing-point between the various downtown areas. Though the streets around it are oddly quiet considering the vitality of surrounding districts, the 855-foot tower, San Francisco's tallest, is a hinge marking the transition from the towers of the Financial District to the low-level tangle of North Beach and Chinatown. The pyramid rose amid a city-planning furore that earned it the name of "Pereira's Prick," after its LA-based architect William Pereira. However, since then it has been accepted as a notable addition, in these days of plump speculative buildings, as a rare example of an architecture which sacrifices the pragmatic to the symbolic. As it tapers to its slender spire, the floors which fetch the highest rents diminish in area. In other words, the pyramid, from a real estate perspective, would be far more valuable upside down. The 48-story structure is capped by a 212-foot hollow spire, lit from within, making it one of the largest architectural ornaments. There are regular art exhibits in the lobby and an observatory on the 27th floor, though this is fairly unremarkable, and you get the feeling that it should be higher. Nonetheless it's free during business hours, and for that reason alone is worth a ride up in the elevator. Look in also on the small

redwood grove on the east side of the building, landscaped with eighty redwoods from the Santa Cruz mountains, giving the building the appearance of a man-made mountain with its own forest at its feet.

A brass plaque in the lobby and the pretentious *Bank Exchange* bar on the ground floor of the Pyramid are the sole reminders that this was once the site of San Francisco's prime literary and artistic crossroads, the **Montgomery Block**. From 1853, when it was built, until 1959, when it was torn down and made into a parking lot, the four-story Montgomery Block was the city's most important meeting place. Though built as offices for lawyers, doctors, and businessmen, it was soon taken over by writers and journalists, and evolved into a live-in community of bohemian poets, artists and political radicals. Ambrose Bierce, Bret Harte, and Joaquin Miller were frequent visitors to its first-floor bar and restaurant, and Mark Twain met a fireman named **Tom Sawyer**—who later opened a popular San Francisco saloon—in the basement steam baths. Later habitués included George Sterling, Maynard Dixon, and **Sun Yat-sen**, who devised the successful overthrow of the Manchu Dynasty while running a local newspaper, *Young China*, from his second-floor office.

Jackson Square: the Barbary Coast

A century or so ago, the eastern flank of what is now the Financial District was part of the so-called "**Barbary Coast**," a rough-and-tumble waterfront district packed with saloons and brothels where hapless young male visitors were given "Mickey Finns" and "shanghaied" into involuntary servitude on merchant ships. Centered on Pacific Street—which was known as "Terrific Street" up until World War II, when its wicked reputation made it off-limits to military personnel—many of the old dives died an inevitable death, but a few structures survived the 1906 earthquake and fire, and, during the 1930s, the Barbary Coast became a low-rent district that attracted artists and writers, including Diego Rivera, who had a studio on Gold Street at the height of his fame as the "communist painter sought after by the world's biggest capitalists." Most of these old structures have since been renovated and preserved as the **Jackson Square Historic District**—not in fact a square, but a rectangle formed by Jackson, Montgomery, Gold, and Sansome streets, making up a few dense blocks of low-rise, mostly brick buildings that now house the offices of advertising agencies and design firms, as well as the requisite cafés and watering holes.

It's more a place for aimless wandering—**Gold Street** and **Hotaling Place**, the narrow alleys off Jackson Street, are best—than for searching out specific highlights, although there are a few noteworthy sights. Now an office building, 415 Jackson Street was the original Ghirardelli chocolate factory, later moved north to what's now Ghirardelli Square, close by Fisherman's Wharf. At the heart of the district, the survival of **Hotaling's Whisky Distillery** at 455 Jackson inspired this post-earthquake poetic ditty:

If, as they say, God spanked the town
for being over frisky
Why did He burn His churches down
and save Hotaling's Whisky?

Pacific Avenue, originally Pacific Street, the old heart of the Barbary Coast, is now perhaps the most anodyne stretch of the Jackson Square district, though Montgomery Street, at its western edge, holds a number of handsome facades, many with further literary and libertine associations. Just down from Jackson Street, 732 Montgomery Street was the home of San Francisco's first literary magazine, the *Golden Era*, which in the 1850s helped launch the careers of Bret Harte and Mark Twain. Writers John Steinbeck and William Saroyan later spent many a night drinking in the vanished *Black Cat Cafe* down the street, and in the middle of the block, **722–728 Montgomery Street**, where Oscar Wilde paid a visit to the artist Jules Tavernier during his whirlwind visit to San Francisco in 1882, has had its original stucco stripped and been fixed up in overwrought Victorian mode. In its time, the building has been a theater, Turkish bath, tobacco warehouse, and auction room; today you can peer through the windows and see the fascinating, if excessive, clutter and career mementoes of flamboyant San Francisco lawyer Melvin Belli, which fill the place.

The Embarcadero

At the northeastern edge of the Financial District, the small waterfront district known as **THE EMBARCADERO** separates the city from the bay. Before the building of the bridges that connect the city to Oakland and Marin County in the 1930s, the Embarcadero was the main point of arrival for 50,000 cross-bay commuters daily. It's still a transport hub, but the main focus of the area is now a satellite city of offices, hotels, and shops housed in four huge modern complexes, overshadowed by the redundant earthquake-damaged freeway.

At the water's edge sits the **Ferry Building**, at the foot of California Street where commuters from Marin County still arrive. Modeled on the Moorish cathedral tower in Seville, it's a small-scale, dignified structure that's positively dwarfed by the looming structures of the Financial District. These days it sits rather forlornly in the shadow of the Embarcadero freeway, and the characterless office units inside do little to suggest its former importance. Since the earthquake of 1989, the Embarcadero freeway has been closed to traffic after sustaining severe damage. Debate rages among city officials who can't decide whether to spend $10 million on repairing it, or slightly more to tear it down. The issue doesn't look set to be resolved for some time: traders in Chinatown and North Beach have complained about a drop in trade since the closure of the freeway (which gave main access to them)—and while everyone agrees that it's an ugly blight on the cityscape, driving across it at night, level with about the tenth floor of the skyscrapers, was something of a thrill.

North and south from the foot of Market Street (which focuses on a fine view of Twin Peaks), stretches San Francisco's once-vital five-mile-long **waterfront**. Though now deathly quiet, during the first half of the century it was alive to the sights and sounds of huge ships loading and unloading cargo at what was still the main point of arrival for goods and people to the city. It was also the site of one of the more notorious episodes of twentieth-century

San Francisco, when, on the eve of America's involvement in World War I, on July 22, 1916, ten members of a massive pro-war demonstration were killed by a bomb. Though there was no tangible evidence of any link, opposition to US intervention in the war led to the city's union leaders being held responsible for the attack, and charged and found guilty (on perjured testimony) of murder. Tom Mooney, a prominent longshoremen's activist, was sentenced to death, and it took twenty years of lobbying and protest (by Emma Goldman among others) before he was freed and his name cleared. His alleged co-conspirator, Warren Billings, spent most of his life behind bars before being pardoned in 1961. Ironically, the site of the bombing is now filled by the brick fortress headquarters of the **Southern Pacific Railroad Corporation**.

Across the street, wander inside the angular **Hyatt Regency** hotel and gaze up into its twenty-story-high atrium lobby, filled with pot plants, trees, and a fountain/sculpture set in a reflecting pool. An amusing novelty is the rooftop *Equinox* revolving bar. The hotel is part of the enormous **Embarcadero Center** development, sponsored by the celebrated eastern family and originally to have borne their name, but somehow "Rockerfeller Center West" was an appellation that didn't sit so well on the Barbary Coast: San Francisco sees itself in no sense as subordinate to the Big Apple and is only begrudgingly part of the same state as the Big Orange. The four tower-slabs of the Center rise from a multi-level base of offices, shops, and cafés that stretch for several blocks east around the **Justin Herman Plaza**. A large paved space, this is largely unused except for the skateboarders who alone can appreciate such vast stretches of concrete, although it did see some excitement when U2 staged an unannounced concert here in February 1988. For the best part of the day the city came to a standstill as people left their offices and abandoned their shopping, hoping to catch a glimpse of the visiting megastars. Someone hung a banner from an office window that read "SF loves U2"—lead singer Bono misinterpreted the SF for Sinn Fein and after a vitriolic outburst threatened to cancel the gig. Whoops.

Nearby at 101 Market Street, the **Federal Reserve Bank** (Mon–Fri 10am–4pm; free) is an unbeatable amusement if you're at all interested in the machinations of money in the city. Computer games allow you to engineer your own stock market disasters, while gallery exhibits detail recent scandals and triumphs in the financial world.

Outside the bank is the starting point of the California Street cable car line, which leads you out of the Financial District, past Chinatown, and up to Nob Hill.

ACCOMMODATION Hotels *Hyatt Regency Hotel.*

BARS *The Carnelian Room, Equinox, London Wine Bar.*

RESTAURANTS American and Californian *Bix, Fog City Diner, Jack's;* **French** *Le Candide, Ernie's;;* **Chinese, Thai and Indonesian** *Wu Kong Restaurant, Yank Sing.*

Nob Hill

Nob Hill, the hill of palaces, must certainly be counted the best part of San Francisco. It is there that the millionaires are gathered together vying with each other in display. From thence, looking down over the business wards of the city, we can decry a building with a little belfry, and that is the stock exchange, the heart of San Francisco: a great pump we might call it, continually pumping up the savings of the lower quarter to the pockets of the millionaires on the hill.

Robert Louis Stevenson

If the Financial District is where money is made in the city, the smart hotels and masonic institutions of **NOB HILL**, just above, are where it is shown off. In a city famous for its hills, this one tops the lot. It is, as Joan Didion wrote, "the symbolic nexus of all old California money and power" and remains San Francisco's most revered address, its mansions, exclusive hotels, and restaurants looking snootily down over the lower areas of the city. Traditionally, San Francisco's monied elite preferred level streets, and it was the invention of the cable car in the 1870s that turned this from an inaccessible backwater into a slice of prime real estate. At its summit, the hill is 338 feet above sea level, offering fantastic views of the city below. When the transcontinental railroad barons made their fortune, they had no doubts about where to invest it. While there are very few real sights as such, just nosing around, or dropping into the grand hotels for a drink in their rooftop bars, is pleasant enough, taking in the aura of privilege and luxury that distinguishes the neighborhood and enjoying the views over the city and beyond.

Originally called the California Street Hill, the area became known as Nob Hill after **the Big Four** robber-baron industrialists, Collis P. Huntington, Charles Crocker, Mark Hopkins, and Leland Stanford, who had made millions on the Central Pacific Railroad, and the bonanza kings of the silver mines of the Comstock Lode, built their mansions here in the 1880s. Sadly, only one of these ostentatious piles survived the 1906 fire, the brownstone mansion of James C. Flood, which cost a cool $1 million in 1886—now the **Pacific Union Club**, a private retreat for the ultra-rich on California Street at Mason. Behind the club sits **Huntington Park**, not the finest of San Francisco's small parks but a good place to watch nannies push the power-brokers of the future around in their baby carriages. The mansions of other millionaires were not so fortunate, and are now the sites of some of San Francisco's grandest **hotels**: the *Mark Hopkins*, with its spectacular rooftop bar, the *Stanford Court*, the elegant *Huntington*, and the strikingly-lobbied *Fairmont* all line up along California Street quietly competing for the top-dollar trade.

Impressive though they are, none of these buildings can compete for effect with the hill's biggest hunk of aspirational architecture, the mock-Gothic **Grace Cathedral** across Huntington Park from the Pacific Union Club (daily 7am–6pm, with free tours Mon–Fri 1–3pm, Sat 11:30am–1:30pm & Sun 12:15–2pm—the highlight is definitely the choral service on Sundays at 11am with a coffee hour afterward). Originally, the block the cathedral stands on was occupied by the homes of the Crocker family, who donated the site to the Episcopal Church after losing their houses in the 1906 fire. Construction began soon after, though most of it was built of faintly disguised reinforced concrete in the early 1960s. The interior shelters an eleventh-century French altar and Renaissance reredos, but the carillon in the bell tower is a contemporary addition from Croydon, England. One part that's worth a look is the entrance, adorned with faithful replicas of the doors of the Florence Baptistry; study, too, the allegorical stained glass around the cathedral walls.

The Cable Car

The invention that made high-society life on the hills possible and practical, the **cable car** (the sort that runs along the ground, not swings precipitously from mountainsides), is another of Nob Hill's dominant features. Since 1873, when Scotsman Andrew Hallidie piloted the first of these little trolleys up the Clay Street hill to Portsmouth Square, they have been an integral part of life in the city. At their peak, just before the 1906 earthquake, over 600 cable cars traveled 110 miles of track throughout the city, though by 1955 their use had dwindled to such an extent that they were due to be closed altogether until nostalgic citizens voted to preserve the remaining 17 miles of track as a moving historic landmark. The streets along which the tracks lie were due for a multi-million-dollar facelift in 1984, and because of the high cost involved, city officials again considered abandoning the system. But public indignance (and some worried maneuvering by the tourist industry) set the restoration in motion. Today some forty-odd cars are in daily operation along three lines, two from Powell Street to Fisherman's Wharf, and the steepest one climbing Nob Hill along California Street from the Embarcadero. The lines cross at the crest of Nob Hill, at the intersection of California and Powell streets.

To climb the hills, the cable cars have to fasten on to a moving two-inch cable which runs beneath the streets, gripping on the ascent then releasing at the top and gliding down the other side. These cables are pulled along by huge motorized pulleys which you can see in the **Cable Car Barn**, two blocks from Grace Cathedral at Washington and Mason streets. This 1887 building has recently been renovated as a working **museum** (daily 10am–6pm; free) with exhibits of vintage cable cars and associated memorabilia.

ACCOMMODATION Hotels *Fairmont Hotel, Huntington Hotel, Mark Hopkins Hotel.*
BARS *The Big Four, 1001 California, Top of the Mark.*
RESTAURANTS American *The Brasserie.*

Chinatown

Hemmed in by moneyed neighbors, plumb at the foot of Nob Hill and just three blocks from Union Square, the two dozen square blocks of constant chaos that make up **CHINATOWN** are completely distinct from any other neighborhood in the city. The gateway arches that mark Chinatown's borders seem barely able to contain the district, and it's by far the city's most thickly populated quarter, with over 80,000 residents in a quarter-mile area. Though home to the second largest community of Chinese outside of Asia, it's no longer solely Chinese: Vietnamese, Thais, Filipinos, and Koreans have all made inroads over recent years, further adding to the dynamism of the neighborhood. Noisy, smelly, colorful, and overcrowded, Chinatown manages to retain a degree of genuine autonomy, despite its obvious reliance on the tourist dollar, with its own schools, banks, and newspapers alongside the predictable morass of souvenir shops. Fortunately, most of the tourist pandering goes on along the main street, Grant Avenue, off which dark, gloomy alleyways thread between buildings that house the real Chinatown of grocery stores, laundries, temples, and bakeries. Looming ominously and casting tall, dark shadows over the small, often unkempt buildings of the district are the massive gleaming monoliths of the Financial District. Contrasts don't come much cruder.

The first Chinese arrived in Northern California in the late 1840s, many of them fleeing famine and the opium wars at home and seeking the easy fortunes of the Gold Rush. Later, in the 1870s, thousands more came across to build the Transcontinental Railroad. At first the Chinese, or "coolies" as they were called (taken from the words *ku li*, meaning "bitter toil"), were accepted as hard-working laborers, but as the railroad neared completion and unemployment rose, many moved to San Francisco, swelling what was already a sizable community. The city didn't extend much of a welcome: jingoistic sentiment turned quickly into a tide of racial hatred, manifested in sometimes vicious attacks that bound the Chinese defensively into a solid, homogenous community. The population stagnated until the 1960s, when the lifting of the anti-Chinese immigration restrictions swelled the area's numbers to close on 160,000. Nowadays the Chinese are the city's most affluent ethnic group: by day the area seethes with activity and congestion; by night the traffic moves a little easier, but the blaze of neon and marauding diners gives the feeling that it just never lets up. Overcrowding is compounded by a brisk tourist trade, and, sadly, Chinatown boasts some of the most egregiously cheap shops and facades in the city. Genuine snatches of ethnicity are sullied by pseudo-Chinese Americana at every turn.

You can approach Chinatown from all sides: Nob Hill drops down to its center, North Beach blends into its upper reaches, and the Financial District flanks it to the east. Coming from the south and Union Square, you enter through the large **dragon-clad archway** that crosses the intersection of Bush Street and **Grant Avenue**—a gift from the Government of Taiwan and, judging from the look of it, not one that broke the bank. Once through here, Grant Avenue seems suddenly much more narrow, crowded with gold ornamented portals and brightly painted balconies which sit above the souvenir shops and restaurants. Plastic buddhas, floppy hats, and chopsticks assault the eye from every doorway. The least obviously Chinese of these falsefronts, a horseshoe-shaped funnel at 916 Grant Avenue, marks one of the very few **bars** in Chinatown—*Li Po's*, named after the great Chinese poet and still something of a literary hangout. Some of the **restaurants**, too, are historical landmarks, none more so than *Sam Woh's* at 813 Washington Street—cheap and churlish ex-haunt of the Beats and still a popular late-night hang-out in which, legend has it, Gary Snyder taught Jack Kerouac to eat with chopsticks and had them both thrown out for his loud and passionate interpretation of Zen poetry.

Before the days of all-consuming tourism, Grant Avenue was known as Dupont Street, an ensemble of opium dens, bordellos, and gambling huts terrorized by *tongs*—Chinese **gangs** who took it upon themselves to police and protect their district in any (usually extremely violent) way they saw fit. Their original purpose was to retaliate against racial hooliganism, but they developed quickly into Mafia-style family feuding—as bloody as any of the Chicago gang wars. These days there isn't much trace of them on the streets, but the mobs continue to operate, battling for a slice of the lucrative West Coast drug trade.

Parallel to Grant, **Stockton Street** is closer to the real thing—Chinatown's main street, crammed with exotic fish and produce markets, bakeries and spice stores; your dollar will go farther here than anywhere else in the neighborhood and your search for the authentic face of Chinatown will be better rewarded, especially if you can manage to get up early. Between Grant and Stockton streets, at the center of Chinatown, a jumble of alleys holds the most worthwhile stops in the area. The best of these is **Waverly Place**, a two-block corridor that was lined with brothels before the 1906 catastrophe and is now the site of most of Chinatown's many family associations and community support groups. It's also home to two opulently decorated but skillfully hidden **temples** (nos. 109–11 and 123–129), their interiors a riot of black, gold, and vermillion. They're still in use today and open to visitors, but the variable opening times mean it's up to chance whether you get in. Nearby, Chinatown's history is well documented in the **Chinese Historical Society of America** at 650 Commercial Street (daily 9am–4pm; donations), which traces the beginnings of the Chinese in the US and has a small but worthy collection of photographs, paintings, and artifacts from the pioneering days of the last century.

Another, more accessible, point of interest is **Buddha's Universal Church** at 720 Washington Street, where America's largest Zen sect gives tours on the second and fourth Sunday of each month. This five-story building was painstakingly built by the sect members from an exotic range of polished woods, adorned everywhere by mosaic images of Buddha. Across the street at 743 Washington, the triple-tiered pagoda of the **Bank of Canton** once housed the multilingual operators of the Chinatown telephone exchange, and the site was earlier the home of the *California Star* newspaper—the city's first daily and the one that announced the discovery of gold in 1848. Not as rich with history, the **Chinese Cultural Center**, tucked away inside the *Holiday Inn* at 750 Kearny Street (Tues–Sat 10am–4pm), does nonetheless have a regular program of art shows, mostly contemporary, that gives much needed exhibition space for the Chinese artistic community, which, traditionally, is poorly represented. A concrete footbridge connects the *Holiday Inn* and the Cultural Center with the larger of Chinatown's two green spaces, **Portsmouth Square**. This was the old center of the city and the place where Sam Brannan announced the discovery of gold—an event that transformed San Francisco from a sleepy Spanish pueblo into a frontier town. Though not the most attractive of parks these days—like Union Square, it's built on top of an indoor parking lot—it's nonetheless an oasis in a very cramped part of town. Old men come to play chess while younger ones fly past on skateboards. In the northwest corner there's a statue of the galleon *Hispaniola* from *Treasure Island*, a monument to Robert Louis Stevenson—who, while waiting for his lover's divorce to come through in 1879, used to come here and write. The other, smaller park, **St Mary's Square**, two blocks south, is dwarfed by a wall of Financial District skyscrapers and marks the western edge of their permitted development. The square holds a bold, modernist sculpture of Sun Yat-Sen, founder of the Chinese republic. Its modern lines would look out of place anywhere in the neighborhood, but do so particularly here, where the old women do their modest Tai Chi routines every morning.

ACCOMMODATION Hotels *Beverly Plaza Hotel, Grant Plaza Hotel.*
BARS *Li Po's.*
RESTAURANTS Chinese, Thai, and Indonesian *Celadon, Empress of China, Lychee Garden, New Asia, Pot Sticker, Sam Woh's, Woey Loy Goey Cafe, Yuet Lee.*

CHAPTER TWO

NORTH BEACH AND THE NORTHERN WATERFRONT

F rom the highly exclusive to the downright offensive, San Francisco's **NORTHERN WATERFRONT** gives you the best and the worst of the city. Before the area came to rest on landfill, the original water-front was the aptly named **North Beach**, a sunny neighborhood in a wind-sheltered valley between two hills in the northeastern corner of the peninsula, which despite chronic gentrification has managed to weather the changes with its Italian foundations intact. As one of the city's oldest neighborhoods, it has a lived-in feeling that will appeal; it's a wonderful area for just hanging around cafés and bars and weaving through its gently sloping streets. Within walking distance, flanking either side of North Beach,

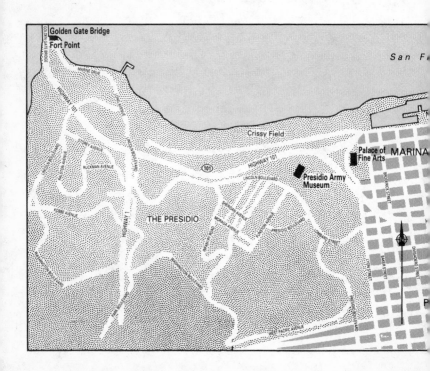

Russian and **Telegraph hills** are more residential in flavor and have few attractions as such, though they, too, are good for strolling and taking in the views of the waterfront—an attractive stretch on the whole, apart from the eyesore that is **Fisherman's Wharf**. As the major focus of tourist activity, you'll have to plow through a lot of overpriced kitsch and commercial gimmicks here to find what remains of the almost obsolete fishing industry: thronged by hundreds of dollar-dropping visitors, it is as crowded as it is unappealing. Moving west from the Wharf, things start to improve: **Aquatic Park** is a small **beach** that draws a few hardy swimmers, though it's known more for being home of the **Maritime Museum**. It's used as a walk-through on the way to **Fort Mason**—an old military installation that was rescued from the clutches of development and now has an impressive grouping of small museums, workshops, theaters, and an excellent youth hostel. Continuing west, the waterfront becomes a focus for the fancy yacht clubs that make up the northernmost tip of the **Marina** district, with its neighbor **Pacific Heights**, a desirable district that thrives on its exclusivity and has little to offer the visitor beyond a mild envy and the distinctive **Palace of Fine Arts**, which rises majestically above the skyline of expensive homes. If you're a keen walker, you may want to trudge the extra mile to the sizable chunk of open green space that covers the remainder of the northern waterfront. **The Presidio**, as it's known, is an army base which is winding down its

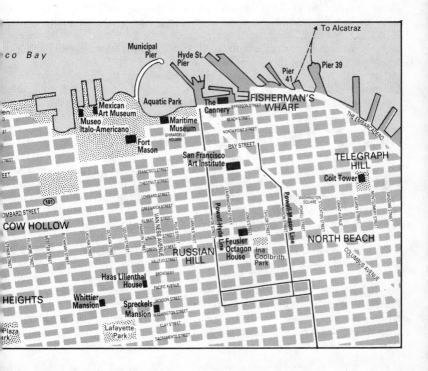

operations as a military site and gradually being turned over to public use. Very little of the base is off-limits, but there's not an awful lot there. However, its eucalyptus groves provide an inspiring approach to the orange spires of the city's most famous landmark, the **Golden Gate Bridge**.

North Beach

From the base of the Transamerica Pyramid, **Columbus Avenue** cuts diagonally through the heart of one of San Francisco's most wanderable quarters, **NORTH BEACH**. This was indeed a beach before landfill pushed back the bay; nowadays, resting in the hollow between Russian and Telegraph hills, North Beach likes to think of itself as the happening district of San Francisco. Originally it was the city's Italian quarter, with, at its peak in the 1940s, some 60,000 mostly northern Italians living within its boundaries. With the prosperity and mobility that followed the war, many left, and with the decongestion rents came down, and the disenchanted children of a bourgeois, postwar America moved in. Since this migration of the 1950s, when the more prominent figures of the **Beat movement** gathered here, it has been among the city's most sought-after sectors for anyone vaguely alternative. There's still an Italian slant to the neighborhood, and it's home to some of the city's best bars and restaurants, but rocketing real estate prices are inevitably bringing about change, and die-hard free-thinkers wrestle to maintain their territory amid the growing numbers of suave young professionals slumming it at North Beach's traditionally seedy cafés. That said, there's still a solid core, and the anecdotes connected with North Beach remain legion—get chatting to any barfly over fifty, they seem to know them all.

The southern edge of the district is visually anchored by the green flatiron **Columbus Tower**, situated on the island formed by Columbus, Kearny, and Jackson streets and looking somewhat surreal against the corporate backdrop of the downtown skyline. Developers have been trying to knock this down for years, but the efforts of its owner, San Francisco-based filmmaker Francis Ford Coppola, have so far ensured its survival. Across Columbus, the now defunct *Purple Onion* nightclub, and the *Hungry i* down Jackson Street, hosted some of the biggest names of the 1950s San Francisco scene. Politically conscious comedians like Mort Sahl, Dick Gregory, and the legendary Lenny Bruce performed here, as did San Francisco author Maya Angelou, in her earlier guise of singer and dancer. These landmarks have now closed or changed beyond recognition, but the district still trades on a reputation earned decades ago.

Another North Beach literary landmark, the **City Lights Bookstore**, stands two blocks up Columbus. The nation's first all-paperback bookshop, established in 1953 and still owned by the poet and novelist Lawrence Ferlinghetti, it's open until midnight seven days a week, and its vast collection of avant-garde, contemporary, and Beat writings keep it very much at the core of the San Francisco literary scene. To encourage the creative juices, almost every local with literary aspirations has spent some time at **Vesuvio's**, handily placed next door. The likes of Dylan Thomas and Jack Kerouac regularly got loaded here, and while times have changed considerably since then, it remains a haven for the lesser-knowns to get blind drunk with impunity and pontificate on the state of the arts. Across Columbus two other Beat bars, *Spec's* and *Tosca's*, should satisfy all but the most unquenchable thirst.

Assuming you leave any of these places with your brain intact, you'll find yourself at the intersection of **Columbus and Broadway**, where poetry meets porn in a raucous assembly of slowly dying strip joints, rock venues, and drag queens. Most famous of these is the *Condor Club*, where the sight of Carol Doda's silicone-implanted breasts thrilled a decade of voyeurs before she quit the stage for a quieter life. Her nipples, once immortalized in neon above the door as a tribute to the years of mammary fascination, have ceased to flash with the closure of the club, signaling lean times for the other clubs along the strip and what seems to be the end of the sex-club era. Beat tourists will want to stop for a look at the building two blocks down, on the northeast corner of Broadway and Montgomery Street, where Allen Ginsberg lived during 1955 when he wrote the definitive Beat poem, *Howl*.

THE BEAT GENERATION

North Beach has always been something of a literary hangout, but it was the emergence of the **Beat Generation** in the late 1950s that really put the place on the map, focusing media attention on the area as literary capital of California. The first Beat writers—Jack Kerouac, Allen Ginsberg, and others—came out here from New York City; like many, they were frustrated by the conservative political climate of the time, and their lifestyle and values emphasized libertarian beliefs that America wasn't perhaps ready for. Nothing really crystallized, however, until they moved out West, settling in North Beach and linking up with an esoteric cluster of writers, poets, musicians, and inevitable hangers-on around the *City Lights* bookstore.

It wasn't long before the Beats were making news. In 1957 a storm of controversy rose up when police moved in to prevent the sale of Ginsberg's poem *Howl* under charges of obscenity—an episode the press latched onto immediately, inadvertently hyping the Beats to national notoriety, as much for their hedonistic antics as for the literary merits of their work. Within six months, Jack Kerouac's *On the Road*—inspired by his friend Neal Cassady's benzedrine monologues and recorded in a marathon two-week session in New York six years earlier—shot to the top of the bestseller lists, having been previously rejected by all the publishers he had offered it to. As well as developing a new, more personalized style of fiction and poetry, the Beats eschewed most social conventions of the time, and North Beach soon became a virtual symbol of their wild and subversive lifestyle, the road trips and riotous partying, the drug-taking and embrace of eastern religion revered and emulated nationwide. Whether the Beat "message" was an important one is a moot point; in any case, the movement—and Kerouac in particular—became more of an industry than anything else, and whatever impact the Beats might have had was quickly trivialized as tourists poured into North Beach for "Beatnik Tours" and the like. But the legend has yet to die, not least in North Beach itself, where—in a campaign vigorously led by Lawrence Ferlinghetti—many of the city's streets have been renamed as a tribute to the famous figures who have graced the neighborhood: the small alley which runs down the side of *City Lights* is called "Jack Kerouac Street."

Continuing north on Columbus the bright lights fade and you enter the heart of the old Italian neighborhood, an enclave of restaurants, cafés, and delicatessens set against a background of narrow streets and leafy enclosures. **Fugazi Hall** at 678 Green Street, between Columbus and Powell, is the neighborhood's grandest symbol of Italian pride. Donated to the community in 1912 by their most prominent figure, John Fugazi, a banker who founded the Transamerica Corporation, this elaborate terracotta-ornamented building was used as a community center and is now host to San Francisco's longest running show, *Beach Blanket Babylon* (see "Theater," Chapter Eight), as well as an upper-floor room that holds photographs depicting the history of San Francisco's Italian community. A couple of hundred yards along, at Columbus Avenue and Union Street, **Washington Square Park** isn't, with five sides, much of a square; nor, due to urban overcrowding, is it much of a park either. However, it's big and green enough for the elder Italians to rest on the benches and the neighboring Chinese to do their Tai Chi routines here on a Sunday morning. On the north side of the park the lacy spires of the **Church of St Peter and Paul**, where local baseball hero Joe DiMaggio married Marilyn Monroe, dominate the center of the neighborhood. There's a statue of Benjamin Franklin in the center of the park, donated by an active prohibitionist who installed faucets at the base of the monument, in the unlikely hope that people would drink water from them rather than try to get their hands on bootleg liquor.

A quick diversion along any of the side streets—Grant is one of the best—will lead you to small landmarks like the *Cafe Trieste*, on Grant and Vallejo streets, a literary waking-up spot since the days of the Beats and still a reminder of more romantic times. On Saturday mornings the owners treat customers to renditions of their favorite opera classics; at other times the café packs in a heavy-duty art crowd, toying with their cappuccinos and browsing through slim volumes of poetry. *The Lost and Found Saloon*, half a block up Grant next to the ancient *Fugazi Hardware Store*, is another survivor: except for a name-change it's much as it's always been, still a favorite with the jazz-and-poetry brigades. There are dozens of bars and cafés jumbled throughout the neighborhood, the best of which are listed in Chapter Seven, *Drinking and Eating*.

ACCOMMODATION Hotels *San Remo Hotel;* **Bed & Breakfast** *Art Center Bed & Breakfast, Washington Square Inn.*

BARS *Enrico's Sidewalk Cafe, The Saloon, San Francisco Brewing Co., Savoy Tivoli, Spec's, Tosca's, Vesuvio's, Washington Square Bar & Grill.*

CAFÉS *Bohemian Cigar Store, Cafe Francisco, Cafe Roma, Cafe Trieste.*

RESTAURANTS Budget *Clown Alley;* **Pizza** *Calzone's, Golden Boy, North Beach Pizza, Tommaso's;* **American and Californian** *Washington Square Bar & Grill;* **Italian** *Capp's Corner, Gold Spike, Green Valley Restaurant, Il Pollaio, Little Joe's, North Beach Restaurant, Raf, Ristorante Firenze;* **Chinese, Thai, and Indonesian** *Brandy Ho's;* **Mexican** *El Tapatio.*

Russian Hill and Telegraph Hill

The two hills that rise steeply to either side of Columbus Avenue are where the bar- and café-hoppers go home to. To the east of Columbus Avenue, **Telegraph Hill**—named after an old wire station that once stood here and now capped by Coit Tower—is a neighborhood of small alleys and eclectic architecture perched on 45-degree inclines. To the west, **Russian Hill** is known to some for Lombard Street—the much-photographed "Crookedest Street in the World"—and to others as the home of writer Armistead Maupin's *Tales of the City* crew. Both hills have the lion's share of the city's most desirable, if not most prestigious, residences, and if you've got strong legs the network of enticing paths, leafy alleys, and stairways that climb their heights can make for a great day's wander.

Russian Hill

Bounded by North Beach to the west and Nob Hill to the south, **RUSSIAN HILL** is an immaculately maintained residential neighborhood of steep slopes and small parks, whose population could be termed as the high-end of bohemia. The hill takes its name from a mysterious legend that tells of a group of Russian sailors who died and were buried here on an expedition from the fur trading companies north of the city in the early 1800s. Excavations carried out some years ago uncovered some unidentified graves, but no tangible proof exists to either deny or confirm the story. At its summit, the hill is some 295 feet high, and it wasn't until cable car lines crossed it during the 1880s that any houses were built. Since that time, it has had an artistic reputation supported only by a few literary figures who inhabited its slopes—Jack Kerouac, Ambroce Bierce, Joaquin Miller, Frank Norris, and California's first Poet Laureate, Ina Coolbrith—and its art institute, although for the most part it's a quiet, fairly wealthy enclave in a crowded corner of town: figuratively, and literally, above it all. A sensible city ordinance prohibits tour buses in the neighborhood, and the most you'll see of other visitors will be those hanging off the Powell–Hyde cable car that traverses Russian Hill on its way to Fisherman's Wharf.

Whether you tour the area by day or night, it's sensible to use **Hyde Street** as your point of reference. It's central to anything you might want to see as well as being well served from the downtown area, and waterfront by cable cars. Come before nightfall, if only to visit the **San Francisco Art Institute** at 800 Chestnut Street (galleries open Tues–Sat 10am–5pm; free) on the eastern slope of the hill. The institute is the oldest art school in the Western United States and as such has been central to the development of the arts in the Bay Area. Housed in a hybrid structure that is one part Mission-style from the 1920s and another part concrete brutalism from the 1960s, it has four galleries, three dedicated to painting and one to photography, mainly exhibiting the work of the students and rotated on a regular basis. The highlight of the institute is unquestionably the **Diego Rivera Gallery**, which has an outstanding mural done by the painter in 1931, at the height of his fame. There's a **cafeteria** on a deck at the back of the building that's a cheap place to refresh yourself and look at the great views of North Beach, Telegraph Hill, and the bay.

Two blocks away on the 1000 block of Lombard at Hyde, you'll run into the cars lining up to drive down the **"Crookedest Street in the World"**—a narrow, tightly curving street with a 5-mph speed limit to make descending its steep gradient less than hazardous. It's featured as often as the Golden Gate Bridge in publicity shots for the city, and is usually surrounded by camera-wielding tourists by day—better to see it at night after they're gone and city lights twinkle below. Its contours make for a thrilling descent by car. At the top of the street is the tiny but immaculate **Alice Marble Park**, good for taking a breather and stretching out in the sun. To continue on from here, head south to Union Street and then one block east until you come to **Macondry Lane**, a walkway made famous as "Barbary Lane" in Armistead Maupin's *Tales of the City*. The lane's leafy enclosure makes for a pleasant stroll across the cobblestones, leading to a rickety old staircase that descends to the intersection at Taylor Street, also featured prominently in Maupin's narrative.

From here it's a steep, two-block uphill walk to **Russian Hill Place**, off Vallejo between Jones and Taylor. This is the hill's summit, and after ascending the steep staircase you're rewarded with a 180-degree view of the city that includes the skyscrapers of the Financial District, the candy-colored houses of North Beach and Telegraph Hill, the Bay Bridge, and, of course, the shimmering bay. After all the climbing you'll probably be eager to get back to Hyde and recover on a cable car, but before leaving you should take a walk down **Russell Street**, a small lane west of Hyde between Grant and Union. Check out the modest (by San Francisco standards) little house at no. 29, whose attic Jack Kerouac lived in for six months in 1952 with Neal and Carolyn Cassady. It was here, with Neal's encouragement, that Kerouac began an affair with Carolyn that endured for many years. Kerouac produced some of his best work during this period, inspired by tape-recorded sessions with Neal Cassady, and went on to write *Doctor Sax* and *Visions of Cody* as well as revising earlier editions of *On the Road*. If you're interested, Carolyn Cassady's rich memoir, *Heartbeat*, chronicles this time, describing Kerouac's development as an artist, and their affair, and offering some physical descriptions of San Francisco.

The prolific turn-of-the-century San Francisco architect **Willis Polk** lived nearby, at the head of the Vallejo Street staircase between Jones and Taylor, in an attractive, shingle house of his own design. Not the work of Willis Polk, but worth a peek, is the 1000 block of Green Street, where one of the few remaining octagonal houses in the city survives thanks to the services of the *Colonial Dames of America*. The **Feusier Octagon House** was built in the 1870s and is open on the first Sunday and the second and fourth Thursdays of each month (1–4pm; free). An alternative to taking the Hyde Street cable car back downtown is to walk a couple of blocks east to the Powell–Mason cable car line, passing on the way the **Ina Coolbrith Park**, another postage stamp piece of greenery, but quiet and pretty enough for a sit-down before negotiating the crowds.

Telegraph Hill

Once an extension of the wilder North Beach territory, but now a firmly settled community in its own right, the pastel clapboard homes of **TELEGRAPH HILL** dangle precipitously from the steep inclines. Quite apart from the stiff walk, there's no easy way up, unless you're willing to sit on *Muni* bus #39 while it makes the slow climb through the always packed tourist traffic, and anyway the walk may make you appreciate the dramatic panorama, from the Golden Gate Bridge in the west to the hills of Berkeley across the bay to the east.

The most direct path to the top of the hill is to take **Filbert Street**, a steep climb from Washington Square Park past the flowery gardens of a line of cottages, up to Telegraph Hill Boulevard. The best viewpoint is from the top of **Coit Tower** (daily 10am–5pm; $3), a phallic concrete monument to the fire-fighters who doused the flames of 1906, designed by Arthur Brown, the archi-tect of City Hall.

While waiting for the elevator to the top of the tower, check out the marve-lous social realist WPA **murals**, inspired and supervised by Diego Rivera. All the frescoes are thematically linked, though the style varies greatly. One section depicts musclebound Californians working on the land; another shows a man reading Marx in front of a wall of books by left-leaning authors like Upton Sinclair and Jack London, while others contemplate apocalyptic newspaper headlines. The murals were completed in 1934, during a long-shoremen's dispute that escalated into a general strike after two union members were killed by police during demonstrations. When rumors about the "subversive" frescoes reached the authorities, the Art Commission ordered that a hammer and sickle be removed from one and even tried to close the tower until tempers had cooled. A picket of the tower was mounted by local unions, keeping it in the headlines until the authorities gave in and allowed it to open several months later.

Heading back down you may feel more able to stop and savor the subtle charms of the hill's many fine houses, and there are a few places you definitely won't want to miss.

If you've ever seen the classic Bogart and Bacall film *Dark Passage*, the fine Art Moderne apartment block she lived in still stands, just down from Coit Tower on the eastern side of the hill at 1360 Montgomery Street. From Montgomery the beautifully landscaped **Filbert Steps** drop steeply down, looking out over the Bay Bridge and giving access to narrow footpaths like **Darrell Place** and **Napier Lane** that cut off to either side. Napier Lane is one of the few remaining boardwalks in the city, lined with cottages and over-flowing greenery.

ACCOMMODATION *Leland Hotel.*
RESTAURANTS Budget *International House of Pancakes;* **Italian** *Allegro Ristorante Italiano;* **Indian** *Golden Turtle, The Peacock.*

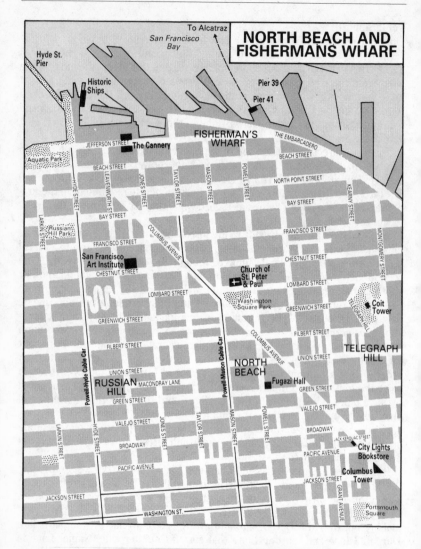

Fisherman's Wharf and Alcatraz

San Francisco doesn't go dramatically out of its way to please the tourist on the whole, but with **FISHERMAN'S WHARF** it makes a rare exception, pulling in over a million visitors a year with its crowded and hideous ensemble of waterfront kitsch and fastfood stands. A series of refurbished piers have been converted into souvenir complexes and places to pick up a pleasure cruise around the bay; stalls selling sweatshirts and baseball caps crowd out the few places of any real interest, and all in all it makes for a sad spectacle—and a rather misleading introduction to San Francisco. It looks like it's taken a hundred years of steady endeavor to make the place so awful, but in fact the Wharf (as it now stands) is only thirty years old. Though it might seem hard to believe now, this was originally a serious fishing port, hauling in real crabs and not the frozen sort now masquerading as fresh fish on the stands. The few fishermen that can afford the exorbitant mooring charges now, however, are usually finished by early morning and get out before the tourists arrive. The shops and bars here are among the most overpriced in the city, and crowd-weary families do little to add to the ambience. There are a few good seafood restaurants and a handful of mildly interesting spots, but, frankly, the best thing you can do with the Wharf is skip it altogether.

At the eastern edge of the Wharf, **Pier 39** marks the beginning of a high volume strip that continues for eight blocks west. You can take a boat from here and cruise the bay (see "Getting Around the City"), but the central focus is a large complex of shops and restaurants, not all awful but certainly all expensive and usually swarming with people. Walking west along Jefferson Street, known as the **Amusement Zone**, you'll come across a cluster of exorbitantly priced museums and exhibitions designed to relieve you of more of your money: a **Wax Museum** (daily 9am–10:30pm; $7.95) with laughable replicas—the one of Cleopatra is uncannily like that of Elizabeth Taylor; **Ripley's "Believe It or Not" Museum** (Sun–Thurs 10am–10pm, Fri & Sat until midnight; $6); even a **Guinness World of Records Museum** (daily 10am–10pm; $5.95). Sadly, even for people with kids to amuse, none is really worth expending very much energy or money on. Better to walk to **Pier 45** at the foot of Taylor Street to see the last vestiges of the working wharf. It still pulls in some twenty million pounds of fish a year, although up to ten times that amount arrives by truck to serve the restaurants of the Bay Area. Unless you're there early morning, you won't see much action, but the boats and storage sheds are there to poke around. At the very end of the pier is the **USS Pampanito** (daily 9am–9pm; $3), a submarine that sank five Japanese ships during its operation in World War II. It's hardly a must but rates highly as an attraction compared to other sights in the area.

There are more seafaring vessels on the **Hyde Street Pier** (daily 8am–5pm; free) at the foot of Hyde Street, which boasts a collection of historic ships. Originally the pier was used to serve the Sausalito ferries before the opening of the Golden Gate Bridge, and today it is home to five ships, three of which are open to the public. The *Balclutha* is the most interesting, a hard-working ship of the late 1800s that doubled Cape Horn, returning with wine and liquor from London, coal from Wales, and hardware from Antwerp. She was put into retirement in the 1930s, to be dragged out and done up for bit parts in films like *Mutiny on the Bounty*, before her current job as a showboat. The *Eureka* was once the largest passenger ferry in the world and is now loaded with a historic fleet of cars and trucks worth a cursory glance; the *Alma* is a flat-bottomed workhouse that used to carry hay and lumber around the bay.

The two other main attractions at the Wharf are both refurbished **shopping complexes**. The first, **The Cannery** on Jefferson Street at Leavenworth, was a fruit-packing factory that was done up in the 1960s when the tourism drive really took off. Escalators take you up and around the three floors of shops. **Ghirardelli Square** at 900 N. Point Street marks the western edge of the Wharf, a boutiquey mall that is a far cry from its days as a chocolate factory, its red neon sign a consumer landmark for miles around. A little more upmarket than The Cannery, it took six years to carefully refurbish and to its credit contains some very good restaurants (see Chapter Seven, *Drinking and Eating*) and one thing you don't need money to enjoy. The **California Crafts Museum** (daily noon–6pm; free) is better than its name suggests and, unlike the batik and macramé knick-knacks you'd expect, has some innovative stuff. A non-profit organization dedicated to exhibiting work in various media (wood, metal, glass, and clay) often unrecognised by galleries, you'll be able to see some designer furniture and unusual sculpture as well as the more traditional ceramics and suchlike. To travel back downtown, you can either tackle the lines at the cable car turnaround in **Victorian Park**, at Hyde and Beach streets, or catch the downtown loop bus #19 at the same intersection.

Alcatraz

Visible from the waterfront, its beacon flashing eerily in the fog, is the prison island of **Alcatraz**, commonly known as "The Rock"—a craggy little islet rising out of the bay that was originally home to nothing more than thousands of pelicans ("Alcatraz" means pelican in Spanish). In the late nineteenth century the island became a military fortress, and in 1934 it was converted into America's most dreaded high-security prison, in an attempt to control the hitherto uncontrollable heavyweights of the penal system. Surrounded by freezing, uncrossable water, it was an ideal place for a jail and safely kept some of America's most wanted criminals behind bars—Al Capone and Machine Gun Kelly were just two of the villains imprisoned here, and Robert "Bird Man" Stroud had a film made about him and his time here.

The conditions were about as inhumane as you'd expect: most inmates were kept in solitary confinement, in cells no larger than five by nine feet, some without light; they were not allowed to converse with the guards, read newspapers, have a game of cards, or even talk to the other inmates; relatives were allowed to visit for only two hours each month. The psychological toll it took on the prisoners is said to have been devastating. Frustration culminated in several riots, including one particularly bloody affair that ended in the deaths of several guards and inmates. Escape was impossible, despite many ingenious attemps, and of the thirty-six men who tried to escape, some were shot to death, most were captured in the water, and five vanished, presumed dead.

For all its usefulness as a jail, however, the island turned out to be a fiscal as well as penitential nightmare, and after years of generating massive running costs, not to mention whipping up a storm of public protest when it started to imprison petty criminals, it closed in 1963. The remaining prisoners were distributed among decidedly less horrific detention centers, and the island remained abandoned until 1969, when a group of Native Americans staged an occupation as part of a peaceful attempt to claim it for their people—citing treaties which designated all federal land not in use as automatically reverting to their ownership. Using all the bureaucratic trickery they could muster, the government finally ousted them in 1971, claiming the operative lighthouse qualified Alcatraz as active. Nowadays the only people to set foot on the island are the annual 750,000 tourists, many of whom take one of the excellent hour-long audio-tours ($4) of the abandoned rows of cells—though you can wander about on your own if you wish. On the tape are sharp anecdotal commentaries by several of the surviving inmates, recalling the horror and desperation of their time and the conditions of the prison. There's also the opportunity to spend a minute (it feels like forever) locked in a darkened cell. The area around the main prison building is, in parts, quite pretty, and the views of the city from the island are impressive. Speculation about the future of the island has included plans to turn it into an offshore gambling haven (gambling is illegal in California), although the latest proposal—and one that looks set to stick—is a scheme to let the island revert to its natural state and develop a series of hiking trails. Boats to Alcatraz leave hourly from Pier 41, beginning at 8:15am, with the last boat back at around 6pm ($8 per person).

ACCOMMODATION Hotels *Holiday Inn, Howard Johnson Motor Lodge, Van Ness Motel, Wharf Inn.*
BARS *Buena Vista Cafe, Lou's.*
CAFÉS *Eagle Cafe.*
RESTAURANTS Pizza *Vicolo Pizzeria;* **Indian** *Gaylord;* **Chinese, Thai, and Indonesian** *Mandarin.*

Aquatic Park and Fort Mason

A little way west of the Wharf lies an area known as the **Golden Gate National Recreation Area**, which was organized in 1972 to provide much-needed central park space for the city by pulling together vacant parts of the waterfront. It encompasses almost seventy square miles of waterfront property, from the beach areas of the city to the south, right up to the cliffs of Marin County on the other side of the Golden Gate Bridge. By claiming this property for public use only, commercial enterprise has been pushed back, and the waterfront feels very much on the fringes of the city. Just a few blocks can take you from urban density to seafront openness.

Immediately west of Fisherman's Wharf, at the foot of Hyde Street, is a small **beach** and an impressively long, windy pier known as **Aquatic Park**. Few brave the choppy waters of the bay, however, and most use the beach as a sunny spot to walk dogs, take picnics, and generally laze about. At weekends, bands set up on the broad semicircle of steps above the beach and often draw crowds away from the congestion of the Wharf to hear the salsa and reggae that's usually on offer. The three-and-a-half-mile scenic walk that begins here, known as the **Golden Gate Promenade**, wraps along the waterfront to the Golden Gate Bridge, passing through attractive spots like Marina Green and the Palace of Fine Arts (see below).

Adjacent to the park is **Fort Mason**, a military site dating originally from the late 1700s that was maneuvered into public hands in 1972, when a powerful congressman and environmentalist, Philip Burton, blocked plans to turn the land over to private speculation and in doing so forced the creation of the Golden Gate National Recreation Association that now owns the land. Used initially by Spanish soldiers from the Presidio in 1797, it came under the auspices of the US Army in 1850, but failure to occupy the land immediately led to squatters building homes here. The squatters took thirteen years to evict, in a gradual program of building, but the fort was to shelter the homeless again as a refugee center after the 1906 earthquake and fire. It saw its greatest action during World War II when 1.6 million soldiers passed through on their way to the Pacific War Zone, and again in the early 1950s during the Korean War when it was a logistical support center. Its current use as a home for arts organizations, known collectively as the **Fort Mason Center**, came after pressure for free or low-cost cultural activities in the city. It has grown tenfold since its opening in 1976 and today is known locally as "Fort Culture."

You can enter Fort Mason by car at Bay and Franklin streets, or climb the stairs at the foot of Van Ness Avenue up to a bluff with spectacular views of the bay. The old shed-like buildings are now home to various art groups, a **hostel** (see "Finding a Place to Stay"), workshops, a few stores, and several **museums** that stage a mixture of permanent and temporary exhibitions. The largest and most visited is the **Maritime Museum**, at the foot of Polk Street (daily 10am–6pm; free; ☎556-3002), housed in a former casino known as the "Boathouse"—a bold, Art-Deco, streamlined imitation of a luxury liner, with three curving levels, steel railings, and porthole windows. The permanent exhibits inside trace the saga of the people and merchant ships that shaped the development of the city back in the days of the Barbary Coast. There are hundreds of artifacts, photographs, and documents charting San Francisco's seafaring history, but the most interesting item is Hilaire Hiler's 1939 **mural** in the main room, symbolizing the lost continent of Atlantis in 37 individual hallucinogenic panels.

Lesser known, but significantly more interesting, is the **Mexican Museum**, Building D, Fort Mason (Wed–Sat noon–5pm; $3, free the first Wed of each month; ☎441-0404). With minimal exhibition space, not much larger than the average classroom, this place nonetheless manages to pack in rare pieces of Hispanic, colonial, and folk art. Originally intended to represent the talents of local Mexican artists, the museum also occasionally scores coups over the larger museums and shows the works of artists like Diego Rivera and Frida Kahlo. There's a small shop where you can buy postcards, prints, and a limited selection of hand-made crafts from Mexico, the proceeds from which go toward maintaining the museum.

A short walk from here, the **Museo Italo Americano**, Building C, Fort Mason (Wed–Sun noon–5pm; free; ☎673-2200) is similar in conception, if vastly different in proportions. Over 5000 square feet of gallery space are dedicated to mainly temporary installations showing the works of local Italian-American artists and sometimes more prestigious traveling shows. Styles vary with the exhibitions, but you can usually rely on the accent being heavily contemporary. Much of the collection is geared toward an under-standing of Italian architecture and culture and is more broadly based than the other cultural museums at the Fort. If you can stand another museum in one day, the **African American Historical and Cultural Society**, Building C, Fort Mason (Wed–Sun noon–5pm; free; ☎441-0640), is an organization dedicated to preserving the history of black Americans. As well as a library, gift shop, and meditation room, there's an excellent **museum** and **gallery**. The museum is of scholarly interest only with specialist artifacts and archival materials, but the gallery shows excellent work by new and master artists of African-American descent.

Though predominantly a daytime venue, crowds come to the Fort by night for performances at the acclaimed **Magic Theater** (see "Theater," Chapter Eight). Now in its 25th season, the theater is one of the oldest and largest theater companies on the West Coast. If you are here by night, take time for a stroll along the Fort's bluff. Pretty by day, by night it becomes one of the most terrifically romantic spots in the city.

ACCOMMODATION Hostels *San Francisco International Hostel.*
RESTAURANTS Vegetarian *Greens.*

The Marina, Palace of Fine Arts, and Union Street

Perched prettily on the edge of the bay, with its Mediterranean revival houses and shops tastefully arranged, the **MARINA** is a fitting neighborhood for the young, image-conscious, money-no-object sort of professionals who inhabit it. Flanked by the Presidio to the west and Fort Mason to the east, it's one of the city's greenest districts, and its prestigious yacht club, joggers, and kite-flyers all add to the ambience of a neighborhood that would rather be a resort. Ironically, the Marina, built specifically to celebrate the re-birth of the city after the massive earthquake of 1906, was the worst casualty of the earth-quake of 1989—tremors tore through fragile landfill and a good number of homes collapsed into a smouldering heap. Rebuilding was immediate, however, and the only signs of damage are the obviously new structures that went up to replace the lost dwellings. Even disaster was not enough to bring rents down, and the Marina remains, despite its hazardous foundations, home to a well-heeled and very smart young set.

The Marina's commercial center runs along **Chestnut Street** between Broderick and Fillmore streets. As a neighborhood, it has a reputation for being something of a haven for swinging singles: the local watering holes are known as "High-intensity breeder-bars" and even the local *Safeway* has been dubbed the "The Body Shop" because of the inordinate amount of cruising that goes on in the aisles. Union Street (see below) is better for ordinary shopping, but if you just need to grab a bite to eat, have a drink, and look at the locals, Chestnut is just the job.

Before the 1915 Panama Pacific International Exhibition to commemorate the rebuilding of the city after the 1906 earthqake and fire, the Marina didn't exist at all. On the bay north of Pacific Heights, a sea wall parallel to the shoreline was built, and the marshland in between was filled in by dredging up sand from the bottom of the ocean. Dredging left enough deep water for the creation of the **St Francis** and **Golden Gate Yacht Clubs**, which sit prestigiously at the foot of Baker Street. Slightly to the east is **Marina Green**, a large stretch of turf frequented for the most part by fitness fanatics. For less strenuous exercise, walk the **Golden Gate Promenade** which runs parallel to Marina Boulevard and runs for a couple of miles before reaching the bridge.

The Palace of Fine Arts and Exploratorium

Marking the westernmost point of the neighborhood is the Marina's most notable landmark, the magnificent **Palace of Fine Arts** at Baker and Beach streets. It is not, as the name suggests, a museum, but a huge, freely inter-preted classical ruin by Bernard Maybeck, whose dream-like columns and rotunda were also created for the Panama Pacific Exhibition in 1915. The weeping figures on the colonnade were the work of sculptor Ulric Ellerhusen and are said to represent the melancholy of life without art. Whatever the implicit message, the lachrymose ladies are the ultimate decorative detail on a structure conceived out of great optimism for post-earthquake San Francisco. It was saved from immediate demolition after the exhibition by sentimental San Franciscans and crumbled with dignity until the late 1950s when a wealthy resident put up the money for its reconstruction. It's the sole survivor of many such triumphal structures built for the Exhibition, which stretched from here all along the waterfront to Fort Mason. Surrounded by Monterey cypresses, a swan-filled lagoon, and other nice touches of urban civility, it beats Marina Green hands down as a picnic spot and makes for the best idling in the neighborhood.

The rather unsightly shed-like building next door is the **Exploratorium** (Wed 1–9:30pm, Thurs & Fri 1–5pm, Sat & Sun 10am–5pm; $5), which, like the Palace of Fine Arts, is a product of high ideals, founded in 1969 on the somewhat idealistic premise that a better understanding of the sciences is the key to solving the world's problems. The museum has over 500 exhibits on light and color, sound and music, patterns of motion, language, and other natural phenomena. Each year over half a million people come to peer through lenses, look in mirrors, stare through filters, experiment with magnets and electricity, spin wheels, swing pendulums, and supposedly, in the process, "learn more about their environment and themselves." A good pacifier for restless children, although some of the exhibits can be a bit tedi-ous for anybody with an elementary grasp of science.

Union Street

Known by some as **COW HOLLOW**, **Union Street** is the busy commercial strip which rests between the Marina and its slightly wealthier neighbor, Pacific Heights, to the south. It takes its name from the days when cows rather than shoppers grazed the valley between Russian Hill and the Presidio, and washerwomen would bring their loads to what was one of the very few sites of fresh water in the city. Problems with open sewage, and complaints from the neighbors up on Pacific Heights about the stench from the cows, brought its pastoral days to an end, and these days cattle markets of an altogether different variety set the tone of the neighborhood: Union Street, like the Marina, is quite the place for single straight people come sundown, the bars full of well-paid young professionals, dressed to death and very expectant, slinging down cocktails and waiting for their luck to change. It's a scene.

Indeed, despite stumbling across some attractive flower-filled courtyards, shopping and bar-hopping is what Union Street is all about. Second only to the downtown area, the seven-block stretch between Fillmore and Franklin streets is crammed with boutiques, fancy eateries, antique shops, cafés, and bars. Even the most fainthearted consumer will find it hard to ignore the classy Italian designer stores and bookstores.

ACCOMMODATION Hotels *Bel Aire Travelodge, Manor Motel Friendship Inn, Marina Motel, Marina Inn.*
BARS *Balboa Cafe, Blue Light Cafe, Chestnut Street Grill, Curtain Call, Margaritaville, Mulhern's, Perry's, Tar & Feathers.*
RESTAURANTS Budget *Joji's House of Teriyaki;* **American and Californian** *Johnny Rockets.*

Pacific Heights

Sharply defined by California Street to the south, Van Ness Avenue to the east, the Marina to the north, and the hulking green landmass that is the Presidio to the west, **PACIFIC HEIGHTS** is a beautifully poised million-aires' ghetto. It's a common source of amusement that when the bright young things of the Marina grow up and have kids, they climb the hill to Pacific Heights and look down on all the fun they used to have. Even when these were bare hills back in the 1860s, their panoramic views of the ocean had them earmarked as fashionable territory as soon as the gradient-conquering cable cars could link them with downtown. Lavishly proportioned mansions teeter precipitously atop hills that are the chosen domain of the stockbroker, business magnate, and the odd best-selling novelist. Pulp-romance writer Danielle Steele lives here in a 42-room mansion, as did Perry Mason creator, Erle Stanley Gardner, with his one man fiction-factory that produced 82 novels selling some three hundred million copies.

The neighborhood is neatly divided by Fillmore Street: to the west are the large dwellings that earned the neighborhood its reputation; to the east swanky Art-Deco apartment buildings that do little to damage it. Known as the **Upper Fillmore**, the stretch of Fillmore Street above California Street is where locals go to shop, dine, and generally lash their cash—a street that merits your exploration if you're to get a clear idea of exactly the kind of people who can afford to live here. Approaching the area from the south where California crosses Fillmore, you should ascend the latter through the maze of fancy pet stores, florists, and restaurants toward the more residential territory to the north, taking in the air of casual wealth and sophistication. The shops, while pricey, are not that remarkable, and unless you're a shophound, skipping the boutiques and heading straight for a walk around the mansions would not constitute a loss. The western portion of the neighborhood is centered around the quiet and restful **Alta Plaza Park**, one block west of Fillmore at Clay and Steiner. A lovely piece of urban landscaping, this is where local dogwalkers earn their keep, exercising the pretty pooches, and you can enjoy the good views of St Mary's Cathedral and Civic Center from its crest. Streisand fans will recognize the park as the site of the famous scene in *What's Up Doc?*, in which she drives the car down the steps on the south side of the park. Close inspection reveals cracks left in the steps after shooting the scene. North of the park, the territory becomes solidly residential, home to well-tended gardens around immaculately maintained houses, apart from one rogue structure on the southwestern corner of Baker and Broadway. This Italian Renaissance Palace, probably built around the turn of the century, is in a romantic stage of decay and from its fancy perch overlooks the Getty Mansion down the street. One block over, at the intersection of Broadway and Lyon, you'll reach the fenced-off Presidio and won't be able to go any farther west. From here, a set of steps leads south down a steep incline and out to the water's edge, passing grandiose homes and presenting a magnificent view of the Palace of Fine Arts and the bay.

To do anything other than mooch about, you'll need to cross Fillmore and explore the eastern side of the neighborhood, filled for the most part with luxury apartment buildings that replaced the great Victorian piles the modern rich found too gloomy to live in. There are, however, still a couple where you can actually get a look around the inside. The **Whittier Mansion**, 2090 Jackson Street (Wed, Sat & Sun 1:30–3pm; free) is home to the *California Historical Society* and has a good collection of nineteenth-century Californian art and immaculate Queen Anne furniture. One block east, the **Haas-Lilienthal House**, 2007 Franklin Street (Wed noon–4pm, Sun 11am–4:30pm; $3), is the headquarters for the *Foundation for San Francisco's Architectural Heritage*—a fully furnished Queen Anne-style house, again good for casual browsing. The unchallenged star, but unfortunately one you can't venture inside, is the **Spreckles Mansion** at Gough and Washington, whose ostentatious, faded elegance, grand in every detail, is as unrestricted in its design as in its decay. Follow the house around to its lovely sloping garden at the back and look at it in its entirety – although this may not be possible for much longer, as it is (sadly) rumored that if the owners are ever to give the mansion the facelift it needs, funds will be raised by selling the grounds that surround the home to developers.

ACCOMMODATION Hotels *Bel Aire Travelodge, Edward II, The Mansion.*
BARS *Alta Plaza, Harry's.*
RESTAURANTS American and Californian *Oppenheimer;* **Japanese and Korean** *Osome, Yoshida-Ya.*

The Presidio and Golden Gate Bridge

Occupying most of the northwest tip of the San Francisco peninsula, the **PRESIDIO** covers some 1600 acres and is home to 75 miles of forested roads. After a hundred years of sporadic military use, it looks set to be handed over to the public, and although no one has ever been denied access to this beautiful corner of the city, apart from functioning as an unofficial auxiliary to the city's parks, there's never been much else to do other than taking a drive through its eucalyptus-scented highways or choosing a section to hike through. A significant symbol of the military's role in the city of San Francisco, it remains the headquarters of the Sixth Army and employs over 6000 troops. However, it has seen too many years of decreasing usefulness as a strategic site, and activity has dwindled to the point of it being a favored last posting (great golf course and officer's club) for about-to-retire army brass. A favorite spot with cyclists and hikers, the Presidio lacks the congestion of Golden Gate Park and makes for a pleasant, if lengthy, stroll on the way to the beaches (see Chapter Five).

In the 1770s the Presidio was a frontier outpost for the Spanish Empire, which garrisoned the distant peninsula to prevent the British and Russian claims on the San Francisco Bay. In 1822 it was ceded to the Mexicans and became the northernmost outpost of the new Mexican republic. After the Americans took over in 1847, the US Army started to develop the inherited adobe structures, but the Presidio didn't take on its present appearance until the 1880s, when an environmentally minded major initiated a program of forestation that changed it from a windswept, sandy piece of coastline into the dense thicket it is today. Afterwards it served mainly as a medical and administrative army base, and the only time its harbor defenses were activated was for a brief period during World War II.

The main entrance to the Presidio is by way of Lombard Street, between Pacific Heights and the Marina. A huge gate bearing the figures of Liberty and Victory leads you inside to the main quadrangle of buildings that is the military headquarters. There's a small chapel and adobe officers' dining room, but entrance is prohibited and the only thing you can actually visit is the **Presidio Museum**, on Lincoln Boulevard and Funston Avenue (Tues–Sun 10am–4pm; free)—the original hospital building, converted into exhibition space and showing not just military history but also a detailed explanation of the development of the city. Its models and maps show how San Francisco's appearance has changed throughout its history and which parts of the city were wiped out by the 1906 earthquake.

Beyond here, development is spread thinly around the large base, the most startling aspect of which is the **National Military Cemetery**, a site that has rather sadly grown from ten acres to around twenty-nine acres, mainly due to the death toll of the Korean and Vietnam wars. The modern Letterman Hospital nearby was the focus of much attention during the Vietnam War when the most severely traumatized soldiers were cared for here: injuries sustained were so severe that many have yet to leave. Other buildings on the site are unremarkable, but a drive along its roads turns up some interesting signs of military life—one building is curiously tagged as a "Religious Activity Center," but most amusing of all is the sign outside the parachute store which reads "Try jumping without us."

The Presidio's (and perhaps even San Francisco's) most dramatic location is the **Fort Point National Historic Site**, a brick fortress built in the 1850s to guard the bay. From here, where the surf crashes and the Pacific stretches to infinity, you get a good sense of the place as the westernmost outpost of the nation. It was originally to have been demolished to make way for the Golden Gate Bridge, but the redesign of the southern approach left it intact. It's a theatrical site, with the ocean pounding away beneath the great span of the bridge high above—a scene made famous by Kim Novak's suicide attempt in Alfred Hitchcock's *Vertigo*. It is alleged that the water here makes for one of the best (if most foolhardy) surfing spots in the area, exponents of which can be seen riding the waves. There's a small **museum** inside the fort (daily 9am–4pm; free), showing some rusty old cannons and firearms, although the military collection at the Presidio Museum is far superior (see above).

The Golden Gate Bridge

The orange towers of the **Golden Gate Bridge**—probably the most beautiful, certainly the most photographed, bridge in the world—are visible from almost every point of elevation in San Francisco. As much an architectural as an engineering feat, the bridge took only 52 months to design and build and was opened in 1937. Designed by Joseph Strauss, it was the first really massive suspension bridge, with a span of 4200 feet, and until 1959 ranked as the world's longest. It connects the city at its northwesterly point on the peninsula to Marin County and Northern California, rendering the hitherto essential ferry crossing redundant, and was designed to withstand winds of up to a hundred miles an hour and swing as much as 27 feet. Handsome on a clear day, the bridge takes on an eerie quality when the thick white fogs pour in and hide it almost completely.

You can either drive or walk across. The drive is the more thrilling of the two options as you race under the bridge's towers, but the half-hour walk across it really gives you time to take in its enormity and absorb the views of the city behind you and the headlands of Northern California straight ahead. Pause at the midway point and consider the seven or so suicides a month who chose this spot, 260 feet up, as their jumping-off spot. Monitors of such events speculate that victims always face the city before they leap. Perhaps the best-loved symbol of San Francisco, in 1987 the Golden Gate proved an auspicious place for a sunrise party when crowds gathered to celebrate its fiftieth anniversary. Some quarter of a million people turned up (a third of the city's entire population); the winds were strong and the huge numbers caused the bridge to buckle, but fortunately not to break.

CHAPTER THREE

CIVIC CENTER, SOUTH OF MARKET, AND THE MISSION

While much of San Francisco is often depicted as some kind of urban utopia—and, in some cases, almost lives up to the promise—the districts of **Civic Center, South of Market, and the Mission** reveal a city of harsh realities. Pretty tree-lined streets, hills and stunning views are conspicuously absent down here, and for the most part these areas are a gritty, blue-collar reminder that not everybody here has it so easy. **Civic Center**, supposedly the bastion of civic pride, has big problems. The offices of the mayor overlook a park that for the last year or so has been the chosen abode of over 300 homeless people, much to the embarrassment of City Hall. Immediately north of Civic Center, **Polk Gulch,** on the other hand, thrives on its slightly seedy edge, a flourishing commercial strip of bars, theaters, and shops that nicely balances the comparatively staid nature of gay life in the Castro. Running parallel to Polk Gulch, north of Civic Center, the main north–south city artery of **Van Ness Avenue**, a traffic-swarmed stretch of Highway 101, runs along the westernmost edge of the downtown area and makes the clearest division between San Francisco's commercial and residential districts.

Tucked between the southern end of Van Ness Avenue and downtown, the **Tenderloin** is San Francisco's most notorious neighborhood, which despite attempts at gentrification remains a stronghold of low-rent dwellings, the homeless, and the soup kitchens and shelters that sustain them. **South of Market** (SoMa), the large chunk of land that takes its name from its position immediately south of Market Street, has responded rather better to recent investment: an area of formerly industrial wasteland turned hip club turf that is facing a massive commercial and housing development program which will change its now fairly empty blocks beyond recognition. The last part of it to change will be the old dock around **Mission Rock** and **China Basin**—still romantically desolate, save the odd waterfront venue for a beer and burger. In sharp contrast, the **Mission** is San Francisco's largest and liveliest neighborhood, another low-rent area that has long been the city's first stop for immigrants. It's been home to many different nationalities over the years, but

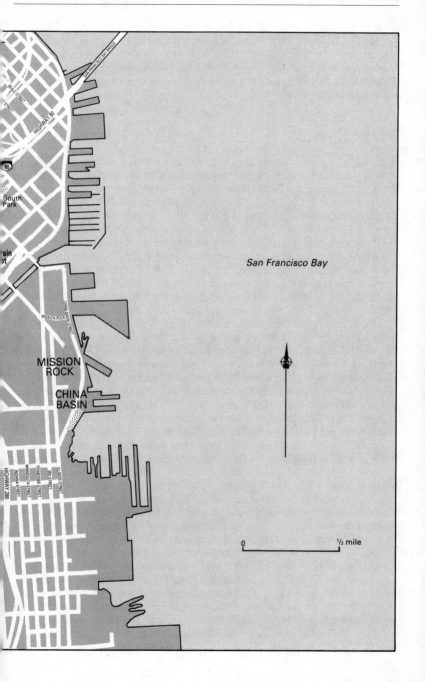

for the last couple of decades it has been solidly and increasingly Hispanic, and it's this culture which lends the neighborhood its character. Nestling in a hilly corner west of the Mission, **Potrero Hill** couldn't be more different, a small enclave of brightly painted houses on slopes offering panoramic views of downtown San Francisco and the waterfront, determinedly village-like and resistant to change.

Civic Center

Born out of a grand, celebratory architectural scheme, **CIVIC CENTER**, a little way southwest of the downtown area, is an impressive layout of majestic federal and municipal Beaux Arts buildings focusing on the grand dome of City Hall, designed by Arthur Brown and completed in 1915 just in time for the Panama Pacific International Exhibition. The surrounding complex is a watered-down version of city planner Daniel Burnham's ambitious schemes for the city, which would have seen grand avenues fanning out across San Francisco, including one extending to the Panhandle of Golden Gate Park. Drawn up with the help of architect Willis Polk, the plans won the whole-hearted approval of city leaders, only to be delayed by the massive earthquake and fire of 1906. Political difficulties after the quake delayed the project further, and, although Burnham doggedly pursued his vision of a "City Beautiful," the project was only finished after his death. He no doubt would be saddened by the complex today: it's still a fine collection of buildings, but the elegant layout has become the focus of San Francisco's most glaring social problem—the homeless. In 1990 police moved to evict over 300 street-people who had set up makeshift homes on the plaza opposite City Hall and on the grass borders around the quadrangle, moving them to temporary shelters in response to a growing rage at the lack of decent public housing in the city. As San Francisco's center for the performing arts—by night, beautifully lit and swarming with tuxedo-clad San Franciscans heading in and out of the opera, ballet, and symphony—the problem was not one that could be easily hidden, and, although the authorities have since established a number of shelters, Civic Center, along with the adjacent Tenderloin, remains the most intensely down-and-out area of town.

Using the Civic Center *Muni* and *BART* station as your starting point, you'll emerge from underground facing the **United Nations Plaza** just south of the main quadrangle. Built as a memorial to the founding of the UN here in 1949, it is an attractive design with fountain and flags which has become the largest public urinal in the city—if the stench doesn't deter you, the characters who hang around it will. Wednesdays are the exception, when the site serves as the city's largest and cheapest fruit and vegetable market. Moving north, you enter the main square of Civic Center, where, on McAllister and Larkin, the **San Francisco Public Library** is three floors of regal turn-of-the-century architecture, classical columns adorning the entrance to a fairly standard collection of reading material apart from the excellent **San Francisco History Room and Archives** (Tues–Sat 10am–

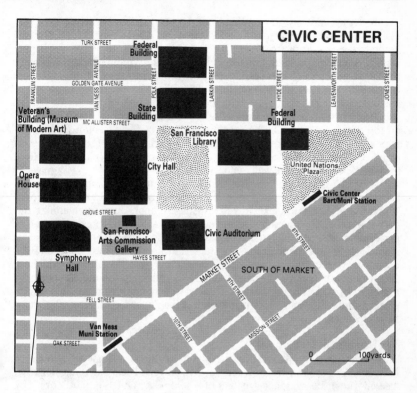

CIVIC CENTER

TURK STREET

Federal Building

FRANKLIN STREET

GOLDEN GATE AVENUE

VAN NESS AVENUE

POLK STREET

LARKIN STREET

HYDE STREET

LEAVENWORTH STREET

JONES STREET

Veteran's Building (Museum of Modern Art)

MC ALLISTER STREET

State Building

San Francisco Library

Federal Building

City Hall

United Nations Plaza

Opera House

Civic Center Bart/Muni Station

GROVE STREET

San Francisco Arts Commission Gallery

Civic Auditorium

8TH STREET

Symphony Hall

HAYES STREET

MARKET STREET

9TH STREET

SOUTH OF MARKET

FELL STREET

10TH STREET

MISSION STREET

Van Ness Muni Station

OAK STREET

0   100 yards

6pm; free) on the third floor. Used mainly as a research library, it's a quiet, crowd-free space to explore the documents and fascinating photographs of San Francisco from its beginnings in the 1700s to the present day. The books are mainly of scholarly interest, but the glass cases are packed with bits and pieces evoking the history of the city—newspaper clippings, old coins, photographs, and paraphernalia from the Gold Rush years.

Dominating the quadrangle at its far end on Polk Street, **City Hall** is arguably the best-looking building in town. Modeled on St Peter's Basilica in Rome, this huge, green-domed baroque building of granite and marble is the city's most grandiose structure and forms the nucleus of Civic Center. The interior of the building is as grand as its facade: a large baroque marble staircase dominates the center, which you should ascend after gazing up into the gold-inlaid dome, and wander beneath the opulent arches. It was here in 1978 that Dan White got past metal-detecting security by climbing through a basement window and assassinated Mayor George Moscone and gay Supervisor Harvey Milk. Later, when White was found guilty of manslaughter (not murder), it was the scene of violent demonstrations, as gay protesters set fire to police vehicles and stormed the doors of City Hall—an event that has come to be known as the "White Night Riot."

Directly behind City Hall on Van Ness Avenue are San Francisco's cultural mainstays, most elegant of which is the **War Memorial Opera House**, home to the *San Francisco Opera* and *Ballet* (see "Performing Arts," Chapter Eight). A suitably refined structure, its understated grandeur puts to shame the giant fishbowl of the **Louise M. Davies Symphony Hall** next door. Constructed in 1980 at a cost of almost 35 million dollars, the symphony hall has none of the restraint of its dignified neighbor, and, despite having fans in the Modernist architecture camp, the general consensus is that it's a blight on the otherwise tastefully harmonious scheme of Civic Center. Both buildings enjoy a healthy patronage, and come nightfall the formally dressed arrive by the busload. Sadly, few performances are subsidized, and they remain the domain of the well-to-do.

If you can't afford the luxury of a night at the opera, you can at least get a sense of its history and successes at the **San Francisco Performing Arts Library and Museum**, 399 Grove St. (Mon–Fri noon–5pm; free), around the corner between the opera house and symphony hall. The largest collection of performing arts material outside of New York, the museum has over a million historic programs, photographs, posters, and press clippings concentrating on music, dance, theater, and opera. Painstakingly collected and exhibited, performing arts fans could spend hours raking through the memorabilia, the highlight of which is the Isadora Duncan collection—programs, old photographs, and other souvenirs of the influential American dancer who ran a ballet school in Berkeley for a while.

The Museum of Modern Art

The Civic Center's biggest crowd-puller is the excellent **Museum of Modern Art**, on Van Ness Avenue at McAllister (Tues–Sat 10am–4pm; $4, free on Tues). Pending construction of a bold new home South of Market by Swiss architect Mario Botta (a move that will double its exhibition space and enable the museum to pull in the bigger traveling exhibits it hitherto has had to decline), the museum for the moment occupies the top two floors of the Veteran's Building, built in tribute to those who fought in World War I. The first museum on the West Coast devoted solely to twentieth-century art, it opened in 1935 but failed to achieve any international prestige until the mid-1970s when new leadership shook up the collection. Owing to its limited amount of space, it has never ranked as a big-league gallery, but the material it does have is well chosen and representative of a diversity of media and styles. Small but bold, it was the first California museum to set up an architecture and design department and has recently widened its net further and started exhibiting video installations—an emerging art form that most established museums have, at best, been lukewarm to. Its proposed expansion in 1993 will almost certainly place it up with the likes of the New York MOMA and the Los Angeles MOCA. Also, unlike other, larger museums, San Francisco's size enables you to take it all in at once.

The permanent collection is distinguished by some major paintings from the **American Abstract Expressionist** school, most notably Clyfford Still, Jackson Pollock, and Philip Guston. Works by Paul Klee are set to arrive by mid-1991, and the museum shows strength in **German Expressionism**, **Fauvism**, and **Mexican Painting** by Frida Kahlo and Diego Rivera. There's a smattering of works by Dali, Matisse, Picasso, and Kandinsky, but by no means their best, and the museum excels most with its collection of twentieth-century **photography**, which includes work by both European and American photographers—Cartier-Bresson and Brassai, as well as Man Ray and Ansell Adams, all get a look in. By appointment, there's also access to a comprehensive **Fine Arts Library** with over 12,000 volumes for the committed archivist, though most will be happy with the **bookshop**'s exhaustive stock of posters and art-related literature.

There are also a couple of **private galleries** in the neighborhood that are worth looking into. The **San Francisco Arts Commission** has a gallery at 155 Grove St., the foremost exhibition space for up-and-coming artists in the Bay Area. Standards are usually high and some of the work affordable. Less prestigious but worth a look is the **San Francisco Women Artists' Gallery** at 370 Hayes Street, which displays mostly photographic work, alongside some paintings and crafts. By far the most superior commercial gallery is the **Vorpal Gallery** at 393 Grove Street—a large space with fine contemporary work that merits at least half an hour's browse.

ACCOMMODATION Hostels *YMCA Central Branch;* **Hotels** *Albion House, Argyle Suite, Gough Hayes Hotel, San Francisco Central Travelodge, UN Plaza Hotel;* **Bed & Breakfast** *Pensione San Francisco.*
BARS *Bulls' Texas Cafe, Max's Opera Cafe, Bahia Tropical.*
RESTAURANTS Budget *Zim's;* **Pizza** *Vicolo Pizzeria;* **American and Californian** *Ivy's, Stars, Zuni Cafe;* **Chinese, Thai, and Indonesian** *Cloisonne;* **French** *Zola's;* **Hispanic** *Bahia Tropical.*

Van Ness Avenue and Polk Street

Running parallel to each other from Market Street near Civic Center to the waterfront way to the north, the major thoroughfares of **Van Ness Avenue** and **Polk Street**, though no more than a block apart, have quite distinct characters. Clearly separate, too, from the affluent neighborhoods that use them (Russian and Nob hills), each has enough movie houses, restaurants, bars, and shops to count as an autonomous strip, and strict social distinctions can be made between those who shop and dine on one as opposed to the other. They may not be at the top of your sightseeing list, but you'll certainly use them at some point to traverse the city.

Van Ness, by far the busier of the two, is the widest street in the city and major carrier of northbound traffic headed for the Golden Gate Bridge and beyond. Not surprisingly, it rarely sees a quiet moment. Traffic flow is pretty much 24 hours a day, and as one of the city's most relentlessly car-choked streets, it isn't recommended for casual strolling. Though it seems hard to believe now, when originally laid out in 1854 it was a quiet, prestigious boulevard of graceful mansions, though these were dynamited in 1906 to break the fire that raged through downtown San Francisco and would have consumed it had the firefighters not managed to stop it here. The few surviving houses were used as temporary retail outlets during the rebuilding downtown, and, apart from a couple of condominium complexes, the avenue has not been residential since. During the 1920s a stately row of luxury car showrooms was built, and these remain today as the places to shop for Rolls Royces, Jaguars, and Cadillacs. Most interesting is the Cadillac showroom at **901 Van Ness Avenue**, designed by Bernard Maybeck in 1928 and a temple-like construction for the worship and consumption of luxury automobiles. It's doubtful that you'll find yourself car-shopping, however; more likely you'll be here at night to eat in one of Van Ness's many restaurants or take in a movie at one of its theaters.

While Van Ness is a place to pass through, **Polk Street** is more a place to pause, improving the farther north you go, the bulk of its interest centered on the southwestern side of Russian and Nob hills, close to the junction with California Street at the end of the cable car line—an area better known as **POLK GULCH**. It's a refreshingly sleazy strip after the sometimes tedious charm of San Francisco's better neighborhoods, thriving on a subculture of rent boys, bums, and a steady stream of people looking for a bit of action— although as areas like this go it's pretty benign, and you can have a good look around without fear of being mugged or even hassled: the streetpeople know their turf and customers, and it's unlikely that you'll be of much interest to them. Also, after years of being a largely undesirable neighborhood, home to the sleazier side of the city's gay culture, apartment prices along Polk Street are now among the most expensive in the city, and it looks like the strip is in for big changes.

At the same time, Polk Gulch remains a center for interesting and affordable small shops, several good movie theaters, San Francisco's best oyster bar, and some rollicking good drinking holes. The characters who hang out here are far from dull—the poet John Wieners wrote the "Hotel Wentley" poems in Polk Gulch, and Frank Norris lived here for a while and now has a small side street off the strip named after him—and it still nurtures a small contingent of poets in its diners and coffee shops, muttering at their notebooks. Go by day for inexpensive snooping around its bookstores and clothes stores (see *Shops and Galleries*, Chapter Six), but Polk Street is best appreciated at night when the streets fill up with people eating on the cheap, going to the movies (Chapters Seven and Eight), or visiting the neighborhood's **gay bars**, which have a raw (though not inhospitable) edge that's a far cry from the down-home feel of the Castro's watering spots, and still rock to a beat more reminiscent of the free-wheeling 1970s. It's hardly intimidating, but if the thought of open solicitation bothers you, you're probably better off giving it a detour.

If you're here at the end of June or beginning of July, make an effort to attend the **Polk Street Fair**, possibly the largest assembly of leather-clad gay men you're ever likely to see (see "Festivals and Parades" in *Basics*) as they gather for a weekend of gay celebration and high-spirited revelry.

ACCOMMODATION Hotels *Embassy Motor Hotel, Pensione San Francisco.*
BARS *Bulls', The Cinch, Max's Opera Cafe.*
RESTAURANTS American and Californian *Hard Rock Cafe, Maye's Original Oyster House;* **Italian** *Enoteca Lanzone;* **Indian** *The Golden Turtle, The Peacock;* **Greek** *Steve the Greek.*

The Tenderloin

On the north side of Market Street, squashed between Union Square's Theater District and Civic Center, is San Francisco's most notorious neighborhood, the **TENDERLOIN**, a small, uninviting area no more than four blocks by five, which, despite a prime location beneath Nob Hill, remains one of the shabbiest—and poorest—spots in the city. The fact that Duke Ellington, Billie Holliday, and Nat King Cole all had homes here will probably do little to endear you to its seedy glamor.

The streets are the dirtiest and most litter-strewn in the whole city and form a kind of base for the city's increasing numbers of homeless, who cram the area's soup kitchens and flophouses, while, between the poorhouses and the porn shops, prostitutes do a brisk trade. Despite complaints from the recent wave of Vietnamese and Laotian immigrants who have moved in here with their young families, nothing seems likely to change, at least not in the immediate future, which is a pity because some of San Francisco's cheapest hotels are located here, and a tight budget may force you to stay in this part of the city. If this is the case, you'll do best to treat this area as a place to crash and move on to the more interesting parts of town for your entertainment.

The Tenderloin's location, smack in the middle of town, is at least convenient, and most things you'll want to see will be within walking distance; also, thanks to the Vietnamese immigrants, there are several places for ultra-cheap food-on-the-run. There are some lively if grimy bars a few blocks away in the Theater District. Partly as an attempt to spruce the area up for the immigrant influx, the city has gone to great lengths to design a "bum-proof" park on Jones and Eddy, replete with every imaginable barrier to dissuade the locals from establishing residence—on a good day, and with heavy patrolling by local police, it can claim to be a success.

Efforts to dignify the strip of **Taylor** around **Eddy** and **Turk** have been less successful; despite the constant police patrols, and city programs to make the streets safer, gangs have made this their territory and loitering is not recommended.

ACCOMMODATION Hostels *Youth Hostel Central;* **Hotels** *Amsterdam Hotel.*
BARS *The Blue Lamp.*
RESTAURANTS Italian-American *Original Joe's.*

South of Market

As Market Street bisects the city, the division it makes is more than simple geography. Its north side, with perhaps the exception of the Tenderloin, is affluent, bristling, and lively; the south side, from Embarcadero to about 12th Street, is a half-used industrial and transportation area that, on the face of things, is among the city's least appealing quarters. This is **SoMa** (South of Market), a district of old factory spaces that have been converted into galleries, fashionable restaurants, and nightclubs. The first factories and foundries appeared South of Market as early as the 1850s, but the area boomed as an industrial base in the 1940s after World War II, and, with its extensive docks and railyards, became the largest transportation hub on the West Coast. The decline of shipping and the rail freight system in the 1960s left much of the area desolate, but in the last ten years or so SoMa has experienced a dramatic renaissance and is nowadays the only place any serious San Franciscan night owl will be seen after dark. It's reminiscent, in a way, of New York's SoHo, and while by day it can seem a bleak expanse of largely deserted warehouse spaces, by night it can fairly claim to be the epicentre of San Franciscan nightlife.

SoMa divides into three main areas: the increasingly developed area **around the Transbay Terminal**, the nightclub plexus along four blocks of **Folsom Street**, and the as yet undeveloped dockland areas of **Mission Rock and China Basin**. The area has been through several sporadic periods of decline and recovery, particularly the 1980s when a construction ban in the Financial District pushed development south. The massive redevelopment came in the wake of major projects like the **Moscone Convention Center**—named after the mayor who was assassinated along with Harvey Milk—where Walter Mondale (remember him?) was nominated as the Democratic Party candidate for president in 1984, and the **Yerba Buena Center**, an enormous project of offices and condominiums. But the biggest changes are yet to come, and, when they do, they will alter the face of SoMa forever. After years of wrangling and public protest, the **Mission Bay Project**—a huge and contentious expansion scheme aimed at restoring the disused docks and railyards to lucrative industry—looks set to bring some 200,000 extra residents into town. Of all the planned buildings, the most exciting will be the new home of the **Museum of Modern Art** designed by Mario Botta, which will more than double the current exhibition space in the Veterans' Building at Civic Center and—optimists predict—make San Francisco the foremost center for contemporary art on the West Coast.

The Transbay Terminal and Around

The corner of SoMa closest to the Embarcadero holds a large concentration of buildings that were prohibited residence in the Financial District. The densest part of SoMa, this includes the **Transbay Terminal** at First and Mission streets, swarming twice daily with commuters, and the first in a proposed series of yuppie housing developments, **Bayside Village**, the whole overlaid by a network of freeways feeding onto the Bay Bridge. City ordinances state that any commercial downtown developer must make funds available for medium- to low-cost housing for the extra workforce that is drawn to the city. With rents approaching the $900 per month mark, it's a questionable definition of low-cost housing, though terrifically handy for the Financial District whizz-kids who have only a ten-minute walk to work. The **Rincon Center**, 101 Spear Street, is worth a look, not for architectural interest but for the permanent exhibition of murals by Anton Refregier in its skylighted atrium. In all there are 27 murals depicting life during the Depression and industrial themes, supervised by Diego Rivera, who left his mark in several sites around the city during the 1920s and 1930s. Walking west from the Rincon Center along Mission you hit the 200 block of New Montgomery Street and the **Pacific Telephone Building**, a product of architecture's golden age in the 1920s: it's a gently tapered, subtly shadowed mountain, detailed in terra-cotta—really just another office building, but one that aspires to greatness. A couple of blocks over is the **Cartoon Art Museum**, 665 3rd St. (Mon–Fri 10am–5pm; free), showing the original artwork—sketches and separations—from which cartoons are made, including examples of newspaper cartoons, magazine panels, comic book illustration, and animation art.

Though most people only visit at night, a daytime stroll will reveal some interesting, if unexpected, corners of SoMa. Nestled between Brannan and Bryant, Second and Third streets, **South Park** is an odd fish in the heavy industrial landscape, a small open space designed by an English architect to mimic the squares of London. The few surviving bits have been recently rediscovered and increasingly house the offices of architects and designers, who can be seen lunching at the chic and genuinely French *South Park Cafe* on the square. Around the corner, where Third Street meets Brannan, a **plaque** marks the birthplace of *Call of the Wild* writer Jack London, though he soon escaped what were then pretty mean streets, enjoying his better days in Oakland and the valleys of Sonoma.

Folsom Street

Folsom Street between Seventh and Eleventh streets is the main artery of clubland. A former gay strip, it was once the center for much lewder goings on than the now respectable Castro (Chapter Four). A few gay clubs and bars remain, but for the most part the mix is pretty diverse and you should expect to find everything except the very tame. The kernel of activity is around Folsom and 11th, where the largest collection of clubs and bars draws crowds who don't mind standing in line at weekends. Comparatively little traffic uses this intersection during the day, and it comes as a surprise to see the bumper-to-bumper and double-parked cars after midnight. If you find yourself here during the day, and want to check out the area, take a walk along Folsom to the block between 7th and 8th streets: *Brainwash* at 1122 Folsom is the epitome of SoMa, a café where you can also do your laundry; opposite, *Buster's Newsstand* has an exhaustive collection of magazines and guides to SoMa and the nightlife scene. There is a handful of small galleries in the area, most interestingly **Artspace** at 9th and Folsom—an avant-garde space for the exhibition of unusual works and video installations.

Rising impressively out of the desolation of the area, the **Old Mint Museum**, Fifth and Mission streets (Mon–Wed 10am–4pm; free), is an unexpected sight. Classically styled from brick and stone, the building is no longer used as a mint, but a stroll around still allows you to glimpse an awful lot of money. As well as a million dollars' worth of gold bars stacked in a pyramid, there's a million-dollar coin collection and lots more valuables besides. Before you enter the movement of Market Street again, stop at the **Tattoo Museum**, 30 7th Street, actually a working tattoo parlour, and check out Lyle Tuttle's bizarre collection of the flesh canvases that have fallen under his needle. You may find yourself tempted by the glamor of a renowned tattooist who'll let you design your own.

Mission Rock and China Basin

With all the new development in progress, it can be hard to imagine what SoMa looked like before. But the real spirit of blue-collar, industrial San Francisco can still be found around the abandoned docks and old shipyards known as **Mission Rock** and **China Basin**. They cover a large area on the eastern edge of the peninsula, and unless you're wildly energetic you'll probably need a car to get the best out of them. Deserted apart from a few spots along the water, it's strange to think that this was once the busiest port along the West Coast, employing thousands of men, most of whom were members of San Francisco's famous (and radical) Longshoremen's Union. Few of the docks are operational now, and the most the area is good for is an indolent stroll, taking in the views of the East Bay across the water and stopping off for a drink at the couple of places that dot the shoreline.

The easiest way to reach the district is to follow 3rd Street south from Market as it curves around to meet the dock area. Starting at the **switchyards** where the drawbridge crosses China Basin Channel at 3rd Street, you'll see a small hut-like building on the south side of the bridge—formerly *Blanche's*, a tiny café that drew attention to the problems of development here when the city tried to get Blanche to move. Despite having her trading license taken away, she opened up the small pier, which juts out over the channel switchyards, for all-comers to bring their sandwiches and wine at lunchtime and look at her collection of antiques from the mills of San Francisco's boomtown days. Sadly, financial deprivation pushed Blanche into retirement, and the site has now been taken over by a Vietnamese family who can never quite capture Blanche's ambience. It was on the switchyards below that Jack Kerouac worked as a brakeman in the 1950s for Southern Pacific, at the same time writing the material that was later to appear in *Lonesome Traveler*, detailing scenes of SoMa skid row hotels, drunks, and whores.

A short walk south takes you to the heart of China Basin, the old water inlet, and Mission Rock—the old Pier 50 that juts out into the bay. This was the focus of the old port where freight ships used to dock from Asia. Occasionally the odd ship will sail by, but these days it's more likely to be the military ships from the Oakland Naval Base cruising the bay than the freight liners that used to jam the waterways. A few small boat clubs have sprung up along the waterfront, but most people come to visit the *Mission Rock Resort* or *The Ramp* (see

Chapter Seven)—two creaky wooden structures that are local landmarks. *The Ramp* in particular is the place to be seen on Sundays when people gather to hear live jazz on the small pier. Locals are determined that these two places should not be sacrificed in the rush for development, but frankly their chances of survival are slim once the Mission Bay Project picks up steam.

ACCOMMODATION Hostels *Globe Hostel, European Guest House;* **Hotels** *Bay Bridge Motel, Golden City Inn.*

BARS *Bouncers Bar, Brainwash, Cadillac Bar & Grill, The Chatterbox, Julie's Supper Club, Milestones, Mission Rock Resort, Paradise Lounge, The Ramp, Rockin Robin's, Zeitgeist.*

RESTAURANTS Budget *Hamburger Mary's, Limbo, Pauline's Pizza Pie;* **American** *Julie's Supper Club;* **French** *Cafe Landais, South Park Cafe;* **Chinese, Thai, and Indonesian** *Manora's Thai Cuisine;* **Japanese and Korean** *Moshi Moshi;* **Vegetarian** *Marty's.*

The Mission

Low-rent, hip, colorful, occasionally dangerous, and solidly blue-collar, the **MISSION** is easily San Francisco's funkiest neighborhood. Positioned way south of the downtown area, it is also the city's warmest, avoiding the fogs which blanket most of the peninsula during the summer. Stretching from the southern end of SoMa down to Army Street in the south, the Mission is a large district, although with *BART* stations at each end, getting here isn't a problem. It is in the eight blocks between the two *BART* stations (16th and 24th St.), along Mission, Valencia, and Dolores, that most of the action happens. Both streets are lined with thrift shops, bookstores, cafés, and bars in which it isn't difficult to empty your pockets. Overall, it's a noisy melange of garages, furniture, and junk stores, old movie houses and parking lots: food is cheap and there's a fair concentration of lively nightspots, making the Mission a good base if you're staying in the city for any length of time.

As a first stop for arriving immigrants to the city, the Mission is something of a microcosm of the history of San Francisco. It was first inhabited by the Scandinavians and Germans, later the Irish, then the Italians, and most recently and significantly, it has been the home of San Francisco's Hispanic population. There's a marked political edge to the area, with active Hispanic campaigning and a multitude of **murals** depicting aspects of the Latin American struggle. Sadly, it is also one of the few areas in town where women are likely to encounter the cat-calling and hissing of Latin men, and perhaps as a defiant result of this it has become a lesbian stronghold, with women's bars, feminist bookstores, and meeting places dotting the streets. There is, too, a flourishing arts scene—theater groups, cultural centers, and a thriving Latin literary network, possibly San Francisco's most vibrant since the Beats, that feels far away from the middle-class complacency of much of the rest of the city.

The district takes its name from the old **Mission Dolores** on 16th and Dolores (daily 9am–4pm; $1), San Francisco's oldest building—its fragile adobe structure surviving the earthquakes of 1906 and 1989. Founded in 1776, it was the sixth in a series of missions built as Spain staked its claim to California. California's Mission period is often hard to uncover, distorted as it is in pious romanticism. Tales of kindly Franciscan friars coming to save the native peoples is misguided fantasy, and the sad truth is that the Spanish Franciscans all but obliterated the native Americans in San Francisco and indeed California. You should go to see the eerie, still cool interior of the mission, filled with paintings and an old Mexican statue of Saint Francis tucked away in one corner. There are few reminders of the Costanoan Indians that were enslaved here, and in the adjoining cemetery there is little to suggest that this is where over five thousand of them are buried. As well as the Indians, the gravesites are occupied by Spanish, Mexican, and Yankee pioneers, California's first governor, and San Francisco's first mayor. The **Basilica** adjacent to the mission is hardly worth entering, but its Churrigueresqe Revival design makes it one of the most beautiful block-fronts in town.

Dolores Street itself is an attractive boulevard divided by a line of palm trees that forms the western border of the neighborhood. A few blocks east, **Dolores Park** sits high on a hill commanding the best view of the downtown skyline—a pretty, quiet place to rest during the day, plagued though it is with children on BMX bikes and defecating doggies. By night it's a little more sinister and has a reputation for being one of the central exchanges for San Francisco's drug trade.

Valencia Street is a curious mix of housing projects, lesbian bars, chronically low-profit progressive **bookstores** (see Chapter Six), and restaurants. There are few sights proper along here, but the **Levi Strauss & Co. Factory** at 250 Valencia Street (Mon–Fri 10am–5pm; ☎565-9153), where you can see how the world's most famous jeans are made, is definitely worth a visit. The Levi Strauss empire started in the Gold Rush days when leftover tent material was used to make work jeans, and has gone on to become the biggest manufacturer of jeans in the world. Tours of the plant include a look at the cutting and sewing operations and how to "stonewash" your new pair to make them look old. The tours are conducted on Wednesdays and Fridays, though you should call ahead to book. Two blocks up at 446 Valencia, **Intersection for the Arts** is a non-profit organization that hosts cultural and theatrical events. The program changes constantly, but occasionally they have good exhibitions of local artists and it's worth popping in just to see what's on. Similarly the **Women's Building** at 18th and Valencia supports gay, lesbian, peace, and progressive groups and often has interesting lectures and exhibitions. Across the first floor of the building a mural depicts local feminist heroines.

Mission Street is a slightly more congested version of Valencia, and unless you're bargain-hunting in the thrift shops (see Chapter Six) or hanging around its bars, you should take it as far as **24th Street**—the axis of Latino shopping, with Nicaraguan, Salvadorean, Costa Rican, Mexican, and other Latin American shops and restaurants. Apart from being the most authentic Latin street in the neighborhood, it's a good place to start a self-guided tour of the Mission's 200-odd **murals**, the fruits of an idea proposed by City Hall to occupy the creative talents of the Mission's poor and not unusually disaffected youth before their energies were channelled into the more conventional criminal activities. They have become the major attraction in a neighborhood that until recently rarely saw tourists. There are hundreds peppered all over the Mission, but the biggest concentration is along 24th Street between Mission and South Van Ness. The largest is a tribute to local hero **Carlos Santana**, adorning three buildings where 22nd Street meets South Van Ness; for more controversial subject matter take a walk down **Balmy Alley** between Folsom and Harrison off 24th Street, where every possible surface is covered with murals depicting the political agonies of contemporary Central America. It was started in 1973 by a group of artists and community workers and has become the most quietly admired public art in San Francisco. Several organizations conduct walking tours of the Mission, but none more amusing or authentic than the four-foot-ten dynamo who runs *Helen's Walking Tours* (see "Tours" in *Basics*).

More Latin artwork is on display at the **Mission Cultural Center**, 2868 Mission Street (daily 10am–6pm; ☎821-1155), founded in 1977 with the aim of preserving and promoting Latino cultural arts. As well as theatrical productions, poetry readings, and classes, there is a large exhibition space for the changing contemporary exhibitions of local paintings and drawings.

Potrero Hill

Cut off from the rest of the Mission by the freeway, rising above San Francisco General Hospital, **POTRERO HILL** is a tiny community that's easy to miss. Its quiet streets and brightly painted houses sit high on a hill overlooking the Mission to the west and the SoMa docks to the north. Blue-collar and solidly residential, it's a peaceful neighborhood that prides itself on its isolation, a lack of tourist traffic, and a pace more evocative of a rural town than a major city; it even has its own weekly newspaper. There's precious little to do, but its leafy streets are perfect for a morning stroll, taking in the views of downtown San Francisco and the docks and pausing for coffee; there are also several excellent **restaurants** in the area (see "Eating," Chapter Seven).

ACCOMMODATION Hostels *International Network Cotel;* **Hotels** *Dolores Park Inn.*

BARS *The Chatterbox, El Rio, Molloy's, The Uptown, Zeitgeist.*

RESTAURANTS Budget *Hamburger Nancy's;* **American** *The Connecticut Yankee, Goat Hill Pizza and Brunch;* **Italian** *La Traviata;* **French** *Le Trou;* **Chinese, Thai, and Indonesian** *Bangok 16, Pazzaz;* **Mexican and Hispanic** *El Cubane, El Tazumal, El Toro, Las Guitarras, Mission Villa Restaurant, Mom's Cooking, New Central Restaurant, La Taqueria, La Victoria.*

CHAPTER FOUR

THE CENTRAL NEIGHBORHOODS

Residential, well-tended, and, for the most part, almost anodynely pleasant, San Francisco's **CENTRAL NEIGHBORHOODS** don't have the cachet or excitement of downtown, nor, on the whole, the hip qualities of North Beach or South of Market, but they're most of the reason San Franciscans find their city so easy to live in. Self-sufficient and independent, these neighborhoods are an inviting collection, each with its own distinct national and social identity, the result of years of immigrant waves and political activity. Bounded by the fancy reaches of Pacific Heights and the Presidio to the north, and stretching from the Civic Center to the Pacific Ocean beaches, they sit snugly in a series of sunny valleys and gentle slopes that makes up the core of living space in San Francisco, their ornate Victorian architecture, interspersed with open spaces and parks, sidewalk cafés, and small shops, revealing something of the city's true identity.

The area as a whole is definitely on the way up. The largest and most depressed neighborhood, the **Western Addition**, is shrinking rapidly, as money from Pacific Heights trickles down in the search for real estate, its borders being redefined by a gentrification boom that shows little sign of slowing. Formerly a solidly black community, its northern reaches have gradually evolved into a pristine enclave known as **Japantown**, spruced up by affluent Japanese families who have bought up lots, opened stores, and transformed the streets from their previously neglected state. South of here, dilapidated housing developments give way at Haight Street to the eponymous **Lower Haight**, another recently poor but now terminally aspiring neighborhood that threatens to overshadow its famous neighbor to the west, the **Haight-Ashbury**.

The Haight, as it's known, is long past its 1960s heyday of druggy hedonism, but traces of its anti-Establishment past do linger in bookstores and cafés that continue to draw a steady subculture. The Haight's biggest draw is perhaps its proximity to the urban idyll of **Golden Gate Park**, which stretches west for two miles as far as the ocean, its museums, gardens, and lakes something of an oasis for San Franciscans struggling to find relief from the congestion of their city. Beautifully landscaped and immaculately maintained, its vast grounds have enough room for the joggers, bike-riders, and busloads of tourists that flock here seeking some refuge and peace away from the downtown area.

The **Castro**, southeast of the Haight and at the far end of Market Street from downtown San Francisco, is perhaps the city's most distinctive neighborhood, though for its people more than for any great sights. As the focus of San Francisco's gay community, it has been through the struggles of the 1960s which culminated in widespread recognition and acceptance in the freewheeling 1970s, only to be knocked off its feet by the advent of AIDS in the 1980s. Gay pride is starting to re-emerge, but the neighborhood's outrageous days are clearly over. In a sunny valley over the hill from the Castro, **Noe Valley** is a restful, attractive district that has changed little over the years—family oriented, with a rooted suburban feel. **Twin Peaks**, the city's most distinctive summit, looms over Noe Valley and the Castro, offering fresh air and unbeatable 360-degree views out over the city below.

The Western Addition, Japantown, and the Lower Haight

Looking at any map of San Francisco, you'll see several blocks labeled the **WESTERN ADDITION**, smack in the middle of the peninsula—a central position which belies its status as one of the city's most unrelentingly poor neighborhoods. Also known as "the Fillmore" after its main thoroughfare, the large, mostly black area spreads along both sides of Fillmore Street from Geary Boulevard south to around Haight Street, marked by block after block of semi-abandoned and low-rent dwellings where unemployment, drugs, and violence are tangible evidence of the community's failure to share in the prosperity of the rest of the city.

Over the last few years the city has taken steps to improve conditions here, though only by moving the problem elsewhere. Whole blocks of the Western Addition have been demolished and crime-infested housing projects ripped out and replaced with new structures. These new apartment buildings have been constructed with some architectural sympathy for those who will inhabit them, but whether they manage to avoid the deterioration that blighted their predecessors remains to be seen. In an effort to reform the area, private blocks are being sold on the basis of their proximity to Civic Center and downtown areas. They're built, claim officials, for middle-income families, though they're more likely to be snatched up by the increasing tide of well-to-do professionals, which leaves the city with a bigger social problem than the one it's trying to cure, with poor, dispossessed, and now homeless black families inevitably being squeezed out to other areas.

The most obvious changes have been taking place in the northern parts of the district, where **JAPANTOWN** fills the area between Fillmore and Webster streets, with Geary Boulevard marking its southern border and Pine Street separating it from Pacific Heights. Japanese immigrants first came to the area via Hawaii, where they worked on the sugar plantations at the turn of the century. Slowly, they built up businesses in the Western Addition that grew to occupy some forty blocks, later selling their property reluctantly and in haste

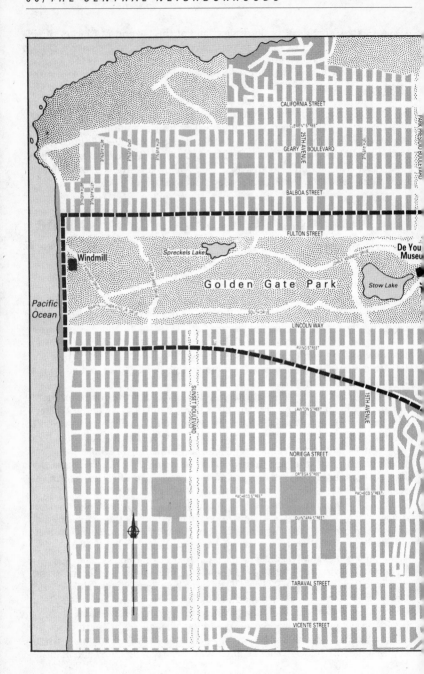

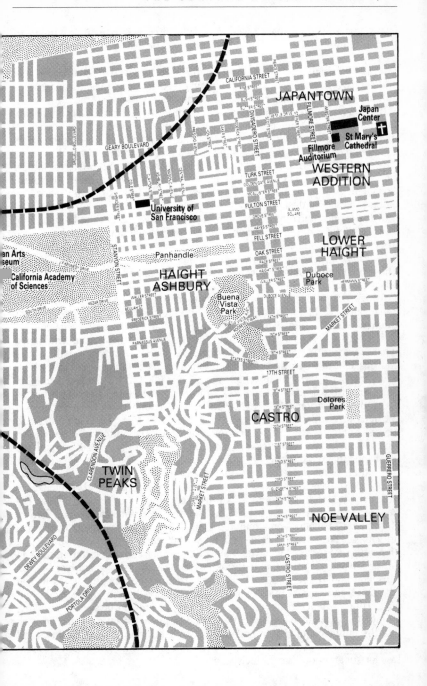

JAPANTOWN

Japan Center

St Mary's Cathedral ✝

Fillmore Auditorium

WESTERN ADDITION

University of San Francisco

LOWER HAIGHT

Panhandle

an Arts seum

California Academy of Sciences

HAIGHT ASHBURY

Buena Vista Park

Dubose Park

CASTRO

Dolores Park

TWIN PEAKS

NOE VALLEY

CALIFORNIA STREET
GEARY BOULEVARD
DIVISADERO STREET
TURK STREET
GOLDEN GATE AVENUE
FULTON STREET
ALAMO SQUARE
GROVE STREET
HAYES STREET
FELL STREET
OAK STREET
PAGE STREET
HAIGHT STREET
WALLER STREET
HERMANN STREET
DUBOCE AVENUE
FILLMORE STREET
WEBSTER STREET
STANYON STREET
KEZAR DRIVE
SOUTH DRIVE
FREDERICK STREET
PARNASSUS AVENUE
STATES STREET
MARKET STREET
GUERRERO STREET
CASTRO STREET
CLARENDON AVENUE
DEWEY BOULEVARD
PORTOLA DRIVE
17TH STREET

in 1942, when anti-Japanese hysteria swept California in response to the Pearl Harbor bombing. Several years later, some Japanese drifted back and tried to pick up the threads but found their old neighborhood occupied by the black community which now inhabits most of the area. Today, divided from the rest of Western Addition by the Geary Boulevard expressway, Japantown occupies only six blocks and doesn't look set to expand any farther.

In contrast to the old, ad hoc, and concentrated development of Chinatown, Japantown is well tended and new—and really quite indigenous. It's something of a misnomer for what is basically a shopping center—the Japanese Cultural and Trade Center (*Nihonmachi*)—albeit one with a distinctly eastern flavor and a five-tiered, 100-foot pagoda at its heart. Better known as the **Japan Center**, it's the home of a few Japanese restaurants and stores, the Japanese Consulate, and, more interestingly, the excellent **Kabuki Complex**—an ultramodern industrial design in glass with eight movie theaters. For most of the year these show current-release and popular movies, but at the beginning of May they host the **San Francisco Film Festival** which runs for about three weeks (see Chapter Eight). The Japan Center's other main highlight is the **Kabuki Hot Springs** (1750 Geary Boulevard, ☎922-6000; 10am–10pm). These genuine community baths offer shiatsu massage, steam baths, and other luxuriating facilities for around $35 a session.

Away from the Japan Center complex there are some signs of a more traditional Japanese lifestyle working alongside the new. Over on Pine Street at Octavia, the **Buddhist Church of San Francisco** has a multiracial congregation and offers services in both English (Sun 10am) and traditional Japanese (Sun 1pm) to serve the diversity of San Franciscans that have chosen Buddhism as their faith. The building itself is plain and gives little indication of the sumptuous temple inside. It is filled with what are claimed to be relics of the Buddha, donated by the King of Siam in 1935. Two blocks over, where Geary meets Gough, is the monumentally provocative **St Mary's Cathedral**. Visible from the heart of downtown, St Mary's is San Francisco's newest Roman Catholic cathedral, built in 1971—elaborate and ostentatious, with a comparatively functional, modern interior. Take a walk around the inside and look up into the 190-foot dome.

Another, much more sinister quasi-religious relic once stood on the now-empty lot six blocks to the west, on Geary between Scott and Steiner. This was the site of the **People's Temple**, in which, during the 1970s, the Reverend Jim Jones established the cult that was later to go and live in "Jonestown," Guyana—an attempted utopia of common-living and egalitarian principles. The mass suicide in 1978 that came to be known as the "Jonestown Massacre" involved mainly San Franciscans, devastating the city just as it was trying to come to terms with the recent assassination of George Moscone and Harvey Milk. Today there is little reference to Jones in San Francisco, and rumors that the old temple was jinxed seem to have had some supporting evidence. Several years after the Jonestown Massacre, a wealthy, anonymous man filled the temple with riches, priceless antiques and artwork that the public could visit free of charge. After a series of small mishaps and accidents, a mysterious fire burned it to its foundations last year—no great loss for superstitious San Franciscans.

Other local landmarks have been luckier. The **Fillmore Auditorium**, the large three-story yellow brick building at the corner of Fillmore and Geary, saw some of rock music's biggest heroes at its zenith in the mid-1960s. The first official home of psychedelia, it was in this small (1000 capacity) ballroom that Bill Graham staged weekend dance concerts featuring the acid-drenched sounds of the Grateful Dead, Jefferson Airplane, and Janis Joplin, sometimes all on the same bill—and the now legendary light shows that went on to become a major component of the psychedelic experience during the "Summer of Love."

Heading south on Fillmore Street through the heart of the Western Addition (*Muni* bus #23 runs all day and night), you pass through one of the few parts of San Francisco that survived the 1906 earthquake and fire. For a few years afterward, Fillmore Street was the city's main commercial stretch, with houses turned into hotels and front parlors converted into banks and grocery stores. However, as the rest of San Francisco returned to normal, the Fillmore area was abandoned, a state of affairs which has continued more or less to the present day. But despite the general shabbiness it's safe enough to walk through. Should you do so, take a diversion a block west of Fillmore along Fulton Street to **Alamo Square**. A small gem of a park, Alamo Square is quiet, pastoral, and at its peak has one of the city's nicest views: sit on the crest and look east across Steiner Street at the multicolored **Painted-Ladies**—six identical, marvelously restored 1894 Victorian houses set against the skyline of the Financial District, which feature in most brochures on San Francisco. Though you might take the presence of these houses as a sign of yet more impending gentrification, they've been in good shape for a number of years while the surrounding area in fact remains one of the city's most uncared for. A number of similar houses nearby have been restored, but with such a large stock of public housing in its environs, a total yuppie invasion looks unlikely.

The few newcomers, particularly around the junction of Fillmore Street and Haight Street, have had an effect but have so far managed to strike the right balance of bringing better stores and restaurants to the area without evicting its residents or radically changing its character. Nowadays the area, known as the **LOWER HAIGHT**, is in a period of transition and has become a major stomping-ground of the sort of fashion victims usually spotted hanging out South of Market, and home to some of the city's best bars and meeting places (see "Drinking," Chapter Seven). There's a growing mix of foreign restaurants, and, given its good access to downtown and proximity to the Castro and Haight-Ashbury, its desirability as a place to live for good-time boys and girls on a budget is undeniable—a fine place to get a cheap breakfast, browse the bookstores, rake through vintage clothing shops, and drink yourself silly.

ACCOMMODATION *Casa Loma Hotel, Queen Anne.*

BARS *Jack's Bailey Bar, Jimmy's West Point, Mad Dog in the Fog, Noc Noc, Toronado, Tropical Haight.*

RESTAURANTS Budget *Spaghetti Western;* **Japanese** *Sushi Bar, Mifune, Asuka Brasserie, Isuzu, Osome, Yoshida-Ya;* **Thai** *Thep Phanom.*

The Castro

Arguably San Francisco's most progressive, if no longer most celebratory, neighborhood, **THE CASTRO** is the city's avowedly Gay Capital and, as such, the best barometer for the state of the AIDS-devastated gay scene. People say many things about the changing face of the Castro—some insist it still ranks as one of the wildest places in town, others reckon it's a shadow of its former self. But all agree that things are not the same. As a district, the Castro occupies a large area which stretches from Market Street to as far south as Noe Valley (see below), but in terms of visible street life the few blocks from Market to 20th Street contain about all there is to see. These streets, once brimming with gay emancipation, have sobered to a state of restraint and resolution. A walk down the Castro ten—or even five—years ago would have had you gaping at the non-stop revelry, and while most of the same bars and hangouts still stand, these days they're host to an altogether different, younger, and more conservative breed. It is still undeniably the province of the gay man, and dignity and determination have survived, but the energy that was once invested in hard-won, open hedonism has been squarely diverted to the formation of AIDS support groups, care for the sick, and enough political dexterity to maintain their mainstream influence in the city's political arena.

The Castro *Muni* station at Market Street is about the best place to begin a tour, at **Harvey Milk Plaza**, dedicated to the extremely popular gay city Supervisor who before his assassination in 1978 owned a camera shop on Castro Street and was the community's most prominent figure. Milk's and Mayor George Moscone's assailant, Dan White, was a disgruntled ex-Supervisor who resigned when the liberal policies of Moscone and Milk didn't meet with his conservative views. A staunch Catholic, White was a spokesman for San Francisco's many blue-collar Irish families and, as an ex-policeman, saw himself in the vanguard of the family values he believed gay rights were damaging. He later tried to get his post back but was refused by Moscone, and soon after climbed through a basement window in City Hall, sauntered into their offices, and shot them both. At the trial, during which the prosecution never once used the word "assassination" or recognized a political motive for the killings, White pleaded temporary insanity caused by harmful additives in his fast-food diet—a plea which came to be known as the "Twinkie defense"—and was sentenced to five years' imprisonment for manslaughter. The gay community reacted angrily to the brevity of White's sentence, and the riots that followed were among the most violent San Francisco has ever witnessed, protesters marching into City Hall, turning over and burning police cars as they went. White was released in 1985 and moved to Los Angeles, committing suicide shortly afterward. The anniversary of the murders, **November 27**, is marked by a candlelight procession from the Castro to City Hall.

Before heading down the hill into the heart of the Castro, take a short walk across Market Street to the headquarters of the **Names Project** at 2362 Market Street (daily 10am–7pm). The organization was founded in the wake of the AIDS crisis and sponsored the creation of "The Quilt"—a gargantuan blanket composed of panels, each 6ft x 3ft (the size of gravesites) and bearing the name of a man lost to the disease. Made by their lovers, friends, and families, the panels are stitched together and regularly toured around the country; it was spread on the Mall in Washington DC in 1987 and 1988 to dramatize the epidemic to the seemingly unconcerned government. Sections of the quilt, too large to be exhibited in any one place in its entirety, continue to tour the world to raise people's awareness of the tragedy, and funds to help keep the care programs alive. Inside the showroom, you can see the thousands of panels stored on shelves: some are hung up for display, and machinists tackle the endless task of stitching the whole thing together.

Back on Castro Street, one of the first things you see is the **Castro Theater**, self-described as "San Francisco's landmark movie palace" and undeniably one of San Francisco's better (if not best) movie houses, as popular for its pseudo-Spanish baroque interior as it is for its billing, which includes revival fare, twenty-minute performances on a Wurlitzer organ, and some plush velvet surroundings (see "Films," Chapter Eight). Half a block down the hill, the junction of **Castro and 18th streets**, known as the "gayest four corners of the earth," is the heart of the Castro, and the site of much political activity, particularly at weekends, when people set up petition stands, canvas for votes, and the bums hang out capitalizing on the throng. **The Sisters of Perpetual Indulgence**, a now world-famous group of local figures who won their notoriety by dressing up as nuns and roaring about on motorbikes and roller skates, spend a lot of time at this junction canvassing for some cause or other, usually in full regalia and always surrounded by an amused crowd. Cluttered with bookstores (some particularly noteworthy: see "Gay & Lesbian Bookstores," Chapter Six), clothing stores, cafés, and bars, this junction is as dense as the neighborhood gets and a sure sign that, despite the losses of the last few years, the survival of the community is assured.

Noe Valley

NOE VALLEY, immediately south of the Castro, is remarkable only for its insignificant status in the pantheon of San Francisco neighborhoods; in fact, so good is it at failing to capture imaginations that it is fondly tagged "Noewhere Valley" by those who have any notion of where and what it's like. Sitting snugly in a sunny valley, the main vein of which runs along 24th Street from the borders of the Mission, it has an air of rugged unfashionableness manifest in clean streets, visible signs of family life, blue-collar sports bars, small human-scale stores and a noticeable lack of street crime and vagrancy—in some degree refreshing after the contrivedness and sleaze of the Haight, Mission, or SoMa.

A good balance of commercial activity along 24th Street gives you reason enough to spend an afternoon wandering in and out of the book and record stores, good delicatessens, and clothing stores. The neighborhood is served by the J-Church streetcar, which, from downtown, winds prettily past Dolores Park and around leafy, curving hills before stopping at Church and 24th

Street, where you should disembark. It is surprisingly close to the center of town, and with San Francisco real estate prices climbing way beyond the means of most, it's perhaps a matter of time before the rents squeeze out the families to make room for wealthy professionals.

As well as the 24th Street strip, Church Street between 24th and 30th has an unusual (and thankfully uncrowded) hotch-potch of weird little junk stores, nail parlors, and hair salons. Noe Valley is *the* place to get your appearance sorted out: there are about seven hairdressers between 24th and 30th alone, and all along 24th Street beauty salons vie for your business with some pretty cut-throat prices. There's even a **hot tub** and sauna place called *Elisa's Health Spa* (4026 24th Street), where you can get half an hour in an outdoor hot tub for $7.50 and half an hour's shiatsu massage for $20.

Diverting slightly onto Sanchez Street, the **Noe Valley Ministry** (1021 Sanchez) is a place to keep an eye out for. Originally built in the late nineteenth century as a Presbyterian Church, this attractive Gothic-style building now serves as the neighborhood community center and, in addition to providing a forum for worship, lectures, and a nursery school, hosts a good program of concerts each Saturday, ranging from classical and chamber choir to modern jazz and soul.

Twin Peaks

Real estate prices in San Francisco are gauged in part by the quality of the views, and with this in mind it's no surprise that the curving streets which wind around the slopes of **TWIN PEAKS** hold some of the city's most outrageously unaffordable homes. If the peaks themselves were up for sale they'd command millions, but fortunately they're among the few hills in San Francisco that have been saved from being entirely covered with houses and so offer spectacular, 360-degree views that you should make every effort to see.

It's a stiff but rewarding climb or bike-ride up Twin Peaks Boulevard from the top of Market Street (*Muni* bus #37 saves most of the work), or you can join one of the many guided **bus tours** of the city—they all stop here. If you've got a car, it's beautiful by night as well, though it can get terribly cold and windswept.

Before all the skyscrapers went up downtown, Twin Peaks was San Francisco's most distinctive landmark—Market Street was laid out expressly to focus sightlines on its voluptuous symmetry. Before that, local Native American tribes believed that the peaks were created when a married couple argued so violently that the Great Spirit separated them with a clap of thunder; they were later tagged "Breasts of the Indian Girl" by Spanish explorers, but Americans finally settled on the more literal name of Twin Peaks. Architect Daniel Burnham spent time here in 1905 working on a master plan for the city which would have replaced the relentless urban grid with more curving streets and broad parkways. Despite the opportunity offered by the earthquake and fire of the following year, commercially minded civic authorities lacked the vision to carry any of it out, and the ideas were largely forgotten, except for his plans for Civic Center.

ACCOMMODATION *Beck's Motor Lodge, Inn on Castro, San Francisco Apartments, 24 Henry, Twin Peaks Hotel.*
CAFÉS *Cafe Flore.*
BARS *The Bear, Castro Station, Cafe San Marcos The Corral, Francines, Jack's Bailey Bar, Midnight Sun, Moby Dick, Noe's, The Phoenix, Rat & Raven, Twin Peaks, Uncle Bert's Place.*
RESTAURANTS Budget *Bagdad Cafe, Church St. Station, Hot N Hunky, Orphan Andy's;* **American** *The Patio;* **Pizza** *Noe Valley Pizza;* **Japanese** *Ma Tante Sumi;* **Greek** *Panos.*

Haight-Ashbury

Two miles west of downtown San Francisco, the neighborhood of **HAIGHT-ASHBURY** lent its name to an era, giving it a fame that far outstrips its size. Small and dense, "The Haight," as it is known, spans no more than eight blocks in length, centered around the junction of Haight and Ashbury streets. It emerged in the Sixties as the mecca of the counter-cultural scene, since when it has gone slightly upmarket while remaining one of San Francisco's most racially and culturally mixed neighborhoods, with radical bookstores, laid-back cafés, record stores, and second-hand clothing stores recalling its era of international celebrity.

The area was no more than a pile of sand dunes that had been claimed in part by squatters until 1865, when a forward-thinking Supervisor called Frank McCoppin spearheaded the development of the dunes into the area that is now known as Golden Gate Park. The landscaping of the Panhandle that leads into the park, the creation of a cable car line along Haight Street, and an amusement park drew people out to the western edge of town; development continued, and by the 1890s the Haight was a thriving middle-class neighborhood. After the 1906 earthquake, new building gathered pace and the neighborhood's desirability grew—something that was checked by the 1930s Depression, which turned many of the respectable Victorian homes into cheap boarding houses. The 1950s saw inroads of students from the then-nearby San Francisco State College, and a youth culture began to develop that later blossomed into Flower Power, the hippies, and the Summer of Love.

The first hippies were an offshoot of the Beats, many of whom had moved out of their increasingly expensive North Beach homes to take advantage of the cheap rents and large spaces in the run-down Victorian houses of the Haight. The post-Beat bohemia that subsequently began to develop here was a small affair at first, involving the use of drugs and the embrace of Eastern religion and philosophy, together with a marked anti-American political stance. Where Beat philosophy had emphasized self-indulgence, the hippies, on the face of it at least, attempted to be more embracing, emphasizing concepts like "universal truth" and "cosmic awareness." The use of drugs was crucial and seen as an integral, and positive, part of the movement—LSD especially, the effects of which were just being discovered, despite an esoteric following in psychoanalytical circles for decades before.

Naturally it took a few big names to get the ball rolling, the pivotal occasion coming in January 1966 when Ken Kesey and his Merry Pranksters hosted a Trips Festival in the Longshoremen's Hall at Fisherman's Wharf. Attended by thousands, most of whom had dropped acid, it set a precedent for wild living, challenging authority, and dropping out of the social and political establishment. At the time LSD was not illegal and was being hyped by groups like the Pranksters as an avant-garde art form, consciousness-raising in its effects. Pumped out in private laboratories and promoted by the likes of Timothy Leary with the prescription "Turn on, tune in, drop out", LSD galvanized a generation into believing that it could be used to raise the creativity of one and all. Before long, life in the Haight took on a theatrical quality: Pop Art found mass appeal, light shows became legion, dress flamboyant, and behavior dissociated from any notion of respectability. The Grateful Dead, Jefferson Airplane, and Big Brother and the Holding Company began to make a name for themselves, and, backed by the business weight of Bill Graham, the psychedelic music scene became a genuine force nationwide.

It wasn't long before kids from all over America started turning up in the Haight for the free food, free drugs . . . and free love. Money became a dirty word, the hip became "heads," the others "straights," and by the time of the massive "Be-In" in Golden Gate Park in 1966 and the so-called "Summer of Love" the following year, this busy little intersection had attracted no fewer than 75,000 transitory people in its short life as the focus of alternative culture.

But along with all the nice middle-class kids who simply wanted to get stoned came the outcasts, the crazies, and the villains. Charles Manson recruited much of his "family" in the Haight, and the enormous flow of drugs through the small neighborhood made it inviting prey for organized crime. Hunter S. Thompson, too, spent his time here researching and writing his book *Hell's Angels*, and was notorious for inviting Angels around to his apartment on Parnassus Street for drinking and drug-taking sessions which were invariably noisy, long, and sometimes—given Thompson's predilection for firearms—even dangerous.

The Haight today has few real sights, relying instead on the constant turnover of hip clothing stores, popular cafés, and bookstores to sustain its legend. Two blocks east of the Haight-Ashbury junction, **Buena Vista Park** is a mountainous forest of Monterey pines and California redwoods, enjoyed in daylight by dogwalkers and other people who take in the stunning views of the city, but come nightfall the locale of much open-air sex. Around the park are examples of some of the most lavish Victorian architecture to be found in the city, not unusually decorated to death with turrets, false gables, columns, corner towers, and elaborate window design; indeed for all its hipness and supposed disdain for bourgeois living, the Haight has all the trappings (or at least the architecture) of an exclusive, chi-chi community. Still, some determinedly psychedelic venues remain. The **Holos Gallery** at 1792 Haight Street, has the largest collection of holograms in California: a dimly-lit affair that comes across as a microcosm of the 1960s—trashy and ultimately empty, but a good idea at the time. A more worthwhile hangover is the **Haight-Ashbury Free Clinic** at 558 Clayton Street. It's quite a phenomenon, providing free health care since the 1960s when drug-related illnesses became a big problem in the Haight. It survives—barely—on contributions and continues to treat drug casualties and the poor, both disproportionately large groups in this part of the city.

Otherwise, stroll along the Haight and take advantage of what is still one of the best areas in town to **shop**. It shouldn't take more than a couple of hours to update your record collection, dress yourself up, and blow money on good books. If you're looking for food, some interesting restaurants are starting to appear along Haight Street, although there's still a better line in bakeries, cafés, and lunch-type joints. Moving west along Haight Street things get livelier the nearer you approach to the **Panhandle**, the finger-slim strip of greenery that eventually leads to Golden Gate Park but is generally considered to be part of the Haight. The Panhandle was landscaped before the rest of the park back in the 1870s and for a while was the focus for High Society carriage rides, where the well dressed would go to look and be looked at. In post-quake 1906 it became a refuge for fleeing families, with some thirty thousand living in tents. During the 1960s it was the scene of outdoor rock concerts which caused considerable wear and tear on the delicate landscape. Today it's rather seedy: home to vagrants and the few guitar-strumming hippies that remain.

ACCOMMODATION *Red Victorian Bed and Breakfast, Stanyan Park Hotel.*
BARS *Achilles Heel, The Gold Cane, The Deluxe, Nightbreak.*
RESTAURANTS Budget *Pall Mall Bar and Grill.*

Golden Gate Park

Unlike other American cities, San Francisco is not short on green space, but **GOLDEN GATE PARK** is its largest, providing a massively bucolic antidote to the city center. Despite the throngs of joggers, polo players, roller-skaters, cyclists, and strollers it never gets overcrowded, and you can always find a spot to be alone. Inspired by Frederick Law Olmsted, creator of Central Park in New York, and designed by park engineer William H. Hall in 1871, it's one of the most beautiful and safest corners of the city, with none of the menace of New York's park. Spreading three miles or so west from the Haight to the Pacific shore, it was constructed on what was then an area of wild sand dunes buffeted by the spray from the nearby ocean, with the help of a dike to protect the western side from the sea. John McLaren, the Scottish park superintendent for fifty-odd years, planted several thousand trees here, and it's nowadays the most peaceful—and most skillfully crafted—spot to relax in the city.

The park is huge, no question, and exploration of all its corners could take days of footwork, though it's best to wander aimlessly, getting lost and seeing what you can stumble across. Sloping gently from east to west, it divides roughly into two sections. The eastern side, nearest the Haight, has all the main attractions—art and science museums, horticultural palaces, tea

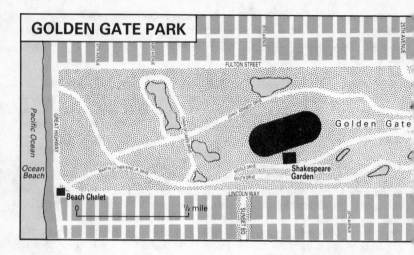

gardens, and bandstands. The west is fairly isolated, with more open space and a less sculpted landscape better suited to horse riding and other outdoor activities.

Fell Street runs along the side of the Panhandle, becoming John F. Kennedy Drive where it enters the park. You should follow this for half a mile to reach the busiest section of the park, near the **museums**. The park's largest, the **M. H. de Young Memorial Museum** (Wed–Sun 10am–5pm; $4, free first Wed of month and Sat mornings), is the city's most diversified, with a permanent collection of American art, from colonial times to the twentieth century—rated as one of the best on the West Coast. The museum had its origin in the California Midwinter International Exposition of 1894, a venture that was so successful that the Fine Arts Building (around which the current museum was built) was turned over to newspaper publisher M. H. de Young with the purpose of establishing a permanent museum. Overall the collection is very impressive, in particular the core of over a hundred paintings from the collection of Mr. and Mrs. John D. Rockefeller III that features works by John Singleton Copley, Rembrandt Peale, and John Singer Sargent. The works in the new British Galleries date from the reign of George III in the latter half of the eighteenth century and continue into the early years of the nineteenth— an era of potent achievement in the neo-Classical and Rococo periods. Among the major painters represented are John Constable, Sir Joshua Reynolds, Thomas Gainsborough, and Henry Raeburn. Least interesting is the museum's showing of the traditional arts of Africa, Oceania, and the Americas, with the display of ancient arts of Egypt, Greece, and Rome faring slightly better.

Next door, the **Asian Art Museum** (Wed–Sun 10am–5pm; $4, free first Wed of month and Sat mornings) opened in 1966 after Avery Brundage, longtime head of the International Olympic Committee, donated his world-famous collection to the city of San Francisco—an assembly of works so large that it

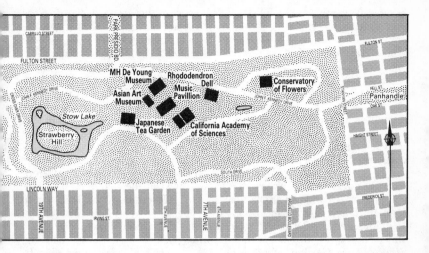

has to be rotated periodically, as it can never be exhibited in its entirety at one time. Highlights include the **Jade Room**, showing pieces that date back as far as 3500 years and the oldest-known dated **Chinese Buddha** image (338 AD). The addition of a new **Indian Gallery** has done much to improve the museum. On display are over twenty miniature paintings, heavy stone sculptures from the Jain period, and textiles.

Opposite, the **California Academy of Sciences** (daily 10am–5pm; $5, children under 6 free) is the perfect place to amuse restless children. There's a natural history museum with a thirty-foot skeleton of a 130-million-year-old dinosaur and life-size replicas of humans throughout the ages. But the show stealer is the collection of 14,500 specimens of aquatic life in the **Steinhart Aquarium** (same times and ticket). The feeding of the seals and dolphins at 10:30am is always worth seeing, as is the doughnut-shaped tank known as the Fish Roundabout: the viewing area is in the center of this 200-foot-circumference tank and the impression of being underwater with the fish swimming all about you is uncannily realistic. Reptile fans will enjoy watching the scaly beasts in The Swamp—a simulated habitat for lizards, alligators, and tortoises. Adults will get more out of a trip to the Academy of Sciences if they can catch the **Morrison Planetarium** (schedule varies; ☎387-6300) at the right time. Laser light shows and rock music often draw an acid-crazed crowd for the evening performances.

Slightly west of the museums is the usually crowded **Japanese Tea Garden** (daily 8am–6pm; $2 admission charged 9am–5pm). Built in 1894 for the California Midwinter Exposition, the garden was beautifully landscaped by the Japanese Hagiwara family, which was also responsible for the invention of the fortune cookie, despite the universal belief that fortune cookies are Chinese. The family looked after the garden until World War II, when, along with other Japanese-Americans, they were sent to internment camps. A massive bronze Buddha dominates the garden, and all around are the bridges, footpaths, pools filled with shiny carp, bonsai, and cherry trees that—but for the busloads of tourists that pour in regularly throughout the day—lend a peaceful feel. The best way to enjoy the garden is to get there around 8am when it first opens and have a breakfast of tea and fortune cookies in the tea house.

Surprisingly perhaps, the park's biggest crowd-puller is neither a museum nor place of refreshment. Considering the abundance of flowers throughout the park in general, it would seem that an enormous exhibition space for them was unnecessary, but the **Conservatory of Flowers** on John F. Kennedy Drive (daily 10am–5pm; free), a huge Victorian glass palace modeled on the Palm House at Kew Gardens in London, has an impressive collection of tropical plants and flowers. Still, it seems a bit foolish to endure the heat of this giant greenhouse when you can stroll the park, free of crowds, and see more or less the same thing. Of the hundreds of flower gardens in the park, two are particularly lovely: **Rhododendron Dell**, where John F. Kennedy Drive meets Sixth Avenue, is a twenty-acre memorial to John McLaren, filled with over 500 species of his favorite flower, as well as a statue of him and one of his favorite poet, Robert Burns; and the **Shakespeare Garden**, where Middle Drive meets Martin Luther King Jr. Drive, has every flower or plant ever mentioned in the writer's plays.

The best things to do at the park are outdoors and free. On Sundays, in the central space near the museums, **music** can be heard for free at the **Music Pavilion** bandstand; to enjoy the quieter corners of the park head west through the many flower gardens and eucalyptus groves towards the ocean. Although most people head for the western end of the park to do nothing whatsoever, activities are many, and quite cheap, if you're feeling energetic. **Boat rental** is available on the beautiful, vast, and swampy **Stow Lake**—in the middle of which is **Strawberry Hill**, a large man-made mountain that's perfect for a picnic and a laze in the sunshine. Boat rental is around $8 per hour and most enjoyable midweek when the lake is almost deserted.

Perhaps the most unusual thing you'll see in the park is the substantial herd of bison, roaming around the **Buffalo Paddock** off JFK Drive near 38th Avenue; you can get closest to these noble giants at their feeding area, at the far west end. Moving toward the edge of the park at Ocean Beach, passing a tulip garden and large windmill, you'll come to the **Beach Chalet** facing the Great Highway. This two-story, white-pillared structure designed by Willis Polk is home to some of San Francisco's lesser-known public art. A series of frescoes painted in the 1930s depicts the growth of San Francisco as a city and the creation of Golden Gate Park.

CHAPTER FIVE

THE BEACHES AND OUTLYING DISTRICTS

B eyond the downtown area and the central neighborhoods, San Francisco's **OUTLYING DISTRICTS** lack much of the character that has helped define the city—peripheral areas that resemble the familiar suburbs of so many cities. What you do get, though, are large green spaces, a feeling of openness and room to breathe, and, although often shrouded in fog, a magnificent shoreline—a mere twenty-minute drive from downtown San Francisco bringing you to the edge of the Pacific Ocean.

As you'd expect, the **outlying districts** are mainly residential in character, inhabited by families and those who either can't afford—or don't care—to live in the city proper. Whichever way you look at it, they're unlikely to be at the top of your agenda on a short visit; and public transit connections can be a hassle. But with more time, there may be spots that could draw you out, not least some of the city's best **beaches**. The most popular of these, **Baker's Beach**, and the less-visited **China Beach**, are easily accessible from downtown, curving around the peninsula from the Golden Gate Bridge to meet **Land's End**—a usually uncrowded set of hiking trails and cliffs above the shoreline that makes for a perfect break from the city. A little way inland, the **Palace of the Legion of Honor**, San Francisco's finest arts museum, stands in majestic isolation on a bluff near the ocean. The least patronized of all the city's museums, you could easily spend an unhurried half-day here, enjoying its high-calibre collection.

Around Point Lobos, the peninsula's westernmost tip, you'll reach the parked tour buses and camera-toting tourists that signal arrival at the **Cliff House**, **Sutro Baths**, and **Seals Rocks**—a trio of seaside attractions that forms the busiest point along the coast. Stretching for miles from here is the vast expanse of **Ocean Beach**: better suited to dog-walking than sun-worship, it's not a crowd-puller and is used mostly by the residents of the often fog-bound **Richmond** and **Sunset** neighborhoods which hug the ocean's edge nearby. Continuing south you reach the city's prettily land-scaped **zoo** and the leafy ravine of **Stern Grove**, both good options for rest-less children, either to see the animals or just to kick a ball about. Similarly, **Lake Merced**, a little farther south, is a fine place to stop for lunch, take a boat out, or sit around waiting for the fog to lift. Better still, head west to reach the beautiful cragginess of **Fort Funston**, San Francisco's southern-most and probably most attractive stretch of beach. The place you're least likely to visit is San Francisco's notorious **Hunter's Point**, over on the south-

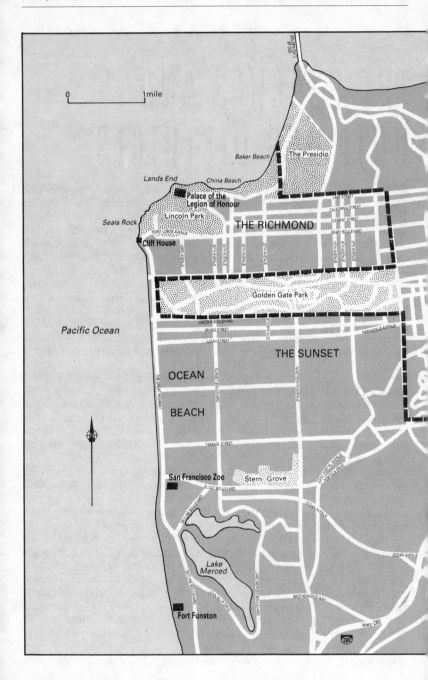

0   1mile

Baker Beach

The Presidio

Lands End   China Beach

Palace of the
Legion of Honour

LAKE STREET

Lincoln Park

CALIFORNIA STREET

Seals Rock

CLEMENT STREET

THE RICHMOND

GEARY BOULEVARD

POINT LOBOS AVENUE

Cliff House

Golden Gate Park

Pacific Ocean

LINCOLN BOULEVARD

IRVING STREET

PARNASSUS AVENUE

JUDAH STREET

THE SUNSET

OCEAN

BEACH

THE GREAT HIGHWAY

TARAVAL STREET

San Francisco Zoo

Stern Grove

SLOAT BOULEVARD

SLOAT BOULEVARD

OCEAN AVENUE

OCEAN AVENUE

Lake
Merced

LAKE MERCED BOULEVARD

BROTHERHOOD WAY

SKYLINE BOULEVARD

Fort Funston

Hwy 280

280

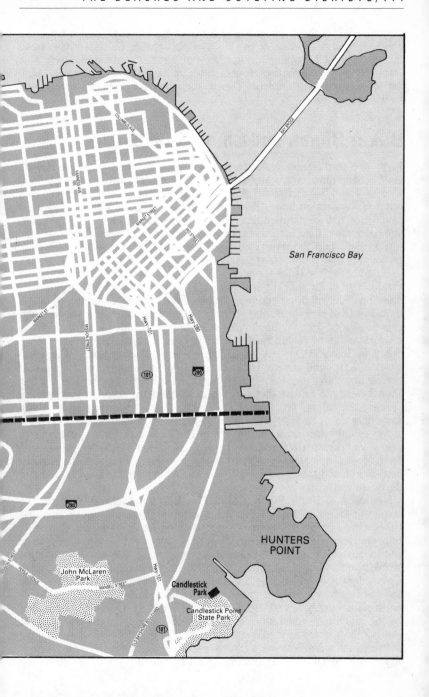

eastern edge of the peninsula near a massive Navy shipyard—a run-down neighborhood with some of the city's worst urban problems—though you may find yourself traveling through on your way to **Candlestick Park**. This is the city's main outdoor sports center, where the *San Francisco 49ers*—local heroes—and the *San Francisco Giants*, keep the civic pride intact with regular winning streaks.

Baker Beach and China Beach

Partly due to the weather, partly due to the people, **beach** culture doesn't exist in San Francisco the way it does in Southern California, and people here tend to watch the surf rather than ride it. Powerful currents and very cold water make it almost impossible to swim comfortably and with any degree of confidence outside high summer (though people *do* swim all year round), and more often than not nude sunbathing is as adventurous as it gets. As a result, you'll find San Francisco's beaches blissfully uncrowded, free from parading bimbos and the surf mobs they follow.

Baker Beach extends for almost a mile along the jagged cliffs below the Presidio, great for walking or fishing but not recommended for swimming. *Muni* bus #29 will bring you here, but if you're driving or cycling, approach from the Golden Gate Bridge: it's a breathtaking route along winding and cypress-shaded Lincoln Boulevard, with the green hills of the Presidio to your left and the crashing Pacific Ocean to your right. Far from being a pleasure zone, Baker Beach was originally used as the hiding place for an enormous 95,000-pound cannon that the army placed in an underground concrete bunker just above the shore in 1905 to protect the bay from intruders. When aircraft began to replace the army's land defenses, the cannon was decreed obsolete and after World War II was melted for scrap, having never seen a day's fighting in its forty-year career. A replacement cannon (for exhibition purposes only) was set up on the site in 1977, and at weekends the rangers give a brief demonstration of how the huge thing would have been aimed and fired. Most people who come here seem quite happy to ignore the massive lump of iron and steel, preferring to laze about taking in the fantastic views of the ocean and bridge.

Southwest of Baker Beach, **China Beach** is a tiny cove nestling at the bottom of the exclusive Sea Cliff neighborhood. It takes its name from the 1870s, when Chinese fishermen camped along its crescent and fished its comparatively calm waters. Later, when the government slapped immigration restrictions on the Chinese, China Beach was supposedly used to smuggle people into San Francisco. During the 1920s there was much wrangling over developing the beach and the land above, but busy campaigning won the day and the beach remained in public hands. These days it is San Francisco's safest swimming beach but despite this is seldom used, most people opting for the much larger and more easily accessible Baker Beach. During good weather, however, you should make the effort to get there—dressing rooms, showers, and a sundeck are all freely available, making it the best option if you want to spend a whole day sunning and swimming.

Lands End and the Palace of the Legion of Honor

Balanced precariously at the city's edge, **Lands End** is as wild and remote as its name implies. Situated on the tip of land that divides Baker and China from Ocean Beach to the south, this lonely bluff has hiking trails and a sublime lookout across the ocean. Beneath the jagged cliffs are the shells of ships which foundered in the treacherous waters—when the tide is out you can see the wrecks. This is one of the few wilderness areas left in the city: ice-plant grows across the sandy cliffs and dazzling wild flowers appear in random clumps; catch it on a good sunset and the experience is quite humbling. A mile-long circular trail that snakes through the cypress groves and along the grassy cliffs is a popular cruising spot for gays, who favor the privacy it offers—but apart from a few lurkers, expect to be alone.

At the south end of the Lands End trail, the **Palace of the Legion of Honor** (Wed–Sun 10am–5pm; $4, free first Wed of month) is a white-pillared twin of the more famous Légion d'Honneur in Paris. Arguably San Francisco's best museum, it is probably also its most beautifully located—the romantic setting, graceful architecture, and colonnaded courtyard combining to lend a truly elegant impression.

Thanks to a donation from the wealthy San Franciscan Spreckels family, the Legion of Honor was built in 1920 and dedicated on Abraham Lincoln's birthday in 1921. Until a major re-sort a couple of years ago, the collection was mainly French and not particularly strong, but with many new additions it has emerged as the city's best collection of fine art. Divided into 23 galleries across two floors, the collection on display is almost entirely permanent, with only one gallery dedicated to traveling, and usually contemporary, exhibits. The **Renaissance** is represented with the works of Titian, El Greco, and sculpture from Giambologna, hung in high-ceilinged, well-lit, spacious marble halls. Some great canvases by Rembrandt and Hals are highlights of the seventeenth-century Dutch and Flemish collection, as is Rubens' magnificent *Tribute Money*. The **impressionist** and **post-impressionist** galleries contain works by Courbet, Manet, Monet, Renoir, Degas, and Cezanne, although the section dedicated to the sculpture of **Rodin** steals the show—bronze, porcelain, and stone pieces including *The Athlete, Fugit Amor, The Severed Head of John the Baptist, Fallen Angel*, and a small cast of *The Kiss* are scattered around an enormous hall, said to be one of the world's finest collections of Rodin sculptures. Stanford University's art museum (see Chapter Ten) makes a similar claim, but the works here certainly take some beating.

Cliff House, Sutro Baths, and Seal Rocks

About a mile southwest along the coast from the tip of Lands End, the **Cliff House**, judging by the number of tour buses parked outside, is one of the top sightseeing spots in the city. At the edge of the Pacific Ocean where Geary

Boulevard meets the Great Highway, the house itself is not spectacular (or even the original), but its setting on a mammoth rock perched over the Pacific, with the broad sands of Ocean Beach stretching for miles to the south, is a memorable one. The original building on this site in the 1850s was known as Seal Rock House and used by hiking and horse-riding San Franciscans as a rest spot after the long journey from the city center. It closed at the end of the 1850s, but the idea for a seaside resort stuck, and with the completion of the first road from the city to the beach, the first Cliff House was constructed, thriving for two decades as an exclusive resort for the leisured classes—the Stanfords, Crockers, and Hearsts of late nineteenth-century San Francisco—and soon earning a reputation for gambling and prostitution. A Prussian immigrant Adolph Sutro bought the original Cliff House, only to watch it burn to the foundations in 1894, and it was he who built the Cliff House that is best remembered today. A stunning Gothic monolith of glass and spires, it had dozens of dining rooms, an art gallery, and twenty private luncheon rooms, enjoying a much celebrated existence until it, too, was destroyed by fire in 1907. Sadly, today's Cliff House can't compare—though the view from the bar at sunset makes it worth braving the hordes.

Adolph's other opulent creation, the **Sutro Baths**, was more enduring: a hundred thousand feet of stained glass covering over three acres of sculpted swimming pools and tanks of fresh and salt water. It came to be known as California's "Tropical Winter Garden," and for ten cents you could enter through a classical columned entrance that led to gardens of fountains, flowers, and trees, and swim all day amid sculptures, tapestries, and ancient artifacts that Sutro had collected from around the world. It all got to be too expensive to maintain, and the baths crumbled elegantly until they were razed by a fire in 1966. Today, some very ancient-looking ruins remain, and if you can manage the clamber down the steep staircase down the cliff face, it makes for an interesting, if occasionally wet, trek through the old ramparts and tunnels. It's a bit frightening here at night, when the surf really starts crashing, but there's atmosphere, too, and on a rare warm evening it becomes one of the city's favorite romantic spots. By day, you'll get the best and closest view of **Seal Rocks**, the clump of boulders a little way out to sea that has been bleached white by the hundreds of seagulls. The rocks take their name from the seals trying to secure themselves a sunny place on the rock.

The Richmond, Sunset, and Ocean Beach

Quite apart from being awkward destinations to reach on public transit, the **Richmond** and **Sunset** districts, often referred to as "The Avenues," are disappointing. Large areas, populated for the most part by families, the neighborhoods are neat, clean, respectable—and terrifically dull. Divided by Golden Gate Park, they have many similarities: flat—and often fog-bound—orderly avenues surrounded by some great open spaces. Stretching north to the Presidio and south of the Golden Gate Park, they extend westward for miles before ending abruptly at the ocean's edge.

The Richmond

Solidly middle-class, **THE RICHMOND** was first settled by Russian and Eastern European Jews after World War I. Later came the Japanese and now, most predominantly, Chinese families are moving their businesses here away from the overcrowding and noise of Chinatown, lending the area the name "New Chinatown." It's a vast neighborhood, divided into **inner** and **outer** districts, separated by Park Presidio Boulevard (Hwy-1). The outer portion is only for passing through on your way out to Sutro Baths and the Cliff House, and, assuming that you're going to bother with it at all, you should confine your wanderings to the inner Richmond around **Clement Street** between Arguello Street and Eighth Avenue. This is the neighborhood's commercial strip, with some good Asian restaurants, a couple of cafés, a movie theater, some rowdy Irish pubs, and San Francisco's oldest comedy club, *Holy City Zoo*, at 407 Clement Street (see "Nightlife," Chapter Eight).

The Sunset and Ocean Beach

There are few places in San Francisco that could be termed unpleasant, but neighborhoods like **THE SUNSET** can certainly be described as monotonous—clean, quiet streets, spread out across a large area, and leading eventually to **Ocean Beach**, the largest and least arresting stretch of San Francisco's shoreline. Some surfing and fishing go on, but mostly the beach is the domain of dog-walkers and strollers out for some fresh air. A strong undertow and unexpected riptides render swimming out of the question, and the often gray color of the sand makes sunbathing unappealing. Like Golden Gate Park and the Richmond district, the Sunset was once just windswept sand dunes until a massive FHA program after World War II paved over the area and put up houses that then cost $5000 each. The same modest structures, occupied largely by the original owners (the Sunset has the highest population of residents over sixty), are reckoned to be worth around half a million at today's prices. There's a build-up of stores and a few restaurants around the area of Judah and Ninth Avenue, but nothing worth making an effort for; indeed, if you never saw the neighborhood you wouldn't be missing a thing.

ACCOMMODATION *Ocean Park Motel, Oceanview Motel, Sunset Motel.*

BARS *Blue Danube Cafe, Last Day Saloon, The Plough and Stars.*

CAFÉS *The Blue Danube.*

RESTAURANTS Italian *Cafe Riggio;* **Chinese and Thai** *Chiang Mai, Java, Pinyo, Straits Cafe;* **Japanese** *Silver Moon;* **Indian** *The Grapeleaf.*

The Zoo, Lake Merced, and Fort Funston

There may be precious little to do in the Sunset, but if you journey a short way **south** your options widen considerably. Some of the city's prettiest green spaces are locked into a square bordered by Hwy-1 to the east, the San Francisco county line to the south, and the best part of Ocean Beach to the west. Take a picnic and spend a day exploring San Francisco's least-visited attractions.

Where Sloat Boulevard meets the Pacific coast, just off the end of the *Muni* L Taraval trolley line, **San Francisco Zoo** (daily 10am–5pm; $5, under-12s free) is a small, but expertly designed institution, organized around the principle that the animals should be housed in an environment most closely resembling their natural habitat. Rather than the usual spectacle of animals listlessly slumped in their small cages, the 1000 or so exotic beasts at San Francisco Zoo swing happily from trees, roam across fields, and lounge on islands. One of the most innovative enclosures is the **Primate Discovery Center**, a complex of fenced-in atriums in which you can get intimate with sixteen playful varieties of primate. It also has an interactive computer facility where you can design a primate to your own specification. There are also the more standard exhibits of lions and tigers, a special **Children's Zoo** ($1) where the under-12s can go and feed a barnyard full of domestic animals, and a **Zebra Zephyr Train** that will take them on an informative tour of the entire zoo.

A little way east, where Sloat Boulevard crosses Nineteenth Avenue (Hwy-1), **Stern Grove** is a leafy ravine of eucalyptus, redwood, and fir trees that shelters a natural amphitheater. For most of the year it's used by picnickers and schoolchildren on nature hikes, but during the summer between June and August, **free concerts** are held each Sunday at 2pm. An excellent variety of programs from classical to jazz are presented—take a picnic and get there early to be sure of a good spot.

For something more active, head south along Skyline Boulevard to **Lake Merced**. A standby reservoir for the city, this large freshwater lake is a peaceful, uncrowded spot to rent a rowing boat or have a picnic. There's a **boathouse** with bar and restaurant where you can sit out on the deck overlooking the lake and have a cheap lunch while waiting for the fog to lift. Seldom used, it's a great spot for the crowd-weary and those who need a large open space to let their children toss a ball about.

Even if you skip all of the above, it's well worth making the effort to visit **Fort Funston**, above San Francisco's most windswept and beautiful stretch of beach, where the sand is fine and white and wild flowers grow along the cliff-tops. The southernmost point of the city's coastline, it is here that San Francisco's hang-gliders leap off the cliffs to float above the ocean's edge. On a sunny day, clamber down the cliff face, lie on the sand, and gaze up at the gliders soaring above.

Hunter's Point and Candlestick Park

San Franciscans speak of **HUNTER'S POINT** with some trepidation. The neighborhood has the city's largest concentration of public housing stock and is rife with the social problems that are endemic to many such projects. Situated south of the SoMa docks on its own mini-peninsula, in the far southeast corner of San Francisco, it was chosen as the site of a major Navy shipyard during World War II. The temporary housing that went up to shelter the

35,000 employees who came to work during the war is still in use, seemingly housing the same people who were made redundant at the war's end, when the shipyards were closed down. It's perhaps the city's most isolated and forgotten corner, and the entire area has a distinct air of neglect about it, with unemployment, crime, and drug abuse major problems in the community. Few people ever venture into the neighborhood from the outside, and to be honest, as a visitor, there's little reason to come.

About the only occasion you're likely to pass through this part of town is if you're trying to beat the often blocked-up traffic on the Bayshore Freeway (US-101)—the main route to and from the airport—or if you're taking Third Street to a *Giants* or *49ers* game at **Candlestick Park**, just south of Hunter's Point. *Muni* puts on special buses on game days, and most take this route. It was here at Candlestick during the 1989 World Series that the big earthquake hit. The panic of the startled crowds in the shaking stadium was broadcast nationwide as they fled the site—hardly what they'd expected but certainly something they'll never forget. If you want to see a game, phone ☎468-2249 for *49ers* tickets, ☎467-8000 for the *Giants*; and see "Sport" in *Basics* for more details.

If stadium mania doesn't appeal, opt instead for a walk around **Candlestick Point State Park**, a fine example of the 1970s asphalting craze, when hitherto unkempt pieces of land were paved into fitness courses, with trails that lead you from push-up bench to chin-up bar, with markers for you to gauge your progress. Skip that and walk toward the pier at the easternmost point of the park where old men and young boys fish indolently and share the views over the quiet stretch of the bay. To describe the park as beautiful, or even attractive, would be pushing it, but it's a pleasant enough place to picnic or just lie about and enjoy the peace.

CHAPTER SIX

SHOPS AND GALLERIES

San Francisco doesn't have the big prestige department stores of New York or Chicago, or even Los Angeles, but scores instead on smaller-scale emporia, great for picking up odd and unusual things you might not find at home. Though all the international names are displayed in downtown store windows, the great majority of places are low key and unpretentious. Not only does this mean slightly lower prices, but it also makes shopping a more pleasant, stress-free activity all round.

If you want to run the gauntlet of designer labels, or just watch the style brigades in all their consumer fury, **Union Square** is the place to aim for. Heart of the city's shopping territory, it has a good selection of big-name and chic stores—expense account stuff admittedly, but good for browsing, especially in the district's many art galleries.

For things that you can actually afford to buy, you'll have a less disheartening and more interesting time in neighborhoods like **Haight-Ashbury** and the **Mission**, where the second-hand, quirky, and plain bizarre are in abundance, fascinating to pick through if you're at a loose end or on the lookout for some good Californian kitsch and unique souvenirs; the Mission, especially, has some marvelous second-hand clothing stores. The city in general is home to a small but excellent array of **bookstores**, and its one-off, independent **record stores** are unbeatable for rare birds to add to your collection.

Most places are open Monday to Saturday, from 9am until 6pm, with quite a number of places open on Sunday, too, particularly for basic things like food and drink; many **supermarkets** are open 24 hours a day, so you'll never have to do without. **Credit cards** are accepted in most shops for purchases above a minimum of $15, though the only supermarket chain that accepts them is Safeway, which takes *Visa*; **travelers' checks** are as good as cash, provided they're in US dollar denominations and you have some form of identification.

Department Stores and Shopping Malls

If you want to pick up a variety of things in a hurry, without having to roam all over town, it's hard to beat the convenience of **department stores** or **shopping malls**. Though even San Francisco's most opulent stores aren't in the same league as *Bergdorf's* or *Bloomingdales*, and the few urban shopping malls still feel like they'd be happier in the suburbs, they are useful and can even be quite lively.

Department Stores

Emporium-Capwell, 835 Market St., near Powell St. *Muni* (☎764-2222). San Francisco's largest department store with a very average range of merchandise—everything the suburban home could possibly need.

I. Magnin, Geary and Stockton St. (☎362-2100). A stylish, if rather conservative store selling well-made clothes at not terribly outrageous prices. Top designer names.

Macy's, Stockton and O'Farrell St. (☎397-3333). Probably the city's best-stocked store, and as such a good place for general shopping, though it's not a patch on its New York counterpart. Nonetheless, brimming with the trinkets of the consumer society, and a dangerous place to go with a wallet full of money. Beautifully presented merchandise, which is hawked noisily from all sides.

Nieman Marcus, 150 Stockton St. (☎362-3900). The sheer chutzpa of the pricing department has earned this store the nickname "Needless Mark-up." Undoubtedly Union Square's most beautiful department store, however, with its classic rotunda, and good for enjoyable browsing.

Nordstrom's, 865 Market St. (☎243-8500). Since it opened in late 1988, shoppers have flocked here for the high-quality fashions, as well as a chance to ride on the spiral escalators that climb the four-story atrium.

Sak's Fifth Avenue, 384 Post St. (☎986-4300). Pathetic compared to its New York sister store. A dodgy selection geared toward the middle-aged shopaholic.

Woolworth's, 898 Market St. (☎286-2164). This is the original five & dime—great for essentials (batteries, film, and the like) as well as for kitsch souvenirs.

Shopping Malls

Crocker Galeria, Kearny and Post St. (☎392-5522). The most recent in the new wave of shopping malls, this has been built to as modern and attractive a design as possible, and features some very pricey showcase boutiques. It's all very nice for a wander, but don't plan on spending money unless your reserves are bottomless.

Embarcadero Center, The Embarcadero, Market St. (☎772-0500). Ugly, four-plaza shopping complex with almost 200 shops, distinguished from other anesthetic shopping malls only by the occasional work of art and a reasonably carefully planned layout. The place where San Franciscans indulge in a spot of consumer therapy.

Japan Center, three blocks bounded by Post, Sutter, Laguna, and Fillmore streets, Japantown (☎922-6776). A five-acre complex of shops, movie theaters, and restaurants run by and for the Japanese community. Interesting, costly shopping.

Drugs, Beauty Products, and Toiletry Stores

There are standard **drugstores** in every San Francisco neighborhood. A few are open 24 hours a day, selling essentials like film and batteries for your Walkman, and all have a pharmacy that can dispense medications and fill prescriptions. **Walgreen** is the largest chain pharmacy with numerous branches throughout the city, selling prescription drugs and general medical supplies, as well as cosmetics and toiletries. Most are open long hours (Mon–Sat 8am–10pm, Sun 9am–8pm). For **more indulgent things**, such as body oils and bubble bath, there are a number of suitable outlets, though these, not surprisingly, tend to congregate in the more exclusive shopping districts.

24-HOUR PHARMACIES

The following branches of **Walgreen** are **open 24 hours**: 498 Castro St. (☎826-8998) and 3201 Divisadero St. (☎931-6415).

Drugstores

Embarcadero Center Pharmacy, 1 Embarcadero Center (☎788-4511). Prescription drugs and general medical and toiletry supplies.

Fairmont Pharmacy, 801 Powell St. (☎362-3000). Huge pharmacy, perfumery and toiletry supply store that also has a good selection of maps and books on San Francisco.

Mandarin Pharmacy, 895 Washington St. (☎989-9292). This amiable, well-stocked drugstore is a sanctuary in the bustle of Chinatown.

Thrifty JR, 2030 Market St.; 4045 24th St. (☎626-7387). General prescription and non-prescription drug and medical needs.

Walgreen Drugs, 135 Powell St. (☎391-4433). Central and open long hours. Also at 498 Castro St. and 3201 Divisadero St.

Toiletries and Beauty Supplies

Beauty Supplies Store, 3600 16th St. (☎861-2019). Make-up, hair dye, and massage oils. Another branch at 1560 Haight St.

The Body Shop, 2072 Union St. (☎922-4076). Since it opened across the bay in Berkeley in the late 1960s, this now national chain has been putting out a full range of aromatic natural bath oils, shampoos, and skin creams.

Common Scents, 3920 24th St. (☎826-1019). Natural oils, cures, remedies, and bath salts.

Crabtree and Evelyn, 50 Post St., in the Crocker Galleria (☎392-6111). Anglophile toiletries shop which is full of perfumed body care products and potpourri.

Clothes and Accessories

Perhaps more than anywhere else in the US, San Francisco's power-dressing **designer clothes** shops are quite distinct from the bulk of the city's clothing outfitters. Though Ralph Lauren-style chic definitely rules the Financial District, style elsewhere in the city is a much more open concept. If you want to play it safe there are dozens of shops—*Esprit* and *The Gap* are two of the bigger names—selling very Californian **casual wear**, mainly jeans and polo shirts in pastel colors, but if you're feeling adventurous check out the dozens of **second-hand clothes** stores specializing in period costume, from Twenties gear to leftover hippy garb. Better still, explore the myriad charitable **thrift stores**, where you can pick up high-quality discards for next to nothing.

Designer Clothes

Betsey Johnson, 2031 Fillmore St. (☎567-2726). One of the few American designers who doesn't see women in business suits. Her clothes are stylish and have flair without being silly—and, by designer standards, they are also affordable.

Brooks Brothers, 201 Post St. (☎397-4500). The original preppy clothes store, with traditional men's clothing, well-tailored and conservative; it's where the Financial District clones go to get their clobber. Now owned by the English Marks and Spencer.

Bullock and Jones, 340 Post St. (☎392-4243). Much the same as *Brooks Brothers*, but if you have to buy suits and look the part, this is the better choice and even has its own barber shop.

California, 2343 Market St. (☎864-1534). Castro women's clothing store—designer patterns, beautifully copied, well made, and not overpriced.

Comme Des Garçons, 70 Geary St. (☎3620-6400). Beautiful clothes that only the lucky few can afford to get decked out in. The store is a total design environment—minimal decor and clothing sparsely scattered around the large space. Good fantasy browsing.

MAC (Modern Appealing Clothing), 812 Post St. (☎775-2515). Showcase for up-and-coming contemporary designers like Workers for Freedom. Where the young and beautiful go to get dressed and pay heartily for the pleasure.

Ralph Davies, 77 Maiden Lane (☎397-3200). Bare, elegant boutique stocking Issey Miyake, Jean Paul Gaultier, Katherine Hamnett, and Romeo Gigli. Fabulous and expensive.

Rolo, 535 Castro St. (☎431-4545). Tiny shop, crammed with unusual and attractive one-offs by lesser-known designers. Moderately priced and well-made clothing.

Wilkes Bashford, 375 Sutter St. (☎986-4380). Five floors of fabulous designer finery for men. A fashion victim's fantasy.

Designer Accessories: Bags, Shoes, Hats, Jewelry

China Gem Co, 500 Grant Ave. (☎397-5070). Good place for jade, opals, and gold.

The Coach Store, 3 Embarcadero Center (☎392-1772). Well-made, simple and expensive handbags and luggage. Definitely worth the investment if you've got the money, *Coach* bags are timeless in their style and come with a lifetime guarantee.

Gucci, 253 Post St. (☎392-2808). Classic Italian shoes, bags, and apparel that you need a trust fund to indulge in. Snoop around the store and be fascinated by the rich ladies that come in and say "I'll have one of those, two of those, one of those," etc.

Hats on Post, 201 Post St. (☎392-3737). Interesting, odd designs, very contemporary, but only worth shelling out for if you're *really* into hats.

Hermes, 1 Union Square (☎391-7200). Classy French luggage and accessories for the super-rich. Again, good only for spying on those who can afford it.

Kenneth Cole, 2078 Union St. (☎346-2121). State-of-the-art boutique selling the well-designed shoes of this New York designer. His men's shoes are imaginative and funky, but the women's stuff is pretty mediocre.

Kenneth Lane, 110 Geary St. (no phone). Beautiful copies of Van Cleef and Bulgari classics, but at the price you'd be better off spending a bit more on the originals.

Pearl of the Orient, Ghirardelli Square, Fisherman's Wharf (☎441-2288). Reputedly the largest stock of pearls in the Bay Area, and very nice, too.

Shapur, 245 Post St. (☎392-1200). Unusual fittings for uniquely cut diamonds and various other gems; each piece is created individually.

Shreve & Co, 200 Post St. (☎421-2600). The oldest jewelers in town and quite possibly the best. Known for their fine silverware and flawless diamonds.

Tiffany, 252 Grant Ave. (☎781-7000). The staff are extraordinarily courteous and will let you try the stuff on even if it's obvious that you can't afford it.

Casual Wear

Banana Republic, 224 Grant Ave. (☎777-0250). Stylish clothes for the traveling yuppie, in this main branch of the San Francisco-based nationwide chain.

Esprit, 16th St. at Illinois (☎648-6900). Warehouse-sized store in SoMa that is the flagship of the wildly successful international chain selling sporty "California-style" casual wear in ghastly colors. For basics, t-shirts, etc, it's pretty good.

The Gap, 934 Market St. (☎397-2266). Hugely successful chain store selling Levi's and own-brand jeans, t-shirts, and casual wear. A second branch at 1975 Market St., by the Powell St. *Muni* station.

Groger's Western Wear, 1445 Valencia St. (☎674-0700). Mission store selling cowboy boots, Stetson hats, boot tips, and traditional brand-name Western clothes. Fun shopping.

North Beach Leather, 190 Geary St. (☎362-8300). Leather everything, and in some pretty sickly colors, but for basic black jackets and simple pieces, there are some pretty well-made styles. Actually in the Union Square district, depsite the name.

Patagonia, 770 North Point, Fisherman's Wharf (☎771-2050). Functional, outdoor clothing that has a cult, semi-yuppie following.

Second-hand Clothes

Aardvarks Odd Ark, 1501 Haight St. (☎621-3141). Large second-hand clothing store in Haight-Ashbury: some junk, but also some priceless pieces and an infinite supply of perfectly faded Levis.

American Rag Co, 1305 Van Ness Ave. (☎474-5214). A store newly opened after a fire, with a bigger, better selection of vintage clothing than before. As second-hand clothing stores go, this one is expensive, but it's probably also superior to most others in San Francisco.

Bargain Mart, 1823 Divisadero St. (☎921-7380). Downscale second-hand clothes that look like they're about to fall apart, but ideal if you need to get decked-out on the cheap.

Buffalo Exchange, 1800 Polk St. (☎346-5726). Cheap and occasionally tawdry Polk Gulch store, but if you've got the patience to search through the piles of clothing, you may turn up some gems.

Mascara Club, 1408 Haight St. (☎863-2837). Vintage clothing in the heart of Haight-Ashbury, heavy on the psychedelic and more recently Wild Western garments.

Past Tense, 665 Valencia St. (☎621-2987). Mission district store selling 1930s to 1960s collectable vintage clothing. One of the smarter second-hand stores.

Spellbound Vintage Clothing, 1670 Haight St. (☎863-4930). Not cheap, but truly classy rags from yesteryear.

Third Hand Store, 1839 Divisadero St. (☎567-7332). As other second-hand stores cash in on the craze for vintage clothing, this Western Addition shop keeps its prices reasonable and stocks some interesting pieces.

The Way You Wore, 1838 Divisadero St. (☎346-1386). Directly opposite the shop above, there isn't much to choose between them, but a trip to the neighborhood will double your chances of finding what you're looking for.

Worn Out West, 1850 Castro St. (☎431-6020). Gay second-hand cowboy gear store—a trip for browsing, but if you're serious about getting some Wild West kit, this is about the cheapest place in town to pick out a good pair of boots, stylish western shirts, and chaps.

Thrift Stores

Community Thrift, 625 Valencia St. (☎861-4910). Gay thrift store in the Mission with clothing, furniture, and general junk. All proceeds are plowed back into gay groups in the community.

Goodwill, 2279 Mission St. (☎928-6200). There are *Goodwill* outlets all over the city; the Mission branch is their biggest and best with everything from pocketbooks to living room furniture.

Purple Heart, 1855 Mission St. (☎621-2581). Top-quality junk and kitsch.

Recollections, 17th and Valencia St. (☎626-3104). Great Fifties furniture and household goods. Not the cheapest in town but perhaps the least nasty.

San Francisco Symphony Thrift Store, 2223 Fillmore St. (☎563-3123). Top-rate vintage clothing store in Pacific Heights, with flamboyant and original pieces going for top dollar.

St Vincent de Paul, 1519 Haight St. (☎863-3615). Ace of the junk shops, St Vinnies, as it's known, will keep you amused for hours. You could spend money all day and still have change from $50. Also at 4452 Mission St. in the Mission.

Thrift Town, 2101 Mission St. (☎861-1132). Quite upmarket for a thrift shop, with some of San Francisco's better quality trash as well as some pretty stylish second-hand clothing bargains.

Food and Drink

Foodies will have a field day in San Francisco's many **gourmet stores**, which are on a par with the city's restaurants for culinary quality and diversity. The simplest neighborhood deli will get your taste buds jumping, and the most sophisticated places will be enough to make you swoon. While you may well be happy to fill up on proven favorites, be sure to try **local specialties** like *Boudin*'s sourdough bread, *Gallo* salami, and *Anchor Steam* beer. Bear in mind, too, that however overwhelming the food on offer in the city may seem, some of the very best places are across the bay in Berkeley. For more basic stocking up there are, of course, **supermarkets** all over the city (*Safeway* is probably the most widespread name), and these are often the best places for picking up essentials, edible and otherwise, sometimes 24 hours a day. Any of the above will sell you an array of beers, wines, and spirits – provided you're over 21, and have a photo ID to prove it – but for the best selection head to a specialist retailer.

Delis and Groceries

Auntie Pasta, 3101 Fillmore St. (☎921-7576). Fresh pasta and sauces for you to heat and eat. Great if you don't want to dine out or cook.

Canton Market, 1135 Stockton St. (☎982-8600). One of the more exotic Chinatown delis, the decor may be a bit stark and the store unbearably crowded but the selection (and prices) makes it worth the effort.

Caravanasary, 262 Sutter St. (☎922-2705). Gourmet cheese and coffee shop. Very expensive.

Casa Lucas, 2934 24th St. (☎826-4334). Mission store with an astonishing array of exotic fruits and vegetables that includes a dozen varieties of banana.

The Cheesery, 427 Castro St. (☎552-6676). Reasonably priced coffees and cheeses from around the world.

David's, 474 Geary Blvd. (☎771-1600). The consummate Jewish deli, open until 1am and a downtown haven for the after-theater crowd and night owls.

Flying Salmon, 2512 Sacramento St. (☎567-4444). Pacific Heights store that stocks smoked fish, seafood, and caviar from around the world.

La Ferme Beaujolaise, 2000 Hyde St. (☎441-6913). French country market-type store, with mouthwatering meats, cheeses, sausages, pastries, and bread, as well as a good selection of imported wines.

Lucca Ravioli, 1100 Valencia St. (☎647-5581). Pasta factory that you can spy on through the big picture windows before you go in to the shop.

Molinari's, 373 Columbus Ave. (☎421-2337). Bristling North Beach Italian deli, jammed to the rafters with goodies.

Rainbow Wholefoods, 1899 Mission (☎863-0620). Progressive politics and organic food in this Mission wholefood store.

San Francisco Health Store, 333 Sutter St. (☎392-8477). Dried fruits, juices, and wholefood.

San Francisco Herb Company, 215 14th St. (☎861-3108). SoMa-based store with large quantities of fresh herbs at wholesale prices.

Sunrise Deli and Cafe, 2115 Irving St. (☎664-8210). Specialty Middle Eastern foodstuffs—stuffed vineleaves, eggplant, and hummus.

Tokyo Fish Market, 1908 Fillmore St. (☎931-4561). Every type of fish. Makes for fun looking even if you don't want to buy.

Williams Sonoma, 576 Sutter St. (☎421-7900). Gourmet foods and cookware.

Bread, Pastries, and Candies

The Acropolis Bakery and Deli, 5217 Geary Blvd. (☎751-9661). Greek/Russian bakery selling unusual filo pastries and baklavas.

Bakers of Paris, 449 Castro St.; 3989 24th St. (☎626-4076). Castro and Noe Valley bakeries selling lots of baguettes and croissants.

Boudin, 156 Jefferson St., Fisherman's Wharf (☎928-1849). They only make one thing—sourdough bread—but it's the best around.

Godiva Chocolates, 50 Post St. in the Crocker Galleria (☎982-6798). Rich Belgian chocolates at around a dollar a nibble. Heaven for the chocaholic.

La Petite Boulangerie, Market St. at Van Ness (☎433-0533). Good selection of breads, but better known for their mouthwatering pastries and muffins.

Liguria Bakery, 1700 Stockton St., North Beach (☎421-3786). Marvelous old-world Italian bakery, with deliciously fresh *focaccia*.

Tea, Coffee, and Spices

Bombay Bazaar, 548 Valencia St. (☎621-1717). Exotic spices and tons of pulses, grains, and other staples.

Freed, Teller & Freed, 1326 Polk St. (☎673-0922). Polk Gulch coffee, tea, and spice emporium. Every conceivable legal addiction and all the paraphernalia that goes with it.

Graffeo Coffee, 733 Columbus Ave. (☎986-2420). Huge sacks of coffee are piled up all around this North Beach store—you can smell the place from half a block away. Great coffees, reasonably priced.

Haig's Delicacies, 642 Clement St. (☎752-6283). Way out in the Richmond, but for Indian and Middle Eastern spices and delicacies, this is the place.

Peet's Coffee, 1156 Chestnut St. (☎931-8302). Russian Hill-based San Francisco flagship of this venerable Berkeley coffee roaster, offering some 25 different blends and roasts, and pint cups for 50¢ a go.

24-HOUR STORES

If you're overcome by hunger in the middle of the night, the following stores are open **24 hours**: the big *Safeway* at 15 Marina Boulevard in the Marina, 1355 Webster Street in the Western Addition, and 2300 16th Street in the Mission. In the Castro, there's *Cala Foods* at 4201 18th St., another at the end of Haight Street opposite Golden Gate Park.

Wines and Liquors

California Wine Merchant, 3237 Pierce St. (☎567-0646). Before you make for the Wine Country, pick up a sample selection at this Marina wine emporium so you know what to look out for.

Cannery Wine Cellars, The Cannery, Fisherman's Wharf (☎673-0400). Astounding selection of wines and imported beers, as well as Armagnac and scotch, lines the walls

Coit Liquors, 585 Columbus Ave. (☎986-4036). North Beach specialty wine store, with the accent on rare Italian vintages. Good stock of regular drinks.

Connoisseur Wine Imports, 462 Bryant St. (☎433-0825). SoMa store that is the city's best place for French, Spanish, Italian, Portuguese, or German wines if you tire of the Californian variety.

D & M Liquors, Fillmore and Sacramento St. (☎346-1325). Great selection of Californian wines, but their specialty is champagne.

Marasco's, 3821 24th St. (☎824-2300). The dipsomaniac's dream—hundreds of wines and exotic liquors taking shopping to alcoholic heaven.

Books

The range of reading material around in San Francisco is surprisingly small for a city with such a literary reputation, and although there are some truly excellent **bookstores** the range is nowhere near as varied as, say, that of food and drink options. The established focus for literature has long been in North Beach, around the legendary *City Lights* bookstore, but increasingly the best spots, particularly for contemporary creative writing, are to be found in the lower-rent Mission district, which is home some of the city's more energized—and politicized—bookstores. There are a few **second-hand booksellers** (the best bargains are found in thrift shops; see above), but these can't compare with the diverse bunch across the bay in Oakland and Berkeley (see Chaper Nine for details). Most bookstores tend to open every day, roughly 10am–6pm, though *City Lights* is open daily until midnight.

General Bookstores

The Booksmith, 1644 Haight St. (☎863-8688). Good general Haight-Ashbury bookstore with an excellent stock of political and foreign periodicals.

City Lights Bookstore, 261 Columbus Ave. (☎362-8193). America's first paperback bookshop, and still San Francisco's best, with a range of titles including *City Lights*' own publications (see p.72).

A Clean, Well Lighted Place for Books, Opera Plaza, 601 Van Ness Ave. (☎441-6670). Good selection of the latest titles.

Crown Books, 1245 Sutter St. (☎441-7479); 518 Castro St. (☎552-5213). The San Francisco branches of the nationwide chain, selling new general books at discounted prices.

Doubleday Bookshop, The White House, 265 Sutter St. Main San Francisco branch of the nationwide chain.

Philosopher's Stone Bookshop, 3814 24th St. General bookstore with a decent range of titles, though rather heavy on the New Age stuff.

Tillman Place Bookstore, 8 Tillman Place, off Grant Ave., near Union Square (☎392-4668). Downtown's premier general bookshop and certainly one of the oldest, with a beautifully elegant feel.

Discount and Second-hand Bookstores

Around the World, 1346 Polk St. (☎474-5568). Musty, dusty, and a bit of a mess, this is a great place for hours of poring over first editions, rare books, and records.

Columbus Avenue Books, 540 Broadway (☎986-3872). North Beach store with a good selection of new and used books, and a large guide and travel books section.

Hunter's Books, 151 Powell St. (☎397-5955). Desirable range of publishers' remainders and other bargain books, with a good line in travel guides.

Maelstrom Books, 572 Valencia St. (☎863-9933). One of the Mission's many second-hand bookshops, they trade almost anything. Could be useful for offloading the paperbacks you finished on your travels.

Specialist Bookstores

About Music, 375 Grove St. (☎647-3343). Tiny, hole-in-the-wall place crammed with books on classical and contemporary music.

Bound Together Anarchist Collective Bookstore, 1369 Haight St. (☎431-8355). Haight-Ashbury store specializing in radical and progressive publications.

China Books, 2929 24th St. (☎282-2994). Mission bookstore dealing in books and periodicals from China, although they also stock a good number of publications on the history and politics of the Third World.

Fanning's Bookstore, 2nd Floor, Ghirardelli Square, Fisherman's Wharf. Specialty bookstore offering the works of only Northern Californian writers—Hammett, London, Twain, and Steinbeck among others.

Field's Bookstore, 1419 Polk St. (☎673-2027). Metaphysical and New Age books.

Great Expectations, 1512 Haight St. (☎863-5515). Radical liberal bookstore with hundreds of t-shirts bearing political slogans, some funnier than others.

Greenpeace Shop, Ghirardelli Square, Fisherman's Wharf (☎474-1870). Books, posters, and a small gallery document the activities of the environmental group.

Kinokuniya, 2nd floor, Japan Center, 1581 Webster St. (☎567-7625). Large stock of Japanese- and English-language books, but they really excel in art books.

Modern Times, 968 Valencia St. (☎282-9246). Largely radical feminist publications, but a hefty stock of Latin American literature and progressive political publications.

Opera Shop, 199 Grove St. (☎565-6414). A must for opera buffs, with good selections of recordings and t-shirts, as well as an exhaustive stock of everything ever written about the opera.

Rand McNally, 595 Market St. at 2nd St. (☎777-3131). Brand new store selling travel guides, maps, and paraphernalia for the person on the move.

Revolution Books, 1541 Grant Ave. (no phone). What it says.

Small Press Traffic, 3599 24th St. (☎285-8394). Situated down in the Mission, don't be misled by the unprepossessing storefront: this is San Francisco's prime outlet for independent, contemporary fiction and poetry, with an astounding range of books, chapbooks, and literary magazines (and postcards, too). It's also the best place, along with *City Lights*, to find out about readings and writing workshops.

William Stout Architectural Books, 804 Montgomery St. (☎391-6757). One of San Francisco's world-class booksellers, with an excellent range of books on architecture, building, and urban studies.

Gay and Lesbian Bookstores

Books Etc, 538 Castro St. (☎621-8631). Stocks the gamut of gay publishing, from psychology to soft-core porn.

A Different Light, 489 Castro St. (☎431-0891). Well-stocked, diverse, and usually crammed with people.

Records

San Francisco's **record stores** are of two types: massive, anodyne ware-houses pushing all the latest releases, and impossibly small specialist shops crammed to the rafters with obscure discs. The big places like *Tower Records* are more or less identical to those anywhere back home. More exciting is the large number of **independent** retailers and **second-hand and collectors' stores**, where you can find anything you've ever wanted, especially in West Coast jazz or psychedelic rock.

New Records

American Music Store, 2388 Mission St. (☎647-2098). Mission record store selling music from all over the continent, including South America.

Aquarius Music, 3961 24th St. (☎647-2272). Small neighborhood store with friendly, knowledgeable staff and an admirable reluctance to stock CDs. Emphasis on indie rock, jazz, and blues.

Discolandia, 2964 24th St. (☎826-9446). Join the snake-hipped groovers looking for the latest in salsa and Central American sounds in this Mission outlet.

Discoteca Habana, 24th and Harrison St. (no phone). Caribbean and samba recordings.

Embarcadero Discs and Tapes, 2 Embarcadero Center, the Embarcadero (☎956-2204). Not a piece of vinyl in sight—up-to-the-minute CDs and tapes.

Magic Flute, 756 Columbus Ave. (☎661-2547). Fine classical music store with a smattering of rock, jazz, and vocals.

Rainbow Records, 2222 Fillmore St. (☎922-4474). Branches all over town but this is the biggest and has the best stock of rock and pop new albums, tapes, and CDs.

Reckless Records, 1401 Haight St. (☎431-3434). If you can't complete your Sixties collection here, you never will.

Record Finder, Noe and Market St. (☎431-4443). One of the best independents, with a range as broad as it's absorbing. Take a wad and keep spending.

Record House, 1550 California St. (☎474-0259). Nob Hill archive library of over 25,000 Broadway and Hollywood soundtracks. Great record-finding service.

Record Rack, 3987 18th St. (☎552-4990). Castro 12"-single emporium with a few albums, but the accent is definitely on stuff you can dance to.

Recycled Records, 1377 Haight St. (☎626-4075). Good general new and used store for records, tapes, and CDs, as well as a good selection of music publications.

Rough Trade, 1529 Haight St. (☎621-4395). Because of its London connec-tions, this is the first place in town to get imports. Good reggae department in particular and indie rock in general.

Streetlight Records, 3979 24th St. (☎282-3550). Great selection of used records, tapes, and CDs. Good way to add to your collection on the cheap. Also at 2350 Market St.

Tower Records, Columbus Ave. and Bay St., Fisherman's Wharf (☎885-0500). Main San Francisco location of the multinational records empire.

Wherehouse Records, 2083 Union St. (☎346-0944). Large, general record store, with a wide range of new releases, etc.

Second-hand Records

Bay Area Records and Tapes, 1444 Polk St. (☎441-0777). Inclusive assortment of new and used records and tapes.

Butch Wax Records, 4077 18th St. (☎431-0904). A hangover from 1970s gay disco-mania, this Castro shop is the best place in town for hard to find 12" singles, rare grooves, and Euro-beat.

Jack's Record Cellar, 254 Scott St. (☎431-3047). The city's best source for American roots music—R&B, jazz, country, and rock & roll. They'll track down rare discs and offer the chance to listen before you buy.

The Jazz Quarter, 1267 20th Ave. (☎661-2331). A bit of a trek to get to, out in the Richmond, but if you're a jazz fiend on the lookout for rarities, it's worth the effort.

Kaleidoscope Records, 575 Haight St. (no phone). Funky, new and used record store. Not a comprehensive collection, but a good one.

Let It Be Records, 2434 Judah St. (☎681-2113). Out in the Sunset, and selling Beatles memorabilia and rock rarities.

Rooky Ricardo's, 448 Haight St. (☎864-7526). Formerly an exclusive purveyor of 45s, they've recently introduced a few albums, but the theme remains the same: 1960s and 1970s soul and funk. Brilliant.

Star Records, 551 Hayes St. (☎552-3017). Rap, soul, jazz, gospel, and reggae specialist, out in Western Addition. Any track ever cut by a black artist, you'll find here.

Art Galleries

At first glance the low-profile San Francisco **art scene** seems provincial compared to the glamorous internationalism of New York and Los Angeles. And in many respects it is. But there is a scene of sorts, and it could be argued that artists here have the freedom to be more concerned with the quality of their own work than with the stylistic vagaries of the world art market. It's doubly difficult for visitors to get a sense of what's going on since most younger artists shun **commercial galleries**, especially the mainstream ones around Union Square, preferring to show their work in their favorite cafés and bars. That said, there is a core of relatively innovative galleries around the South of Market area—though even here the prices asked can be pretty steep.

Union Square and Around

The Allrich Gallery, 251 Post St. (☎398-8896). Contemporary painting and sculpture as well as textiles.

American Indian Contemporary Arts, 685 Market St. (☎495-7600). The only non-profit gallery in the country run by Native American artists. Shows native American contemporary art.

Atelier Dore, 771 Bush St. (☎391-2423). Salon-style gallery hung floor-to-ceiling with top-quality paintings. Historical genre paintings from California, including WPA works, and about the only place that carries the work of nineteenth- and twentieth-century black American painters.

Axis Gallery, 699 Sutter St. (no phone). Contemporary fine art from Europe and Japan.

Breckenridge Gallery, 545 Sutter St. (☎397-7090). Space for emerging Californian, and particularly Bay Area, artists.

Caldwell Snyder Gallery, 357 Geary St. (☎296-7896). Modern contemporary graphics regularly featuring Andy Warhol, David Hockney, and Jurgen Gorg. Expensive, coveted stuff.

Circle Gallery, 140 Maiden Lane (☎989-2100). Expensive contemporary American and European art, plus ceramics and glassware in a Frank Lloyd Wright building.

Japonesque, 50 Post St. (☎398-8577). Museum-quality Japanese art, including pottery, sculpture, and watercolors.

Miller Brown Gallery, 77 Geary St. (☎861-2082). Mixed media includes photography, textiles, sculpture, and paintings.

Modernism, 685 Market St. (☎541-0461). Futurism, Expressionism, Pop Art, Minimalism, and American modern art.

Moss Gallery, 55 Grant Ave. (☎433-7224). Latin American art and sculpture.

Pascel de Sarthe Gallery, 315 Sutter St. (no phone). Impressionist and twentieth-century masters.

John Pence Gallery, 750 Post St. (☎441-1138). Realist painting and sculpture.

Richard Thompson Gallery, 80 Maiden Lane (☎956-2114). Twentieth-century American Impressionism with occasional European Impressionistic works.

Vorpal Gallery, 393 Grove St. (☎397-9200). Contemporary international work.

James Willis Gallery, 109 Geary St. (☎989-4485). Tribal artifacts from India, Africa, and Indonesia. Unusual carvings and fabrics.

SoMa and Elsewhere

Art Lick Gallery, 4147 19th St. (no phone). A rare gallery that shows work in all media: sculpture, paintings, photography, graphic art, and furniture.

Artspace, 9th and Folsom St. (no phone). Adventurous, avant-garde gallery that often exhibits video installations.

Joanne Chappel Gallery, 625 2nd St. (☎777-5711). Works by nationally known, and West Coast, artists.

Joseph Chowning Art Gallery, 1717 17th St. (☎626-7496). Massive forum for humorous and bizarre art.

Contemporary Realists Gallery, 506 Hayes St. (☎863-6556). One of the more interesting galleries and the first California gallery dedicated to promoting current realist drawing.

Crown Point Press, 871 Folsom St. (☎974-6273). With a showcase that changes monthly, you never know what to expect from one of SoMa's most eclectic galleries, which has a reputation for taking a chance on new talent.

Erickdon & Elins Fine Art, 398 Kansas St. (☎861-1080). Nineteenth- and twentieth-century fine art.

Folk Art International, Ghirardelli Square, Fisherman's Wharf (☎441-6100). African, Indian, Chinese, and Mexican folk art.

New Langton Arts, 1246 Folsom St. (☎626-5416). Non-commercial gallery space showing cutting-edge works in all media and hosting lectures, readings, and performances.

San Francisco Art Institute, 800 Chestnut St. (☎771-7020). Local avant-garde contemporary art and student work.

SF MOMA Rental Gallery, Building A, Fort Mason (☎441-4777). Large exhibition space for over 500 artists trying to break into the commercial art world.

William Sawyer Gallery, 3045 Clay St. (☎921-1600). New work in a variety of styles.

Six-oh-One, 601 Minnesota St. (no phone). SoMa gallery known for its controversial and alternative works.

Smile, A Gallery With Tongue In Chic, 1750 Union St. (☎771-1909). From the whimsical to the very serious, this gallery is one of very few into it just for the fun of it. They'll exhibit anything.

Bruce Velick Gallery, 371 11th St. (☎626-9055). Drawing, photography, printing, and sculpture.

Vision Gallery, 1155 Mission St. (☎621-2107). Photography by the well-known and the unknown.

Specialty Shops

In among the designer clothes stores and art galleries of the Union Square area are a handful of interesting shops selling **antiques and other treasurable objects**; though prohibitively expensive, many repay a look-in at least. We've also pulled together in this section some of the city's odd stores specializing in things you often need desperately but never know where to find—stationery, birthday cards, nuts and bolts, flowers, camping gear, children's toys, etc . . .

Antiques and Collectables

Antonio's Antiques, 701 Bryant St. (☎781-1737). Three floors of antiques from around the world. Good porcelain and sculpture.

Asakichi Japanese Antiques and Art, Japan Center (☎921-2147). Lovely pieces, but definitely geared toward the tourist dollar.

Biordi, 412 Columbus Ave. (☎392-8096). North Beach store selling lovely hand-painted Italian dinnerware and ornaments. It's unlikely that you'd ever buy this kind of stuff while traveling, but it makes for very enjoyable browsing.

J. Canes, 530 Folsom St. (☎495-3579). Small store with some interesting and reasonably priced collectables and antiques.

Genji Kimonos, 1731 Buchanan St. (☎931-1616). Expensive oddments and beautiful wooden chests.

Gumps, 250 Post St. (☎982-1616). Famous for its jade, oriental rugs, and objects cast in crystal, silver, and china. More fuel for fantasies than genuine consumption.

Heartland, 1801 Fillmore St. (no phone). Pacific Heights shop that stocks handicrafts from around the US, including lovely granny-style patchwork quilts, baskets, and pottery.

Originals of Nature, Ghirardelli Square, Fisherman's Wharf (☎928-1592). Unusual selection of minerals, fossils, and gems.

Primitivo, 2241 Fillmore St. (☎563-0505). Native and folk art from the US, Central America, and Brazil. Great stuff that you may be tempted to buy if you have the cash.

Miscellaneous

Brooks Cameras, 45 Kearny St. (☎392-1900). Huge, high-quality camera store with full repair department.

FAO Schwartz, 180 Post St. (☎391-0100). This mega-toystore is paradise for tinies of all ages.

Figoni Hardware, 1351 Grant Ave. (☎392-4765). Ancient-looking North Beach hardware store that's incredibly well stocked.

Headlines, 1217 Polk St. (☎776-4466); 838 Castro St. (☎626-8061). Kitsch and novelty gift items that make for a fun browse even if you'd never want to spend money on such indulgent rubbish.

Star Magic, 4026 24th St. (☎641-8626). Situated down in Noe Valley, this is the ultimate New Age shop, full of crystals to cleanse your chakras and the like.

Union Street Papery, 2162 Union St. (☎563-0200). Excellent, pricey stationers selling fine writing paper and a range of cards and pens.

CHAPTER SEVEN

DRINKING AND EATING

To experience San Francisco as the locals do, you're going to have to spend a lot of your time **eating** and **drinking** in the city's many cafés, restaurants, and bars. Wining and dining is second nature to most San Franciscans, and, given the reasonable prices and sheer number of bars and restaurants in the city, it should also prove to be the most pleasurable of activities. The city prides itself on its fresh gourmet foods and fine wines, and in some places the taking of nourishment is treated with a reverence—and done with a protocol—normally reserved for affairs of state. That's not to say that simple fare and casual snacks can't be found, just that food and drink receive an uncommon amount of attention.

We've listed **bars** geographically by neighborhood, followed by a rundown of **cafés**, and a section detailing the city's many and varied **gay and lesbian** watering holes. **Restaurants** are listed by cuisine together with a round-up of where to eat around-the-clock. For convenience in locating a place on your explorations of the city, we've also listed all establishments by name at the end of each neighborhood account in Chapters One to Five. See also *Basics*, "Food and Drink," for the **full rundown on eating and drinking** in the Bay Area.

DRINKING: BARS AND CAFÉS

Since its lawless, boomtown days, San Francisco has been a **drinking** town. Even as the rest of California cleans up its act and guzzles mineral water, San Franciscans continue to indulge with impunity, and the city's huge array of bars, varying from seedy late-night dives to rooftop piano lounges boasting glittering views, can be one of its real pleasures. San Francisco is also home to a higher proportion of **cafés** than most cities—informal places, patronized more during the day than at night, and with the emphasis more on good coffee than alcohol. Both bars and cafés normally have some kind of food available, even if it's only sandwiches or pretzels, though cafés will often have hot meals, too. Unsurprisingly, the city has many specifically **gay bars**, most plentifully in the Castro—although few bars are at all threatening for either gay men or lesbians, or women on their own.

Bars

There are some two thousand **bars** in San Francisco, spread all over the city but particularly numerous in North Beach, the Haight, SoMa, and the Mission, with North Beach your best bet for serious bar-hopping, where they're literally lined up next to each other. On the whole San Francisco's bars are rough-hewn, informal affairs, although slicker places can be found around the downtown area and in the Financial District. Most open mid-morning (the legal opening time is 6am) and close around 2am, although after-hours drinking is not uncommon in the smaller neighborhood joints. We've listed the best of the bunch below, but you should refer, too, to the listings in the "Nightlife" section of Chapter Eight, which includes many places that make good spots for a drink before things hot up later in the evening.

Downtown

The Big Four, *Huntington Hotel*, 1075 California St. Classy hotel bar with cocktails and piano music.

The Blue Lamp, 561 Geary St. For daytime slumming within five minutes of Union Square, this is unbeatable.

Dashiell's, *Hotel Union Square*, 114 Powell St. Stylish hotel bar playing up its Hammett connections—he wrote a number of his "Thin Man" stories from one of the upstairs rooms.

Li Po's Bar, 916 Grant Ave. Named after the Chinese poet, *Li Po's* is Chinatown's only bar and something of a literary hang-out among the Chinatown regulars. Enter through the false cavern front and sit at the very dimly lit bar where Wayne Wang filmed *Chan is Missing*.

The London Wine Bar, 415 Sansome St. Dubiously tagged as "America's first wine bar," this place is a suitably pretentious and expensive hang-out for the Financial District clones that flock here after work.

1001 California, 1001 California St. A swish Nob Hill hang-out where you can sit and watch the rich get loaded. Worth it for the premium liquor and polished piano playing.

The Redwood Room, *Clift Hotel*, 495 Geary St. Gorgeous redwood-paneled, Art-Deco-style lounge, dulled only slightly by the wealthy geriatric hotel guests who frequent it. Definitely worth a look.

ROOFTOP BARS

The Carnelian Room, 555 California St., in the Bank of America building. Best of the rooftop cocktail lounges, the *Carnelian Room* is 53 floors up and a truly elegant spot for some refined drinking. Bring lots of cash.

Equinox, *Hyatt Regency*, the Embarcadero. Good for novelty value only, this rooftop cocktail lounge revolves so that you get 360-degree views of the city without ever leaving your seat. Have a drink, revolve, and leave.

The Starlight Roof, top floor of the *Sir Francis Drake Hotel*, 450 Powell St. Totally glitzy, the *Starlight Roof* is nonetheless an experience to be had. Panoramic views of the city and free food at happy hour compensate for the expensive cocktails.

Top of the Mark, *Mark Hopkins Hotel*, California St. at Mason. Its reputation surpasses the actual experience of drinking up here, but if you're determined to do all the rooftop cocktail lounges, this should be on your agenda.

North Beach and the Northern Waterfront

Balboa Cafe, 3199 Fillmore St. A favorite with the young, upmarket singles of the Marina. Very good food, too.

The Blue Light Cafe, 1979 Union St. Relaxed Cow Hollow piano bar for low-key drinking. Not the place for a stag night.

Chestnut Street Grill, 2231 Chestnut St. A neighborhood bar and grill that is a fine place for some well-made cocktails before dinner.

Curtain Call, 1980 Union St. Quiet, relaxed piano bar. Not the sort of place for rowdy partying.

Enrico's Sidewalk Cafe, 504 Broadway. Busy little place for listening to jazz and having your milkshake spiked with the liquor of your choice.

Harry's, 2020 Fillmore St. A bona fide saloon, this elegantly decorated hang-out serves a mixed, unpretentious crowd and makes for a great night's drinking.

Margaritaville, 1787 Union St. Lively cocktail bar for the professional swinging singles of the Marina.

Mulhern's, 3653 Buchanan St. Right across from the Marina *Safeway*, this is where you bring your date once you've picked them up in the supermarket. Horny yuppies abound.

Perry's, 1944 Union St. Sophisticated meat market, featured in Armistead Maupin's *Tales of the City* as the quintessential breeder bar.

The Saloon, 1232 Grant Ave. This bar has stood for over a hundred years and seen use as a whorehouse and prohibition speakeasy. Today the old structure creaks nightly as blues bands and crowds of enthusiastic dancers do their thing.

San Francisco Brewing Co, 155 Columbus Ave. A must for beer fans who tire quickly of the insipid home-grown variety, this North Beach hang-out makes its own full-flavored brews on the premises.

Savoy Tivoli, 1434 Grant Ave. Definitely North Beach's most attractively decorated and populated bar, and also serving good, reasonably priced food—although the emphasis is definitely on liquid enjoyment.

Spec's, 12 Adler St. Long-standing North Beach bar with a good, jocular drinking crowd enjoying the cocktail shakers full of martini for just $3. Particularly handy for women drinking alone: the barman will hand a card which reads "Sir, the lady is not interested in your company" to anyone that hassles you. A most civilized place to get plowed.

Tosca's, 242 Columbus Ave. The theme is opera here, in more stylish surroundings; mingle with media people and pay through the nose for a drink. Worth the investment if you like to dress up and be seen.

Vesuvio's, 255 Columbus Ave. Legendary North Beach Beat haunt in the 1950s, and still catering to an arty but friendly crowd who prop up the bar into the small hours. Situated next to *City Lights Bookstore*, it's a good place for browsing through your new purchases with a drink.

Washington Square Bar & Grill, 1707 Powell St. Primarily a restaurant, but worth checking out for the great bar and the chance to spy on the media and literary crowd who have made it their second home. A regulars' bar.

Civic Center, SoMa, and the Mission

The Edinburgh Castle, 950 Geary St. Most of San Francisco's so-called pubs are embarrassingly cutesy, but this one pulls it off quite well and features bagpipes on Fri and Sat. Good fish and chips, too.

Bouncers Bar, 64 Townsend St. Old waterfront hang-out, with free live music and a very earthy crowd.

Brainwash, 1122 Folsom St. Great idea—café/bar and laundromat where you can have breakfast and a beer while you do your washing. Needless to say, it's popular with the young and novelty-conscious.

Bulls' Texas Cafe, 25 Van Ness Ave. Tacky Tex-Mex bar-cum-restaurant, but a great place to wolf down the free food at happy hour and imbibe some very cheap pitchers of margarita.

Cadillac Bar and Grill, 1 Holland Court. Noisy Mexican-style bar with good food available, although most people come just to drink the margaritas.

The Chatterbox, 853 Valencia St. Mainly a night spot but good for drinking with the goth and leather brigades anytime.

The Dovre Club, 3541 18th St. Solid Irish bar, full of gaelic charmers.

El Rio, 3158 Mission St. When it isn't staging one of its specials (samba on Sun, comedy on Wed, and dancing on Fri), this is a great place for a quiet drink and a game on the best-looking pool table in town.

Henry's, 2 Showplace Square. A real mixed bag—soul, jazz, and rock music, and enthusiastic crowds of drinkers who are not averse to the odd dance on the table.

Julie's Supper Club, 1123 Folsom St. A popular restaurant, but best for sitting at the bar munching good-value Cajun snacks and listening to the free live jazz.

Max's Opera Cafe, Opera Plaza, Van Ness Ave. Highly stylized and clinically clean, it's not the ideal surroundings for downing a few, but makes for very interesting people-watching when the tuxedo-clad opera, ballet, and symphony fans pop in for a quick one before and after performances at the Civic Center venues.

Milestones, 376 5th St. Low-key SoMa jazz bar with good music and the occasional live band. Perfect for leisurely drinking and chatting.

Mission Rock Resort, 817 China Basin. Seedy, blue-collar bar down on the old dockyards, great for a cheap beer and views of the bay.

Molloy's, 1599 Howard St. Favoured by construction workers over fifty and the habitual drunk. Toughest of all the bars down this way.

Paradise Lounge, 1501 Folsom St. Mainly a venue for bands, but the upstairs bar has lots of room and pool tables—good for early evening beers and a game.

The Ramp, 855 China Basin. Way out on the old docks, this is well worth the half-mile trek (you'll probably want a car unless you're a seasoned walker) to sit out on the patio and sip beers overlooking the abandoned piers and the new boatyards. Free jazz on Sun afternoons.

Rockin Robin's, 133 Beale St. Fifties rock and roll music and lots of boys in leather. Good fun if you can stand to hear that much Elvis in one evening. Mon–Fri only.

The Travel Lounge, 4 Valencia St. As dives go, this one is pretty lively and beginning to achieve a certain downbeat glamor status with local pool-playing pseuds.

The Uptown, 200 Capp St. Best of the Mission's neighborhood bars, embracing an eclectic crowd who shoot pool, drink like fiends, and fall around on the crummy leatherette upholstery. Some simply go to watch the ball game on TV. A more bizarre collection of characters would be hard to find. Don't miss it.

Zeitgeist, 199 Valencia St. A favorite in the Mission with bikers and those who like to dress in black. Comfortably seedy.

The Central Neighborhoods

Achilles Heel, 1601 Haight St. Attractive, Victorian-style English pub in the Haight-Ashbury.

Casa Loma Hotel, 600 Fillmore St. Very neighborly Lower-Haight hang-out for a well-behaved young crowd. A must for the Lower-Haight bar-hopping schedule.

The Deluxe, 1511 Haight St. Formerly a hang-out for older gays, the *Deluxe* is now gaining a well-earned reputation as one of the better pool halls in town.

The First Inning Lounge, 4026 24th St. Home of the sports fan and rabble rouser. Great jukebox.

The Gold Cane, 1569 Haight St. Beer for $1 and shots for $1.50 in what is admittedly a career-drunk senior citizen hang-out.

Ground Zero, 783 Haight St. Regular exhibits by local artists adorn the surreal walls of this Lower-Haight café—worth the trip to check out the decor if not the menu.

Jack's Bailey Bar, 26th and Church St. Comfy neighborhood bar with proper armchairs so that you can really recline into a brew.

Jimmy's West Point, 669 Haight St. The joint is jumping most nights at this black neighborhood bar, where Philadelphia soul and Motown blare out relentlessly from the jukebox. Sleazed to perfection in 1970s vinyl upholstery, this is the perfect place for one last shot before you stagger home.

The Mad Dog in the Fog, 530 Haight St. Aptly named by the two London lads who own the joint, this is one of the Lower Haight's most loyally patronized bar with darts, English beer and tabloids, and a typical pub menu that includes bangers and mash (sausages and mashed potatoes), hearty ploughmans (cheese, salad, relish, and a roll), and the like.

Noc Noc, 557 Haight St. Decorated like an Egyptian tomb. Draws a fashionable but informal young crowd in for new wave music and flasks of hot sake.

Noes, 1199 Church St. Blue-collar sports bar; come here to catch a game on the giant video screen and have a jeer and cheer with the locals who can't take their eyes off it.

The Rat and the Raven, 4054 24th St. Friendly, hard-drinking neighborhood bar with pool, darts, and, if you're into country music, one of the best jukeboxes in town.

Toronado, 547 Haight St. With over twenty varieties on tap, this is definitely a—mostly male—beer-drinker's haven.

Tropical Haight, 582 Haight St. Best-decorated bar in the district; the theme is tropical, the crowd most definitely is not. Impromptu performances on Tuesdays provide the biggest laugh you're likely to have.

Outlying Districts

Last Day Saloon, 406 Clement St. Very lively bar in the Richmond with regular blues and soul acts, often no cover.

The Plough and Stars, 116 Clement St. Irish ex-pat bar with live music some evenings.

THE DIVE GUIDE

If you've ever had a romantic image of the seedy bar with a pithy bartender and solitary drunks, the checklist below should help you to live this particular little fantasy out. These bars are in no way threatening, though some may be a little daring for women alone. Usually they're old, crumbling, and haven't seen a coat of paint in thirty years. But most importantly they're cheap and open all day, every day, until 2am. See the listings for full comments.

The Blue Lamp, 561 Geary St.

The Dovre Club, 3541 18th St.

The First Inning Lounge, 4026 24th St.

Francine's, 4149 18th St.

The Gold Cane, 1569 Haight St.

Molloy's, 1599 Howard St.

The Travel Lounge, 4 Valencia St.

Cafés

Cafés are slightly different from bars inasmuch as there will virtually always be newspapers and other reading material available and at least a small contingent of people who are not drinking alcohol: really, they're more suited to daytime socializing, many of them serving full meals.

Blue Danube Cafe, 306 Clement St. Café society alive and well in the suburbs? Not quite, but about as alternative as you'll get in the Richmond.

Bohemian Cigar Store, 566 Columbus Ave. Small, informal North Beach hang-out for sipping coffee or slinging beers.

Buena Vista Cafe, 2765 Hyde St, Fisherman's Wharf. If you like your coffee with a kick, this is the place for you. Claims to be the home of the world's first Irish coffee, which is hard to believe, but who cares—it's certainly the best in town, and the crowds which pack the place are testimony to the generously laced coffee. Good, inexpensive food, too, making it a decent stop-off for a sightseeing lunch.

Cafe la Boheme, 3138 24th St. A staggering range of coffees brings in the Mission's caffeine addicts from morning until late at night.

Cafe Flore, 2298 Market St. Lively, partly gay café near the Castro serving meals until 3pm. A popular cruising spot for the locals—drown in a sea of newspapers and pretty faces.

Cafe Francisco, 2161 Powell St. North Beach home of the ponderous coffee drinker.

Cafe Picaro, 3120 16th St. Very popular, no-frills spot where you can get cheap lunches and browse through the hundreds of books that line the walls. Opposite the *Roxie* movie theater in the Mission.

Cafe Roma, 414 Columbus Ave. Not big on atmosphere, but worth a visit to check out the classical, cherub-adorned murals and ornate decor with a cup of coffee.

Cafe Trieste, 609 Vallejo St. Noisy North Beach Italian café, popular with a serious literary crowd which hangs out and listen to the opera classics which boom from the jukebox. Saturday lunchtimes are a treat—the family which runs the place gets up and sings. Get there by noon if you want a seat.

Community Blend Cafe, 233 Fillmore St. Enjoy an excellent breakfast (served all day) or glass of wine in the contrived shabbiness of this Lower-Haight gallery-cum-café where groovy people go to write in their journals. Beer and wine only.

Eagle Cafe, Pier 39, Fisherman's Wharf. Cheap eatery by day and venue for drinks and free live music at night, this place survives remarkably untarnished amid all the waterfront kitsch at Fisherman's Wharf.

Gay and Lesbian Bars

San Francisco's **gay or lesbian bars** are many and varied, ranging from cosy cocktail bars to full no-holds-barred leather-and-chain hang-outs. It's true to say the scene is no longer as wild as its reputation would have you believe, but at its best it can still be hard to beat. The **Castro** holds the thickest concentration of gay men's bars, though its establishments have matured in recent years, and you need to visit **SoMa**, **Polk Street**—or to a lesser extent the **Mission**—for anything outside the mainstream. Take note that places we've listed as bars may switch on some music later on and transform into a club; we've listed the better ones that do this in the following chapter—*Nightlife*. Specifically women's bars are fewer than you might expect, and right now are pretty much confined to the Mission, but the numbers are growing constantly as the lesbian social scene continues to pick up steam.

Bear in mind, though, that the increasingly integrated nature of the gay scene means that formerly exclusively male bars now often have a sizable lesbian contingent. Most, too, are perfectly welcoming places for straight people, especially those in the Castro. If you can't decide where to head for, just ask: gays in San Francisco are on the whole a friendly and communicative lot, and will normally be glad to point you to the kind of thing you're looking for.

Mixed

The Bear, 440 Castro St. Friendly neighborhood bar that draws a chatty, non-cruisy crowd—nice patio out back.

Cafe Flore, 2298 Market St. Very much the in spot before dark. Attractive café with leafy outdoor area and no shortage of people sizing each other up.

Cafe San Marcos, 2367 Market St. Restaurant downstairs and bar and pool tables upstairs. Bit of a couples place, though it gets cruisier at weekends.

The Corral, 2140 Market St. Country and western bar with large dance floor and cheerful crowd. Dolly Parton fans alight here.

The Mint, 1942 Market St. Relaxed piano bar with occasional acts and a mellow crowd.

Uncle Bert's Place, 4086 18th St. Lives up to its name—a cosy, neighborhood watering hole.

Mainly for Men

Alta Plaza, 2301 Fillmore St. Upscale, gay Pacific Heights hang-out for professional, well-dressed men.

Black Rose, 335 Jones St. Raunchy Tenderloin bar popular with transvestites and transexuals. Good cabarets.

Castro Station, 456 Castro St. Noisy disco bar that manages to pack 'em in even in the middle of the day. Very much the die-hard scene of the 1970s with a fair number still in leather gear.

The Cinch, 1723 Polk St. Rowdy bar with pool tables and an animated crowd.

Deluxe, 1511 Haight St. Large, comfy bar with pool tables and slightly older gay guys, but getting a reputation as a good pool hall and drawing an increasingly mixed crowd.

Eagle, 12th & Harrison St. Legendary SoMa biker bar. Not for wimps.

El Rio, 3158 Mission St. Mixed crowds gather for cabaret on Wednesdays but most nights of the week this is an exclusively gay bar popular with Hispanics from the local Mission district. Dancing to live samba on Sunday afternoons. Recommended.

La India Bonita, 3089 16th St. Casual neighborhood bar, mostly Latin but anybody welcome, with occasional drag acts.

Midnight Sun, 4067 18th St. Young, white boys dressed to the nines and cruising like maniacs in this noisy Castro video bar.

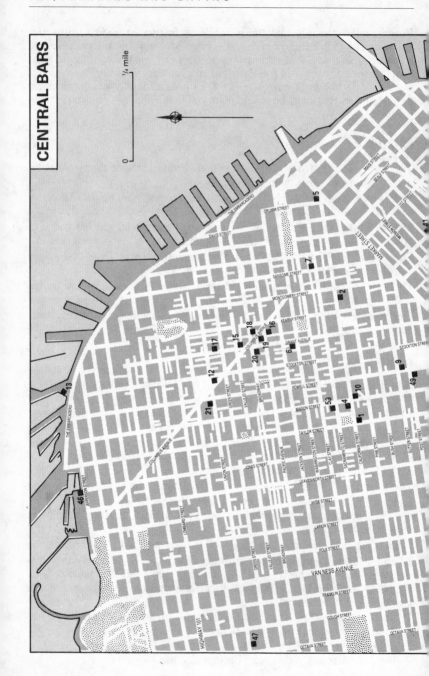

CENTRAL BARS

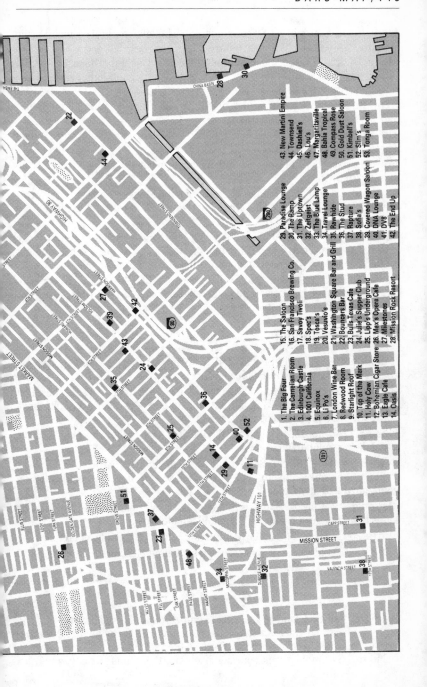

CHINA BASIN

THE EMBARCADERO

HIGHWAY 80

MARKET STREET

MISSION STREET

VALENCIA STREET

HIGHWAY 101

1. The Big Four
2. The Carnelian Room
3. Edinburgh Castle
4. 1001 California
5. Equinox
6. Li Po's
7. London Wine Bar
8. Redwood Room
9. Starlight Roof
10. Top of the Mark
11. Holy Cow
12. Bohemian Cigar Store
13. Eagle Cafe
14. Oasis

15. The Saloon
16. San Francisco Brewing Co.
17. Savoy Tivoli
18. Spec's
19. Tosca's
20. Vesuvio's
21. Washington Square Bar and Grill
22. Bouncer Bar
23. Bull's Texas Cafe
24. Julie's Supper Club
25. Lipp's Underground
26. Max's Opera Cafe
27. Milestones
28. Mission Rock Resort

29. Paradise Lounge
30. The Ramp
31. The Uptown
32. Zeitgeist
33. The Blue Lamp
34. Travel Lounge
35. Rawhide
36. The Stud
37. Rapture
38. Sofia's
39. Covered Wagon Saloon
40. DNA Lounge
41. DV8
42. The End Up

43. New Martini Empire
44. Townsend
45. Dashiell's
46. Lou's
47. Margaritaville
48. Bahia Tropical
49. Compass Rose
50. Gold Dust Saloon
51. Kimball's
52. Slim's
53. Tonga Room

Lion Bar & Lounge, 2898 Sacramento St. The affluent, professional Pacific Heights crowd packs this place out.

Moby Dick, 4049 18th St. Beautifully decorated neighborhood bar in the Castro with music and video, but the accent definitely on light-hearted chatting and a few drinks.

Pendulum, 4146 18th St. Cruisy black men and their admirers. Pool tables and TV screens for sporting events.

The Phoenix, 482 Castro St. The Castro's only dance bar, it not surprisingly draws a large, lively crowd.

Powerhouse, 1347 Folsom St. Full-on leather boys. Definitely not for the faint-hearted.

Rawhide, 280 7th St. If men in chaps are your scene, go no farther than this dimly lit SoMa bar/dance club that plays country and western and bluegrass favorites.

The Stud, 399 9th St. A favorite dancing spot with a mixed but mostly gay crowd. No cover charge and some raucous times and shameless freaking out on the dance floor. Definitely recommended.

Twin Peaks, 17th and Castro St. The Castro's first blatantly gay bar with large see-through windows and generally an older crowd who gather for quiet drinks and conversation.

Mainly for Women

Amelia's, 647 Valencia St. Favored hang-out for mostly younger, fashion-conscious women. The lipstick lesbian scene.

Baybrick Inn, 1190 Folsom St. One of the newer women's venues that describe themselves as "upscale but not uptight"—basically a slick dance club with live entertainment at weekends.

Female Trouble, 1821 Haight St. Wednesday dance club with female bands and dancing. A lot of fun.

Francine's, 4149 18th St. Something of a female biker bar in the Castro—a friendly (if butch) joint with pool tables and the sort of women you'd want on your side if a fight started.

Maude's, 937 Cole St. Situated in one of the busier parts of the Haight, this tends to be full most nights with a mixed female crowd.

Skirts, 300 De Haro St. Sunday dance club. Informal, friendly, good fun.

Sofia's, 527 Valencia St. Popular women's meeting place in the Mission.

EATING

With over four thousand restaurants crammed on to the small peninsula, and scores of bars and cafés which are open all day (and many all night), **eating** in San Francisco is never difficult. Perhaps the most cuisine-oriented place in California, San Franciscans gourmandize expertly around the city, and most people will have at least four restaurant recommendations up their sleeve. It's worth knowing, too, that eating out isn't all that expensive—in some cases not greatly more expensive than cooking your own food—especially if you stick to the **budget places**. Options for cheap eating range from the usual array of pizza and burger joints to a broad selection of **Chinese** restaurants in Chinatown and the **Mexican** eateries of the Mission—really, the two cuisines San Francisco does best. More expensively, **Italian** restaurants are common, in North Beach and around much of the rest of the downtown area, **Thai** cuisine is becoming rapidly more popular, and **French** food is a perennial favorite, at least with the power-broking crowd; and although *nouvelle cuisine* is finally beginning to loosen its grip on San Franciscan menus, its obsession with the beautifully presented tiny portion lives on in the city's **California cuisine** eateries. **Japanese** food, notably sushi, is also still massively popular though not always affordable.

Not surprisingly, health-conscious San Francisco also has a wide range of **vegetarian** and **wholefood** restaurants, and it's rare to find anywhere that doesn't have at least one meat-free item on the menu. Remember, also, that the vineyards of Napa and Sonoma Valley are on the city's doorstep and produce prize-fighting grapes that are good—and cheap—enough to make Europeans nervous and quality **wine** a high-profile feature in most San Francisco restaurants. It's worth knowing, also, that there's much restaurant life beyond the city limits, and that a trip over to the East Bay is always a good idea, where prices will often be cheaper and in some cases, particularly Berkeley, the food better. See the eating and drinking listings in Chapter Nine, *The East Bay*, for suggestions.

For **more on eating** in San Francisco and the Bay Area, see *Basics*, "Food and Drink." We've also included a list of American food terms, and, since some of the foreign restaurants, especially the Asian ones, don't have English-language menus, and the staff are unlikely to be able to translate for you, a glossary of dishes.

Budget Eating: Breakfasts and Burgers

It's surprisingly easy to eat well *and* cheaply in San Francisco, especially if you eat a late breakfast, available in **diners**, **coffee shops**, and the like all over town. The rest of the day the same places serve burgers, sandwiches, and full meals, and can often be the best-value option for lunch.

Bagdad Cafe, 2295 Market St. (☎621-4434). Good hearty breakfasts and burgers served 24 hours a day.

Church Street Station, 2100 Market St. (☎861-1266). Big steak-and-salad-type restaurant. Possibly the largest portions you'll find for the price—around $5 for a burger and fries.

Clown Alley, 42 Columbus Ave. (☎421-2540). Full-blown sleaze with a questionable clientele, but it does serve huge breakfasts 24 hours a day.

David's Delicatessen, 474 Geary St. (☎771-1600). Kosher food in giant portions. Eat until you expire for under $10.

Hamburger Mary's Organic Grill, 1582 Folsom St. (☎626-5767). One of the rowdier eateries in town, in which punky waiting staff will slap burgers, sandwiches, and several vegetarian options on your table for less than $7. Usually full of ravenous SoMa club-goers.

Hamburger Nancy's, 2001 17th St. (☎863-6777). Not wildly different from *Hamburger Mary's*, but more appealing to the office worker crowd with its cheap happy hour.

Hot 'N Hunky, 4039 18th St. (☎621-6365). As the name suggests, the burgers are on the large side, masses of red meat straining under their buns, in what is generally considered San Francisco's best burger joint. The atmosphere is negligible but an average single serving could feed a family of four.

Holey Bagel, 1206 Masonic St. (☎626-9111). Every type of bagel you could think of, stuffed with the filling of your choice and served with coffee for around $1.75.

International House of Pancakes, 2299 Lombard St. (☎921-4004). Popular all over California, "Ihops" are famous for pancakes with every conceivable topping.

Johnny Rockets, 2201 Chestnut St. (☎931-6258). Fifties-style diner with juicy burgers and shakes thick enough to constitute a meal in themselves.

Joji's House of Teriyaki, 1919 Union St. (☎563-7808). Fast food spiced way out of the range of most taste buds, but priced to make you try anyway. Burgers and pizzas from $2.50.

Limbo, 299 9th St. (☎255-9945). Super cheap and ultra-cool, so you can be sure that you won't be alone if you come for dinner here. Wholefood and burgers from under $4.

Mission Rock, 817 China Basin (☎621-5538). Good cheap breakfasts and lunches, served outside on the wharf when the weather's good.

Orphan Andy's, 3991 17th St. (☎864-9795). Favorite hang-out in the Castro for filling burgers, omelettes, and breakfasts.

The Pine Crest, 401 Geary St. (☎885-6407). Bit of a greasy spoon, but ideal for getting rid of your spare change and hunger at the same time.

The Pall Mall Bar & Grill, 1568 Haight St. (no phone). Dark and dingy, with a crowd that's more interesting than the food. But cheap at around $3.50 for burgers and $3 for the all-day breakfasts.

Patio Cafe, 531 Castro St. (☎621-4640). Casual terrace restaurant, great for cheap wholesome food and slinging back inexpensive cocktails.

Seltzer City Cafe, 680 8th St. (☎621-5010). New York-style deli, ideal for large breakfasts and big sandwiches at lunchtime.

Sparky's Diner, 240 Church St. (☎621-6001). Inexpensive 24-hour diner cooking up burgers, pastas and pizzas, and delicious breakfasts, particularly a marvelous eggs florentine. Beer and wine as well.

Spikes, 139 8th St. (☎255-1392). Newly opened Sixties-style diner that often has coupons for cheap dinners in the local press. Even without a discount card, you can get a big breakfast or cheap lunch.

Spaghetti Western, 576 Haight St. (☎864-8461). Best breakfasts in town and a lively Lower-Haight crowd to look at while you chow down.

Zim's, 1498 Market St. (☎431-0600). Steaks, burgers, omelettes, breakfasts, salads—usually for less than about $6.

Happy Hours and Free Food

Bars in San Francisco don't have quite the same deal with free food during happy hours that you'd find in New York, but there are a few places where you can stuff your face for the price of a drink, mainly in the Financial District, though beware—often the drinks tend to be pricey in these haunts. Should you find yourself completely destitute, the city also has several organizations (mainly church-run) who'll give you a warm meal, though these are, not surprisingly, generally the haunts of homeless people and down-and-outs.

Happy Hour Food

Achilles Heel, 1601 Haight St. Mon–Fri 5–7pm.

Bull's Texas Cafe, 25 Van Ness Ave. Mon–Fri 4–6pm.

Cadillac Bar, 1 Holland Court. Mon–Fri 4–7pm.

Dewey's, *St Francis Hotel*, Union Square. Mon–Fri 4–7pm.

Starlight Roof, *Sir Francisco Drake Hotel*, Union Square. Mon–Fri 4–7pm.

Free Food

Food not bombs, Civic Center Plaza, east side of Golden Gate Park (☎330-5030). Wed–Sun 7–7:30pm, Mon & Tues noon–4pm.

Glide Memorial Church, 330 Ellis St. (☎441-6501). Daily 8–9am and noon–1pm.

Haight Ashbury Food Program, 1525 Waller St. (☎566-0366). Open Tues–Fri 1–2pm.

Krishna Temple, 64 Carl St. (☎753-8648). Open daily 7:45–8:30pm. Don't be surprised if you have to attend the Krishna service before they'll feed you.

Martin de Porres, 225 Potrero Ave. (☎552-0240). Mon–Fri 6–7:30am, Sat noon–3pm, Sun 9–10:30am.

Missionaries of Charity, 1330 4th St. (☎821-9687). Daily 5–6:30pm.

St Anthony's Dining Room, 45 Jones St. (☎552-3838). Daily 10am–12:30pm. Showers, laundry, and haircuts also available.

St Peter and Paul Catholic Church, 666 Filbert St. (no phone). Daily 4–5pm.

Pizzas

There are numerous places where you can eat **pizza** in San Francisco. Quick-stop cafeteria-style pizzerias dot every street corner, standard places serving pizza by the slice and with little to choose between them. Most Italian restaurants also have a good selection of pizzas on their menus. Look out, too, for the very much in vogue "designer" pizza, topped with exotic, inventive ingredients and available at a number of specialist places.

Blondie's, 63 Powell St. (☎282-6168). Union Square pizzeria, usually packed out; they do well-topped pizzas for $1.25 a slice.

Calzone's, 430 Columbus Ave. (☎397-3600). Busy bar and restaurant smack in the middle of North Beach, serving lush pizzas and fat calzones, as well as regular Italian fare, to a noisy crowd.

Goat Hill Pizza and Brunch, 300 Connecticut St. (☎647-7676). Designer pizzas and stylish brunches for the fashion-conscious crew which flocks out to Potrero Hill.

Golden Boy, 542 Grant St. (☎982-9738). North Beach venue that's the best place to sample slices of exotic pizza without spending a bomb.

Noe Valley Pizza, 3898 24th St. (☎647-1664). If you love garlic this is your place—every pizza is loaded up with it.

North Beach Pizza, 1499 Grant Ave. (☎433-2444). Good location in the middle of one of the best bar-hopping areas in town. Tasty and cheap, it's just the ticket for a drink-induced munchie.

Pauline's Pizza Pie, 260 Valencia St. (☎552-2050). Something of a truck stop as far as decor goes, but serving some inventive combinations, in big portions and at cheap prices.

Tommaso's, 1042 Kearny St. (☎398-9696). Always a wait for tables, but worth it to stuff yourself with these delicious pizzas and admire the seedy decor and classical murals.

Vicolo Pizzeria, 201 Ivy St. (☎863-2382); Ghirardelli Square, Fisherman's Wharf (☎776-1331). The consummate designer pizza parlors, these two turn out some very fancy fare and charge for the privilege. The Civic Center restaurant has a better atmosphere for a sit-down dinner—the Wharf branch is a bit of an eat-and-run joint.

American and Californian

Restaurants serving **American** food make up a wide-ranging category: basically it encompasses everything from brasserie-type bar-and-grill places to oyster bars and Jewish delis. Those offering **California cuisine** are quite distinct places, serving dishes made with the freshest ingredients combined in unusual ways—the more bizarre the better. In the latter, at least, you can always reckon on spending a fortune.

Bix, 56 Gold St. (☎433-6300). Jackson Square restaurant decked-out like a majestic ocean liner, with torch singer, sax player, and pianist—even if the food was rubbish you'd be enchanted with the place. Actually the food is great—straightforward, classic dishes. Not surprisingly, a hot spot you'd be well advised to book. Dinner for two will probably cost around $50, but if you're into elegant dining experiences you should definitely go.

The Brasserie, basement of the *Fairmont Hotel*, Mason and California St. (☎772-5000). Plush and incredibly pricey, this is, however, the only place to satisfy a 4am craving for lobster thermidor.

Cafe Majestic, *Majestic Hotel*, 1500 Sutter St. (☎776-6400). Totally out of place in the Japantown neighborhood, but nonetheless a lovely place for dinner. The full-on classical decor includes high ceiling and columns, and the food is exquisite.

The Connecticut Yankee, 100 Connecticut St. (☎552-4440). Not cheap, but this Potrero Hill restaurant does great weekend brunches served with generous cocktails.

Fog City Diner, 1300 Battery St. (☎982-2000). Expensively done up to look like a top-class diner, this place is pricey, but provided you don't mind paying for the decor, the food ain't half bad.

Hard Rock Café, 1699 Van Ness Ave. Standard *Hard Rock* clone. Loud music, rock-and-roll decor, and the sort of crowd that doesn't mind standing in line for hours to get in.

Homeboy's Barbeque, 1117 Fillmore St. (☎563-3020). Western Addition eatery serving up steak, ribs, and chicken American-style—LARGE. Good way to load up your protein (and cholesterol) levels.

Ivy's, 398 Hayes St. (☎626-3930). Civic Center restaurant that makes a nice stopoff for lunch, though it's worth avoiding in the evening when it tends to be thronged with the opera-going crowd—and is consequently more expensive.

John's Grill, 63 Ellis St. (☎986-0069). Straight out of the *Maltese Falcon*, this place hasn't changed since Dashiell Hammett was a regular here. Burgers, steaks, and other all-American fare.

Mayes Original Oyster House, 1233 Polk St. (☎474-7674). In business since the 1860s, this is one of San Francisco's oldest restaurants, turning out reasonably priced, well-cooked fish dishes. Oysters by the half-dozen with a beer at the bar for the budget-conscious or less hungry.

Oppenheimer, 2050 Divisadero St. (☎563-0444). Upscale delicatessen, with a full range of kosher foods.

Original Joe's, 144 Taylor St. (☎775-4877). Inexpensive Italian-American restaurant, good for steaks, ribs, salads, pasta, and the like.

Pazzaz, 3296 22nd St. (☎824-8080). American food with a Chinese twist. Inexpensive and usually crowded.

Stars, 150 Redwood St. (☎861-7827). Definitely the place to be seen for cocktails before—or a full-blown dinner after—the opera or a symphony. Expensive, but the food is exquisite, the fixtures and fittings opulent, and the clientele inevitably high class.

Trader Vic's, 20 Cosmo Place (☎776-2232). Virtually a San Francisco institution, *Trader Vic's* has been the restaurant of choice for San Francisco "Society" for many years. Although the food has a Polynesian/Indian bent, this is very much dining monied-American style. Atmosphere stops at the dinner plate.

Washington Square Bar & Grill, 1707 Powell St. (☎982-8123). Stylish American grill with an Italian tilt and a media/politico patronage. Food cooked to rich and heavy perfection and martinis that are little short of sublime. A wander down the cheaper side of the menu (burgers, sandwiches, etc) should get you out unscathed for around $15 per head with a few drinks. If you want to see the upper echelons of San Francisco society power-lunching, this is your scene.

Zuni Cafe, 1658 Market St. (☎552-2522). The chic place to be and be seen, with Californian nouvelle cuisine portions as minimal as the elegant decor for around $30 a head with wine. If you don't want to spend that kind of money, sit at the bar and down a few cocktails with oyster shooters (6 for around $8).

Italian

Though the city may be better known for its Asian eateries, some of San Francisco's best meals are to be had in one of a range of fine **Italian** restaurants, many of which are concentrated around the North Beach area.

Allegro Ristorante Italiano, 1701 Jones St. (☎928-4002). Russian Hill hang-out popular with those in the know. If you want to join such enlightened company, you presumably won't mind paying for it.

Cafe Riggio, 4112 Geary Blvd. (☎221-2114). Out in the Richmond, this is the original Italian trattoria, a genuinely earthy haunt that serves solid, if unexceptional, food and the cheapest Italian wine in town.

Capp's Corner, 1600 Powell St. (☎989-2589). Funky, family-style Italian restaurant in North Beach, with a fashionable clientele which lines up for the big portions.

Enoteca Lanzone, Opera Plaza, 601 Van Ness St. (☎928-0400). A favorite with opera-goers, this one has a menu that's beyond the price range of most, but it's worth a visit to check out the "Grappa Room," offering 140 different varieties of firewater.

Gold Spike, 527 Columbus Ave. (☎986-9747). More like a museum than a restaurant, with enough photographs, mooseheads, and war souvenirs to keep you occupied for what can be a long wait for the excellent-value $12 six-course dinner.

Green Valley Restaurant, 510 Green St. (☎788-9384). Good, hearty fare in a basic but busy place, full of local North Beach families and birthday celebrants. Eat till you drop for under $10.

Il Pollaio, 555 Columbus Ave. (☎362-7727). You'll be hard pushed to spend more than $6 for a blow-out in this minuscule restaurant, in which the great deal more than compensates for the lack of elbow-room.

La Traviata, 2854 Mission St. (☎282-0500). Friendly, noisy, and cheap Mission Italian restaurant.

Little Joe's, 523 Broadway (☎433-4343). Always a wait for tables, but worth it for the cheap, enormous portions of well-cooked food in this North Beach institution.

North Beach Restaurant, 1512 Stockton St. (☎392-1587). Extensive menu, moderately priced. Great cocktails.

Raf, 478 Green St. (☎362-1999). Another place where you get the feeling that you're paying for the expensive decor and not the food. However, it's a great spot for seeing the terminally chic spend their cash and enjoying some fairly exotic dishes.

Ristorante Firenze, 1421 Stockton St. (☎421-5813). Modern decor, traditional food, quick service—an attractive combination.

French

French food has always been the favored cuisine of wealthy San Franciscans, and most places are well beyond the budget of most travelers. However, there are a couple of places in which you can have a good meal without having to send home for more cash.

Cafe Landais, 489 3rd St. (☎495-6944). SoMa bistro that's about the cheapest place for French food in town. Popular with connoisseurs on a budget.

Le Candide, 301 Kearny St. (☎981-2213). Reasonably priced standard French fare. You can rub shoulders with the well-dressed Financial District crowd.

Ernie's, 847 Montgomery St. (☎397-5969). Certainly not cheap, but a lovely Victorian interior and a *haute cuisine* menu made famous by Hitchcock's *Vertigo*—it figured in some of the crucial scenes.

South Park Cafe, 108 South Park (☎495-7275). Chic SoMa gathering place for aficionados of all things French, especially pastries and good brandy.

Le Trou, 1007 Guerrero St. (☎550-8169). About as reasonably priced as you'll get, this is French food on a budget.

Zola's, 395 Hayes St. (☎864-4824). Very fancy, beautifully prepared and presented French *nouvelle cuisine* in stylized surroundings. Smoke-free and quite expensive.

Chinese, Thai, and Indonesian

Chinese is the food most people imagine when they think of foreign food in San Francisco, and it does predominate even outside Chinatown's boundaries. However, as increasing numbers of other Asian restaurants are opening, it's being strongly challenged from all sides. **Thai** food, with its emphasis on fresh herb and citrus flavorings, was popular during the health-conscious late 1980s, while **Indonesian** restaurants are popping up all over town.

Bangkok 16, 3214 16th St. (☎431-5838). Moderately priced Thai restaurant down in the Mission, with a great selection for vegetarians—and for meateaters they do a mean lamb saté.

Brandy Ho's Original Hunan, 217 Columbus Ave. (☎788-7527). Excellent long-established Hunan cuisine restaurant. Another, new branch at 450 Broadway (☎362-6268).

Burma Restaurant, 309 Clement St. (☎751-4091). Authentic Burmese cuisine, not cheap but the portions are so massive that two could split a main course.

Celadon, 881 Clay St., Chinatown (☎982-1168). One of the fancier Cantonese restaurants in town. Far from bargain-basement food, but worth coughing up for the beautifully presented, fragrant dishes.

Chiang Mai, 5020 Geary Blvd. (☎387-1299). Cheerful little Thai restaurant out in the Richmond with delicious inexpensive food. Huge range of seafood dishes.

China Moon Cafe, 639 Post St. (☎775-4789). Standard Cantonese cuisine, but the restaurant is more notable for its excellent, cheap dim sum lunches.

Cloisonne, 601 Van Ness Ave. (☎441-2232). First-class Cantonese cooking, moderately priced and served in luxurious surroundings. Draws most of its business from the opera crowds down the road, so it tends to be quite formal. You won't be refused if you turn up in jeans, but you might feel out of place.

Empress of China, 838 Grant Ave. (☎434-1345). The smartest place in town to get to grips with Chinese cuisine, with an incredible selection of dishes and amazing views over neighboring North Beach. You'll be lucky to pay less than $18 for a main course, but if you're in the mood for a blow-out it's definitely the place to be decadent.

Indonesian Restaurant, 678 Post St. (☎474-4026). Small, unassuming, and affordable restaurant.

Java, 417 Clement St. (☎752-1541). No-frills cheap Richmond Indonesian.

Jing Wah, 1634 Bush St. (☎922-5279). Highly-rated Cantonese cuisine served at reasonable prices in very unpretentious surroundings in the middle of Polk Gulch.

Lychee Garden, 1416 Powell St. (☎397-2290). High-quality Cantonese cuisine, favored by families and large groups because of the quick and tolerant service and the way they'll improvise items on the menu to suit children.

The Mandarin, Ghirardelli Square, Fisherman's Wharf (☎673-8812). Stylish conversion of industrial space stuffed with Asian antiques. The Chinese food is expensive but excellent—ideal for a special night out.

Manora's Thai Cuisine, 1600 Folsom St. (☎861-6224). Massively popular, and you may have to wait, but it's worth it for light, spicy, and fragrant Thai dishes at around $6 each.

Marnee Thai, 2225 Irving St. (☎665-9500). The food is pretty average, but it's worth a trip out to the Sunset just to sit in a restaurant virtually carpeted in fresh flowers. Small and very lovely.

New Asia, 772 Pacific Ave. (☎391-6666). Considering the neighborhood is so pressed for space, it's amazing that a place this big survives. It serves some of the most authentic dim sum in town, with waitresses pushing carts down the aisles, shouting out their wares as they pass.

Pazazz, 3296 22nd St. (☎824-8080). Chinese food for the non-adventurous—they serve up Americanized (very tame) Chinese fare that you don't have to eat with chopsticks.

Pinyo, 4036 Balboa St. (☎221-2161). Way out near the ocean in the farthest reaches of the Richmond, and a bit of a trek to reach, but so cheap you could afford to take a taxi there and back and still save money. Main dishes from $3.50.

Pot Sticker, 150 Waverly Place (☎397-9985). Extensive menu offering Szechuan and Hunan dishes in this popular and often crowded Chinatown favorite. Inexpensive meals, served with beer or wine only.

Sam Woh's, 813 Washington St. (☎982-0596). Much tamer since the death of hilariously surly waiter Edsel Ford Fong some years ago, this late-night (until 3am), very basic eatery—you have to clamber up dubious old steps through the kitchen to reach the eating area—still manages to attract the North Beach crowds when the bars turn out.

South Pacific, 2500 Noriega Ave. (☎564-3363). Seafood, tropical cocktails, live music, and hula dancers on weekends. Every bit the novelty eatery, though way out in the Sunset district.

Straits Cafe, 3300 Geary Blvd. (☎668-1783). Affordable Singaporean cuisine in authentic surroundings.

Thep Phanom Restaurant, 400 Waller St. (☎431-2526). Simple, delicate decor and beautifully prepared dishes make this Lower Haight restaurant seem more expensive than it really is. Expect to pay no more than $7 for a main course, but also expect to wait.

Woey Loy Goey Cafe, 699 Jackson St. (☎982-0137). Like Sam Woh's, this is very much an after-hours place and is similarly priced—it also has wine at 85¢ a glass.

Wu Kong Restaurant, 1 Rincon Center, 101 Spear St. (☎957-9300). Popular with workers from the Financial District, the excellent Shanghai cuisine here commands some pretty steep prices, but if you just nip in for some dim sum, you shouldn't be left penniless.

Yank Sing, 427 Battery St. (☎362-1640). Join the Financial District workers at lunchtime and eat dim sum in the fanciest of surroundings.

Yuet Lee, 1300 Stockton St. (☎982-6020). Cheap and cheerful Chinese restaurant with a good seafood menu and enthusiastic crowds of diners. No alcohol but you can take your own beer or wine.

Japanese and Korean

Japanese people, and **Japanese** food, had a low profile in San Francisco until the 1970s, when the building of the Japan Center brought half a dozen new restaurants. In contrast there are only a few **Korean** restaurants in the city, but although the cuisine lacks the ready identification afforded sushi and other Japanese dishes, the barbecue-based cooking is catching the eye of more and more San Francisco foodies.

Asuka Brasserie, *Miyako Hotel*, 1625 Post St. (☎922-3200). Very flash indeed. Great Japanese food in beautiful surroundings, priced beyond the means of most. For celebratory meals or special occasions only.

Benkay, *Hotel Nikko*, 222 Mason St. (☎394-1111). Hi-tech, minimal and ultra-modern, *Benkay* is the Jean-Paul Gaultier of the restaurant biz. The theme is *Kaiseki*, a succession of many exquisite courses served by kimono-clad waitresses. If you've got $100 to blow on dinner for two, you'll love it.

Isuzu, 1581 Webster St. (☎922-2290). Fashionable Japan Center restaurant featuring seperate sushi and tempura bars. Rub shoulders with up-to-the-minute restaurant-goers.

Ma Tante Sumi, 4243 18th St. (☎552-6663). Unusual Japanese restaurant run by French food freaks, producing an interesting combination of dishes ranging from the very light to the incredibly rich. A popular Castro dining spot.

Mifune, 1737 Post St. (☎922-0337). Moderately priced seafood and Japanese fare to take away.

Mitoya, 1855 Post St. (☎563-2156). Inexpensive sushi and seafood served from a bar where you sit on cushions. The adjoining bar has singers and is an excellent place to warm up before dinner.

Moshi Moshi, 2092 Third St. (☎861-8285). Oscure SoMa restaurant full of people who pride themselves on finding such an out-of-the-way gem. Excellent Japanese sushi and seafood, moderately priced.

Mun's, 401 Balboa St. (☎668-6007). Western Addition venue serving inexpensive, simple Korean fare.

New Village, 4828 Geary Blvd. (☎668-3678). Good-value set meals at this Richmond restaurant, with barbecue short ribs, chicken, or seafood plus a half-dozen Korean specialties for around $10.

Osome, 1923 Fillmore St. (☎346-2311). Chic, popular restaurant serving highly rated sushi and seafood.

Sanppo, 1702 Post St. (☎346-3486). Small, busy, and unpretentious Japantown eatery—the decor might be negligible but the food is cheap and first rate.

Silver Moon, 2301 Clement St. (☎386-7852). Seafood and vegetarian Japanese fare. Very light, healthy dishes.

Sushi Bar, 1800 Divisadero St. (no phone). Bright, cheap, and quick.

Yoshida-Ya, 2909 Webster St. (☎346-3431). There are countless sushi bars in San Francisco but few places you can actually kick off your shoes and eat at low tables on futoned floors. This is just such a place: expect to pay around $20 a head for a good selection of sushi and a few drinks.

Indian, Greek, and Middle Eastern

Like most other US cities, San Francisco has never been particularly big on **Indian** cuisine, but its spicy dishes have caught on more of late, and there are now a dozen or so restaurants in the city. **Greek** and **Middle Eastern** food is similarly rare, though where they exist, both make for good, cheap options.

Asimakopoulos Cafe, 288 Connecticut St. (☎552-8789). Upscale Greek cooking, although you get the feeling you're paying for the psuedo-authentic decor and not the food.

Gaylord, Ghirardelli Square, 900 North Point, Fisherman's Wharf (☎771-8822). One of very few Indian restaurants in San Francisco and probably the best, though you should expect to pay around $15 for a main course. Still, if you must have a curry . . ..

The Golden Turtle, 2211 Van Ness Ave. (☎441-4419). Though primarily a Vietnamese restaurant, this Russian Hill venue has a large selection of kebabs and other Middle Eastern dishes, all for under $10.

The Grapeleaf, 4031 Balboa St. (☎668-1515). Way out in the western suburbs, this small Lebanese bistro serves unusual and spicy food, but what really makes it are the spirited belly-dancers who gyrate round the restaurant.

India House, 350 Jackson St. (☎392-0744). Again, not cheap, but lavish decoration and extraordinarily punctilious service help soften the blow when the check arrives.

Mamounia, 441 Balboa St. (☎752-6566). Eat Moroccan food with your fingers and pay through the nose for it.

The Peacock, 2800 Van Ness Ave. (☎928-7001). Indian restaurant near Fort Mason serving hot tandoori dishes and fragrant Indian breads. Very tasty, moderately priced, and quite formal.

Steve the Greek, 1431 Polk St. (no phone). Authentic Greek (including plastic tablecloths) and ultra cheap.

Mexican and Hispanic

Mexican food accounts for a good proportion of San Francisco's eating options and is one of the best ways to eat well at no great cost. The largest concentration of places is in the Mission, though taco and burrito stands can be found all over the city. It's a heavy but filling cuisine, and in many places the best thing about it is the beer served to wash it all down: almost everywhere will have a range of imported Mexican *cervezas* by the bottle, and—equally thirst-quenching—fresh fruit juices called *licuados*. A number of restaurants also do a variety of Central and South American dishes, not least **Peruvian** and **Salvadorean**.

Cadillac Bar, 1 Holland Court, off Howard St. (☎543-8226). As Mexican restaurants go, this one is fairly upmarket and has live guitar music to help your burritos go down.

El Cubane, 1432 Valencia St. (☎824-6655). Big portions of Cuban food with a Tues–Fri lunch special for $4.

El Tapatio, 475 Francisco St. (☎981-3018). Not as cheap as the Mexican restaurants of the Mission, but the food in this North Beach eatery is notably better—and the margaritas larger than most.

El Tazumal, 3522 20th St. (☎550-0935). Interesting Salvadorean restaurant where you can try tripe, tongue, and spicy rice dishes for around $5 for a lunch and up to $9 for a dinner. Small but lively, and with an interesting crowd.

El Toro, 3071 16th St. (☎431-3351). Always a line outside for the massive burritos.

Ensenada Restaurant, 2976 Mission St. (☎826-4160). One of the more cheerful-looking of the Mission's inexpensive Mexican restaurants, with Mexican art on the walls and a standard menu with full meals for around $4–5.

Las Guitarras, 3200 24th St. (☎285-2684). Noisy Mission Mexican favored by the locals. Don't expect a fine dining experience, but you can count on a good hearty dinner.

Mission Villa Restaurant, 2391 Mission St. (☎826-0454). Enormous burritos and tacos for around $2–3.

Mom's Cooking, 1192 Geneva St. (☎586-7000). Small and crowded, on the fringes of the Mission. You may have to wait for a table, but it's well worth it for the super-cheap fresh Mexican food.

New Central Restaurant, 301 South Van Ness Ave. (☎431-8587). Small, family-run restaurant serving moderately priced, hearty dishes to a ravenous crowd.

La Taqueria, 2889 Mission St. (☎285-7717). Always busy with locals, which is as good a recommendation as any for its fairly standard Mexican menu.

La Victoria, 1205 Alabama St. (☎550-9309). Small, intimate South American cafeteria run by two old women. Service is slow, but the food is fresh and delicious.

Vegetarian and Wholefood

Though its roots may well be closely intertwined with 1960s Flower Power hippiedom, San Francisco's **vegetarian and wholefood** restaurants go far beyond the brown rice worthiness that is usually associated with this kind of cooking, into the distant realms of *haute cuisine*. While many of the places listed below are fairly basic and inexpensive, a couple, especially *Greens* in Fort Mason, are incredibly refined—and correspondingly expensive.

Amazing Grace, 216 Church St. (☎626-6411). Rated highly by local vegetarian buffs, with standard veggie fare for around $4 a dish.

Greens, Building A, Fort Mason Center, Fort Mason (☎771-6222). A converted Army supply warehouse that's now San Francisco's only Zen Buddhist restaurant, serving unusual and delicious macrobiotic and vegetarian food to an eager clientele. Always busy, so book in advance, and count on spending around $30 a head for a five-course dinner.

Marty's, 508 Natoma St. (☎621-0751). Stuck down a little alley, this isn't the sort of place you'd stumble over, but if you're into macrobiotic food, you should definitely make the effort. Thurs–Sun only.

Real Good Karma, 501 Dolores St. (☎621-4112). Hearty and nutritious portions of vegetarian and wholefood dishes in informal surroundings.

24-HOUR EATS

This is simply a checklist of places where you can get reasonably priced food **all night**. For details and comment see the appropriate restaurant listings above.

Baghdad Cafe, 2295 Market St. (☎621-4434).

The Brasserie, in the basement of the *Fairmont Hotel* on Mason and California St. (☎772-5199).

Church St Station, 2100 Market St. (☎861-1266).

Orphan Andy's, 3991 17th St., the Castro (☎864-9795).

Clown Alley, 42 Columbus Ave. (☎421-2540).

International House of Pancakes, 2299 Lombard St. (☎921-4004).

Lori's Diner, 336 Mason St. (☎392-8646).

The Pine Crest, 401 Geary St. (☎885-6407).

Sparky's Diner, 240 Church St. (☎621-6001).

Zim's, 1498 Market St. (☎931-5890).

CHAPTER EIGHT

NIGHTLIFE

Compared to many US cities, where you need money and attitude in equal amounts, San Francisco's **nightlife** scene demands little of either. This is no 24-hour city, and the approach to socializing is often surprisingly understated, with little of the pandering to fads and fashions that goes on in New York or LA. It's a casualness which is contagious and manifest in a **club scene** that—far as it is from the cutting edge of hip—is encouragingly cheap compared to other cities: $30 can get you a decent night out, including cover charge, a few drinks, and maybe even a taxi home. The city's **live music** scene is similarly economical—and, frankly, what the city does best: San Franciscans may be relatively out of touch with fashion, but there are decent rock, jazz, or folk venues all over town, many entertaining you for no more than the price of a drink.

The city has a somewhat better reputation for **opera** and **classical music**, its orchestra and opera association among the country's most highly regarded, though obviously opera-going and nights at the symphony or ballet take money: there are few cheap deals to be had beyond getting a ticket at the top of the balcony, and even then seats can be pricey. **Theater** is more accessible and much cheaper, with discount tickets available, but most of the mainstream downtown venues are mediocre, mainly staging Broadway re-runs, and you'd do better to take some time to explore the infinitely more interesting fringe circuit. The city's **cabaret and comedy** scene is more uptempo: there are some excellent clubs, hosting an increasingly healthy and varied diet of good comedians. **Film**, too, is almost as big an obsession as eating in San Francisco, and you may well be surprised by just the sheer number of movie theaters—repertory and current release—that flourish in the small city.

LISTINGS AND TICKET INFORMATION

Other than keeping an eye out for the flyers stuck up around town, the *Sunday Chronicle*'s "Pink Pages" supplement is about the best source of **listings and what's on information**; you might also check the free weekly *Bay Guardian*, the *San Francisco Weekly*, and a host of other more specific publications listed below under the relevant sections. For **tickets**, *BASS* (☎893-2277) and *Ticketron* (☎392-7469) are the major Bay Area booking agencies. You can either reserve with a credit card on these numbers, or in person at one of their branches in record stores like *Tower Records* or *Wherehouse*; for addresses of these, see Chapter Six, *Shops and Galleries*. For **theater tickets**, there's the *STBS* ticket booth on Union Square; see "Theater" for details.

Live Music: Rock, Jazz, and Folk

San Francisco's **music scene** reflects the character of the city: laid-back, eclectic, and not a little nostalgic. The options for catching **live music** are wide and the scene is definitely on the up and up, with the city spawning some good young bands. However, it has never recaptured its crucial Sixties role and these days lacks the influence of many other American cities, better as a venue for good R&B, psychedelia, folk and rock standards, and—of late—country and western and Latin American bands. Sadly, not all jazz haunts are commensurate with the amount of talent in the greater Bay Area—if you want to hear some really good stuff, you'll need to head over to the East Bay, where a couple of excellent clubs more than make up for the relative paucity in the city.

The best thing about the city is the fact that live bands are so easy to catch: ordinary neighborhood bars regularly host decent groups, often for free, and there are any number of good small venues charging minimal covers. Bigger names, too, play the Bay Area regularly, although you should expect to pay about $20 to see anybody halfway popular.

Unlike the club scene, which is concentrated in the South of Market area, **live music** tends to be more spread out across the city, though the Haight, North Beach, and the Mission tend to have more venues than most. Few of them fall into any particular camp, with most varying their bill throughout the week, and it can be hard to specify which venues feature a certain music style. Many also double as clubs, hosting some kind of disco after the live music has stopped. Below is a pretty comprehensive list of established venues, but be sure to check the music press, the best of which is San Francisco's free *BAM* (*Bay Area Music*)—which has exhaustive listings of events in the city and Bay Area as a whole and is available in most record stores.

The Large Performance Venues

The best way to reserve seats for the following venues is through *BASS* or *Ticketron*, either with a major credit card several weeks in advance, or at one of their record store branches. You can try contacting the theaters direct for tickets, but most now operate solely through booking agencies. Bear in mind that some of the Bay Area's best large-scale venues are actually across the bay in Oakland and Berkeley, and that this is where the big names will often be playing. For a full rundown you should see the listings in Chapter Nine, *The East Bay*.

Great American Music Hall, 859 O'Farrell St. (☎885-0750). Theater District venue too small for major names, but too large for local yokels. It hosts a range of musical styles from balladeers to thrash bands. Seating for several thousand.

The Warfield, 982 Market St. (☎775-7722). *The Warfield* can usually be relied on to stage major rock crowd-pullers. Chart bands, big-name indie groups, and popular old-timers keep the place packed.

Rock, Folk, and Country

The Albion, 3139 16th St. (☎552-8558). Mostly just a Mission neighborhood bar, though occasionally hosting local bands on its tiny stage. Small, inexpensive, and intimate, it's ideal for a night out on the cheap. No cover.

The Blue Lamp, 561 Geary St. (☎885-1464). Quite the deserted dive, this is a great place to listen to small folk and country acts, usually of the struggling solo artist variety. No cover.

Bouncers Bar, 64 Townsend St. (☎397-2480). Near the SoMa waterfront, this was originally a rowdy sailors' hang-out. These days the sailors are gone, but the rowdiness lives on in this hardcore drinkers' bar staging obscure country, blues, and R&B bands. No cover.

Full Moon Saloon, 1725 Haight St. (☎775-6190). You'll have to take your chances with this one—expect anything from reggae and funk to bluegrass. Consistently lively clientele and good fun. No cover.

I-Beam, 1748 Haight St. (☎668-6023). Haight-Ashbury's most famous venue, usually host to some fairly big names. It's not the place to see bands on the cheap, although midweek you can generally get in for around $5–10.

JJ's, 2225 Fillmore St. (☎563-2219). Pacific Heights hang-out in vogue for the better-dressed live music fan. Good bar and cruisy singles crowd. Usually a cover charge of $6–12.

Last Day Saloon, 406 Clement St. (☎387-6343). A bit out of the way, but if you find yourself in the Richmond and you're wondering where to find some action, this is the best the area has to offer. Mostly soul, blues, and R&B. Cover $3–6.

Lost and Found Saloon, 1353 Grant St. (☎397-3751). Informal North Beach hang-out with a catch-all selection of music styles. No cover.

Lou's, 300 Jefferson St. (☎771-0377). Country/rock and blues bar down on Fisherman's Wharf that hosts some good local bands. Weekend lunchtimes are a good time to check out the lesser-knowns in relative peace. Come nightfall it's madness. No cover before 9pm.

Nightbreak, 1821 Haight St. (☎221-9008). Slightly shabby, small Haight venue for a lot of new wave and goth bands playing to a matching crowd. Very dark, very loud, very crowded, and charging a small cover only at weekends.

Paradise Lounge, 11th and Folsom St. (☎861-6906). Good, cheap SoMa venue to see new wave, rock, and occasionally country bands. See the band and dance downstairs, or take a break and a game of pool upstairs. Free Sun–Thurs, $5 cover Fri and Sat.

Paul's Saloon, 3251 Scott St. (☎922-2456). Stands alone in San Francisco as the only place to see genuine, foot-tappin' bluegrass bands who twang and fiddle hard nightly from 9pm until 1am. Drinks are remarkably cheap, and the place is one of the city's most comfortable old watering holes.

The Plough and Stars, 116 Clement St. (☎751-1122). Quite a way from downtown but worth the trip if you're into Irish folk music. Very much the haunt of the Irish ex-pat community. Usually a small cover.

The Saloon, 1232 Grant St. (☎397-3751). Always packed to the gills, this is North Beach's best spot for some rowdy R&B. No cover.

Slim's, 33 11th St. (☎621-3300). Slick but reliable venue for rock and R&B.

The Stone, 412 Broadway (☎391-8282). Solid San Francisco venue with consistently good billing of rock and new wave bands. Open until 6am Fri and Sat for a very danceable rock disco after the bands finish. Young, fun clubbers, cover around $8.

Tar & Feathers, 2140 Union St. (☎563-2612). Young, casual, country and western. The Marina's place to go for a few beers and a singalong when you can't face the singles bars.

Jazz and Latin American

Bahia Tropical, 1600 Market St. (☎861-8657). Expensive, yuppie hang-out and supper club with good Brazilian and samba bands. Cover $7.

Bajone's, 3140 Mission St. (☎648-6641). Unusual—and refreshing—age-range for San Francisco, ranging from 25 to 65. Excellent Latin jazz that plays nightly. Casual, unpretentious, and genuine. $5 cover at weekends.

The Compass Rose, Lobby of the *St Francis Hotel*, Union Square (☎397-7000). With a string quartet at cocktail hour and jazz trio in the evenings, this is quite the place for sitting in deluxe surroundings and sipping expensive drinks.

Gold Dust Saloon, 247 Powell St. (☎397-1697). So close to Union Square it's a bit of a tourist hang-out, but good for a sing-song and some old-fashioned Dixieland jazz. No cover.

Jack's, 1601 Fillmore St. (☎567-3227). Small, intimate bar with jazz and blues seven nights a week. Recommended. No cover.

Kimball's, 300 Grove St. (☎861-5585). Slick establishment jazz-club-cum-restaurant with a clientele bordering on middle-age. Luckily, you don't have to eat, which is handy as the cover tends to be high. Open daily until 3am.

Lascaux, 248 Sutter St. (☎391-1555). So mellow the crowd is in danger of nodding off, but nonetheless a fine place for a meal and some soft jazz. Open Mon–Sat.

Le Montmartre, 2125 Lombard St. (☎931-9921). Bit of a pick-up place, but cheap drinks and good salsa music make the sometimes unwanted attention worth it. Cover $3.

Pasand Lounge, 1875 Union St. (☎922-4498). Unusual club where you can come to eat Indian food and listen to very mellow jazz in the comfortable lounge. Open Wed–Sat. Sometimes a small cover.

Pearl's, 256 Columbus Ave. (☎291-8255). Cosy North Beach supper club for those who like their jazz sitting down with a good meal in front of them. No cover, but you must eat.

The Rite Spot Cafe, 2099 Folsom St. (☎552-6066). Informal, café-style club with jazz and R&B bands. Open Mon–Sat, and serving snacks, drinks, and coffee until 1am. Small cover at weekends.

Roland's, 2513 Van Ness Ave. (☎567-1063). Classic and Latin jazz for the serious jazz fans who like their music a bit on the esoteric side in a dark, smoky atmosphere. Open Tues–Sun. Small cover at weekends.

Slim's, 333 11th St. (☎621-3330). Slick, medium-sized venue staging mainly jazz bands with the occasional big name topping the bill. Friendly, comfortable club. Cover depends on the check, usually $7–10.

The Tonga Room, basement of the *Fairmont Hotel*, 950 Mason St. (☎772-5000). An absolute must for fans of the ludicrous or just the very drunk. Decked out like a Polynesian village with a pond and simulated rain storms, the grass-skirted band play terrible jazz and pop covers on a raft in the middle of the water. Worth every penny of the cover charge and outrageously priced cocktails. Cover $4.

Clubbing

Trading on a reputation earned decades ago, the city's **nightclubs** continue to trail vapidly behind those of other large American cities. That said, the compensations are manifold—no standing in line for hours, or high cover charges, ridiculously priced drinks and feverish posing. Instead you'll find a diverse range of small- to medium-sized affordable clubs in which leather-clad goths rub shoulders with the bearded and beaded, alongside a number of gay hang-outs still rocking to the sounds of high-energy funk and Motown.

Unlike most other cities, where the action never gets going until after midnight, many San Francisco **clubs** have to close at 2am during the week, so you can usually be sure to find things well under way by 11:30pm. At weekends, most places stay open until 3–4am, but again you don't have to wait up late for things to get lively. There is rarely any kind of door policy, and only on very busy nights will you have to wait. The greatest concentration of clubs is in **SoMa**, especially the area around 11th Street and Folsom; indeed SoMa is your best bet for club and bar-hopping—most places don't mind you leaving and re-entering provided you've got your regulation hand-stamp. Unlike more style-conscious cities, where serious clubbers only go out during the week, San Francisco isn't really big or club-oriented enough to sport a serious attitude toward weekend out-of-towners; in fact some places are actually more exciting at the weekend. Your best bet is to follow the press, ask around, and take your chances. Note that many **gay clubs**, particularly those listed under "Mixed," are by no means no-go areas for straight people—indeed many rank among the city's best nightspots, whatever your orientation.

Several places charge no **cover** at all, and only the most chi-chi of clubs will charge a fortune for drinks. The entry age to clubs, as with bars, is 21, and it's a good idea to carry an **ID** with you at all times: as a general rule, if you look under thirty you'll definitely need it. Clubs are cracking down in general and becoming very fussy about **drugs** in particular: in keeping with the increasingly conservative attitude in the city a crafty joint is enough to get you thrown out of some places.

The Clubs

Caesar's Latin Palace, 3140 Mission St. (☎826-1179). Possibly the biggest laugh you'll have in the city: Latin, jazz, and disco rock for those who want to relive late 1970s disco-mania. Cheap drinks and late licensing (open until 6am at weekends) all add to the spirit of a place that's appalling enough to have achieved cult status. $6 cover.

Chatterbox, 853 Valencia St. (☎821-1891). Open daily until 2am for good no-nonsense rock'n'roll in a room resembling a pool hall. Mixed, beer-drinking biker crowd; cover around $5.

Covered Wagon Saloon, 917 Folsom St. (☎974-5906). Definitely one of the better SoMa places, especially on Thursday when they have their "Love Shack" hi-tech psychedelic night, and on Saturday for hip-hop. Cover $4–6.

DNA Lounge, 375 11th St. (☎626-1409). Club which changes its music style nightly but draws the same young hipsters. Large dance floor downstairs and when the dancing gets too much you can lounge around in comfy sofas on the mezzanine. Cover $7. Open Tues–Sun 9pm–4am.

DV8, 540 Howard St. (☎777-1419). Huge, ornate, and fashionable, this is the closest San Francisco gets to rivaling the big clubs of New York and Los Angeles, decorated by Keith Haring pop-art and playing high-energy funk and house music. It also has a nice members-only bar that's worth talking your way into if you can. About the only club in town worth dressing up for. Cover $10. Open Wed–Sat.

El Rio, 3158 Mission St. (☎282-3325). Latin, jazz, and samba are the specialty here, with live bands on Sunday, dancing to modern funk on Friday, and cabaret on Wednesday in a friendly, anything-goes atmosphere. Open seven nights 3pm–2am, until 6am at weekends. No cover. See also "Comedy Clubs."

The Endup, Harrison and 6th St. (☎495-9550). A mostly gay crowd, but recently discovered by the weekend clubbers, and a good place for the hard-core party animal—especially so on "Wet jockstrap night." Open continuously from 6am on Sat morning until 2am Mon. Small cover.

Firehouse 7, 3160 16th St. (☎621-1617). Not to be missed, a bar/club with the broadest cross-section of music styles and clientele that you're likely to find. Reggae night Wednesday, live music Friday, and house music on Saturday. Relaxed, informal crowd and pool tables for those not into dancing. $3 cover at weekends.

Full Moon Saloon, 1725 Haight St. (☎775-6190). Typical Haight mixed-bag of styles and people. Low-key, good laugh, no cover.

Holy Cow, 1535 Folsom St. (☎621-6087). Young club-fiends trying hard to be cool, but a good rave once it warms up. A huge plastic cow hangs outside, you can't miss it. Open Tues–Sun. Usually no cover.

I-Beam, 1748 Haight St. (☎668-6006). One of San Francisco's longest-standing rock venues, featuring both familiar names and lesser-knowns for around $5. Tickets for the bigger shows can be pricey, but dancing afterward keeps the place packed until 2am. Tea dances on Sunday afternoons, popular with the gay community.

Kennel Club, 628 Divisadero St. (☎931-9858). Most popular for its "Box" club on Thursday and Saturday for the gay crowd. Friday is "Club Q" for women, and Sunday reggae and worldbeat music. Good fun, mixed crowd. Cover $6.

The New Martini Empire, 1015 Folsom St. (☎626-2899). Club with an international bent where you'll be able to hear some of the more unconventional sounds of Brazilian, salsa, Arabic, African, and Soca. Open Fri–Sun. Cover $4.

Nightbreak, 1821 Haight St. (☎221-9008). Small Haight club that has tagged itself with the slogan "All the funk that's fit to pump"—house, hip-hop, and funk most nights, except for Wednesday when it becomes "Female Trouble," lesbian dance night. Small cover at weekends.

Oasis, 11th and Folsom St. (☎621-8119). One of the few places in town where you have to wait to get in, but usually worth it to dance on the open-air plexiglass-covered swimming pool to new wave, rock, and house music. Tues–Sun; $7 cover at weekends.

The Palladium, 1031 Kearny St. (☎434-1308). Cavernous nightclub with three dance floors, flashing lights, and young, sweaty, disco-serious crowd. Cover $7. Open Thurs–Sun until 6am.

Pierce Street Annex, 3138 Fillmore St. (☎567-1400). The archetypal singles hang-out, known as the "Bermuda Triangle" for its ability to make people disappear overnight with one another. No cover.

Rock & Bowl, 1855 Haight St. (☎752-2366). Try this one for a change—a bowling alley that turns up the music at weekends so that you can dance while you bowl. Definitely good fun if there's a group of you.

Rockin Robin's, 1840 Haight St. (☎221-1960). A real mixture, including rock'n'roll, Motown on Tuesday, and Karaoke (get up on the mike and howl to your favorite tunes) on Thursday. No cover.

Townsend, 177 Townsend St. (☎974-6020). A must for house fans, this place really cranks up the bass and keeps it blaring. Thurs–Sat. Cover $5.

The Underground Club, 201 9th St. (☎552-3466). About the only place in town that you might have trouble getting into, priding itself on its exclusivity, and, as a consequence, with a long line of well-dressed clubbers waiting outside. Thurs–Sun, open till 8am Fri and Sat. $10 cover.

Gay and Lesbian Clubs

Many **gay and lesbian clubs** are bars that host various club nights at least once a week. Pleasingly unpretentious, the city's gay clubs rank among the city's best, and although a number are purely male affairs, with women-only discos few and far between, the majority welcome gay people of both sexes. Bear in mind that the distinction between gay bars and **gay clubs** is a fine one, and many gay and lesbian bars convert to discos in the evening. We've listed the more obviously club-like places below, but it's a good idea to also turn to Chapter Seven, *Drinking and Eating*, for details of other likely spots for revelry.

Mixed

The Box at the *Kennel Club*, 628 Divisadero St. (☎931-9858). Very popular dance club that plays a good selection of funk and house music. Currently the hot favorite for dance-serious men and women. Thurs and Sat.

Crystal Pistol, 842 Valencia St. (☎695-7887). One of the newer clubs and as such enjoying a very healthy patronage. Good dancing, and a young, well-turned-out set make for a good evening.

El Rio, 3158 Mission St. (☎282-3325). Mixed crowds gather for dancing to live samba on Sundays in the open-air courtyard, funk on Fridays, and cabaret Wednesdays. Not to be missed. $4.

Mainly for Men

Esta Noche, 3079 16th St. (☎861-5757). Disco-mania Latin-style. Young men and their pursuers dance to a high-energy disco beat reminiscent of the 1970s.

I-Beam, 1748 Haight St. (☎668-6006). A rock venue most weeknights that on Sunday afternoon transforms itself for gay tea-dancing.

Powerhouse, 1347 Folsom St. (☎861-1790). Full of leather boys. Not for the faint-hearted.

Rawhide, 280 7th St. (☎621-1197). Country and western dance hall. Hysterical good fun if you're into square dancing and the like.

The Stud, 399 9th St. (☎863-6623). An oldie but a goodie. Has been popular for years for its energetic, uninhibited dancing and good times. No cover charge.

Mainly for Women

Club Q at the *Kennel Club*, 628 Divisadero St. (☎931-9858). Friday disco patronized by a young, ethnically mixed group of women. Always packed.

Female Trouble at *Nightbreak*, 1821 Haight St. (☎221-9008). Wednesday is lesbian dance night at *Nightbreak* and draws a pretty mixed female crowd. Not much dancing or posing and as such better for drinking and chatting than serious funking.

Rapture, 1484 Market St. (no phone). Saturday night dance club for women. Tends to draw the younger, well-dressed lipstick-lesbian crowd.

Skirts, 300 de Haro St. (no phone). Sunday dance club. Informal, friendly, good fun.

Classical Music, Opera, and Dance

Though the San Francisco arts scene has a reputation for provincialism, it is the only city on the West Coast to boast its own professional **symphony**, **ballet**, and **opera** companies, each of which has thriving upper-crust social support wining and dining its way through fundraisers and the like. These companies rely entirely on private contributions for their survival, and cheap tickets are rare, if not non-existent.

Louise M. Davies Symphony Hall, 201 Van Ness Ave. (☎431-5400). Permanent home of the San Francisco Symphony, which offers a year-round season of classical music and sometimes performances by other, often offbeat, musical and touring groups. Established in 1909 as a small musical group, the symphony rose to international prominence in the 1950s when it started touring and recording. They've scooped up several awards on the international circuit, though they're by no means world beaters, enjoying instead non-stop recording work which has included sixteen symphonies and the soundtracks for *Amadeus* and *The Unbearable Lightness of Being*. Their reputation was also boosted when, under the direction of Herbert Blomstedt, they debuted at the Salzburg Festival in 1990. Prices obviously depend on the performance but are marginally cheaper than either the opera or ballet, with the least expensive seats going for around $20—and availability is nowhere near as much of a headache.

War Memorial Opera House, 401 Van Ness Ave. (ticket and schedule information: ☎864-3330). The very opulent venue for both the San Francisco Opera Association and the ballet, designed by architect Arthur Brown Jr.— creator of City Hall and Coit Tower—means that a night at the opera in San Francisco is no small-time affair. The Opera Assocation has been performing here since the building opened in 1932 and is currently in its 68th season. By far the strongest of San Francisco's cultural trio, the company has won critical acclaim for its performances of Beethoven's *Fidelio* and Puccini's *La Boheme* and *Madame Butterfly*, as well as obscure Russian productions that other companies prefer not to tackle. The Association carries considerable international weight and pulls in big names like Placido Domingo and Kiri Te Kanawa on a regular basis. Its main season runs from the end of September for thirteen weeks, and its opening night is said to be one of the principal social events on the West Coast. Sporadically, it has a summer season during June and July, and in general these tickets are easier to come by. Performances tend to be booked up far in advance, so unless you plan to spend more than a week or two in the city, your chances of getting tickets may be slim. If you do succeed, expect to pay in the region of $40—for which you do at least get supertitles with the foreign operas.

The San Francisco Ballet (☎893-2277). The city's ballet company is the oldest and third largest in the US, and puts on an ambitious six-month— January to June—program of both classical and contemporary dance annually. Founded in 1933, the ballet was the first American company to stage full-length productions of *Swan Lake* and *Nutcracker*. They've won Emmys, broadcast, toured, and generally earned themselves a reputation for ambition— overreach drove them toward bankruptcy in the 1970s, and they seemed to be sliding until 1985, when the Icelandic Helgi Tomasson, "premier danseur" of the New York City Ballet, stepped in as artistic director. Since his appointment, the company can seem to do no wrong, and some proud San Franciscans are already tagging it "America's premier ballet company." Critical opinion hasn't quite concurred with this statement yet, but investing in tickets would not be an extravagant waste. The demand for tickets doesn't quite match the opera, but a decent seat will cost you around $30.

During the summer months, look out for the **free concerts in Stern Grove** (at 19th Ave. and Sloat Blvd.) where the symphony, opera, and ballet give open-air performances for ten successive Sundays (starting in June).

Theater

The majority of San Francisco's **theaters** congregate downtown around the Theater District. Most aren't especially affordable (although there is a handful of more inventive fringe places in other parts of town, notably SoMa), but tickets are reasonably affordable—up to $20 a seat—and there's usually good availability. You can either buy tickets direct from the box offices of the theaters or, more commonly, book through one of the ticket agencies (see above) using a credit card. Failing that, try the *STBS* ticket booth on the Stockton Street side of Union Square (Mon–Sat 11am–6pm; ☎433-7717), which regularly has last-minute tickets for as much as 30 percent off the price.

Downtown

American Contemporary Theater, *Geary Theater*, 450 Geary St. (☎775-5811). The Bay Area's leading resident theater group, that, despite suffering the wholesale destruction of their theater in the 1989 earthquake, has bounced back and continues to stage the city's most impressive plays from temporary bases around the city. Call the above number for location details of current performances.

Cable Car Theater, 430 Mason St. (☎771-6900). For the last eight years, this has been the home of *Greater Tuna*, a scathing two-man portrait of small-town Texan bigotry that has yet to lose its ability to draw the crowds. Small, comfortable theater and extremely funny production.

Curran Theater, 445 Geary St. (☎243-9001). Tackles bigger productions and musicals of the Andrew Lloyd-Webber genre.

Golden Gate Theater, 1 Taylor St. (☎775-8800). Originally built in the 1920s and recently restored to its former splendor, the *Golden Gate* is San Francisco's most elegant theater, with marble flooring, rococo ceilings, and gilt trimmings. A pity the program doesn't live up to the surroundings—generally a mainstream diet of Broadway musicals on their latest re-run, although they occasionally pull a big name out of the bag for a one-man Vegas-type show.

Lorraine Hansberry Theater, 25 Taylor St. (☎474-8842). Radical young group of black performers whose work covers traditional theater as well as more contemporary political pieces and jazz/blues musical reviews. Impressive.

Mason Street Theater, 340 Mason St. (☎861-6895). Cabaret performances and short, fast-paced plays.

The Orpheum, 1192 Market St. (☎243-9001). Showtime, song and dance performances, and "light" cabaret-style theater.

Stage Door Theater, 420 Mason St. (☎433-9500). Attractive, medium-sized turn-of-the-century theater with a reputation for serious productions.

Theater On The Square, 450 Post St. (☎771-6900). Converted Gothic theater with drama, musicals, comedy and mainstream theater pieces. San Francisco's main fringe venue.

Elsewhere

Beach Blanket Babylon Series, *Club Fugazi Cabaret*, 678 Green St. (☎421-4222). One of the few musts for theater-goers in the city, in its formality it takes itself very seriously, but the shows themselves are zany and fast-paced cabarets of jazz singers, dance routines, and comedy very slickly put together. Currently in its sixteenth year.

Climate Theater, 252 9th St. (☎626-9196). Small, reputable SoMa theater, specializing in fringe/alternative productions. Cheaper and probably a lot more stimulating than some of the downtown efforts.

Cowell Theater, Pier 2, Fort Mason (☎441-8822). Fort Mason's newest theatrical addition, the *Cowell* is a state-of-the-art venue for innovative productions that are critically well-received but still have a way to go before they can hold a candle to their neighbor, the *Magic Theater*.

Intersection for the Arts, 446 Valencia St. (☎626-3311). Well-meaning but at times hopelessly amateurish community-based group that tackles interesting productions in inadequate facilities. Dance, comedy, and straight theater, alternating with art exhibitions and lectures.

The Lab, 1805 Divisadero (☎346-4063). Mixed media center with gallery and changing exhibitions downstairs, a small theater for drama and dance upstairs. Usually something locally based and interesting going on.

The Magic Theater, Fort Mason Center, Building D (☎441-8822). Busiest and largest company after the *ACT*—and probably the most exciting, the *Magic Theater* specializes in the works of contemporary American playwrights and emerging new talent: Sam Shepard traditionally premieres his work here. It has been described as the "most adventuresome company in the West."

Mission Cultural Center, 2868 Mission St. (☎821-1155). An organization dedicated to preserving and developing Latin culture, staging small but worthy productions using the wealth of talented but underrated performers in San Francisco's Latin community.

Phoenix Theater, 301 8th St. (☎621-4423). Small SoMa playhouse that specializes in readings, one-act plays, and sketches.

Theater Artaud, 450 Florida St. (☎621-7797). Very modern theater in a converted warehouse that tackles the obscure and abstract: visiting performers, both dance and theatrical, always something interesting.

Theater Rhinoceros, 2926 16th St. (☎861-5079). San Francisco's only uniquely gay theater group, this company, not surprisingly, tackles productions that confront gay issues, as well as lighter, humorous productions.

Comedy

Comedians have always found a welcoming audience in San Francisco, but in recent years the alternative **comedy and cabaret scene** has experienced a rebirth. Some new, excellent venues have opened up, and while many may be smartening up beyond the tastes of some, they will undoubtedly be able to draw bigger names to the city. It's unlikely that many of the comedians will be familiar: as with any cabaret venue you take your chances, and what could be a good club one week might have dubious acts the next, and vice versa. You should expect to pay roughly the same kind of cover in most of the clubs ($7–10), although be aware that most places impose a two-drink minimum. There are usually two shows per night, the first kicking off around 8pm and a late show starting at around 11pm. For bargains, check the press for "Open Mike" nights when unknowns and members of the audience get up and have a go; there's rarely a cover charge for these evenings, and, even if the acts are diabolical, they can be a lot of fun.

Comedy Clubs

Cobbs Comedy Club, The Cannery, 2801 Leavenworth (☎563-5157). Small venue, popular on the cabaret circuit, where new performers often get the chance of their first live appearance.

El Rio, 3158 Mission St. (☎282-3325). Wednesday night comedy shows, with a choice of performers that is often a lot riskier than in the established clubs. Very alternative and, more often than not, extremely funny.

Finocchio's, 506 Broadway (☎982-9388). A San Francisco institution, *Finocchio's* presents a small cast of female impersonators who run through textbook routines, heavy on the sauciness. At one time it was considered outrageous; these days it's more than a little tame, good for cheap laughs and expensive drinks.

509 Cultural Center, 509 Ellis St. (☎346-1308). Seedy, but worth visiting on Tuesdays for "Open Mike Night."

Holy City Zoo, 408 Clement St. (☎386 4242). Supreme champion of the alternative circuit, *Holy City* plays host to the best of the genre in a small, funky club. Make an effort to go.

The Improv, 401 Mason St. (☎441-7787). The chain store of the comedy world, this is the latest of a string of *Improv*s around the country, which get the acts after the other clubs have finished with them. Nonetheless, it does seem to draw some good established talent and also has an eye for up-and-coming acts. Monday is the cheapest and best night to go, when guest company "Theater of the Deranged" presents a completely improvized night's entertainment.

Morty's, 1024 Kearny St. (☎986-6678). Old North Beach club that evokes the Lenny Bruce era of comedy. None of the acts is quite as good as he was, but the club itself has a genuine feel that makes it worth the trip.

The Punch Line, 444 Battery St. (☎397-7553). Front-runner of the city's "polished" cabaret venues, this place has an intimate, smoky feel that's ideal for downing expensive cocktails and laughing your head off. The club usually hosts the bigger names in the world of stand-up and is always packed.

Film

After eating, watching **films** is the favorite San Francisco pastime. For one thing it's cheap (rarely more than $6, sometimes as little as $2), and secondly there's a staggering assortment of current-release and repertory film houses, with programs ranging from the latest general-release films to Hollywood classics, iconoclastic Sixties pieces, and a selection of foreign and art films that's usually as good as (if not better than) most other US centers. Moviegoing in San Francisco is a pleasure: there are rarely lines, and the movie theaters are often beautiful Spanish-revival and Art-Deco buildings that are in themselves a delight to behold. **The San Francisco Film Festival** is held at various movie theaters around the city, but usually centering on the Kabuki eight-screen theater (see below), in the first couple of weeks in May. It specializes in political and short films you wouldn't normally see. Tickets sell extremely fast, and you'll need to book about four days in advance for all but the most obscure movies. Just as popular is the **Gay and Lesbian Film Festival**, which is held in June at the Castro Theater. If you know you're going to be in town for either and are interested, you should try and call ahead for programs by contacting the theaters. Remember also that Berkeley has some good movie theaters, the best of which is the **Pacific Film Archive**, which has regular offbeat programs of foreign and art films; see Chapter Nine, *The East Bay*, for more details.

The Alhambra, Polk St. and Union (☎775-2137). With its gorgeous, plush, Moorish-looking interior, this movie theater is one of the city's grandest, showing a selection of current releases and re-runs.

The Castro Theater, 429 Castro St. (☎621-6120). Perhaps San Francisco's most beautiful movie house, offering a steady stream of re-runs, Hollywood classics, and (best of all) a Wurlitzer organ played between films by a man who rises up from the stage. A fond favorite with the gay community, it hosts the annual Gay and Lesbian Film Festival each June.

Cinema 21, 2141 Chestnut St. (☎921-6720). Comfy theater for mainly current-release films.

The Clay, 2261 Fillmore St. (☎346-1123). Small, elegant art house theater.

The Four Star Theater, 2200 Clement St. (☎752-2650). Tiny little rep movie house showing a high-brow selection of current-release (but mainly arty) films.

Kabuki Cinemas, Post and Fillmore St. (☎931-9800). Attractive, modern building in the Japan Center complex, housing eight movie theaters showing mainly current-release movies.

The Lumiere, 1572 California St. (☎885-3200). Another opulent Spanish-revival art house, a bit run down but often showing an interesting program of obscure art films as well as a select choice of current-release films.

Opera Plaza, 601 Van Ness Ave. (☎771-0102). Modern cinema complex with four theaters showing the better pick of current-release films.

The Red Vic, 1727 Haight St. (☎282-0318). Friendly collective, formerly housed in a room full of ancient couches where you could put your feet up, and now moved to more upmarket premises up the street. Same idea, though, showing popular re-runs and cult films.

The Regency, Sutter St. and Van Ness Ave. (☎776-8054). Ultra-modern theater that shows the pick of the new releases and cult re-runs.

The Roxie, 317 16th St. (☎863-1087). San Francisco's chic-est independent rep house in the heart of the Mission, showing a steady diet of punk, new wave, and political movies.

The Royal, 1529 Polk St. (☎474-0353). A once elegant, now decaying old theater that looks about a week away from demolition. Varied, innovative programming, though.

The Strand, 1127 Market St. (☎621-2227). Dark, appropriately scruffy surroundings for cult films and B-movies.

The York, 2789 24th St. (☎282-0316). Large, comfortable collective movie house specializing in *film noir* seasons.

PART THREE

THE
BAY AREA

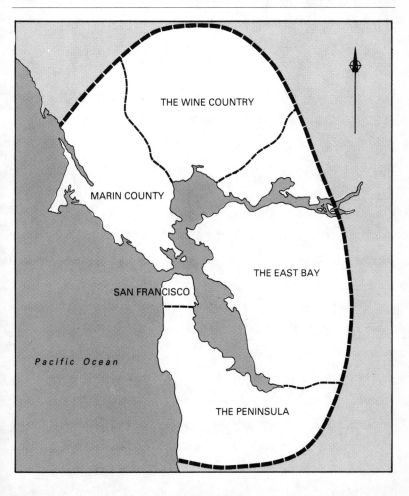

THE WINE COUNTRY

MARIN COUNTY

THE EAST BAY

SAN FRANCISCO

Pacific Ocean

THE PENINSULA

CHAPTER NINE

THE EAST BAY

The largest and most-traveled bridge in the US, the **Bay Bridge** heads east from San Francisco, part graceful suspension bridge and part heavy-duty steel truss. Completed just a year after the more famous (and better-loved) Golden Gate, the Bay Bridge works a whole lot harder for a lot less respect: a hundred million vehicles cross the bridge each year, though you'd have to search hard to find a postcard of it. Indeed, its only claim to fame—apart from the fact that its partial collapse during the 1989 earthquake was captured on videotape and broadcast repeatedly on the TV news—is that **Treasure Island**, where the two halves of the bridge meet, hosted the 1939 World's Fair. During World War II the island became a Navy base, which it remains, but just inside the gates there's a small **museum** (daily 10am–3pm; free) with pictures of the Fair amid maritime memorabilia. The island also gives some great views of San Francisco and the Golden Gate.

The Bay Bridge—and the *BART* trains which run under the bay—finishes up in the heart of the East Bay in **Oakland**, a hard-working, blue-collar city that earns its livelihood from shipping and transport services, evidenced by the massive Port of Oakland whose huge cranes dominate the place, lit up at night like futuristic dinosaurs. Oakland spreads north along wooded foothills to **Berkeley**, an image-conscious college town that looks out across to the Golden Gate and collects a mixed bag of pin-striped Young Republicans, aging 1960s radicals, and Nobel prize-winning nuclear physicists in its many cafés and bookstores.

Berkeley and Oakland blend together so much as to be virtually the same city, and the hills above them are topped by a twenty-mile string of forested **regional parks**, providing much needed fresh air and quick relief from the concrete grids below. The rest of the East Bay is filled out by Contra Costa County, a huge area that contains some intriguing, historically important waterfront towns—well worth a detour if you're passing through on the way to the Wine Country region of the Napa and Sonoma valleys—as well as some of the Bay Area's most insular suburban sprawl. Curving around the **North Bay** from the heavy-industrial landscape of Richmond, and facing each other across the narrow **Carquinez Straits**, Benicia and Port Costa were both vitally important towns during California's first twenty years of existence, after the 1849 Gold Rush; they're now strikingly sited but little-visited ghost towns. In contrast, standing out from the soulless dormitory communities that fill up the often baking hot **inland valleys**, are the preserved homes of an unlikely pair of influential writers: the naturalist **John Muir**, who, when not out hiking around Yosemite and the High Sierra, lived most of his life near Martinez, and playwright **Eugene O'Neill**, who wrote many of his angst-ridden works at the foot of **Mount Diablo**, the Bay Area's most impressive peak.

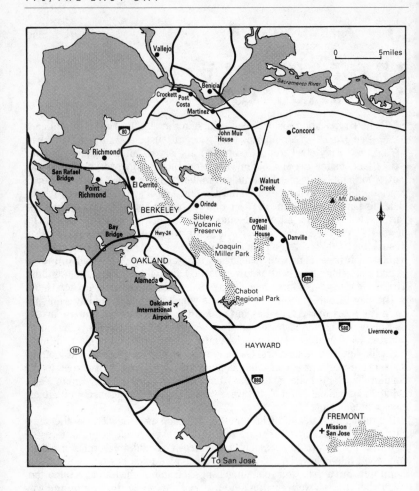

Arrival

You'll probably be staying in San Francisco when you visit the East Bay, though it's also possible, and sometimes cheaper, to fly direct to **Oakland Airport** (see *Basics* for details of airlines), particularly if you're coming from elsewhere in the US. It's an easy trip from the airport into town: take the *AirBART Shuttle* van (every 15min; $1) from outside the terminal direct to the Coliseum *BART* station, from where you can reach Oakland, Berkeley, or San Francisco. There are also a variety of privately operated shuttle buses, costing from $10. Coming **by bus**, Oakland's *Greyhound* station (☎834-3070) is in a dubious part of town, on the north side of Downtown Oakland on San Pablo Avenue at 21st Street. If you come to the Bay Area **by train**, the end of the line is the *Amtrak* station (☎982-8512) on 16th and Wood streets in the depths of West Oakland, though it's a better option to get off at Richmond and change there onto *BART*.

Getting Around

BART (from San Francisco ☎788-BART, from the East Bay ☎465-BART), the ultra-modern *Bay Area Rapid Transit* system, links San Francisco with the East Bay, via the underground transbay tube, Monday to Saturday 6am to midnight and 9am to midnight on Sundays. Three lines run from **Daly City** through San Francisco and on to Downtown Oakland, before diverging to service East Oakland out to **Fremont**, Berkeley, and north to **Richmond**, and east into Contra Costa County as far as **Concord**. Fares range from 80¢ to $3, and the cost of each ride is deducted from the total value of the ticket, purchased from machines on the station concourse. If you're relying on *BART* to get around a lot, you ought to buy a **high-value ticket** ($5 or $10) to avoid having to stand in line to buy a new ticket each time you ride.

From East Bay *BART* stations, pick up a free transfer saving you 25¢ off the 60¢ fares of **AC Transit** (☎839-2882), which provides a good bus service around the entire East Bay area, especially Oakland and Berkeley. *AC Transit* also runs buses on a number of routes to Oakland and Berkeley from the Transbay Terminal in San Francisco. These operate throughout the night and are the only way of getting across the bay by public transit once *BART* has shut down. Excellent free **maps** of both *BART* and the bus system are available from any station.

There are also two smaller-scale bus companies you might find useful on occasion. The *Contra Costa County Connection* (☎676-7500) runs buses to most of the inland areas, including the John Muir and Eugene O'Neill historic houses. The *Benicia Bay Connection* (☎707/642-1168) operates buses between the Pleasant Hill *BART* station and downtown Benicia.

One of the best ways to get around is **by bike**; there's a fine cycle route that follows Skyline Boulevard along the wooded crest of the hills between Berkeley and Lake Chabot. If you haven't got one, touring bikes are available for $15 a day (mountain bikes cost $25) from *Carl's Bikes* (☎835-8763), 2416 Telegraph Avenue in Oakland. For those interested in **walking tours**, the city of Oakland sponsors free "discovery tours" (☎273-3234) of various neighborhoods every Wednesday and Saturday at 10am.

Information

The **Oakland Convention and Visitors Bureau**, at 1000 Broadway near the 12th Street *BART* station downtown (Mon–Fri 8:30am–5pm; ☎839-9000), offers free maps and information on the whole of the East Bay; the **Berkeley Chamber of Commerce**, 1834 University Avenue (Mon–Fri 9am–4pm; ☎549-7000), is less helpful. If you're spending any time at all in the Berkeley area, pick up a copy of *Berkeley Inside/Out* by Don Pitcher (Heyday Books, $12.95), an indispensable and informative guide that'll tell you everything you ever wanted to know about the town and its inhabitants. For information on hiking or horse-riding in the many parks that top the Oakland and Berkeley hills, contact the **East Bay Regional Parks District**, 11500 Skyline Boulevard (☎531-9300). The widely available (and free) *East Bay Express*—in many ways the best newspaper in the Bay Area—has the most comprehensive listings of **what's on** in the vibrant East Bay music and arts scene. The troubled Oakland daily *Tribune* (25¢) is also worth a look for its coverage of local politics and sporting events.

Accommodation

Surprisingly, it's not a great deal cheaper to stay in the East Bay than in San Francisco, and anyway there's not much to choose from. The only hostel is solely for men, but the **motels** and **hotels**, at around $30 a night, are slightly more economical than their San Francisco equivalents. **Bed and breakfast** is a more pleasant option, particularly in Berkeley, one of the first places in the.US to offer this type of accommodation. There are two fine **campgrounds** in the East Bay, though both are hard to reach without a car.

Inexpensive

Berkeley YMCA, 2001 Allston Way at Milvia Street, a block from Berkeley *BART* (☎848-6800). Ideal bargain accommodation for male travelers; single rooms for $22 a night including use of the excellent gym and pool. Men only.

Golden Bear Motel, 1620 San Pablo Avenue, West Berkeley (☎525-6770). The most pleasant of the many motels in the "flatlands" of West Berkeley, though somewhat out of the way; $37 doubles.

Hotel Touraine, on the corner of 16th and Clay St., Downtown Oakland, near 19th Street *BART* (☎800/238-4916). Huge and only slightly seedy, it will always have a room; doubles from $20 a night, $85 a week.

University of California Housing Office, Ida Sproul Hall, 2400 Durant Avenue, Berkeley (☎642-5925). Rents dorm rooms in summer for $32 single, $42 double.

Moderate to Expensive

Best Western Boatel, 21 Jack London Square, Oakland (☎836-3800). A floating hotel moored on the best stretch of the Oakland waterfront, close to the *AC Transit* bus #51 route. Doubles from $80.

Claremont Hotel, 41 Tunnel Road at Ashby Avenue on the Oakland–Berkeley border (☎843-3000). At the top end of the scale, this grand Victorian palace has panoramic bay view rooms from $100 a night. All-inclusive "weekend breaks" are also available.

The French Hotel, 1538 Shattuck Avenue, North Berkeley (☎548-9930). Small and comfortable, in the heart of Berkeley's Gourmet Ghetto. Doubles from $60.

Holiday Inn Bay Bridge, 1800 Powell Street, Emeryville (☎658-9300). Not outrageously pricey considering the great views to be had from the upper floors. Doubles from $80.

Hotel Durant, 2600 Durant Avenue, Berkeley (☎845-8981). Fairly plain but well worn and comfortable, and very handy for the UC Berkeley campus. Doubles $75–85.

Hyatt Regency, 1001 Broadway, Downtown Oakland (☎893-1234). Flashy and modern like the others in the chain; some rooms with views of San Francisco. Doubles from $120 a night.

London Lodge, 700 Broadway, Downtown Oakland (☎451-6316). Spacious rooms, some of which have kitchens, make this a good option for families or groups. Doubles from $60.

Shattuck Hotel, 2086 Allston Way, Berkeley (☎845-7300). Very central and newly refurbished. Doubles from $85.

Victorian Hotel, 2520 Durant Avenue, Berkeley (☎540-0700). Well placed but fairly quiet. Doubles from $50.

Bed and Breakfast

Bed and Breakfast International, 1181-B Solano Avenue, Albany (☎525-4569). Not an inn but a clearing-house that books rooms in private homes throughout the East Bay. There's a two-night minimum, but rooms start at a bargain $35 including breakfast, and it's a great way to get to know some local people.

Gramma's, 2740 Telegraph Avenue, Berkeley (☎549-2145). Pleasant if slightly dull rooms—with fireplaces—in a pretty mock-Tudor mansion half a mile south of UC Berkeley. Doubles from $85.

East Brother Light Station, 117 Park Place in Point Richmond (☎233-2385). A handful of rooms in a converted lighthouse right on the bay. Doubles from $60 a night.

Camping

Chabot Regional Park (☎531-9043), off I-580 in East Oakland. Walk-in, tent-only places, with hot showers and lots of good hiking nearby; in summer, reservations are handled by *Mistix* (☎800/442-7275).

Mount Diablo State Park (☎837-2525). Twenty miles east of Oakland off I-680 in Contra Costa County. RV and tent places; likewise, book through *Mistix* in summer.

OAKLAND

A quick trip across the Bay Bridge or on *BART*, **OAKLAND** is a solidly working-class balance to upwardly mobile San Francisco: the workhorse of the Bay Area, the largest port on the West Coast, and the western terminal of the railroad network. It's not all hard slog, though: the climate is rated the best in the US, often sunny and mild when San Francisco is cold and dreary, and there's great hiking around the redwood- and eucalyptus-covered hills above the city—and views right over the entire Bay Area.

Oakland is better served by historical and literary associations than important sights, of which it has very few. **Gertrude Stein** and **Jack London** both grew up in the city, at about the same time though in entirely different circumstances—Stein a stockbroker's daughter, London an orphaned delinquent. The macho and adventurous London is far better remembered—most of the waterfront, where he used to steal oysters and lobsters, is now named in his memory—while Stein is all but ignored. Perhaps this is due to her book, *Everybody's Autobiography*, in which she wrote: "What was the use of me having come from Oakland, it was not natural for me to have come from there yes write about it if I like or anything if I like but not there, *there is no there there*"—a quote which has haunted Oakland ever since.

Jack London's mildly socialist leanings set a style for the city, and Oakland has been the breeding ground for some of America's most unabashedly revolutionary **political movements** in the years since. The 1960s saw the city's fifty-percent black population find a voice through the militant Black Panther movement, and in the 1970s Oakland was again on the nation's front pages, when the radical Symbionese Liberation Army demanded a ransom for kidnapped heiress Patty Hearst in the form of free food distribution to the city's poor.

Oakland is still very much its own city, one whose diversity and dynamism take time to get a feel for. A good place to start, if you're here in the spring, is at the annual Festival at the Lake, celebrated each June on the shores of Lake Merritt. Also, although civic pride has never fully recovered from the defection of the *Oakland Raiders* to the bright lights of Los Angeles a few years back, sports fans still rally behind the many-times American League and World Series champion *Oakland A's*.

Downtown Oakland

Coming by *BART* from San Francisco, get off at the 12th Street–Civic Center station and you're in **DOWNTOWN OAKLAND**, a compact district of spruced-up Victorian storefronts overlooked by modern hotels and office buildings that has been in the midst of an ambitious program of restoration and redevelopment for the last decade or so. It's a project that's been fraught with allegations of illegal dealings and incompetent planning, and so far it's anything but a success. To make way for the moat-like I-980 freeway—now the main route through Oakland since the collapse of the Cypress Freeway in the 1989 earthquake—entire blocks were cleared of houses, some of which were saved and moved to **Preservation Park** at 12th Street and Martin Luther King Jr. Way, where they now sit empty and slowly falling apart; and the late nineteenth-century commercial center along 9th Street west of Broadway, now tagged **Victorian Row**, underwent a major restoration some years ago, but the buildings have since been boarded up waiting for tenants. Certainly, the centerpiece of the redevelopment—and the one part thus far complete—is the brand-new Oakland Convention Center opposite the *BART* station, hardly an inviting-looking construction, dominated by the space-age international *Hyatt Regency* hotel with its trademark atrium lobby. By way of

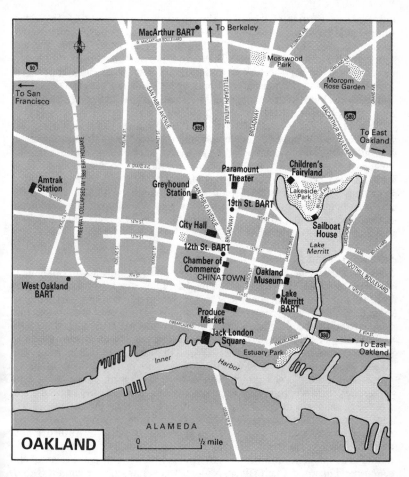

OAKLAND

0   ½ mile

contrast, stroll a block east of Broadway, between 7th and 9th streets, to Oakland's **Chinatown**, whose bakeries and restaurants are as lively and bustling—if not as picturesque—as those of its more famous cousin across the Bay.

Luckily not all of downtown Oakland has the look of a perennial building site. The city experienced its greatest period of growth in the early twentieth century, and many of the grand buildings of this era survive a few blocks north along Broadway, centered on the awkwardly imposing 1914 **City Hall** on 14th Street. Two blocks away, at 13th and Franklin streets, stands Oakland's most unmistakable landmark, the chateauesque lantern of the **Tribune Tower**, home of the *Oakland Tribune* newspaper.

Farther north, around the 19th Street *BART* station, are some of the Bay Area's finest early twentieth-century buildings, highlighted by the outstanding Art-Deco interior of the 1931 **Paramount Theater** at 2025 Broadway (tours Sat at 10am; $5; ☎465-4600). Nearby buildings are equally exuberant in their decoration, ranging from the wafer-thin Gothic "flatiron" office tower of the **Cathedral Building** at Broadway and Telegraph, to the Hindu temple-like facade of the 3500-seat **Fox Oakland** on Telegraph at 19th—the largest movie house west of Chicago when built in 1928—and, across the street, the 1931 **Floral Depot**, a group of small Moderne storefronts faced in black-and-blue terracotta tiles with shiny silver highlights.

West of Broadway, the area around the *Greyhound* bus station on San Pablo Avenue is a fairly dubious one. San Pablo used to be the main route in and out of Oakland before the freeways were built, but many of the roadside businesses are now derelict, especially around the industrial districts of **EMERYVILLE**, a mile north. Some of Emeryville's old warehouses have been converted into artists' lofts and studios, though any gentrification there might be is diffused by the scenes on the street, where prostitutes and drug-dealers hang out under the neon signs of the gambling halls and dingy bars that line the murky sidewalks.

Lake Merritt and the Oakland Museum

Five blocks east of Broadway, the eastern third of downtown Oakland is made up by **Lake Merritt**, a three-mile-circumference tidal lagoon that was bridged and dammed in the 1860s to become the centerpiece of Oakland's most desirable neighborhood. All that remains of the many fine houses that once circled the lake is the elegant **Camron-Stanford house**, on the south-west shore at 1418 Lakeside Drive, a graceful Italianate mansion whose sumptuous interior is open for visits (Wed 11am–4pm, Sun 1–5pm; free). The lake is also the nation's oldest **wildlife refuge**, and migrating flocks of ducks, geese, and herons break their journeys here. The north shore is lined by **Lakeside Park**, where you can rent canoes and row boats ($4 an hour), and a range of sailboats and catamarans ($4–10 an hour) from the Sailboat House (daily 10am–5pm in summer, weekends only rest of year; ☎444-3807)—provided you can convince the staff you know how to sail. There's also a mini-ature Mississippi riverboat ($1) that makes half-hour lake cruises on week-end afternoons, and kids will like the puppet shows and pony rides at the *Children's Fairyland* (daily 10am–5:30pm, weekends only in winter; $1:50), along Grand Avenue on the northwest edge of the park. Every year, on the first weekend in June, the park comes to life during the **Festival at the Lake**, when all of Oakland gets together to enjoy non-stop music and perfor-mances from local bands and entertainers.

Two blocks south of the lake, or a block up Oak Street from the Lake Merritt *BART* station, the **Oakland Museum** (Wed–Sat 10am–5pm, Sun noon–7pm; free, except for special exhibitions) is perhaps a more worthwhile stop, not only for the exhibits but also for the superb modern building in which it's housed, topped by a terraced rooftop sculpture garden that gives great views out over the water and the city. The museum covers many widely differing areas: there are displays on the **ecology** of California, including a simulated walk from the seaside through various natural habitats up to the 14,000-foot summits of the Sierra Nevada mountains; state **history**—with objects ranging from old mining equipment to the guitar that Berkeley-born Country Joe MacDonald played at the Woodstock festival in 1969; and a broad survey of works by California artists and craftspeople, some highlights of which are pieces of turn-of-the-century **arts and crafts furniture**, and excellent **photography** by Edward Muybridge, Dorothea Lange, and Imogen Cunningham. The museum also has a collector's gallery which hires and sells works by California artists.

ACCOMMODATION *Holiday Inn-Bay Bridge, Hotel Touraine, Hyatt Regency, London Lodge.*

CAFÉS *Coffee Mill.*

RESTAURANTS *Byul Mi House, Flint's Barbeque, Gulf Coast Oyster Bar & Specialty Co., Jade Villa, Ratto's.*

The Waterfront, Alameda, and West Oakland

Half a mile down from Downtown Oakland on *AC Transit* bus #51A, at the foot of Broadway on the **Waterfront**, is **Jack London Square**, Oakland's sole concession to the tourist trade. An anesthetic complex of boutiques and eateries along the harbor that was named after the self-taught writer who grew up pirating shellfish around here, but is about as distant from the spirit of the man as it's possible to get. Jack London's best story, *The Call of the Wild*, was written about his adventures in the Alaskan Yukon, where he carved his initials in a small **cabin** that has been reconstructed here; another survivor is *Heinhold's First and Last Chance Saloon*, a seedy bar where London spent much of his wayward youth.

If you're not a keen fan of London (if you are, you'd be better off visiting his Sonoma Valley ranch—see Chapter Twelve), there are still a couple of worthwhile things to do here. One is to take the **ferry boat tour** around the harbor (Thurs and some weekends in summer at 10am & noon; free; ☎839-2300 for reservations), looking at the docks and cranes of one of the world's largest containerized shipping facilities. Or walk a few short blocks inland to the **Produce Market**, along 3rd and 4th streets, where there are some very good places to eat and drink among the railroad tracks (see "Eating" below). This bustling warehouse district has fruit and vegetables by the forklift load and is at its most lively early in the morning, from about 5am.

Alameda

AC Transit bus #51A continues from Broadway under the inner harbor to **ALAMEDA**, a quiet and conservative island of middle-America dominated by a large naval air station, where massive nuclear-powered aircraft carriers sometimes dock. Alameda was severed from the mainland as part of a harbor improvement program in 1902, and the fine houses along the original shore-line on Clinton Street were part of the summer resort colony that flocked here to the *contra costa* or "opposite shore" from San Francisco, near the now-demolished **Neptune Beach** amusement park. The island has since been much enlarged by dredging and landfill, and 1960s apartment buildings now line the long, narrow shore of **Robert Crown Memorial Beach**, along the bay.

West Oakland

WEST OAKLAND—an industrial district of warehouses and railroad tracks, wartime housing projects, and decaying Victorian houses—is the nearest East Bay *BART* stop to San Francisco but is light years away from that city's prosperity. Except for the few artists and others who have ventured into the area—most noticeably at the *PRO-Arts Gallery* (☎763-4361), an artists' collective at 461 Ninth Street which organizes a popular "Open Studios" tour each June—the only time anyone pays any attention to it is when something dramatic happens. Two examples are when Black Panther **Huey Newton** was gunned down here in a drugs-related revenge attack, and when the double decker I-880 freeway which divided the neighborhood from the rest of the city collapsed on to itself in the **1989 earthquake**, killing dozens of commuters.

Local people are resisting government plans to rebuild the old concrete eyesore, and where the freeway used to run through is now the broad and potentially very attractive Cypress Boulevard. But otherwise West Oakland remains the Bay Area's poorest and most neglected neighborhood. If you visit, do so during the day, preferably by car, and don't take anything you'd want to lose.

For a long time the area was known as "the place where the trains stopped"—which it still is: take *Amtrak* to San Francisco and you'll arrive at the old **Southern Pacific Depot** at the end of 16th Street (from where buses run across the bay). The station is interesting for the interior alone, cut by huge blue-tinted arched windows and seemingly untouched for the last fifty years. However, since the structure was damaged in the 1989 quake it may soon be demolished; in the meantime you can peer in and watch the colonies of feral cats who've taken over the lobby. Trains still use the platforms, and a temporary waiting room and ticket office have been built next door.

Half a mile south, near the West Oakland *BART* station, Seventh Street was the heart of the Bay Area's most vibrant entertainment district from the end of Prohibition in 1933 until the early 1970s, when many of the bars and nightclubs were torn down in the name of urban renewal. Seventh Street runs west between the docks and storage yards of the Oakland Army Base and the Naval Supply Depot, ending up at **Portview Park**, one of the best places to watch the huge cargo ships that cruise by. The small park stands on the site of the old transbay ferry landing, used by as many as forty million passengers a year at its peak in the 1930s before the Bay Bridge was completed. Though the park has been closed since the earthquake, you can nip around the fence and join the people fishing from the small pier, or just enjoy the unmatched view of the San Francisco skyline framed by the Bay and Golden Gate bridges.

ACCOMMODATION *Best Western Boatel.*
BARS *Heinhold's First and Last Chance Saloon.*
RESTAURANTS *Acapulco, Alameda Taqueria, Oakland Grill, Time to Eat.*

East Oakland

The bulk of Oakland spreads along foothills and flatlands to the east of downtown, in neighborhoods obviously stratified along the main thoroughfares of Foothill and MacArthur boulevards. Gertrude Stein grew up here, though when she returned years later in search of her childhood home it had been torn down and replaced by a dozen **Craftsman-style bungalows**—the simple 1920s wooden houses that cover most of **EAST OAKLAND**, each fronted by a patch of lawn and divided from its neighbor by a narrow concrete driveway.

A quick way out from the gridded streets and sidewalks of the city is to take *AC Transit* bus #15A from downtown east up into the hills to **Joaquin Miller Park**, the most easily accessible of Oakland's hilltop parks. The park stands on the former grounds of the home of the "Poet of the Sierras," Joaquin Miller, who made his name playing the eccentric frontier American in the literary salons of 1870s London. His poems weren't exactly acclaimed (his greatest poetic achievement was rhyming "teeth" with "Goethe"), although his prose account, *Life Amongst the Modocs*, documenting time spent with the Modoc Indians near Mount Shasta, does stand the test of time. It was more for his outrageous behavior that he became famous, wearing funny clothes and biting debutantes on the ankle. His house, a small white cabin called **The Abbey**, still survives, as do monuments he built to his friends Robert and Elizabeth Browning, and the thousands of trees he planted.

Perched in the hills at the foot of the park, the pointed towers of the **Mormon Temple** look like missile-launchers designed by the Wizard of Oz—unmissable by day or floodlit night. During the holiday season, speakers hidden in the landscaping make it seem as if the plants are singing Christmas carols. Though you can't go inside (unless you're a confirmed Mormon), there are great views out over the entire Bay Area and a small **museum** (daily 9am–9pm; free) that explains the tenets of the faith.

Two miles east along Hwy-13 sits the attractive campus of **Mills College**. Founded in 1852 as a women-only seminary and still decidedly female after a much-publicized recent struggle against plans to make it co-ed, Mills is renowned for its music school, considered one of the best and most innovative in the US, and worth a visit for its **museum** (Sept–June Tues–Sun 10am–4pm; free), which has a fine collection of Chinese, Japanese, and pre-Columbian ceramics. A broad stream meanders through the lushly landscaped grounds, and many of the buildings, notably the central campanile, were designed in solid California Mission style by Julia Morgan, architect of Hearst Castle as well as some 500 Bay Area structures. Farther east, **Oakland Zoo** in Knowland Park is not worth the $2 entry fee, plus $2 to park, but you can hire **horses** (☎569-4428) from the stables at 14600 Skyline Boulevard and ride around **Lake Chabot** in the forested hills above.

Along the bay south to San Jose stretch some twenty miles of tract house suburbs, and the only vaguely interesting area is around the end of the *BART* line in **FREMONT**, where the short-lived Essanay movie studios were based. Essanay, the first studios on the West Coast, made over 700 films in three years, including Charlie Chaplin's *The Tramp* in 1914. Not much remains from these pre-Hollywood days, however, and the only real sight is the **Mission San Jose de Guadalupe** on Mission Boulevard south of the I-680 freeway (daily 10am–5pm; donations), which in the best traditions of Hollywood set design was completely rebuilt in Mission style only a few years ago.

BARS *Rickey's Sports Lounge.*
RESTAURANTS *Alvita's, Flint's, Taqueria Morelia.*

North Oakland and Rockridge

The pretty hillside homes around Broadway in **NORTH OAKLAND** look out across the bay over the flatlands that were the proving grounds of Black Panthers Bobby Seale and Huey Newton, who first studied politics at the old Merritt College campus on Martin Luther King Jr. Way. The area has very few things to see but contains some of the best **nightclubs** in the entire Bay Area (see "Nightlife" below).

The **Oakland Rose Garden**, on Oakland Avenue three blocks north of MacArthur Boulevard (daily April–Oct; free), repays a look if you do come during the day; in between runs one of Oakland's most neighborly streets, **Piedmont Avenue**, lined by a number of small bookstores and cafés. At the north end of Piedmont Avenue, the **Mountain View Cemetery** was laid out in 1863 by Frederick Law Olmsted (designer of New York's Central Park) and holds the elaborate dynastic tombs of San Francisco's most powerful families—the Crockers, the Bechtels, and the Ghirardellis. No one minds if you jog or ride a bike around the well-tended grounds.

Pleasant Valley Road leads back to Broadway, where you can catch *AC Transit* bus #76 and climb the hills up Broadway Terrace to **Lake Temescal** for a swim in summer, or continue on up to the forested ridge at the **Robert Sibley Regional Preserve**, which includes the 1761-foot volcanic cone of Round Top Peak and panoramas of the entire Bay Area. Skyline Boulevard runs through the park and is popular with cyclists, who ride the twelve miles south to Lake Chabot or follow Grizzley Peak Boulevard five miles north to Tilden Park through the Berkeley Hills.

Most of the Broadway traffic, including the *AC Transit* #51 bus, cuts off onto **College Avenue** through Oakland's most upscale district, **ROCKRIDGE**, at the foot of wooded hills and with views out over the bay. Spreading for a half mile on either side of the Rockridge *BART* station, the quirky stores and eateries here are, despite their undeniably yuppie overtones, some of the best around and make for a pleasant afternoon's wander. Both in geography and in atmosphere it's as near as Oakland gets to the café society of neighboring Berkeley.

> **ACCOMMODATION** *Claremont Resort Hotel.*
> **BARS** *Bertola's, The Hut, The Kingfish, The White Horse.*
> **CAFÉS** *Cafe Oliveto, Edible Complex, Fenton's Creamery, Mama Bear's, Mama's Royal Cafe.*
> **RESTAURANTS** *Bay Wolf Cafe, Bertola's, Flint's, Rockridge Cafe, Zachary's Pizza.*

BERKELEY

This Berkeley was like no somnolent Siwash out of her own past at all, but more akin to those Far Eastern or Latin American universities you read about, those autonomous culture media where the most beloved of folklores may be brought into doubt, cataclysmic of dissents voiced, suicidal of commitments chosen—the sort that bring governments down.

Thomas Pynchon, *The Crying of Lot 49*

More than any other American town, **BERKELEY** conjures up an image of dissent. During the Sixties and early Seventies, when university campuses were protesting against the Vietnam War, it was the students of the University of California, Berkeley, that led the charge, gaining a name for themselves as the vanguard of what was increasingly seen as a challenge to the very authority of the state. Full-scale battles were fought almost daily here for a time, on the campus and on the streets of the surrounding town, and there were times when Berkeley looked almost on the brink of revolution itself. If you've seen the Hendrix film *Jimi Plays Berkeley* you'll have some idea of the violent skirmishes that took place when students (and others) throwing stones and gas bombs were met with tear-gas volleys and truncheons by National Guard troops under the nominal command of then Governor Ronald Reagan. It was, of course, most inspired by the mood of the time, and apart from several anti-apartheid rallies in the 1980s, official campus politics are nowadays decidedly conservative. But—despite an influx of non-rebellious students of the Eighties, a thriving bedrock of exclusive California Cuisine restaurants, and the high-tone types they attract—the progressive legacy lingers around the town and campus, noticeable in the many small bookstores and in the agenda of the local city council. Indeed, the "People's Republic" of Berkeley is one of the few small towns in the US with its own foreign policy, supporting the ANC and Sandinistas abroad and left-of-centre theater groups and community politics at home.

The **University of California** completely dominates Berkeley, and, as it's right in the center of town, it makes a logical starting point for a visit. Its many grand buildings and 30,000 students give off a definite energy that spills down the raucous stretch of **Telegraph Avenue**, which runs south from the campus, holding most of the studenty hang-outs, including a dozen or so lively cafés, as well as a number of Berkeley's many fine bookstores. Older students, and a good percentage of the faculty, congregate in the **Northside** area, popping down from their woodsy hillside homes to partake of goodies from the "Gourmet Ghetto," a stretch of Shattuck Avenue that

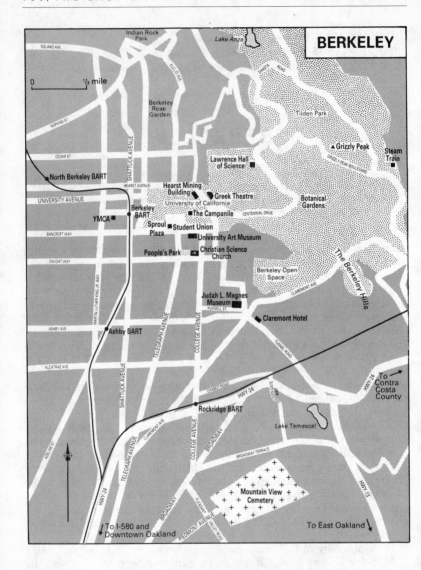

collects many of Berkeley's internationally renowned restaurants, delis, and bakeries. Of quite distinct character are the flatlands that spread through **West Berkeley** down to the bay, a poorer but increasingly gentrified district that mixes old Victorian houses with builder's yards and light industrial premises. Along the bay itself is the **Berkeley Marina**, where you can rent sailboards and sailboats or just watch the sun set behind the Golden Gate.

The University of California

Caught up in the frantic crush of students who pack the **University of California** campus during the semesters, it's nearly impossible to imagine the bucolic learning environment its high-minded founders intended. When the Reverend Henry Durant and other East Coast academics decided to set up shop here in the 1860s, the rolling foothills were still largely given over to dairy herds and wheatfields, the last remnants of the Peralta family's Spanish land-grant *rancho* which once stretched over most of the East Bay. Construction work on the two campus buildings—imaginatively named North Hall and South Hall—was still going on when the first 200 students, including 22 women, moved here from Oakland in 1873. Since then an increasing number of buildings have been squeezed into the half-mile-square main campus, and the state-funded university has become one of America's most highly respected, with so many Nobel laureates on the faculty that it's said you have to win one just to get a parking permit. Overcrowding aside, the beautifully landscaped campus, stepping down from the eucalyptus-covered Berkeley Hills toward the Golden Gate, is eminently strollable—and with maps posted everywhere, you'd have to try hard to get lost—though enthusiastic students will show you around on a free two-hour **tour** (☎642-5215), weekdays during the semesters at 1pm.

A number of footpaths climb the hill from the Berkeley *BART* station on Shattuck Avenue, but the best way to get a feel for the place is to follow Strawberry Creek from the top of Center Street across the southeast corner of the campus, emerging from the groves of redwood and eucalyptus trees at **Sproul Plaza**. It's the newest and largest public space on campus, enlivened by street musicians playing for quarters on the steps of the **Student Union** building and conga drummers pounding away in the echoing courtyard below. **Sather Gate**, which bridges Strawberry Creek at the north end of Sproul Plaza, marks the entrance to the older part of the campus. Up the hill, past the imposing facade of Wheeler Hall, the 1914 campus landmark **Campanile** is modeled after the one in the Piazza San Marco in Venice; you can take an elevator to the top for a great view of the campus and the entire Bay Area (daily 10am–4pm; 25¢). At the foot of the tower stands red-brick **South Hall**, the sole survivor of the original pair of campus buildings.

Inside the plain white building next door, the **Bancroft Library** (Mon–Sat 10am–5pm) displays odds and ends from its exhaustive accumulation of arti-facts and documents tracing the history of California, including a faked brass plaque supposedly left by Sir Francis Drake when he claimed all of the West Coast for Queen Elizabeth I. It also contains an internationally important collection of manuscripts and rare books, from Mark Twain to James Joyce—though you have to show some academic credentials if you want to see any of these. Around the corner and down the hill, just inside the arched main entrance to Doe Library, you'll find the **Morrison Reading Room**, a great place to sit for a while and read foreign magazines and newspapers, or just ease down into one of the many comfy overstuffed chairs and unwind with a book.

Also worth a look if you've got time to kill is the **Museum of Paleontology** in the nearby Earth Sciences Building, which details evolutionary concepts with hundreds of fossils, skeletons, and geological maps displayed along the corridors on the lower floors. From here it's a quick walk to the collection of cafés and restaurants lining Euclid Avenue and Hearst Avenue and the beginning of Berkeley's Northside (see below).

The Hearst family name appears with disturbing regularity around the Berkeley campus, though in most instances this is due not to the notorious William Randolph Hearst but to his altruistic mother, Phoebe Apperson Hearst. Besides inviting the entire senior class to her home every spring for a giant picnic, she sponsored the architectural competition that came up with the original campus plan and donated a good number of the campus buildings, including many that have since been destroyed. One of the finest that survives, the 1907 **Hearst Mining Building** (daily 8am–5pm) on the northeast edge of the campus, conceals a delicate metalwork lobby topped by three glass domes, above aging exhibits on geology and mining—which is how the Hearst family fortune was originally made, long before scion William Randolph took up publishing. Another Hearst legacy is the **Greek Theatre**, an open-air amphitheater cut into the Berkeley Hills east of the campus, which hosts a summer season of rock concerts.

Higher up in the hills, above the 100,000-seat Memorial Stadium, is the lushly landscaped **Botanical Garden** (daily 9am–5pm; free), good for defeating on-campus claustrophobia with its thirty acres of plants and cacti. Near the crest, with great views out over the bay, a full-size fiberglass sculpture of a sei whale stretches out in front of the space-age **Lawrence Hall of Science** (daily 10am–5pm; $3.50, children free), an excellent museum and learning center that features earthquake simulations, model dinosaurs, and a planetarium, plus a number of hands-on exhibits for kids in the Wizard's Lab. Both the gardens and the Lawrence Hall of Science are accessible on weekdays via the free *UC Berkeley Shuttle* bus from the campus or the Berkeley *BART* station.

In the southeast corner of the campus, the **Lowie Museum of Anthropology** in Kroeber Hall (Thurs–Tues 10am–4pm; $2, free Thurs) has a variety of changing exhibits and an intriguing display of artifacts made by Ishi, the last surviving Yahi Indian, who was found near Mount Lassen in Northern California in 1911. Anthropologist (and father of Ursula K. Le Guin) Alfred Kroeber brought Ishi to the museum (then located on the UC San Francisco campus), where he lived under the scrutiny of scientists and journalists—in effect, in a state of captivity—until his death from tuberculosis a few years later. Also in Kroeber Hall, the Worth Ryder Art Gallery in room 116 shows varying degrees of quality in the work of Berkeley's art students.

The brutally modern, angular concrete of the **University Art Museum** across Bancroft Way (Wed–Sun 11am–5pm; $3) is in stark contrast to the campus's older buildings. Its skylit, open-plan galleries hold works by Picasso, Cezanne, Rubens, and other notables, but the star of the show is the collection of Fifties American painter Hans Hofmann's energetic and colorful abstract paintings, on the top floor. The best thing about the museum are its cutting-edge, changing exhibitions: the main space hosts a range of major shows—like Robert Mapplethorpe's controversial photographs—while the Matrix

Gallery focuses on lesser known, generally local artists. Works on paper are shown downstairs outside the **Pacific Film Archive**, which shares the building, showing new films from around the world that you won't see elsewhere, as well as revivals from its extensive library (see "Nightlife" for details).

ACCOMMODATION *University of California Housing Office.*
CAFÉS *Ramona's.*
RESTAURANTS *The Faculty Club.*

Telegraph Avenue and South Berkeley

Downtown Berkeley—basically two department stores, a few banks, a post office, and the City Hall building—lies west of the university campus, around the Berkeley *BART* station on Shattuck Avenue, but the real activity centers on **Telegraph Avenue**, which runs south of the university from Sproul Plaza. This thoroughfare saw some of the worst of the Sixties riots and is still a frenetic bustle, especially the four short blocks closest to the university, which are packed to the gills with cafés and second-hand bookstores. Sidewalk vendors hawk hand-made jewelry and brilliantly colored t-shirts, while down-and-outs hustle for spare change and spout psychotic poetry.

BERKELEY'S BOOKSTORES

Berkeley's **bookstores** are as exhaustive as they are exhausting—not surprising for a college town. Perfect for browsing and taking your time, you won't be made to feel guilty or obliged to buy a book you've been poring over for ages.

Black Oak Books, 1491 Shattuck Ave, North Berkeley (☎486-0698). Some new books, some second-hand; also regular evening readings.

Cody's Books, 2454 Telegraph Ave. (☎845-7852). The flagship of Berkeley booksellers, with an excellent selection of fiction, poetry, and criticism.

Comics and Comix, 2461 Telegraph Ave. (☎845-4091). Great selection of comic books, both current and classic.

The Holme's Book Company, 274 14th St., Downtown Oakland (☎893-6860). Not in Berkeley, but the largest new and second-hand bookstore in the Bay Area. An excellent local history selection.

The Map Center, 2440 Bancroft Way (☎841-6277). Well-stocked map and guide store.

Moe's Books, 2476 Telegraph Ave. (☎849-20-87). The biggest (and most expensive) of Berkeley's bookshops, selling second-hand books at new book prices; there's an excellent art section on the top floor though.

Serendipity Books, 1201 University Ave, Berkeley (☎841-7455). The best second-hand bookstore in California—a must for anyone interested in twentieth-century American fiction and poetry.

Shakespeare and Company, 2499 Telegraph Ave. (☎841-8916). Crammed with quality second-hand books at reasonable prices. The best place to linger and scour the shelves for finds.

People's Park, now a seedy and overgrown plot of land a block up from Telegraph between Haste Street and Dwight Way, was another battleground in the late 1960s, when organized and spirited resistance to the university's plans to develop the site into dormitories brought out the troops, who shot dead an onlooker by mistake. To many, the fact that the park is still a community-controlled open space (and outdoor dosshouse for Berkeley's homeless legions) symbolizes a small victory in the battle against the Establishment, though it's not a pleasant or even very safe place to hang about, especially after dark. A mural along Haste Street remembers some of the reasons why the battles were fought, in the words of student leader Mario Savio: "There's a time when the operation of the machine becomes so odious, makes you so sick at heart, that you can't take part, you can't even tacitly take part. And you've got to put your bodies upon the gears and upon the wheels, upon the levers, upon all the apparatus, and you've got to make it stop"—ideals that can't help but be undermined by the state of the place these days.

The results of a more restrained but no less radical effort faces the vegetable gardens of People's Park across Bowditch Street. One of the finest buildings in the Bay Area, Bernard Maybeck's **Christian Science Church**, built in 1910, is an eclectic but thoroughly modern structure laid out in a simple Greek cross floorplan and spanned by a massive redwood truss with carved Gothic tracery and Byzantine painted decoration. The interior is only open on Sundays for worship and for tours afterward at 11am, but the outside is worth lingering over, its cascade of many gently pitched roofs and porticoes carrying the eye from one hand-crafted detail to another. It's a clever building in many ways: while the overall image is one of tradition and craftsmanship, Maybeck also succeeded in inconspicuously incorporating such unlikely materials as industrial metal windows, concrete walls, and asbestos tiles into the structure—thereby cutting down costs.

Though many of the largely residential neighborhoods elsewhere in South Berkeley ("Southside")—especially the Elmwood and Claremont districts around College Avenue—are worth a wander, there are a couple of specific sights worth searching out. One of these is the **Judah L. Magnes Museum**, a few blocks south of the campus at 2911 Russell Street (Sun–Fri 10am–4pm; free). Located in a rambling old mansion, it has California's largest repository of Judaica, and the exhibits detail the history of Jewish life from ancient times to the present day. The other Southside attraction is much harder to miss, towering as it does over the Berkeley–Oakland border. The half-timbered castle imagery of the **Claremont Hotel** gives a fairly clear hint as to what's inside—it's now one of the Bay Area's plushest resort hotels, with the three-story Tower Suite going for a cool $750 a night. Built in 1914, just in time for San Francisco's Panama-Pacific Exposition, the *Claremont* was designed to encourage day-trippers out across the bay in the hope that they'd be so taken with the area they'd want to live here. The ploy worked, and the hotel's owners (who incidentally also owned the streetcar system that brought people here, and all the surrounding land) made a packet.

ACCOMMODATION *Berkeley YMCA, Hotel Durant, Shattuck Hotel, Victorian Hotel.*
BARS *Larry Blake's, Spat's, Triple Rock Brewery.*
CAFÉS *Au Coquelet, Cafe Mediterranean, Cafe Milano, Cafe Strada.*
RESTAURANTS *Blondie's Pizza, Mario's La Fiesta, The Soup Kitchen, Steve's Barbeque, Top Dog.*

North Berkeley

NORTH BERKELEY, also called "Northside," is a subdued neighborhood of professors and postgraduate students, its steep, twisting streets climbing up the lushly overgrown hills north of the campus. At the foot of the hills, some of the Bay Area's finest restaurants and delicatessens—most famously *Chez Panisse*, started and run by Alice Waters, the acclaimed inventor of California Cuisine—have sprung up along Shattuck Avenue to form the so-called "Gourmet Ghetto" (see "Eating" below for details), a great place to pick up the makings of a tasty *al fresco* lunch.

Above the Gourmet Ghetto on Euclid Avenue (if you want to avoid the fairly steep walk, take bus #7 from Hearst Avenue, the northern edge of the campus), there's no more pleasant place for a picnic than the **Berkeley Rose Garden**, a terraced amphitheater filled with some three thousand varieties of roses and looking out across the bay to San Francisco. Built as part of a WPA job-creation scheme during the Depression, a wooden pergola rings the top, stepping down to a small spring. Opposite the Rose Garden, through a pedestrian tunnel, is **Codornices Park**, a broad expanse of manicured lawn edged by a baseball diamond, basketball courts, and lots of play equipment, best of which is a long concrete helter-skelter that's good fun to hurtle down, and not only for kids. A **footpath** leads up from the park along Codornices Creek, burbling with small waterfalls after a good rain.

Though the hills are steep, the homes here—built in an eclectic range of styles, designed to meld seamlessly into the wooded landscape—are some of the finest and most impressively sited in the Bay Area. All repay many times over the effort it takes to see them, if only for their marvelous setting. Many were constructed by members of the **Hillside Club**, a slightly bohemian group of turn-of-the-century Berkeleyans who also laid out many of the pedestrian paths that climb the hills. Perhaps the single most striking of these hillside homes, the **Rowell House**—a half-timbered chalet built in 1914 by architect John Hudson Thomas—stands alone at the top of the path up from Codornices Park, where it crosses Tamalpais Road. Many of the other houses nearby were designed and built by Bernard Maybeck, architect of the Palace of Fine Arts, Christian Science church, and other notable Bay Area buildings; the homes he built for himself and his family still stand around the junction of Buena Vista Way and La Loma Avenue, a hundred yards south.

Complementing the picturesque houses of the Berkeley Hills are a number of enticing **parks**, all with great views over the bay. The largest and highest of these spreads along the crest of the hills at the top of Grizzley Peak Boulevard (reached from the end of Euclid Avenue via *AC Transit* #7 bus), **Tilden Regional Park**, where you can swim in Lake Anza, ride the old carousel, or take a miniature **steam train** through the redwood trees. Nearer to town, at the north end of Shattuck Avenue and close by the shops and cafés along Solano Avenue, the gray basalt knob of **Indian Rock** stands out from the foot of the hills, challenging rock-climbers who hone their skills on its forty-foot vertical faces. There are steps around its back for those who just want to appreciate yet another good view, and, carved into similarly hard volcanic stone across the street, **mortar holes** which native Ohlone Indians used to grind acorns into flour. In between, and in stark contrast, stands the rusting hulk of a Cold War-era air-raid siren.

ACCOMMODATION *French Hotel.*
BARS *The Pub, Spat's, Triple Rock Brewery.*
CAFÉS *Cafe Espresso, Peet's Coffee.*
RESTAURANTS *Chez Panisse, Saul's Deli, Tambo Cafe, Zachary's Pizza.*

West Berkeley and the Waterfront

From downtown Berkeley and the UC campus, **University Avenue** runs downhill toward the bay, lined by increasingly shabby frontages of motels and massage parlors. The liveliest part of this **WEST BERKELEY** area is around the intersection of University Avenue and San Pablo Avenue—the pre-freeway main highway north—where a community of recent immigrants from India have set up shops and markets and restaurants that serve some of the best of the Bay Area's rare curries. Otherwise there's not much reason to stop.

The area between San Pablo Avenue and the bay is the oldest part of Berkeley, and a handful of hundred-year-old houses and **churches**—like the two white-spired Gothic Revival ones on Hearst Avenue—survive from the time when this district was a separate city, known as Ocean View. The neighborhood also holds remnants of Berkeley's industrial past, and many of the old warehouses and factory premises have been converted into living and working spaces for artists and craftspeople—most successfully the **Kawneer Building** at 2547 8th Street. Though few of these are officially open to visitors, there's no harm in showing an interest. Along similar lines are the cafés, workshops, and galleries built in the late 1970s along **Fourth Street** north of University Avenue, which have since become somewhat yuppified but are still good places to wander in search of handicrafts and household gadgets.

One of the few places you can visit here is the **Takara Sake Tasting Room**, just off 4th Street south of University Avenue at 708 Addison Street (daily noon–6pm; free). Owned and operated by one of Japan's largest producers, this plant is responsible for more than a third of all sake drunk in the US. You can sample any of the five varieties of California strain sake (brewed from California rice), best drunk warm and swallowed sharply. Though no tours are offered, they will show you a slide presentation of the art of sake brewing.

Berkeley Marina

The I-80 freeway, and the still-used railroad tracks that run alongside it, manage to pretty well cut off Berkeley from its waterfront. The best way to get there is to take *AC Transit* bus #51M, which runs regularly down University Avenue. Once a major hub for the transbay ferry services—to shorten journey times, a three-mile-long pier was constructed, much of which still stands stuck out into the bay—the **Berkeley Marina** is now one of the prime spots on the bay for leisure activities, especially windsurfing. If you're interested in having a go on the water, contact the *Cal Sailing Club* (see "Sports and Outdoor Activities" in *Basics* for details). The surrounding area, all of which is landfill largely owned by the Southern Pacific railroad, has long been the subject of heated battles between developers and the environmentalists who want to preserve it as a shoreline park. For the moment, the winds off the bay make it a good place to fly a kite, and there are some short hiking trails.

ACCOMMODATION *Golden Bear Motel.*
BARS *Albatross Pub, Brennan's.*
RESTAURANTS *Bette's Ocean View Diner, Casbah, Fourth Street Grill, Homemade Cafe, Juan's Place, Maharani, Picante, Spenger's.*

THE NORTH BAY AND INLAND VALLEYS

Compared to the urbanized bayfront cities of Oakland and Berkeley, the rest of the East Bay is sparsely populated, and places of interest are few and far between. The **North Bay** area is home to some of the Bay Area's heaviest industry—oil refineries and chemical plants dominate the landscape—but also holds a few, remarkably unchanged, waterfront towns that merit a side trip if you're passing by. Away from the bay, in the **inland valleys**, it's a whole other world, of dry rolling hills dominated by the towering peak of Mount Diablo. Dozens of tract house developments have made commuter suburbs out of what had been cattle ranches and farms, but so far the region has been able to absorb the numbers and still feels rural, despite having doubled in population in the past twenty years.

The North Bay

North of Berkeley there's not a whole lot to see or do. In ALBANY *Golden Gate Fields* has horse-racing from October to June, and EL CERRITO's main contribution to world culture was the band Creedence Clearwater Revival, who did most of their "Born on the Bayou" publicity photography in the wilds of Tilden Park in the hills above. **RICHMOND**, at the top of the bay, was once a boomtown, building ships during World War II at the Kaiser Shipyards, which employed 100,000 workers between 1940 and its closure in 1945. Now it's the proud home of the gigantic Standard Oil refinery, the center of which you drive through before crossing the **Richmond–San Rafael Bridge** ($1) to Marin County. About the only reason to stop in Richmond is that the city marks the north end of the *BART* line, and the adjacent *Amtrak* station is a better terminal for journeys to and from San Francisco than the end of the line in West Oakland.

Though not really worth a trip in itself, if you're heading from the East Bay to Marin County **POINT RICHMOND** repays a look. A cosy little town tucked away at the foot of the bridge between the refinery and the bay, its many Victorian houses are rapidly becoming commuter territory for upwardly mobile professionals from San Francisco. Through the narrow tunnel that cuts under the hill stands the most obvious sign of this potential gentrification: "Brickyard Landing," an East Bay docklands development, with modern bay-view condos, a private yacht harbor, and a token gesture to the area's industrial past—disused brick kilns, hulking next to the tennis courts on the front lawn. The rest of the waterfront is taken up by the broad and usually deserted strand of Keller Beach, which stretches for half a mile along the sometimes windy shoreline.

The Carquinez Straits

At the top of the bay some 25 miles north of Oakland, the land along the **Carquinez Straits** is a bit off the beaten track, but it's an area of some natural beauty and much historic interest. The still-small towns along the waterfront seem worlds away from the bustle of the rest of the Bay Area, but how long they'll be able to resist the pressure of the expanding commuter belt is anybody's guess. *AC Transit* bus #70 runs every hour from Richmond *BART* north to **CROCKETT** at the west end of the narrow straits—a tiny town cut into the steep hillsides above the water that seems entirely dependent upon the massive C&H Sugar factory at its foot, whose giant neon sign lights up the town and the adjacent Carquinez Bridge.

From Crockett the narrow **Carquinez Straits Scenic Drive**, an excellent cycling route, heads east along the Sacramento river. A turn two miles along drops down to **PORT COSTA**, a small town that was dependent upon ferry traffic across the straits to Benicia until the bridge was built at Crockett and the town lost its livelihood. It's still a nice enough place to watch the huge ships pass by on their way to and from the inland ports of Sacramento and Stockton. If you don't have a bike (or a car), you can enjoy the view from the window of the *Amtrak* train, which runs alongside the water twice a day from Oakland and Richmond, not stopping until MARTINEZ, at the eastern end of the straits, two miles north of the John Muir house (see below).

Benicia

On the north side of the Straits, and hard to get to without a car (see "Getting Around," above), **BENICIA** is the most substantial of the historic waterfront towns, but one that has definitely seen better days. Founded in 1847, it at first rivaled San Francisco as the major Bay Area port and was even the state capital for a time; but despite Benicia's better weather and fine deep-water harbor, San Francisco eventually became the main transport point for the fortunes of the Gold Rush, and the town very nearly faded away altogether. Examples of Benicia's efforts to become a major city stand poignantly around the very compact downtown area, most conspicuously the 1852 Greek Revival building that was used as the **first State Capitol** for just thirteen months. The building has been restored as a **museum** (daily except Tues and Wed 10am–5pm; $1), furnished in the legislative style of the time, with top hats on the tables and shining spitoons every few feet.

A walking tour map of Benicia's many intact Victorian houses and churches is available from the **tourist office** at 831 First Street (☎707/745-2120), including on its itinerary the steeply pitched roofs and gingerbread eaves of the **Frisbie-Walsh house** at 235 East L Street—a prefabricated Gothic Revival building that was shipped in pieces from Boston in 1849 (an identical house was put up by General Vallejo at his house in Sonoma; see Chapter Twelve). Across the City Hall park, the arched ceiling beams of **St Paul's Episcopal Church** look like an upturned ship's hull; it was built by shipwrights from the Pacific Mail Steamship Company, one of Benicia's many successful nineteenth-century shipyards. Half a dozen former brothels and saloons stand in various stages of decay and restoration along First Street down near the waterfront, from where the world's largest train ferries used to ply the waters between Benicia and Port Costa until 1930.

In recent years Benicia has attracted a number of artists and craftspeople, and you can watch glass-blowers and furniture-makers at work in the **Yuba Complex**, at 670 East H Street (Mon–Fri 10am–4pm). Judy Chicago is among others who work in converted studios and modern light industrial parks around the sprawling fortifications of the old **Benicia Arsenal** east of the downtown area, whose thickly walled sandstone buildings formed the main Army storage facility for weapons and ammunition from 1851 up through the Korean War. One of the oddest parts of the complex is the **Camel Barn** (Sat & Sun 1–4pm, and Fri in summer; free), now a **museum** of local history, but formerly used to house camels that the Army imported in 1856 to transport supplies across the deserts of the Southwestern US. The experiment failed, and the camels were kept here until they were sold off in 1864.

Vallejo and Marine World/Africa USA

Across the Carquinez Bridge from Crockett, the biggest and most boring of the North Bay towns—**VALLEJO**—was, like Benicia, an early capital of California but now lacks any sign of its historical importance. In contrast to most of the other Gold Rush-era towns that line the Straits, Vallejo has remained economically vital, largely because of the massive military presence here at the **Mare Island Naval Shipyard**, a sprawling, relentlessly gray complex that covers an area twice the size of Golden Gate Park. Its less than glamorous history—the yard builds and maintains supply ships and the like, not carriers or battleships—is recounted in a small **museum** in the old city hall building at 734 Mare Street (Tues–Fri 10am–4:30pm; $1), whose highlight is a working periscope that looks out across the bay. Though not a great thrill, it merits a quick stop; it's right on Hwy-29, the main route from the East Bay to the Wine Country, in the center of town.

The only reason you might conceivably come to Vallejo is for **Marine World/Africa USA** (daily 9:30am–6:30pm; $16.95; ☎707/643-6722), five miles north of Vallejo off I-80 at the Marine World Parkway (Hwy-37) exit. Operated by a non-profit educational group, it offers a standard range of performing sea lions, dolphins, and killer whales kept in approximations of their natural habitats, as well as water-ski stunt shows and a large aviary full of cockatoos, macaws, and other tropical birds. It can be a fun day out, especially for children, and it's not bad as these things go, but nonetheless you can't deny that the creatures pay a much bigger price to be here than the families of tourists who crowd it on summer weekends. The best way to get here from San Francisco is the *Red and White Fleet* catamaran **ferry boat** (☎546-2896) from Fisherman's Wharf, which takes an hour each way and adds another $12 on to the admission price.

ACCOMMODATION *East Brother Light Station.*
CAFÉS *Mabel's Cafe.*
RESTAURANTS *Prevot's,* in the *Union Hotel; The Harbor House.*

The Inland Valleys

Most of the **inland East Bay** area is made up of rolling hills covered by grasslands, slowly yielding to suburban housing developments and office complexes, as more and more businesses abandon the pricey real estate of San Francisco. Dominating the region is the great peak of **Mount Diablo**, twice as high as any other Bay Area summit and surrounded by acres of campgrounds and hiking trails. There are also two historic homes that serve as memorials to their literate and influential ex-residents, **John Muir** and **Eugene O'Neill**.

BART tunnels from Oakland through the Berkeley Hills to the leafy-green stockbroker settlement of ORINDA, continuing east through the increasingly hot and dry landscape to the end of the line at **CONCORD**, site of chemical plants and oil refineries and a controversial nuclear weapons depot. A few years ago, a peaceful, civilly disobedient blockade here ended in protestor Brian Willson losing his legs under the wheels of a slow-moving munitions train. The event raised public awareness—before it happened few people knew of the depot's existence—but otherwise it's still business as usual.

Martinez and John Muir's House

From Pleasant Hill *BART*, one stop before the end of the line, *Contra Costa County Connection* bus #116 leaves every half hour for **MARTINEZ**, the seat of county government, passing the preserved home of naturalist **John Muir** (daily 10am–4:30pm; $1), just off Hwy-4, two miles south of Martinez. Muir, an articulate, persuasive Scot whose writings and political activism were of vital importance in the preservation of America's wilderness as National Parks, spent much of his life exploring and writing about the majestic Sierra

Nevada mountains, particularly Yosemite. He was also one of the founders of the Sierra Club—a wilderness lobby and education organization still active today. Anyone who is familiar with the image of this thin, bearded man wandering the mountains with his knapsack, notebook, and packet of tea might be surprised to see his very conventional, upper-class Victorian home, now restored to its appearance when Muir died in 1914. The house was built by Muir's father-in-law and so doesn't reflect much about Muir himself, except for the parts he added to it, like the massive, rustic fireplace he had built in the East Parlor so he could have a "real mountain campfire." The bulk of Muir's personal belongings and artifacts are displayed in his **study**, on the upper floor, and in the adjacent room an exhibition documents the history of the Sierra Club and Muir's battles to protect America's wilderness.

Behind the bell-towered main house is a large, still productive **orchard** where Muir cultivated grapes, pears, and cherries to earn the money to finance his explorations (you can sample the fruits free of charge, pre-picked by staff gardeners). Beyond the orchard is the 1849 **Martinez Adobe**, homestead of the original Spanish land-grant settlers and now a small **museum** of Mexican colonial culture. It's worth a look if you're out here, if only for the contrast between Mexican and American cultures in early California; also, the building's two-foot-thick walls keep it refreshingly cool on a typically hot summer day.

Eugene O'Neill and Mount Diablo

At the foot of Mount Diablo, fifteen miles south, near DANVILLE, playwright **Eugene O'Neill** used the money he got for winning the Nobel Prize for Literature in 1936 to build a home and sanctuary for himself, which he named Tao House. It was here, before 1944 when he was struck down with Parkinson's Disease, that he wrote many of his best-known plays: *The Iceman Cometh*, *A Moon for the Misbegotten*, and *Long Day's Journey into Night*. Readings and performances of his works are sometimes given in the house, which is open to visitors, though you must reserve a place on one of the free guided **tours** (twice daily at 10am & 1:30pm; ☎839-0249). To get to the house, take the *Contra Costa County Connection* bus #121 from Walnut Creek *BART* station—it stops close by.

As for **Mount Diablo** itself, it rises up from the rolling ranchlands at its foot to a height of nearly 4000 feet, its summit and flanks preserved within **Mount Diablo State Park** ($3 parking; ☎837-2525). The main road through the park (there's no public transit, though the Sierra Club sometimes organizes day trips: see *Basics*) reaches within 100m of the top, so it's a popular place for an outing, and you're unlikely to be alone to enjoy the marvelous view. On a clear day you can see over 200 miles in every direction—from San Francisco to the High Sierra—making it the most extensive panorama in the world, after Mount Kilimanjaro. The 15,000 acres of parkland surrounding the peak offer many miles of hiking and some of the only **camping** in the East Bay.

There are two main entrances to the park, both well marked off I-680. The one from the southwest by way of Danville passes by the **ranger station**, where you can pick up the excellent trail map ($1) which lists a range of day-hikes. The other runs from the northwest by way of Walnut Creek, and the routes join together five miles from the summit. March and April, when the wild flowers are out, are the best times to be here, and since mornings are ideal for getting the clearest view, you should drive to the top first and then head back down to a trailhead for a hike, or to one of the many picnic spots for a leisurely lunch. In summer it can get desperately hot and dry, so much so that parts of the park are closed because of fire danger.

Livermore and Altamont

Fifteen miles southeast of Mount Diablo, on the main road out of the Bay Area (I-580), the rolling hills around **LIVERMORE** are covered with thousands of shining, spinning, hi-tech **windmills**, placed here by a private power company to take advantage of the nearly constant winds. It's one of the largest wind-farms in the world, and you'll probably have seen it used in a number of TV ads, as a space-age backdrop to hype flashy new cars or sexy perfumes. The federal government provides no funding for this non-polluting, renewable source of energy but spends billions of dollars every year designing and testing nuclear weapons and other sinister applications of modern technology at the nearby **Lawrence Livermore Laboratories**, where most of the research and development of the nuclear arsenal and the "Star Wars" Strategic Defense Initiative takes place. There is a small Visitors Center (Mon–Fri 9am–4:30pm, Sat & Sun noon–5pm; free), with hands-on exhibits showing off various scientific phenomena and devices, two miles south of I-580 on Greenville Road.

Up and over the hills to the east, where I-580 joins I-5 for the 400-mile route south through the Central Valley to Los Angeles, stand the remains of **Altamont Speedway**, site of a nightmarish Rolling Stones concert in December 1969. The free concert, which was captured in the film *Gimme Shelter*, was intended to be a sort of second Woodstock, staged in order to counter allegations that the Stones had ripped off their fans during a long US tour. In the event it was a complete fiasco: three people died, one of whom was kicked and stabbed to death by the Hell's Angels "security guards"—in full view of the cameras—after pointing a gun at Mick Jagger while he sang "Sympathy for the Devil." Needless to say there's no historical plaque marking the site.

EAST BAY LISTINGS

Life doesn't end the other side of the Bay Bridge, and even if you're staying and spending most of your time in San Francisco, there are many reasons for zipping across at night. As the birthplace of California Cuisine, the **restaurants** are as varied and no less excellent than those of San Francisco, and the **bar and café scene** compares well—indeed in parts of Berkeley and Oakland it's considerably more exciting. **Nightlife**, too, is dynamic: the East Bay has some of the best of the Bay Area's **live music** venues, not to mention a good sprinkling of offbeat **movie theaters** and fringe **theaters**.

Cafés and Bars

One of the best things about visiting the East Bay is the opportunity to enjoy its many **cafés**. Concentrated most densely around the UC Berkeley campus, they're on a par with the best of North Beach for bohemian atmosphere—heady with the smell of coffee, and from dawn to near midnight full of earnest characters wearing their intellects on their sleeves. If you're not after a caffeine fix, you can generally also get a glass of beer, wine, or fresh fruit juice, though for serious drinking you'll be better off in one of the many **bars**, particularly in rough-hewn Oakland. Grittier versions of what you'd find in San Francisco, they're mostly blue-collar, convivial, and almost always cheaper. Not surprisingly, Berkeley's bars are brimming with students, academics, and those who don't mind mixing with them.

Cafés

Au Coquelet, 2000 University Ave., next to the UC Theater, Berkeley. Late-night coffee house, open until 2am for the midnight movies crowd.

Cafe Mediterranean, 2475 Telegraph Ave., Berkeley. Berkeley's oldest café, straight out of the Beat Generation archives: beards and berets optional, books *de rigueur*.

Cafe Milano, 2522 Bancroft Way, near Telegraph Ave., Berkeley. Airy, artsy warehouse-like space just off the UC campus.

Cafe Strada, 2300 College Ave. at Bancroft Way, Berkeley. Upmarket outdoor café where art and architecture students mix with lawyers and chess wizards.

Coffee Mill, 3363 Grand Ave., Lake Merritt. Spacious room that doubles as an art gallery, and often hosts poetry readings; the coffee's good, too.

Mama Bear's, 6536 Telegraph Ave., North Oakland. Mainly a women's book-store, it doubles as a café and meeting place and has regular readings, often for women only, by lesbian and feminist writers. Open daily 10am–7pm, later for readings.

Peet's Coffee, 2124 Vine St., North Berkeley. Mostly for take-home coffee-buyers; regular cups for 50¢, massive ones for 80¢, minus 10¢ if you bring your own cup. Another branch at 2916 Domingo near the *Claremont Hotel*.

Ramona's, UC Berkeley. Located on the first floor of Wurser Hall and serving cheap coffee and a range of pastries, bagels, and sandwiches.

Bars

Albatross Pub, 1822 San Pablo Ave., West Berkeley. For good beer and a low-key atmosphere this is the place; sign up for the nightly darts contests.

Bertola's, 4659 Telegraph Ave., North Oakland. Loud and hospitable bar with the cheapest drinks in town. It's also an Italian restaurant (see below).

Brennan's, 4th St. and University Ave., Berkeley, under the I-80 freeway overpass. Solid blue-collar hang-out for watching a game on TV, jostling nois-ily at the bar, and escaping the droves of students. Cheap drinks and cafeteria food, with lots of room.

Heinhold's First and Last Chance Saloon, Jack London Square. Authentic waterfront bar that's hardly changed since the turn of the century, when Jack London himself drank here.

The Hut, 5517 College Ave., near Rockridge *BART*. Friendly, low-key pub with cheap pitchers, free popcorn, and a pool table.

The Kingfish, 5201 Claremont Ave., two blocks from Telegraph Ave. in North Oakland. Less a bar than a tumbledown shack, selling cheap cold beer. Popular with UC Berkeley headbangers.

Larry Blake's, 2367 Telegraph Ave., Berkeley. Upstairs there's a small bar, downstairs there's a R&B club and large bar; in between the two there's a good-value restaurant.

The Pub, 1492 Solano Ave., North Berkeley. Good range of English beers, quaffable on their tree-shaded outdoor deck.

Rickey's Sports Lounge, 15028 Hesperian Blvd., San Leandro, near Bayfair *BART* (☎352-0200). With seven giant-screen TVs, and 35 others spread around the cavernous room, this bar-cum-restaurant is *the* place to go to watch sports games, especially the *A's* and *Raiders*.

Spats, 1974 Shattuck Ave., Berkeley. Stuffed animals and bizarre bric-a-brac in this studenty bar, known for creative cocktails more than serious drinking.

Starry Plough, 3101 Shattuck Ave., South Berkeley. An Irish bar with Guinness and Anchor Steam on draft, Powers Whiskey on call, happy hours, and sporadic collections for the IRA. Near Ashby *BART*, and with live music some nights; see "Nightlife," below.

Triple Rock Brewery, 1920 Shattuck Ave., Berkeley. Buzzing, all-American beer bar: the decor is Edward Hopper-era retro, and the beers (brewed on the premises) are heavily carbonated to suit the soda-pop palates of the studenty crowd, but it's still fun.

The White Horse, 6560 Telegraph Ave. at 66th St., North Oakland. Smallish, friendly mixed bar (it was one of the first Bay Area bars to openly welcome gay men and lesbians), with dancing and a pool table.

Eating

Official home of California Cuisine and reputedly with some of the best **restaurants** in the state, Berkeley is an upmarket diner's paradise. But it's also a college town, and you can eat cheaply and well, especially around the southern end of the university, along and around Telegraph Avenue. The rest of the East Bay is less remarkable, except for when it comes to American food like barbecued ribs, grilled steaks, and seafood—or deli sandwiches, for which it's unbeatable.

Budget Food: Diners and Delis

Bette's Ocean View Diner, 1807 4th St., West Berkeley (☎548-9494). Named for the neighborhood and not for the vista. Huevos rancheros and home fries served from 6:30am.

Edible Complex, 5600 College Ave., North Oakland (☎658-2172). Busy soup and sandwich counter, open 8:30am–midnight every day.

Faculty Club, UC Berkeley (no phone). Open to everyone, this serves good-value cafeteria-style food in a marvelous Bernard Maybeck-designed dining room.

Flint's Barbeque, 3314 San Pablo Ave., Downtown Oakland (☎658-9912). Open until the early hours of the morning for some of the world's best take-out barbecued chicken and ribs. Also at 6609 Shattuck Ave., North Oakland (☎653-0593), and 6672 E 14th St. in East Oakland (☎569-1312).

Homemade Cafe, 2554 Sacramento St., West Berkeley (☎845-1940). The best place for breakfast in the East Bay, with fluffy omelettes filled with garden-fresh veggies, world-class home-fried potatoes, and mugs of piping hot coffee; open 7am–3pm, 8am on weekends, when you may have to line up outside for a table.

Lois the Pie Queen, 851 60th St., North Oakland (☎658-5616). Famous for southern-style sweet potato and fresh fruit pies, this cosy diner serves massive down-home breakfasts and Sunday dinners that'll keep you full for a week.

Mabel's Cafe, 635 1st St., Benicia (☎707/746-7068). Timeless American diner food in a homey, small front room.

Mama's Royal Cafe, 4012 Broadway, North Oakland (☎547-7600). Small breakfast joint that does very good omelettes, open daily 7am–3pm.

Ratto's, 9th and Washington St., Downtown Oakland (☎832-6503). Italian delicatessen and grocery store that has excellent soups and sandwiches.

Rockridge Cafe, 5492 College Ave., Rockridge (☎653-1567). Chrome-and-lino breakfast and burger bar with good desserts, opens at 7am every day.

Saul's Deli, 1475 Shattuck Ave., North Berkeley (☎848-DELI). For pastrami, corned beef, kreplach, or knishes, this is the place.

The Soup Kitchen, 2498 Telegraph Ave. at Dwight Way, Berkeley (no phone). Healthy soups, salads, and sandwiches for under $2.

Time to Eat, in Oakland's Produce Market at 325 Franklin St. (no phone). A Chinese bar and café that serves breakfasts from 5am.

Top Dog, 2534 Durant St., Berkeley (no phone). Not just a hot dog stand, and open late for bockwurst, bratwurst, kielbasas, and Louisiana Hot Sausages.

American Food

Bay Wolf Cafe, 3853 Piedmont Ave., North Oakland (☎655-6004). A comfortable restaurant serving moderately expensive grilled steaks and seafood on an ever-changing menu.

Bertola's, 4659 Telegraph Ave., North Oakland (☎547-9301). Cheap and filling Italian-American food—and a good place for cheap stiff drinks.

Chez Panisse, 1517 Shattuck Ave., North Berkeley (☎548-5525). The first and still the best of the California Cuisineries—although at $50 a head prix-fixe you may prefer to try the comparatively cheap *Cafe* upstairs, especially if you haven't made the obligatory three-months-in-advance reservation.

Fourth Street Grill, 1820 4th St., West Berkeley (☎849-0526). Ever-popular, hi-style southwestern desert eatery with plaster cacti and pastel decor, serving grilled meats and fish for around $12 a plate.

Gulf Coast Oyster Bar & Specialty Co., 736 Washington St., Downtown Oakland (☎839-6950). Popular and reasonably priced Cajun-flavored seafood restaurant.

The Harbor House, Harbor Way near the Marina, Vallejo (☎707/642-8984). Fresh seafood at a fair price in an old Victorian house in nautical Vallejo.

Oakland Grill, in the Produce Market at Franklin and 3rd St. (☎835-1176). Good all-American food all day, every day, in an airily remodeled warehouse.

Prevot's, 401 1st St., Benicia, in the *Union Hotel* (☎707/746-0100). Highly rated restaurant serving good-value lunches and dinners in a restored 1880s hotel.

Spenger's, 1919 4th St., West Berkeley (☎845-7111). About as far as you can get from the subtle charms of Berkeley's high-style eateries, this is nonetheless definitely a local institution: the largest restaurant in the whole Bay Area, serving up tons of seafood to thousands of customers every day. Full meals from $8 to $15.

Pizzas, Mexican, and South American Food

Acapulco, 2104 Lincoln Ave., Alameda (☎523-4935). Often packed shoulder-to-shoulder for the huge portions of (admittedly tame) Mexican food. Meals (including margaritas) $15.

Alameda Taqueria, 1513 Park St., Alameda (☎865-9380). Small and family-run, with some of the freshest and best-tasting burritos in the Bay Area.

Alvita's Restaurant, 3522 Foothill Blvd., East Oakland (☎536-7880). Arguably the best Mexican restaurant in the Bay Area, with great *chiles rellenos*, *carnitas*, and a range of seafood dishes.

Blondie's Pizza, 2340 Telegraph Ave., Berkeley (☎548-1129). Takeout New York-style pizza by the slice ($1.25) or by the pie; open late (2am) and always crowded.

Cafe Oliveto, 5655 College Ave., Rockridge (☎547-5356). Popular sidewalk tapas bar with good-sized portions costing around $4 a plate.

Juan's Place, 941 Carlton St., West Berkeley (☎845-6904). The original Berkeley Mexican restaurant, with great food (tons of it) and an interesting mix of people.

Mario's La Fiesta, 2444 Telegraph Ave. at Haste St., Berkeley (☎540-9123). Usually just crowded enough to keep things going at a dull roar, and the food is very good for the little you pay.

Picante, 1328 6th St. at Gilman St., West Berkeley (☎525-3121). Good, cheap tacos with fresh salsa and live jazz at weekends. A happening hang-out.

Tambo Cafe, 1981 Shattuck Ave. near University Ave., Berkeley (☎841-6884). Brilliant, reasonably priced Peruvian food—*papas huacainas* (potatoes in spicy cheese sauce) and *empanadas* (meat or vegetable pies), as well as marvelous *ceviche*—served up fresh and fast.

Taqueria Morelia, 4481 E 14th St., East Oakland (☎261-6360). Excellent burritos and the more unusual but authentic tortas.

Zachary's Pizza, 5801 College Ave., Rockridge (☎655-6385). Good salads and arguably the best pizzas in the East Bay, thick and tasty or thin and crusty. Also at 1853 Solano Ave., Berkeley (☎525-5950).

Asian, African, and Indian Food

The Blue Nile, 2525 Telegraph Ave., Berkeley (☎540-6777). Go here with a group and share the giant platters of Ethiopian stewed meats and veggies, eaten by hand with pancake-like *injera* bread.

Byul Mi House, 308 14th St., Downtown Oakland (☎839-3993). Small, quiet café with excellent *bulgoki*, *kim chee*, and other Korean delicacies; $5 for a set lunch, $9 for dinner.

Casbah, 1920 San Pablo Ave., West Berkeley (☎540-0784). From *cous-cous* to shish-kebabs, the best of North Africa served up in a spacious restaurant, complete with palm trees. Evenings only.

Cha-Am, 1543 Shattuck Ave., North Berkeley (☎848-9664). Climb the stairs up to this unlikely, always crowded small restaurant that serves up deliciously spicy Thai food at bargain prices.

Jade Villa, 800 Broadway, Downtown Oakland (☎839-1688). For dim sum lunches or traditional Cantonese meals, this is one of the best places in Oakland's thriving Chinatown.

Maharani, 1025 University Ave., West Berkeley (☎848-7777). One of the best of the handful of eateries that have sprung up here in Little India, and certainly the cheapest, with $6 all-you-can-eat lunchtime buffets during the week.

Sorabol, 372 Grand Ave., Lake Merritt (☎839-2288). Excellent Korean restaurant, featuring addictive barbecued meats for around $8 a dish.

Steve's Barbeque, in the Durant Center, 2525 Durant St., Berkeley (no phone). Excellent cheap Korean food (*kim chee* to kill for); other cafés in the complex sell Mexican food, healthy sandwiches, slices of pizza, pitchers of beer, and home-made doughnuts.

Ice Cream and Desserts

Edy's, 2201 Shattuck Ave., Berkeley (☎843-3096). If you can bear the orange vinyl booths, the sundaes, banana splits, and milk shakes are great.

Fatapples, 1346 Martin Luther King Way, North Berkeley (☎526-2660). Excellent apple and fruit pies, and a menu full of countless variations on the burger.

Fenton's Creamery, 4226 Piedmont Ave., North Oakland (☎658-4949). A brightly lit 1950s ice cream and sandwich shop, open until midnight seven days a week.

Schuyler's, 1854 Euclid Ave., North Berkeley (☎841-6374). Borrow a book from the wall of paperbacks while you down a hot fudge sundae or two.

Yogurt Park, 2433A Durant Ave., Berkeley (☎549-0570). Frozen yogurt a specialty, open until midnight for the student throngs.

Specialty Shops and Markets

Acme Bread, 1601 San Pablo Ave., West Berkeley (☎524-1327). Small bakery that supplies most of Berkeley's better restaurants; the house specialty is delicious sourdough baguettes.

Cheese Board, 1504 Shattuck Ave., North Berkeley (☎549-3183). Collectively owned and operated since 1967, this was one of the first outposts in Berkeley's Gourmet Ghetto and is still going strong, offering over 200 varieties of cheese and a range of delicious breads.

La Farine, 6323 College Ave., Rockridge (☎654-0338). Small but highly rated French-style bakery, with excellent *pain chocolat*.

Monterey Foods, 1550 Hopkins St., North Berkeley (☎526-6042). The main supplier of exotic produce to Berkeley's gourmet restaurants, this boisterous market also has the highest quality fresh fruit and vegetables available.

Poulet, 1685 Shattuck Ave., North Berkeley (☎845-5932). Famed for their ready-cooked, free-range chickens, the shop also sells a variety of chicken-based pâtés and salads.

Nightlife

Nightlife is where the East Bay really comes into its own. Even more than in San Francisco, dancing to canned music and paying high prices for flashy decor is not the done thing, which means that **discos** are virtually non-existent. Instead there are dozens of **live music venues**, covering the range of musical tastes and styles—from small, unpretentious jazz clubs to buzzing R&B venues—of which Oakland's hotspots are unsurpassed. Berkeley's clubs tend more toward folk and "world" music, with occasional bouts of hardcore thrash, and the university itself holds two of the best medium-sized venues in the entire Bay Area, both of which attract touring big-name stars.

Though not bad by San Francisco standards, the East Bay **theater** scene isn't exactly thriving, and shows tend to be politically worthy rather than dramatically innovative. By contrast, the range of films is first class, with a dozen **movie theaters** showing new releases and Berkeley's *Pacific Film Archive*, one of the world's finest film libraries, filling its screens with obscure but brilliant art flicks.

Check the free *East Bay Express* or the *Berkeley Monthly* for details of who and **what's on** where in the entire East Bay region.

The Large Performance Venues

Berkeley Community Theater, 1930 Allston Way, Berkeley (☎845-2308). Jimi Hendrix played here, and the 3500-seat theater still hosts major rock concerts and community events.

The Oakland Coliseum Complex, Coliseum *BART*, near the airport (☎639-7700). Mostly stadium shows, inside the 18,000-seat Arena or outdoors in the adjacent 55,000-seat Coliseum.

Paramount Theater, 2025 Broadway, Downtown Oakland (☎465-6400). Beautifully restored Art-Deco masterpiece, hosting classical concerts, big-name crooners, ballets, and opera. Tickets $6–15.

Zellerbach Hall and the outdoor **Greek Theater** on the UC Berkeley campus (☎642-9988). Two of the prime spots for catching touring big names in the Bay Area. Tickets cost $15–20.

Live Music Venues

Ashkenaz, 1317 San Pablo Ave., Berkeley (☎525-5054). World music and dance café. Acts range from modern Afrobeat to the best of the Balkans. Kids and under-21s welcome. Admission $5–8.

Caribe Dance Center, 1408 Webster St., Downtown Oakland (☎835-4006). For reggae, rockers, calypso, soca, dub, salsa, or lambada, this new place is hard to beat. Admission $3–8.

Eli's Mile High Club, 3629 Martin Luther King Jr. Way, North Oakland (☎655-6661). The best of the Bay Area blues clubs. Waitresses balance pitchers of beer on their heads to facilitate a safer passage through the rocking crowds. Cover $5–8.

Freight and Salvage, 1827 San Pablo Ave., West Berkeley (☎548-1761). Singer-songwriters in a coffee house setting. Cover $6.

Gilman Street Project, 924 Gilman St., West Berkeley (☎648-3561). On the outer edge of the hardcore punk scene. Admission $3–6.

Kimball's East, 4800 Shellmound St., Emeryville (☎658-2555). Fairly slick, high-style jazz and dancing venue. Cover $10–20.

Koncepts Cultural Gallery, 480 Third St., Downtown Oakland (☎763-0682). Excellent, ground-breaking jazz club, hosting a wide variety of different acts. Admission $8–15.

La Peña Cultural Center, 3105 Shattuck Ave., Berkeley near Ashby *BART* (☎849-2572). More folk than rock, often politically charged. Admission $3–6.

The Omni, 4799 Shattuck Ave., North Oakland (☎547-7655). Heavy metal and touring rock dinosaurs. Admission $5–10.

Starry Plough, 3101 Shattuck Ave., Berkeley (☎841-2082). Nearest thing to a pub-rock venue, with free Irish music every Mon. For live bands, admission is $3–5.

Yoshi's, 6030 Claremont Ave., North Oakland (☎652-9200). Spacious and comfortable jazz and blues club. Cover $8–15.

Your Place, 5319 Martin Luther King Jr. Way, North Oakland (☎65-BLUES). The newest, bluest, blues bar in the East Bay, open nightly. No cover Sun–Thurs; $2 Fri and Sat.

Cinemas

Act One and **Act Two**, 2128 Center St., Berkeley (☎548-7200). Foreign films and non-mainstream American ones.

Coliseum Drive-in, 5401 Coliseum Way, East Oakland (☎536-7491). If you've never been to a drive-in, here's your chance.

Grand Lake Theater, 3200 Grand Ave. (☎452-3556). The grand dame of East Bay picture palaces, right on Lake Merritt, showing the best of the current major releases.

Pacific Film Archives, 2621 Durant Ave., Berkeley, in the University Art Museum (☎642-1412). For the serious film fan, this is perhaps the best cinema in all California, with seasons of contemporary works from around the world, plus revivals of otherwise forgotten favorites. Two films a night; $4.25 each, $5.25 for both.

Piedmont Theater, 4186 Piedmont Ave. (☎654-2727). Old neighborhood theater divided up into multi-screener.

Rialto Theater, 841 Gilman St., West Berkeley (☎526-6669). Recent foreign and independent films, and the better re-releases; $4.

UC Theater, 2036 University Ave., Berkeley, just below Shattuck Ave. (☎843-6267). Popular revival house, with a huge auditorium and a daily double feature; $4.

Theater

Berkeley Repertory Theater, 2025 Addison St., Berkeley (☎845-4700). One of the West Coast's most highly respected theater companies, presenting updated classics and contemporary plays in an intimate modern theater. Tickets $6–20.

Black Repertory Theater, 3201 Adeline St., Berkeley near Ashby *BART* (☎652-2120). After many years of struggling, this politically conscious company moved into their own specially built home in 1987, since when they've been encouraging new talent with great success. Tickets $4–12.

California Shakespeare Festival, Siesta Valley, Orinda (☎548-3422). After 15 seasons in a North Berkeley park, this outdoor festival was forced to move to a larger home for the 1991 season. Tickets $8–15.

8th Street Studio, 2525 8th St. (☎654-9618). Small performance space down by the waterfront that specializes in the classics. Tickets $4–6.

Julia Morgan Theater, 2640 College Ave. (☎548-7234). A variety of touring shows stop off in this cunningly converted old church. $8–15.

Eugene O'Neill Tao House, Danville (☎839-0249). Staged readings and some performances in the preserved home of this Nobel prize-winning playwright.

Zellerbach Playhouse, UC Berkeley (☎642-9988). Occasionally brilliant visiting productions. Tickets $5–15.

CHAPTER TEN

THE PENINSULA

The city of San Francisco sits at the tip of a five-mile-wide **Peninsula**. Home of old money and new technology, this stretches for fifty miles of relentless suburbia south from San Francisco along the bay past the wealthy enclaves of Hillsborough and Atherton, to wind up in the futuristic roadside landscape of the so-called "Silicon Valley" near **San Jose**—though your only glimpse of the area may be on the trip between San Francisco and the airport. There was a time when the region was covered with orange groves and fig trees, but the concentration of academic interest around Stanford University in **Palo Alto** and the continuing boom in computers—since the 1970s the region's biggest industry—has buried any chances of it hanging on to its agricultural past.

Surprisingly, most of the land along the **coast**—separated from the bayfront sprawl by a ridge of redwood-covered peaks—remains rural and undeveloped; it also contains some of the best **beaches** in the Bay Area and a couple of affably down-to-earth farming communities, all well served by public transit.

Getting Around and Information

BART only travels down the Peninsula as far as DALY CITY, from where you can catch **SamTrans** (☎761-7000) buses south to Palo Alto or along the coast to Half Moon Bay. For longer distances, **Caltrain** (☎557-8661) offers an hourly rail service from its terminal at 4th and Townsend in downtown San Francisco, stopping at most bayside towns between the city and San Jose, for $1–5; *Greyhound* runs regular buses along US-101 to and from their San Jose terminal at 70 S. Almaden (☎408/297-8890) as well. **Santa Clara County Transit** (*SCCT*) (☎408/287-4210) runs buses around metropolitan San Jose. If you're going to be spending most of your time down here, it's possible to **fly** direct into **San Jose International Airport** (SJO), surprisingly close to downtown San Jose on the frequent *SCCT* bus #64.

The **Palo Alto Chamber of Commerce**, 325 Forest Avenue (Mon–Fri 9am–noon & 1–5pm; ☎324-3121), has lists of local eateries and cycle routes; for information on nearby Stanford University phone ☎723-2560. To find out **what's on** and where, pick up a free copy of the *Palo Alto Weekly*, available at most local shops. At the southern end of the bay, the **San Jose Convention and Visitors' Bureau**, 333 W. San Carlos Street (Mon–Sat 9am–5pm; ☎408/295-9600), is the best bet for tourist information; for local news and events pick up a copy of the excellent *San Jose Mercury* newspaper or the free weekly *Metro*.

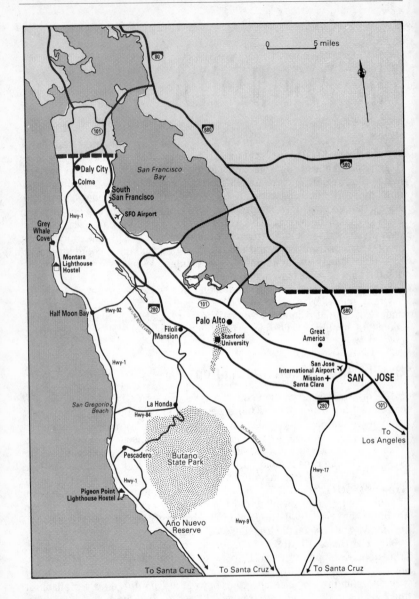

Accommodation

There are dozens of $40-a-night **motels** along Hwy-82, "El Camino Real," the old main highway, and, with a bit of advance planning (and a car), you could save money by staying here rather than in the city. Also, if you're arriving late or departing on an early flight from SFO you might want to avail yourself of one of the many **airport hotels**, listed on p.37. Perhaps the best reason to spend the night down on the Peninsula is its many cheap and pleasant **hostels**, two of which are housed in old lighthouses bang on the Pacific coast.

Hostels

Hidden Villa Hostel, 26807 Moody Rd., Los Altos Hills (☎941-6407). Located on an 1800-acre ranch in the foothills above the Silicon Valley; closed June–Sept. $11 a night.

Montara Lighthouse Hostel, on Hwy-1 in Montara, 25 miles south of San Francisco (☎728-7177). Dorm rooms in a converted 1875 lighthouse, accessible from the city via *SamTrans* bus #1A. $11 a night.

Pigeon Point Lighthouse Hostel, on Hwy-1 south of Pescadero, 50 miles south of San Francisco (☎879-0633). Worth planning a couple days around, this beautifully sited hostel is ideal for exploring the redwoods in the hills above or watching the wildlife in nearby Año Nuevo State Reserve. $11 a night.

Motels and Hotels

Best Western Inn, 455 S. 2nd St., San Jose (☎408/298-3500). Right in downtown San Jose, with pool and sauna for $55 a double.

Best Western Stanford Park Hotel, 100 El Camino Real, Menlo Park (☎322-1234). Doubles from $65.

Hotel California, 2431 Ash St., Palo Alto (☎322-7666). Centrally located small hotel with breakfast included. $75 a double.

San Benito House, 356 Main St., Half Moon Bay (☎726-3425). Twelve restful rooms in a 100-year-old building, just a mile from the beach. Doubles from $80 a night, including breakfast.

Stanford Terrace Inn, 531 Stanford Ave., Palo Alto (☎857-0333). Big rooms and a small pool for not much money. $75 for a double room.

Town House Motel, 4164 El Camino Real, Palo Alto (☎493-4492). A mile from anywhere but the rooms are particularly clean and well-kept. $42 for a double.

The Viking Motel, 4238 El Camino Real, Palo Alto (☎493-4222). Slightly cheaper than the above motels, and slightly farther away. Count on $40 for a double.

Valley Inn, 2155 The Alameda, San Jose (☎408/241-8500). Standard motel not far from the Rosicrucian Museum. Doubles $45.

Camping

Butano State Park, Pescadero (☎879-0173). RV and tent spaces in a beautiful redwood forest. Free camping.

Half Moon Bay State Beach, Half Moon Bay (☎726-6238). Sleep out along the beach for free, or in the campground for $10.

South Along the Bay

US-101 runs south from San Francisco along the bay through over fifty miles of unmitigated sprawl to San Jose, lined by light industrial estates and shopping malls. The only place worth stopping at is the **Coyote Point Museum** (Wed–Fri 9am–5pm, Sat & Sun 1–5pm; free), four miles south of the airport off Poplar Avenue in a large bayfront park, where examples of the natural life of the San Francisco Bay—from tidal insects to birds of prey—are exhibited in engaging and informative displays, enhanced by interactive computers and documentary films.

A more pleasant drive is via **I-280**, the newest and most expensive freeway in California, which runs parallel to US-101 but avoids the worst of the bayside mess by cutting through wooded valleys down the center of the Peninsula. Just beyond the San Francisco city limit the road passes through **COLMA**, a unique place made up entirely of cemeteries (which are prohibited within San Francisco). Beyond Colma the scenery improves quickly as I-280 continues past the **Crystal Springs Reservoir**, an artificial lake which holds the water supply for San Francisco—pumped here all the way from Yosemite. Surrounded by twenty square miles of parkland, hiking trails lead up to the ridge from where San Francisco Bay was first spotted by eighteenth-century Spanish explorers; it now overlooks the airport to the east, but there are good views out over the Pacific Coast, two miles distant.

At the south end of the reservoir, just off I-280 on Canada Road in the well-heeled town of **WOODSIDE**, lusciously abundant gardens surround the palatial **Filoli Estate** (tours Tues–Sat 10:30am & 1pm; $6; ☎364-2880). The 45-room mansion, designed in 1915 in neo-Palladian style by architect Willis Polk, may seem familiar—it was used in the TV series *Dynasty* as the Denver home of the Carrington clan. It's the only one of the many huge houses around here that you can actually visit, although it's the gardens that are most worth coming for, especially in the spring when everything's in bloom.

Palo Alto and Stanford University

PALO ALTO, just south and three miles east between I-280 and US-101, is a small, leafy community with all the contrived atmosphere you'd expect to find in a college town but little of the vigor of its northern counterpart, Berkeley. Though a visit doesn't really merit the expense of a night's accommodation, you could spend a lazy day in the bookstores and cafés that line **University Avenue**, the town's main drag. Or, if you're feeling energetic, try cycling around the town's many well-marked bike routes; a range of bikes is available for $12–25 a day from *The Effortless Bike* at 401 High Street (☎328-3180), near the *Caltrain* station a block west of University Avenue.

Stanford University, spreading south from the end of University Avenue, lends Palo Alto what liveliness it has. The university is one of the best—and most expensive—in California, though when it opened in 1891, founded by railroad magnate Leland Stanford in memory of his dead son, it offered free tuition. Ridiculed by East Coast academics, who felt that there was as much need for a second West Coast university (after UC Berkeley) as there was for "an asylum for decayed sea captains in Switzerland," Stanford was defiantly built anyway, in a hybrid of Mission and Romanesque buildings on a huge campus that covers an area larger than the whole of downtown San Francisco.

Stanford, whose reputation as an arch-conservative think-tank was enhanced by Ronald Reagan's decision to donate his video library to the school, hasn't always been an entirely boring place, though you wouldn't know it to walk among the preppy future-lawyers-of-America that seem to comprise 90 percent of the student body. **Ken Kesey** came here from Oregon in 1958 on a writing fellowship, working nights as an orderly on the psychiatric ward of one hospital here, and getting paid $75 a day to test experimental drugs (LSD among them) in another. Drawing on both experiences, Kesey wrote *One Flew Over the Cuckoo's Nest* in 1960 and quickly became a counter-culture hero. These days Stanford attracts a more prosaic body of students, preferring to bolster its departments in medicine, science, and engineering.

Approaching from the Palo Alto *Caltrain* and *SamTrans* bus station, which acts as a buffer between the town and the university, you enter the campus via a half-mile-long, palm-tree-lined boulevard which deposits you at its heart, the **Quadrangle**, bordered by the phallic **Hoover Tower** and the colorful, gold-leaf mosaics of the **Memorial Church**. Free hour-long walking **tours** of the campus leave from here daily at 11am and 2pm, though it's fairly big and is best seen by car or bike.

The one place worth spending some time, the **Stanford Museum of Art** (Tues–Fri 10am–5pm, Sat & Sun 1–5pm; $3), between "the Quad" and the town, has been closed since the 1989 earthquake and won't reopen till 1992, though you can still have a laugh at the insipid mosaics that decorate its upper story. When the museum reopens you'll be able to check out its assemblage of Asian art and Egyptian sculpture, though it says a lot about the collection that pride of place is given to the golden spike that Leland Stanford drove to join the two halves of the Transcontinental Railroad in 1869: Stanford made his fortune from the railroad monopoly he and his Southern Pacific Railroad colleagues exerted over most of the western US. For now, the best reason to come here is to have a look at the distinguished collection of Rodin sculpture, including a *Gates of Hell* flanked by a shamed *Adam and Eve*, displayed in a attractive outdoor setting on the museum's south side. Also, if you keep up on the latest trends in sub-atomic behavior, you won't want to miss the **Stanford Linear Accelerator** (Mon–Fri by appointment only; ☎854-3300), a mile west of the central campus on Sand Hill Road, where infinitesimally small particles are crashed into one another at very high speeds to see what happens.

ACCOMMODATION *Best Western Stanford Park Hotel, Hotel California, Stanford Terrace Inn, Town House Motel, Viking Motel.*
BARS *Fresco, Pudley's Burger Saloon.*
RESTAURANTS *Barrio Fiesta, Little Garden.*

San Jose

The fastest-growing city in America's fastest-growing state, **SAN JOSE**, save the odd Burt Bacharach song, is not strong on identity, though in area and population it's close to twice the size of San Francisco. Sitting at the southern end of the Peninsula, with a location that's almost in the center of the state, an abundance of cheap land brought developers and businessmen into the area in the 1960s, hoping to draw from the concentration of talent in the commerce-oriented halls of Stanford University. Fueled by the success of computer firms like Apple and Hewlett-Packard, in the past 25 years San Jose has emerged as the civic heart of Silicon Valley, surrounded by miles of faceless hi-tech industrial parks where the next generations of computers are designed and crafted.

Ironically enough, San Jose is one of the oldest settlements in California, though the only sign of it is at the late eighteenth-century **Mission Santa Clara de Asis**, on San Jose's main drag, the Alameda, two miles northwest of the *Caltrain* station via *SCCT* bus #63, where a small museum (Tues–Fri 10am–5pm, Sat & Sun 1–5pm; $1) has artifacts from the Mission era. Otherwise there's only really one good reason to subject yourself to San Jose's relentlessly boring cityscape—to visit the **Rosicrucian Museum**, 1342 Naglee Avenue (Tues–Fri 9am–4:30pm, Sat–Mon noon–4:30pm; $3), reachable from the *Caltrain* station on *SCCT* bus #36. Languishing in the suburbs, this grand structure contains a brilliant collection of Assyrian and Babylonian artifacts, with displays of mummies, amulets, a replica of a tomb, and ancient jewelry.

You could also stop off at the **Winchester Mystery House**, 525 S. Winchester Boulevard, just off I-280 near Hwy-17 (daily 9:30am–4:30pm; $9). Sarah Winchester, heir to the Winchester rifle fortune, was convinced by an occultist upon her husband's death that he had been taken by the spirits of men killed with Winchester rifles. She was told that unless a room was built for each of the spirits and the sound of hammers never ceased, the same fate would befall her. Work on the mansion went on 24 hours a day for the next thirty years, with results that need to be seen to be believed—stairs lead nowhere, windows open on to solid brick—though it's a shameless tourist trap, and you have to run a gauntlet of ghastly gift shops and soda stands to get in or out.

There's one other Peninsula place that might exercise a certain attraction, particularly to those fond of roller coasters, log rides, and all-American family fun: **Great America** (daily 10am–10pm in summer, weekends only in winter; $16.95, $8.95 under-6s)—a huge, 100-acre amusement park on the edge of San Francisco Bay, just off US-101 north of San Jose. It's not in the same league as Disneyland but doesn't suffer from the same crowds and lengthy lines, and the range of high-speed thrills and chills—from the loop-the-looping "Demon" to "The Edge," where you free-fall in a steel cage for over 100 feet—is well worth the entry fee, especially on weekdays when you may well have the place to yourself. The whole park is laid out into heritage-themed areas like "Hometown Square," "Yankee Harbor," or "County Fair," filled up with all sorts of sideshow attractions and funfair games.

ACCOMMODATION *Best Western Inn, Hidden Villa Hostel, Valley Inn.*
BARS *Abigail's Pub.*
RESTAURANTS *Eulipia, Krung Thai Cuisine, Original Joe's.*

The Coast

The **coastline** of the Peninsula south from San Francisco is more appealing than inland—relatively undeveloped, with very few buildings, let alone towns, along the 75 miles of coves and beaches that extend down to the resort city of Santa Cruz. The bluffs protect the many nudist beaches from prying eyes and make a popular launching pad for hang-glider pilots, particularly at Burton Beach and Fort Funston, a mile south of the San Francisco Zoo—also the point where the earthquake-causing San Andreas Fault enters the sea, not surfacing again until Point Reyes. From here Skyline Boulevard follows the coast past the repetitious tracts of proverbial ticky-tacky houses that make up DALY CITY, where it is joined by Hwy-1 (and *SamTrans* bus #1A) for the rest of the journey.

San Pedro Point marks the southern extent of San Francisco's suburban sprawl. Fifteen miles south of the city proper, it's a popular surfing beach, and worth a stop to have a look at the old Ocean Shore Railroad Depot, now a private residence among the handful of shops in the beachfront town. This is one of the few surviving remnants of an ill-advised train line between San Francisco and Santa Cruz that was wiped out during the 1906 earthquake. The line was in any case never more than a third complete, and the few patrons had to transfer back and forth by ferry to connect the stretches of track that were built, much of which you can still see scarring the face of the bluffs. The continually eroding cliffs don't take very well to being built on, as evidenced a mile south by the **Devil's Slide**, where the highway is washed away with some regularity in winter storms. The slide area was also a popular dumping spot for corpses of those who'd fallen foul of rum-runners during Prohibition, and features under various names in many of Dashiell Hammett's detective stories.

Just south of the Devil's Slide, the sands of **Gray Whale Cove State Beach** (daily dawn–dusk; $2 to park) are clothing-optional. Despite the name it's not an especially great place to look for migrating gray whales, but there is a stairway from the bus stop down to a fine beach. Two miles south, the red-roofed buildings of the **Montara Lighthouse**, set among the windswept Monterey pines at the top of a steep cliff, have been converted into a **youth hostel** (see "Accommodation", above, for details), where you can rent bikes for $10 a day. There are a few good places to stop for a drink or a bite to eat in the town of MOSS BEACH, across Hwy-1.

South of the lighthouse, the **James Fitzgerald Marine Reserve** strings along the shore, a two-mile shelf of flat, slippery rocks that make excellent tidal pools. The ranger often gives guided interpretive walks through the reserve at low tide, the best time to explore. At the south end of the reserve, Pillar Point juts out into the Pacific, just east of which, along Hwy-1, fishing boats dock at Pillar Point Harbor. The faintly touristy, ramshackle town adjacent to the waterfront, **PRINCETON-BY-THE-SEA**, has a few stands selling fish and chips, sometimes freshly caught. Farther along, the best of the local surfing areas is just offshore from **Miramar Beach**; after a day in the water or on the beach, the place to head for is the beachfront *Bach Dancing and Dynamite Society*, an informal jazz club and beer bar that faces the sands.

Half Moon Bay

HALF MOON BAY, twenty miles south of the city and the only town of any size between San Francisco and Santa Cruz, takes its name from the crescent-shaped bay formed by Pillar Point. Lined by miles of sandy beaches, the town is surprisingly rural considering its proximity to San Francisco and Silicon Valley, and sports a number of ornate Victorian wooden houses around its center. The oldest of these is at the north end of Main Street: built in 1849, it's just across a little stone bridge over Pillarcitos Creek. The **Chamber of Commerce** (Mon–Fri 9am–5pm; ☎726-5202), housed in an old railroad car at the other end of Main Street, half a mile south, has free walking tour maps of the town and information on the two annual festivals for which the place is well known. These are the **Holy Ghost and Pentecost Festival**, a celebratory parade and barbecue held on the sixth Sunday after Easter, and the **Pumpkin Festival**, celebrating the harvest of the area's many pumpkin farms, just in time for Halloween, when the fields around town are full of families searching for the perfect jack-o'-lantern to greet the hordes of trick-or-treaters. There are free, primitive **campgrounds** all along the coast in Half Moon Bay State Park, a half mile west of the town.

Half Moon Bay is also the southern end of the *SamTrans* bus #1A route; to continue south, transfer here to route #90C, which runs every three hours to Waddell Creek, twenty miles south. **San Gregorio State Beach**, ten miles south of Half Moon Bay, is at its best in the spring, after the winter storms, when flotsam architects construct a range of driftwood shelters along the wide beach south of the parking area. In summer the beach is packed with well-oiled bodies; around the bluffs to the north is quieter, and clothing-optional.

The Butano Redwoods and the Año Nuevo State Reserve

If you've got a car and it's not a great day for the beach, head up into the hills above, where the thousands of acres of the **Butano redwood forest** feel at their most ancient and primeval in the grayest and gloomiest weather. About half the land between San Jose and the coast is protected from development in a variety of state and county parks, all of which are virtually deserted despite being within a half-hour's drive of the Silicon Valley sprawl. Any one of a dozen roads will lead you through endless stands of untouched forest, and even the briefest of walks will take you seemingly miles from any sign of civilization. Hwy-84 climbs up from San Gregorio through the **Sam McDonald County Park** to LA HONDA, from where you can continue on to Palo Alto, or, better, loop back to the coast via Pescadero Road. A mile before you reach the quaint town of **PESCADERO**—which has two of the best places to eat, *Duarte's* and *Dinelli's Cafe*, on the Peninsula—Cloverdale Road heads south to **Butano State Park**, where you can hike and camp overlooking the Pacific.

Back on Hwy-1, five miles south of Pescadero is another great place to spend the night, sleeping in the old lighthouse keeper's quarters or soaking your bones in a marvelous hot tub at the *Pigeon Point Lighthouse Hostel* (see "Accommodation" for details). If you're here in December or January, continue south another five miles to the **Año Nuevo State Reserve** for a chance to see one of nature's most bizarre spectacles—the mating rituals of the northern elephant seal. These massive, ungainly creatures, fifteen feet long and weighing up to three tons, were once found all along the coast, though they were nearly hunted to extinction by whalers in the last century. During the mating season the beach is literally a seething mass of blubbery bodies, with the trunk-nosed males fighting it out for the right to sire as many as fifty pups in a season. At any time of the year you're likely to see a half dozen or so dozing in the sands. The reserve is also good for bird-watching, and in March there's a chance of getting a good look at migrating gray whales.

The slowly resurgent Año Nuevo seal population is still carefully protected, and during the breeding season the obligatory **guided tours** (hourly 8am–4pm; ☎879-0227)—designed to protect spectators as much as to give the seals some privacy—are often oversubscribed. Otherwise tickets are usually made available to people staying at the *Pigeon Point Hostel*, and *SamTrans* (☎348-SEAL) sometimes runs charter bus tours from SAN MATEO on the bay side of the Peninsula. Año Nuevo is the end of *SamTrans* route #90C; there's no way to continue south by public transit to the resort town of Santa Cruz, twenty miles away, though hitchhiking shouldn't be a problem.

ACCOMMODATION *Pigeon Point Lighthouse, San Benito House.*
RESTAURANTS *Dinelli's, Duarte's.*

Eating and Drinking

Though the culinary establishments of the Peninsula hardly compete with those of San Francisco, if you find yourself down here there are a number of places worth searching out, if only because the pace is more relaxed and you get more for your **eating** and **drinking** dollar. Most of the places listed are centrally located in the downtown areas of the various Peninsula cities, though a few others are worth almost any effort to get to. Also, as most of the restaurants are good spots for a drink and vice versa, we've listed them all together. For late-night partaking, check out the clubs described under "Nightlife," below; all serve drinks until the early hours.

Abigail's Pub, 265 N 1st St., San Jose (☎408/294-4111). Ersatz English tavern catering to anglophile computer wizards, but serving good roast beef and Yorkshire puddings for around $12, and a wide range of beers.

Barrio Fiesta, 909 Antoinette Lane, South San Francisco (☎871-8703). Hard to find amid the shopping malls of South City, but well worth it for the huge portions of beautifully presented, delicious Filipino dishes, especially seafood. Full meals cost around $15; bring your own wine or beer.

Dinelli's, 1956 Pescadero Rd., Pescadero (☎879-0106). Probably the best roadside café in the known world, with great burgers and a house specialty, fried artichoke hearts, that brings people from all over the Bay Area.

Duarte's, 202 Stage Rd., Pescadero (☎879-0464). Platefuls of traditional American cooking for around $10, plus wonderful fresh fruit pies.

Eulipia, 374 S. 1st St., San Jose (☎408/280-6161). Upscale and stylish spot featuring well-prepared versions of California Cuisine staples like grilled fish and fresh pastas. Full bar; dinner and drinks will set you back $15–25.

Fresco, 3398 El Camino Real, Palo Alto (☎493-3470). Wide range of pastas, pizzas, and salads with palpably fresh ingredients in unusual combinations. Opens early.

Krung Thai Cuisine, 1699 W. San Carlos St., San Jose (☎408/295-5508). Delicious, unusual seafood dishes—start off with a *po-tak* soup of clams and crab legs in citrus broth—and excellent satays.

Little Garden, 4127 El Camino Real, Palo Alto (☎494-1230). Simple, spicy Vietnamese food—fried chicken on a bed of cabbage, shrimp and hot peppers in peanut sauce—in unpretentious surroundings.

Original Joe's, 301 S. 1st St., San Jose (☎408/292-7030). Grab a stool at the counter or settle into one of the comfy booths and enjoy a burger and fries or a plate of pasta at this San Jose institution, where $10 goes a long way.

Pudley's Burger Saloon, 255 University Ave., Palo Alto (☎328-2021). Burgers ($4) and beers ($1.50) in retro-American 1940s setting.

Nightlife

Though many San Franciscans would deny it and think you were crazy even to suggest the possibility, there's a surprisingly good **nightlife** scene on the Peninsula, particularly in San Jose but also in the studenty environs of Palo Alto.

Cactus Club, 417 S. 1st St., San Jose (☎408/280-1435). One of two very good clubs near each other in downtown San Jose, hosting some of the better up-and-coming bands with music ranging from roots reggae to hardcore thrash. Cover $4–8.

The Edge, 260 California Ave., Palo Alto (☎324-EDGE). Cheap drinks and low (or no) cover charge make this dance club a lively option. Good live bands some nights, when tickets cost $5–7.

FX: The Club, 400 S. 1st St., San Jose (☎408/298-9796). The other San Jose club, more for drinking and dancing; 21 and over only. Closed Mon and Tues, cover $4–6.

Hard Disk Saloon, 1214 Apollo Way, Sunnyvale (☎408/733-2001). Near US-101 at Lawrence Expressway in the heart of the Silicon Valley; live blues most nights, no cover Sun–Wed.

CHAPTER ELEVEN

MARIN COUNTY

A cross the Golden Gate from San Francisco, **Marin County** (pronounced Ma-RINN) is an unabashed introduction to Californian self-indulgence: an elitist pleasure-zone of conspicuous luxury and abundant natural beauty, with sunshine, sandy beaches, high mountains, and thick redwood forests. Often ranked as the wealthiest county in the US, Marin has drawn a sizable contingent of northern California's wealthier young professionals to live in its swanky waterside towns, many of whom grew up during the Flower Power years of the 1960s and lend the place its New Age feel and reputation. Locals get their shitiake-mushroom pizzas delivered in

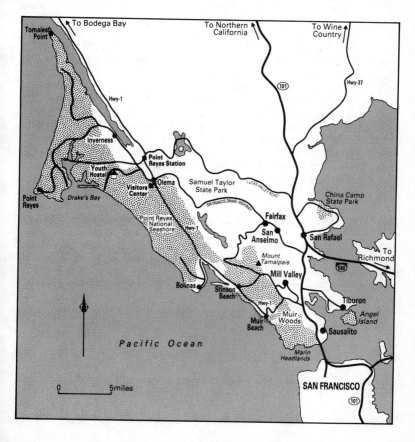

Porsches and think nothing of spending $1000 to see the Grateful Dead play at the Pyramids. Though many of the cocaine-and-hot-tub devotees who seemed to populate the place in the 1970s have traded in their drug habits for mountain bikes, life in Marin still centers around personal pleasure, and the throngs you see hiking and cycling at weekends, and the hundreds of bizarrely esoteric self-help practitioners—Rolfing, Re-Birthing, and soul-travel therapists fill up the classified ads of the local papers—prove that Marinites work hard to maintain their easy air of physical and mental well-being.

Flashy modern ferry boats sail across the bay from San Francisco and give a good initial view of the county: heading past desolate Alcatraz Island, curvaceous **Mount Tamalpais** looms larger until you land at its foot in one of the chic bayside settlements of **Sausalito** or **Tiburon**. **Angel Island**, in the middle of the bay but accessible most easily from Tiburon, provides relief from the excessive style-consciousness of both towns, retaining a wild untouched feeling among the eerie ruins of derelict military fortifications.

Sausalito, Tiburon, and the lifestyles that go with them, are only a small part of Marin. The bulk of the county rests on the slopes of the ridge of peaks which divides the peninsula down the middle, separating the sophisticated harborside towns in the east from the untramelled wilderness of the Pacific coast to the west. The **Marin Headlands**, just across the Golden Gate Bridge, hold time-warped old battlements and gun emplacements that once protected San Francisco's harbor from would-be invaders, and now overlook surfers and backpackers enjoying the acres of open space. Along the coastline that stretches north, the broad shore of **Stinson Beach** is the Bay Area's finest and widest stretch of sand, beyond which Hwy-1 clings to the coast past the rural village of **Bolinas** to the seascapes of **Point Reyes**, where, in 1579, Sir Francis Drake landed and claimed all of California for England.

Inland, the heights of Mount Tamalpais, and specifically **Muir Woods**, are a magnet to sightseers and nature-lovers, who come to wander through one of the few surviving stands of the native coastal redwood trees that once covered most of Marin. The trees were chopped down to build and rebuild the dainty wooden houses of San Francisco, and the long-vanished lumber mills of the rustic town of **Mill Valley**, overlooking the bay from the slopes of Mount Tam, as it's locally known, bear the guilt for much of this destruction; it's the oldest town in Marin County and now home to an eclectic bunch of art galleries and cafés. Farther north, the largest town in Marin, **San Rafael**, is best passed by, though its outskirts contain two of the most unusual places in the county: Frank Lloyd Wright's peculiar Civic Center complex and the preserved remnants of an old Chinese fishing village in China Camp State Park. The northern reaches of Marin County border the bountiful wine-growing regions of the Sonoma and Napa valleys, detailed in the following chapter.

Arrival and Getting Around

Just getting to Marin County can be a great start to a day out from San Francisco. *Golden Gate Transit* (☎322-6600) ferries leave from the **Ferry Building** on the Embarcadero, crossing the bay past Alcatraz Island **to Sausalito and Larkspur**; they run from 5:30am until 8pm, approximately

---

SAN FRANCISCO–MARIN COUNTY FERRIES

GOLDEN GATE TRANSIT FERRIES

San Francisco–Sausalito: depart at 7:50, 9:15, 10:25, and 11:45am, and at 1:10, 2:35, 4:10, 5:30, 6:40, and 8pm.

Sausalito–San Francisco: depart at 7:15, 8:25, 9:50, and 11:05am, and at 12:25, 1:55, 3:20, 4:45, 6:05, and 7:20pm

San Francisco–Larkspur: depart at 6:30, 7, 7:45, 8:50, and 10:45am, and at 12:45, 2:45, 3:40, 4:20, 4:50, 5:20, 6, 6:45, and 8:25pm.

Larkspur–San Francisco: depart at 5:30, 6, 7, 7:30, 8, 8:40, 9:45, and 11:45am, and at 1:45, 3:45, 4:25, 5:05, 5:40, and 7:35pm.

San Francisco–Tiburon: depart at 10am, noon, 2pm, and 3:45pm daily.

Tiburon–San Francisco: depart at 11am, 1pm, 3pm, and 5pm daily.

RED AND WHITE FLEET FERRIES

San Francisco–Sausalito: depart at 11:20am, 12:40pm, 1:50pm, 3:15pm, and 4:50pm.

Sausalito–San Francisco: depart at 11:50am, 1:15pm, 2:30pm, and 4pm.

---

every half hour during the rush hour, less often the rest of the day, and every two hours at weekends and holidays. Tickets cost $3.50 one way to Sausalito, $2.20 to Larkspur Monday to Friday ($3 weekends). Refreshments are served on board. The more expensive *Red and White Ferries* ($9 round trip; ☎546-2805) sail from Pier 43 1/2 at **Fisherman's Wharf to Sausalito** and from the **Ferry Building to Tiburon**—from where the *Angel Island Ferry* ($3 round trip, plus $1 per bicycle; ☎435-2131) nips back and forth to Angel Island State Park daily in summer, weekends only in the winter. The only services between Marin County and the East Bay are offered by *Traveler's Transit* (☎457-7080) minivans, running between the Richmond *BART* station and downtown San Rafael for $2 a trip.

Golden Gate Transit also runs a comprehensive **bus service** around Marin County and across the Golden Gate Bridge from the **Transbay Terminal** in San Francisco (from Marin County, ☎453-2100), and publishes a helpful and free system **map** and timetable, including all ferry services. Bus **fares** range from $1 to $3, depending on the distance traveled. Basic *GGT* bus routes run every half hour throughout the day, and once an hour late at night. *GGT*

MARIN COUNTY BUS SERVICES

#10: San Francisco–Sausalito–Marin City–Mill Valley–Tiburon

#20: San Francisco–Marin City–Larkspur–San Anselmo–San Rafael

#50: San Francisco–Sausalito–Marin City–San Rafael

#24: San Francisco–San Anselmo–Fairfax–Point Reyes Station; once a day at 5:40pm, weekdays only.

#63: Marin City–Stinson Beach; weekends and holidays only at 8:45, 9:45, and 10:45am.

#65: San Rafael–Point Reyes; 9am and 4pm weekends only.

commuter services run only during the morning and evening rush hours but can be the only way to get to some places. Also, San Francisco's *Muni* bus #76 runs hourly from San Francisco direct to the Marin Headlands on Sundays only. The list above includes the most useful routes. If you'd rather avoid the hassle of bus connections, *Gray Line* (☎896-5915; $37.50) offers four-hour guided **bus tours** from San Francisco, taking in Sausalito and Muir Woods, daily at 9am, 11am, and 1:30pm.

One of the best ways to get around Marin is by **bike**, particularly by mountain bike, cruising along the many trails that criss-cross the county. If you want to ride on the road, Sir Francis Drake Highway—from Larkspur to Point Reyes—makes a good route, though it's best to avoid it at weekends, when the roads can get clogged up with cars. All ferry services allow you to bring a cycle from San Francisco, or you can rent one from local outlets like *Ken's Bikes*, 94 Main Street in Tiburon (☎465-1683), or *Point Reyes Bikes*, 11431 Hwy-1 in Point Reyes Station (☎663-1768).

Information

For further **information** regarding Marin County, there are three main on-the-spot sources: the **Marin County Visitors Bureau**, 30 N. San Pedro Road, San Rafael (Mon–Fri 9am–5pm; ☎472-7470); the **Sausalito Chamber of Commerce**, at 333 Caledonia Street (Mon–Fri 9am–5pm; ☎332-0505); and the **Mill Valley Chamber of Commerce**, 85 Throckmorton Avenue (Mon–Fri 9:30am–4pm; ☎388-9700), in the center of the town. For information on **hiking and camping** in the wilderness and beach areas, depending on where you're heading, contact the Golden Gate National Recreation Area, Building 201, Fort Mason Center (daily 9am–4pm; ☎556-0560), Mount Tamalpais State Park, 801 Panoramic Highway, Mill Valley (daily 9am–5pm; ☎388-2070), or the Point Reyes National Seashore, Bear Valley, Point Reyes (daily 9am–5pm; ☎663-1092). For information on **what's on** in Marin, there are widely available local freesheets, like the down-to-earth *Coastal Post* or the New-Agey *Pacific Sun*.

Accommodation

You might prefer simply to dip into Marin County using San Francisco as a base, and if you've got a car or manage to time the bus connections right it's certainly possible, at least for the southernmost parts of the county. However, it can be nicer to take a more leisurely look at Marin, staying over for a couple of nights in some well-chosen spots. Sadly there are few **hotels**, and those that there are often charge in excess of $100 a night; **motels** tend to be the same as anywhere, though there are a couple of attractively faded ones along the coast. In any case, the best bet for budget accommodation is a dorm bed in one of the beautifully situated **hostels** along the western beaches.

Hostels

Golden Gate Hostel, Building 941, Fort Barry, Marin Headlands (closed 9:30am–4:30pm; ☎331-2777). Hard to get to unless you're driving—it's near Rodeo Lagoon just off Bunker Road, five miles west of Sausalito—but worth the effort for its setting, in cosy old army barracks just across the Golden Gate Bridge. On Sundays and holidays only, *Muni* bus #76 from San Francisco stops right outside. Dorm beds $11 a night.

Point Reyes Hostel, in the Point Reyes National Seashore (closed 9:30am–4:30pm; ☎663-8811). Also hard to reach without your own transport; just off Limantour Road six miles west of the visitors center and two miles from the beach, it's located in an old ranchhouse and surrounded by meadows and forests. Dorm beds $11 a night.

Motels and Hotels

Casa Madrona, 801 Bridgeway, Sausalito (☎332-0502). Deluxe hideaway tucked into the hills above the bay; doubles $100.

Motel Alto, 817 Redwood Highway, Mill Valley (☎388-6676). A bit hard to find—take the Seminary Drive exit of US-101, and it's just west of the free-way—but worth it for the low prices. Singles $30, doubles $40.

Ocean Court Motel, 18 Arnold St., Stinson Beach (☎868-0212). Just a block from the beach, west of Hwy-1. Large double rooms with kitchens for $85 a night.

San Rafael Inn, 865 E. Francisco Blvd., San Rafael (☎454-9470). Large road-side motel, just off US-101; doubles $45.

Stinson Beach Motel, 3416 Shoreline Highway, Stinson Beach (☎868-1712). Basic roadside motel right on Hwy-1, ten minutes' walk from the beach. Doubles $45 a night.

Bed and Breakfast

The Bed and Breakfast Exchange, 45 Entrata Drive, San Anselmo (☎485-1971). Not an inn but a letting agency, with rooms available in comfortable private homes all over Marin County from $50 a night for two, ranging from courtyard hideaways on the beach in Tiburon to houseboats in Sausalito.

The Blue Heron Inn, 11 Wharf Rd., Bolinas (☎868-1102). Lovely double rooms in an unbeatable locale for $75 a night.

Lindisfarne Guest House, part of the *Green Gulch Zen Center*, Muir Beach (☎383-3036). Restful rooms in a meditation retreat set in a secluded valley above Muir Beach. Doubles $50 a night, and the price includes excellent vegetarian meals.

Pelican Inn, 10 Pacific Way, Muir Beach (☎383-6000). Very comfortable rooms in a pseudo-English country inn, with good bar and restaurant down-stairs, ten minutes from beautiful Muir Beach. Double rooms $85 a night.

Ten Inverness Way, 10 Inverness Way, Inverness (☎669-1648). Quiet and restful in small village of good restaurants and bakeries on the fringes of Point Reyes. Doubles $80 a night.

Camping

China Camp State Park, off North San Pedro Rd. north of San Rafael (☎456-0766). Walk-in plots (just 200m from the parking lot) overlooking a lovely meadow. First-come, first-camped for $8 a night per plot.

Marin Headlands, just across the Golden Gate Bridge (☎331-1540). The best of dozens of plots here are at Kirby Cove, at the northern foot of the Golden Gate Bridge. Free.

Mount Tamalpais State Park, above Mill Valley (☎388-2070). Free plots for backpackers on the slopes of the mountain, and a few rustic cabins ($20 a night) along the coast at Steep Ravine.

Point Reyes National Seashore, forty miles northwest of San Francisco (☎663-1092). A wide range of free plots for backpackers, near the beach or in the forest.

Samuel Taylor State Park, on Sir Francis Drake Blvd., fifteen miles west of San Rafael (☎488-9897). Deluxe, car-accessible plots with hot showers, spread along a river for $12 a night. In summer, reserve a place through *Mistix* (☎800/445-7275).

Across the Golden Gate: Marin Headlands and Sausalito

The headlands across the Golden Gate from San Francisco afford some of the most impressive views of the bridge and the city behind. Take the first turn past the bridge, and follow the road up the hill into the **Marin Headlands** section of the Golden Gate National Recreation Area—largely undeveloped land, except for the concrete remains of old forts and gun emplacements standing guard over the entrance to the bay. The coastline here is much more rugged than it is on the San Francisco side, and though it makes a great place for an aimless, cliff-top scramble, or a walk along the beach, it's impossible not to be at least a little sobered by the presence of so many military relics—even if none was ever fired in a war. The oldest of these artillery batteries dates from the Civil War and the newest was built to protect against a Japanese invasion during World War II, but even though the huge guns have been replaced by picnic tables and brass plaques—one of the concrete bunkers has even been painted to make a *trompe l'oeil* Greek temple—you can't overlook their violent intent. Battery Wallace, the largest and most impressive of the artillery sites, is cut through a hillside above the southwestern tip, and the clean-cut military geometry survives to frame views of the Pacific Ocean and the Golden Gate Bridge. If you're interested in such things, come along on the first Sunday of the month and take a guided tour of an abandoned 1950s ballistic missile launchpad, complete with disarmed nuclear missiles. The one non-military thing to see, the **Point Bonita Lighthouse**, stands at the very end of the Headlands, where it's open for tours at weekends, except during the winter.

Most of what there is to do out here is concentrated half a mile to the north, around the rocky cliffs and islets of the point. Adjacent to the **Marin Headlands Visitor Center** (daily 8:30am–4:30pm; ☎331-1450)—also the end of the *Muni* bus #76 route from San Francisco on Sundays and holidays—there's a wide sandy **beach** in between the chilly ocean and swimmably

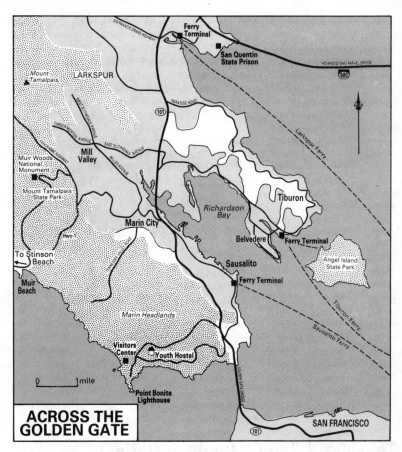

ACROSS THE GOLDEN GATE

warm-water **Rodeo Lagoon**. The visitor center has maps and information and handles reservations for the Headlands' free campgrounds (see above), each three miles from the beach and nearest road. Next to the center, the **Marine Mammal Center** rescues and rehabilitates injured and orphaned sea creatures, which you can visit while they recover; there's also a series of displays on the marine ecosystem and a bookstore that sells t-shirts and posters. The largest of the old army officers' quarters in the adjacent Fort Barry, half a mile to the east, has been converted into the spacious and homey **Golden Gate Youth Hostel** (see above for details), an excellent base for more extended explorations of the inland ridges and valleys.

Sausalito
SAUSALITO, along the bay below US-101, is a pretty, smug little town of exclusive restaurants and pricey boutiques along a picturesque waterfront promenade. Very expensive, quirkily designed houses climb the overgrown

cliffs above Bridgeway Avenue, the main road and bus route through town. Sausalito used to be a fairly gritty community of fishermen and sea-traders, full of bars and bordellos, and despite its upscale modern face it's still a fun day out from San Francisco by ferry, the boats arriving next to the Sausalito Yacht Club in the center of town. Hang out for a while along the marina and watch the crowds strolling along the esplanade, or climb the stairways across Bridgeway and amble among the grand houses which surround Sausalito's one truly impressive structure—the opulent Spanish Revival mansion that's been converted into the renowned *Casa Madrona* hotel and restaurant.

The old working wharves and warehouses that made Sausalito a haven for smugglers and Prohibition-era rum-runners are long gone; most have been taken over by dull steakhouses like the *Charthouse*—fifty years ago one of the settings for Orson Welles' waterfront murder-mystery, *The Lady from Shanghai*. However, some stretches of it have, for the moment at least, survived the tourist onslaught. Half a mile north of the town center along Bridgeway Avenue, an ad hoc community of exotic barges and **houseboats**, some of which have been moored here since the 1950s, is being threatened with eviction to make room for yet another luxury marina and bay-view office development. In the meantime many of the boats—one looks like a South Pacific island, another like the Taj Mahal—can be viewed from the marina behind the large brown shed that houses the Army Corps of Engineers **museum** (summer Tues–Sun 10am–6pm, other times Mon–Sat 9am–4pm; free), which features a massive working model of the San Francisco Bay, simulating changing tides and powerful currents.

ACCOMMODATION *Casa Madrona, Golden Gate Youth Hostel.*
BARS *no name bar.*
CAFÉS *Cafe Trieste.*
RESTAURANTS *Casa Madrona, Greater Gatsby's.*

The Marin County Coast to Bolinas

The Shoreline Highway, Hwy-1, cuts off west from US-101 just north of Sausalito, following the old main highway through the dull outskirts of MARIN CITY. The first turn on the left, Tennessee Valley Road, leads up to the less-visited northern expanses of the Golden Gate National Recreation Area. You can make a beautiful three-mile hike from the parking lot at the end of the road, heading down along the secluded and lushly green **Tennessee Valley** to a small beach along a rocky cove; or you can take a guided tour on horseback from *Miwok Livery* ($15 per hr; ☎383-8048).

Hwy-1 twists up the canyon to a crest, where Panoramic Highway spears off to the right, following the ridge north to Muir Woods and Mount Tamalpais (see below); *Golden Gate Transit* bus #63 to Stinson Beach follows this route every hour on weekends and holidays only. Two miles down from the crest, a small unpaved road cuts off to the left, dropping down to the bottom of the broad canyon to the **Green Gulch Farm and Zen Center** (☎383-3134), an organic farm and Buddhist retreat, with an authentic Japanese tea house and a simple but refined prayer hall. On Sunday mornings the center is opened for a public meditation period and an informal discussion of Zen Buddhist practice, after which you can stroll down to Muir Beach. If you already have some experience of Zen practice, look into the center's Guest Student Program, which enables initiates to stay from three days to several weeks at a time (it costs about $10 a night). If you just want a weekend's retreat, you can also stay overnight in the attached *Lindisfarne Guest House* for about $50 a night including meals, and take part as you like in the communal life. Residents of the center rise well before dawn for meditation and prayer, then work much of the day in the gardens, tending the vegetables that are eventually served in many of the Bay Area's finest restaurants (notably *Greens*, in San Francisco's Fort Mason Center).

Beyond the Zen Center, the road down from Muir Woods rejoins Hwy-1 at **Muir Beach**, surprisingly dark and usually uncrowded, around a semicircular cove. Three miles north—assuming Hwy-1 has been reopened since the massive mudslide of January 1990—**Steep Ravine** drops sharply down the cliffs to a small beach, past very rustic $20-a-night cabins and a $6-a-night campground, bookable through Mount Tamalpais State Park (see above for details). A mile on is the small and lovely **Red Rocks** nudist beach, down a steep trail from a parking area along the highway. **Stinson Beach**, which is bigger, and more popular (it's packed at weekends in summer, when the traffic can be nightmarish) despite the rather cold water, is a mile farther. You can rent surfboards and wetsuits for $10 a day from the *Livewater Surf Shop* (☎868-0333) along the highway at the south end of a short block of stores.

Bolinas

At the tip of the headland, due west from Stinson Beach, is the village of **BOLINAS**, though you may have a hard time finding it—road signs marking the turnoff from Hwy-1 are removed as soon as they're put up by locals hoping to keep their place all to themselves. The campaign may have backfired, though, since press coverage of the "sign war" has done more to publicize the town than any road sign every did; to get there, take the first left beyond the estuary and follow the road to the end. The village itself is a small colony of artists and writers (the late trout-fishing author Richard Brautigan and basketball diarist Jim Carroll among them), and there's not a lot to see—though you can get a feel for the place (and pick up a tasty sandwich and bags of fresh fruit and veggies) at the *Bolinas People's Store* in the block-long village center.

Beyond Bolinas there's a rocky beach at the end of Wharf Road west of the village; and **Duxbury Reef Nature Reserve**, half a mile west at the end of Elm Road, is well worth a look for its tidal pools, full of starfish, crabs, and sea anemones. Otherwise, Mesa Road heads north from Bolinas past the **Point Reyes Bird Observatory** (☎868-0655)—best visited in the morning, though open for informal tours all day. The first bird observatory in the US, this is still an important research and study center: if you time it right you may be able to watch, or even help, the staff as they put colored bands on the birds to keep track of them. Beyond here the road is no longer paved and leads on to the

Palomarin Trailhead, the southern access into the Point Reyes National Seashore (see below). The best of the many beautiful hikes around the area leads past a number of small lakes and meadows for three miles to **Alamere Falls**, which plunge down the cliffs onto tiny **Wildcat Beach**.

ACCOMMODATION *Pelican Inn, Blue Heron Inn.*
RESTAURANTS *Pelican Inn, The Sand Dollar, Stinson Beach Grill.*

Mount Tamalpais and Muir Woods

Mount Tamalpais dominates the skyline of the Marin peninsula, hulking over the cool canyons of the rest of the county in a crisp yet voluptuous silhouette and dividing the county into two distinct parts: the wild western slopes above the Pacific coast and the increasingly suburban communities along the calmer bay frontage. Panoramic Highway branches off from Hwy-1 along the crest through the center of **Mount Tamalpais State Park**, which has some thirty miles of hiking trails and many campgrounds, though most of the redwood trees which once covered its slopes have long since been chopped down to form the posts and beams of San Francisco's Victorian houses. One grove of these towering trees does remain, however, protected as the **Muir Woods National Monument** (daily 8am–sunset; free), a mile down Muir Woods Road from Panoramic Highway. It's a tranquil and majestic spot, with sunlight filtering through the 300-foot-tall trees down to the laurel- and fern-covered canyon below. The canyon's steep sides are what saved it from Mill Valley's lumbermen, and today it's one of the only first-growth redwood groves between San Francisco and the fantastic forests of Redwood National Park, up the coast near the Oregon border.

Being so close to San Francisco, Muir Woods is a popular target, and the trails nearest the parking lot have been paved and are often packed with bus-tour hordes. However, if you visit during the week, or outside midsummer, it's easy enough to leave the crowds behind, especially if you're willing to head off up the steep trails that climb the canyon sides. Winter is a particularly good time to come, as the streams are gurgling—the main creek reaches down to Muir Beach, and salmon have been known to spawn in it—and the forest creatures are more likely to be seen going about their business. Keep an eye out especially for the various species of **salamanders** and **newts** that thrive in this damp environment; be warned, though, that some are poisonous and will bite if harassed. Other colorful Muir Woods denizens are the colonies of ladybugs that spend their winter huddling in the rich undergrowth.

One way to avoid the crowds, and the only way to get here on public transit, is to enter the woods from the top, by way of a two-mile hike from the **Pan Toll Ranger Station** (☎388-2070) on Panoramic Highway—which is a stop on the *Golden Gate Transit* #63 bus route. As the state park headquarters, the station has maps and information on hiking and camping in the region, and rangers can suggest hikes to suit your mood and interests. From here the Pan Toll Road turns off to the right along the ridge to within a hundred yards of the 2571-foot **summit** of Mount Tamalpais, from where there are breathtaking views of the distant Sierra Nevada and close-ups of red-necked **turkey vultures**, listlessly circling the peak.

Mill Valley

From the East Peak of Mount Tamalpais, it's a quick two-mile hike downhill, following the Temelpa Trail through velvety shrubs of chaparral, to the town of **MILL VALLEY**, the oldest and most enticing of the inland towns of Marin County, also accessible every half hour by *Golden Gate Transit* bus #10 from San Francisco and Sausalito. Originally a logging center, it was from here that the destruction of the surrounding redwoods was organized, though for many years the town has made a healthy living out of tourism. The *Mill Valley and Mount Tamalpais Scenic Railroad*—"the crookedest railroad in the world" the blurb goes—was cut into the slopes above the town in 1896, twisting up through nearly three hundred tight curves in under eight miles, a trip which proved so popular with tourists that the line was extended down into Muir Woods in 1907, though road-building and fire combined to put an end to the railroad by 1930. You can, however, follow the old railroad from the end of Summit Avenue in Mill Valley, a route that's popular with daredevils on all-terrain bikes—which were, incidentally, invented here. More sport goes on here each June, when runners and assorted masochists come together for the **Dipsea**, a fiercely competitive seven-mile cross-country race over the mountains through Muir Woods to Stinson Beach.

The town centers today around the *Book Depot and Cafe* (daily 7am–10pm), a popular bookstore, café, and meeting place on Throckmorton and Miller. The **Chamber of Commerce** (Mon–Sat 9am–5pm; ☎388-9700), next door, has listings and maps of the many local cafés and restaurants and information on the wide range of local entertainments, including summer plays in the outdoor Mountain Theater, which also hosts a film festival in October. Though much of Mill Valley's attraction is in its easy access to hiking and mountain bike trails up Mount Tam, its compact yet relaxed center collects a number of cafés and some surprisingly good **galleries**, like *Artisans* at 78 E. Blithedale Road. Besides these, there are few sights worth seeking out, especially since the rustic, water-powered **sawmill** that gave the town its name has been dismantled and removed for restoration. Until last year it stood in the very pleasant, tree-shaded **Old Mill Park**, up Throckmorton Avenue 200 yards from the center of town, where it's due to be reconstructed in mid-1991. From Mill Valley, *Golden Gate Transit* bus #10 heads down Blithedale Avenue east to the bay, crossing US-101, and out along the Tiburon Peninsula.

BARS *Sweetwater*.
CAFÉS *Book Depot and Cafe, The Cantina, Dipsea Cafe, Jennie Low's Chinese Cuisine, Mill Valley Coffee Roastery.*
RESTAURANTS *Mountain Home Inn, da Angelo.*

Tiburon and Angel Island

TIBURON, at the tip of a narrow peninsula three miles east of US-101, is, like Sausalito, a ritzy harborside village to which hundreds of people come each weekend, via direct *Red and White Fleet* ferries from Pier 41 near Fisherman's Wharf in San Francisco and regular buses from elsewhere in Marin. It's a relaxed place, less touristy than Sausalito, and if you're in the mood to take it easy and watch the boats sail across the bay, it's a good place to sit out on the sunny deck of one of many cafés and bars and key in on the life of the town. There are few specific sights to look out for, but it's quite pleasant just to wander around, popping into the odd gallery or antique shop. The best of these are grouped together in **Ark Row**, at the west end of Main Street: the quirky buildings are actually old houseboats that were beached here early in the century. On a hill above the town stands **Old St Hilary's Church** (tours Wed and Sun 4–6pm), a Carpenter Gothic beauty that should be visited in the spring, when the surrounding fields are covered with buckwheat, flax, and paintbrush.

If you're feeling energetic, rent a **bicycle** from *Ken's Bikes*, 94 Main Street (☎465-1683), and cruise around the many plush houses of **Belvedere Island**, just across the Beach Road Bridge from the west end of Main Street, enjoying the fine views of the bay and Golden Gate Bridge. More ambitious cyclists can continue along the waterfront bike path, which winds from the bijou shops and galleries three miles west along undeveloped Richardson Bay frontage to a bird sanctuary at **Greenwood Cove**. The pristine Victorian house here is now the western headquarters of the **National Audubon Society** and open for tours (10am–4pm) on Sundays; there's also a small interpretive center with displays on local and migratory birds and wildlife. Another fine ride heads east from Tiburon along winding Paradise Road, around the mostly unbuilt-on headland three and a half miles to **Paradise Beach**, a county park with a fishing pier and close-up views of passing oil tankers heading for the refinery across the bay in Richmond. If you want to make a full circuit, Trestle Glen Boulevard cuts up and over the peninsula from near Greenwood Cove, linking with Paradise Road two miles northwest of Paradise Beach.

CAFÉS *Sweden House.*
RESTAURANTS *New Morning Cafe, Sam's Anchor Cafe.*

Angel Island

Tiburon is soon exhausted, and you'd be well advised to take the hourly *Angel Island Ferry* a mile offshore ($3 round trip, plus $1 per bicycle; ☎435-2131) to the largest island in the San Francisco Bay, ten times the size of Alcatraz. **Angel Island** is now officially a state park, but over the years it's served a variety of purposes, everything from a home for Miwok Native Americans to a World War II prisoner-of-war camp. It's full of ghostly **ruins** of old military installations and, with oak and eucalyptus trees and sagebrush covering the hills above rocky coves and sandy beaches, feels quite apart from the mainland. It's another excellent place to **cycle**: a five-mile road rings the island, and an unpaved track (and a number of hiking trails) leads up to the 800-foot hump of **Mount Hamilton**, which gives a panoramic view of the Bay Area.

The ferry arrives at **Ayala Cove**, where there's a small **snack bar** selling hot dogs and cold drinks—the only sustenance available on the island, so bring a **picnic** if you plan to spend the day here. The nearby **visitors' center** (daily 9am–4pm; ☎435-1915) has displays on the island's history, in an old building that was built as a quarantine facility for soldiers returning from the Philippines after the Spanish-American War. Around the point on the northwest corner of the island the North Garrison, built in 1905, was the site of a **prisoner-of-war camp** during World War II, while the larger East Garrison, on the bay a half mile beyond, was the major transfer point for soldiers bound for the South Pacific.

Around the point, **Quarry Beach** is the best on the island, a clean sandy shore that's protected from the winds blowing in through the Golden Gate; it's also a popular landing spot for kayakers and canoeists who paddle across the bay from Berkeley.

Sir Francis Drake Boulevard and Central Marin County

The quickest route to the wilds of the Point Reyes National Seashore, and the only way to get there on public transit, is by way of **Sir Francis Drake Boulevard**, which cuts across central Marin County through the inland towns of San Anselmo and Fairfax, reaching the coast thirty miles west at a crescent-shaped bay where, in 1579, Drake landed and claimed all of what he called Nova Albion for England. The route makes an excellent day-long cycling tour, and there are good beaches, a youth hostel, and some tasty restaurants at the end of the road.

The Larkspur *Golden Gate Transit* ferry, which leaves from the Ferry Building in San Francisco, is the longest and, surprisingly, least expensive of the bay crossings. It's primarily a commuter route and docks at the modern space-frame terminal at Larkspur Landing. The monolithic, red-tile-roofed complex you see on the bayfront a mile east is the maximum-security **San Quentin State Prison**, which houses the state's most violent and notorious criminals; at the gate there's a small gallery that displays and sells art and crafts created by men held inside.

It's only four miles west from the ferry landing to **San Anselmo**, the first town of any interest, but unless you're arriving with the homeward-bound commuters, in which case there'll be a connecting bus (*Golden Gate Transit* #19), it's annoyingly difficult to get there. To board the main *Golden Gate Transit* #24 bus—which follows Sir Francis Drake all the way to Point Reyes—you'll have to walk a quarter of a mile west from the ferry terminal, following the creek under US-101 to the bus stop.

San Anselmo, Fairfax, and Point Reyes Station

SAN ANSELMO, set in a broad valley two miles north of Mount Tam, calls itself "the antiques capital of Northern California" and sports a tiny center of specialty shops, furniture stores, and cafés that draws out many San Francisco shoppers at weekends. The ivy-covered **San Francisco Theological Seminary** dominates the town from the hill above, and there's the very green and leafy **Creek Park** along the creek that winds through the town center, but otherwise there's not a lot to do but eat and drink—or browse through fine **bookstores** like *Oliver's Books*, at 645 San Anselmo Avenue.

Center Boulevard follows the tree-lined creek west for a mile to **FAIRFAX**, a town that's much less ostentatiously hedonistic than the harborside towns, though in many ways it still typifies Marin lifestyles, with an array of whole-food stores and bookstores geared to a thoughtfully mellow crowd. From Fairfax, the narrow **Bolinas Road** twists up and over the mountains to the coast at Stinson Beach, while Sir Francis Drake Boulevard winds through a pastoral landscape of ranch houses hidden away up oak-covered valleys—an area that was used as the location for Alan Parker's tear-jerking saga of Marin County life, *Shoot the Moon*, in which slobby Albert Finney starred as a philandering writer.

Ten miles west of Fairfax along Sir Francis Drake Boulevard, **Samuel Taylor State Park** has excellent **camping** (see above for details); five miles more brings you to the coastal Hwy-1 and the town of OLEMA, a mile north of which sits the town of **POINT REYES STATION**, a good place to stop off for a bite to eat or to pick up picnic supplies before heading off to enjoy the wide-open spaces of the Point Reyes National Seashore just beyond. *Point Reyes Bikes*, 11431 Hwy-1 at Main Street (☎663-1768), rents **mountain bikes** for $20 a day, much the best way to get around.

CAFÉS *Caffe Nuvo, Patrick's Bookshop and Cafe.*
RESTAURANTS *Hilda's, Mi Casa, Station House Cafe.*

The Point Reyes National Seashore

From Point Reyes Station, Sir Francis Drake Boulevard heads out to the westernmost tip of Marin County at Point Reyes through the **Point Reyes National Seashore**, a near-island of wilderness that's surrounded on three sides by more than fifty miles of isolated coastline—pine forests and sunny meadows bordered by rocky cliffs and sandy, windswept beaches. The wing-shaped landmass is something of an aberration along the generally straight coastline north of San Francisco and is in fact a rogue piece of the earth's crust that has been drifting slowly and steadily northward along the San Andreas Fault, having started some six million years ago as a suburb of Los Angeles. When the great earthquake of 1906 shattered San Francisco, the land here at Point Reyes, the epicenter, shifted over sixteen feet in an instant, though damage was confined to a few skewed cattle fences.

The park **Visitors' Center** (daily 9am–5pm; ☎663-1092), two miles south-west of Point Reyes Station near Olema, just off Hwy-1 on Bear Valley Road, has engaging displays on the geology and natural history of the region; rangers can suggest good places to hike or cycle to, and have up-to-date information on the **weather**, which can change quickly and be cold and windy along the coast even when it's hot and sunny here, three miles inland. They also handle permits and reservations for the various **campgrounds** within the park. Nearby, a replica of a native Miwok village has an authentic religious roundhouse, and a popular hike follows the Bear Valley Trail along Coast Creek four miles to **Arch Rock**, a large tunnel in the seaside cliffs that you can walk through at low tide.

North of the visitors' center, Limantour Road heads west six miles to the **Point Reyes Youth Hostel** (see above), continuing on another two miles to the coast at **Limantour Beach**, one of the best swimming beaches and a good place to watch the seabirds in the adjacent estuary. Bear Valley Road rejoins Sir Francis Drake Boulevard just past Limantour Road, leading north along the Tomales Bay through the village of **INVERNESS**, so-named because the landscape reminded an early settler of his home in the Scottish Highlands. Eight miles west of Inverness, a turn leads down past *Johnson's Oyster Farm*—where you can buy bivalves by the dozen for half the price you'd pay in town—to **Drake's Beach**, the presumed landing spot of Sir Francis in 1579. Appropriately, the coastline here resembles the southern coast of England, often cold, wet, and windy, with chalk-white cliffs rising above the wide sandy beach. The main road continues west another four miles to the very tip of Point Reyes, where there's a precariously sited **lighthouse** standing firm against the literally crashing surf. The lighthouse, which you can't tour, is reached via a tiring 300 or so steps down the steep cliffs, but even without making the trek all the way out to the lighthouse, the bluffs along here are excellent places to look out for sea lions and, in winter, migrating gray **whales**.

The northern tip of the Point Reyes seashore, **Tomales Point**, is accessible by the Pierce Point Road, which turns off Sir Francis Drake Boulevard two miles north of Inverness. Jutting out into Tomales Bay, it's the least-visited section of the park and a refuge for hefty **tule elk**; it's also a great place for admiring the lupines, poppies, and other wild flowers that appear in the spring. The best swimming (at least the warmest water) is at **Heart's Desire Beach**, a little way before the end of the road; also, down the bluffs from where the road comes to a dead end, there are excellent tidal pools at rocky **McClure's Beach**. North of Point Reyes Station, Hwy-1 continues along the coast, through Bodega Bay up to Mendocino and the northern California coast.

San Rafael and Northern Marin County

You may pass through **SAN RAFAEL** on your way north from San Francisco, but there's little worth stopping for. It's the county seat and the only big city in Marin County, and it has none of the woodsy qualities that make the other towns special, though there are a couple of good restaurants and bars along Fourth Street, the town's main drag. The one sight to see in town is an old Franciscan **Mission** (daily 11am–4pm; free), in fact a 1949 replica that was built near the site of the 1817 original, on Fifth Avenue at A Street. The real points of interest are well on the outskirts: the Marin County Civic Center to the north and the little-known China Camp State Park along the bay to the east.

The **Marin County Civic Center** (Mon–Fri 9am–5pm; free; ☎472-3500), spanning the hills just east of US-101 a mile north of central San Rafael, is a strange, otherworldly complex of administrative offices, plus an excellent performance space that looks like a giant train viaduct capped by a bright blue-tiled roof. These buildings were architect **Frank Lloyd Wright**'s one and only government project, and although the huge circus tents and amusement park at the core of the designer's conception were never built, there are some interesting touches, like the atrium lobbies that open directly to the outdoors.

From the Civic Center, North San Pedro Road loops around the headlands through **China Camp State Park** (☎456-0766), an expansive area of pastures and open spaces that's hard to reach without your own transport. It takes its name from the intact but long-abandoned Chinese shrimp-fishing village at the far eastern tip of the park, the sole survivor of the many small Chinese communities that once dotted the California coast. The ramshackle buildings, small wooden pier, and old boats lying on the sand seem straight out of a John Steinbeck tale, the only recent addition a chain-link fence to protect the site from vandals. At the weekend you can get beer and sandwiches from the old shack at the foot of the pier, but the atmosphere is best during the week, at sunset, when there's often no one around at all. There's a **campground** at the northern end of the park, about two miles from the end of the *Golden Gate Transit* bus #39 route.

Six miles north of San Rafael, the **Lucas Valley Road** turns off west, twisting across Marin to Point Reyes. Although he lives and works here, it was not named after *Star Wars* filmmaker George Lucas, whose sprawling *Skywalker Ranch* studios are well hidden off the road. Hwy-37 cuts off east, eight miles north of San Rafael, heading around the top of the bay into the Wine Country of the Sonoma and Napa valleys (see Chapter Twelve).

ACCOMMODATION *San Rafael Inn.*
BARS *Fourth Street Tavern.*
RESTAURANTS *Rice Table, Millie's, New George's.*

Eating

For all its healthy and wealthy prosperity, Marin County's **eating** options don't really compare with those in the rest of the Bay Area. However, there are plenty of **restaurants** worth searching out if you're in the area, serving anything from pizzas and Mexican food to vegetarian crêpes and standard soup-and-sandwich combos, as well as some fine places whose settings—on the waterfront or high up in the hills—make them quite special indeed.

Restaurants

The Cantina, 651 E. Blithedale Rd. at Camino Alto, Mill Valley (☎381-1070). Some of the best Mexican food in Marin, spiced by what's certainly the hottest salsa for miles.

Casa Madrona, 805 Bridgeway, Sausalito (☎331-5888). Mediterranean staples meet California Cuisine in this delectable hotel-restaurant which does excellent fresh seafood. Great view of the harbor, and service is anything but hurried.

Da Angelo, 22 Miller Ave., Mill Valley (☎388-2000). Good salads and large portions of tasty if unremarkable Italian dishes, especially pasta, for around $10 a plate.

Dipsea Cafe, 1 El Paseo, Mill Valley (☎381-0298). Hearty diner food, especially good for breakfast before a day out hiking on Mount Tamalpais.

Greater Gatsby's, 39 Caledonia St., Sausalito (☎332-4500). Handy, inexpensive pizza parlor a block from the waterfront on the north side of town.

Hilda's, 639 San Anselmo Ave., San Anselmo (☎457-9266). Great breakfasts and lunches in this down-home, cosy café.

Jenny Low's Chinese Cuisine, 38 Miller Ave., Mill Valley (☎388-8868). Whether you're after Cantonese, Hunan, Mandarin, or Szechuan food you'll find it here. Main dishes cost $4–8.

Manka's, 30 Calendar Way, Inverness (☎669-1034). Excellent Czechoslovakian food in a homey dining room near the wilds of Point Reyes.

Milly's, 1613 4th St., San Rafael (☎459-1601). Extremely healthy, wideranging vegetarian dishes like Thai vegetable curries and jalapeño ravioli. Open evenings only.

Mountain Home Inn, 810 Panoramic Highway, above Mill Valley (☎381-9000). Another place that's as good for the atmosphere as for the food, with a range of broiled meats and fish dishes served up in a rustic lodge on the slopes of Mount Tam.

New Morning Cafe, 1696 Tiburon Blvd., Tiburon (☎435-4315). Lots of healthy wholegrain sandwiches, plus salads and omelettes.

Pelican Inn, Hwy-1, Muir Beach (☎383-6000). Great fish and chips ($8) or roast beef and Yorkshire pudding ($15) in a coaching-house atmosphere.

Rice Table, 1617 4th St., San Rafael (☎456-1808). From the shrimp chips through the crab pancakes and noodles on to the fried plantain desserts, these fragrant and spicy Indonesian dishes are worth planning a day around. Dinners only, but excellent value at $5–8 a plate.

Sam's Anchor Cafe, 27 Main St., Tiburon (☎435-2676). Rough-hewn, amiable waterfront café. Good burgers, soups, and sandwiches, plus Sunday brunches.

The Sand Dollar, 3458 Shoreline Highway (Hwy-1), Stinson Beach (☎868-0434). Good-value burgers and sandwiches on a sunny outdoor deck, with a range of seafood dishes indoors in the evenings.

Station House Cafe, Main St. at 3rd St., Point Reyes Station (☎663-1515). Open for breakfast, lunch, and dinner every day but Tuesday, this friendly local favorite brings people from miles around.

Stinson Beach Grill, Hwy-1, Stinson Beach (☎868-2002). Somewhat pricey California Cuisine in a beachfront setting.

Viva Bien Cafe, 225 Corte Madera Ave., Larkspur (☎924-7940). A bit hard to get to—it's on the main route from Larkspur up to Mill Valley—but worth it for the terrific, mostly veggie food, including great filled crêpes, sandwiches, and salads.

Drinking and Nightlife

Almost every Marin town has at least a couple of **cafés** that are open long hours for a jolt of caffeine and, if you're after more relaxing liquid refreshments, any number of saloon-like **bars** where you'll feel at home immediately. And while the nightlife is never as charged as it gets in San Francisco, since most of the honchos of the Bay Area music scene—from impresario Bill Graham to psychedelic rangers Grateful Dead—and dozens of lesser-known but no less brilliant session musicians and songwriters live here, Marin's **nightclubs** are unsurpassed for catching big names in intimate locales.

Cafés

Book Depot and Cafe, 87 Throckmorton Ave., Mill Valley (☎383-2665). Lively café housed in an old train station, which it shares with a bookstore and newsstand.

Caffe Nuvo, 556 San Anselmo Ave., San Anselmo (☎454-4530). Great coffee and pastries, with a large balcony overhanging a creek, plus poetry readings and live music most nights

Cafe Trieste, 1000 Bridgeway, Sausalito (☎332-7770). This distant relative of the North Beach institution serves good coffee, a wide menu of pastas and salads, and great *gelati*.

Mill Valley Coffee Roasters, 2 Miller Ave., Mill Valley (☎383-2912). Boisterous, always crowded coffee house right in the center of town.

Patrick's Bookshop and Cafe, 9 Bolinas Rd., Fairfax (☎454-2428). Coffees and teas, and tasty soups and sandwiches, in this low key hippie holdout; good selection of books and mags, too.

Sweden House, 35 Main St., Tiburon (☎435-9767). Great coffee and marvelous pastries on a jetty overlooking the yacht harbor, all for surprisingly reasonable prices.

Bars

no name bar, 757 Bridgeway, Sausalito (☎332-1392). A thriving ex-haunt of the Beats which still hosts poetry readings and evening jam sessions.

Marin Brewing Company, 1809 Larkspur Landing, Larkspur (☎461-4677). Lively pub opposite the Larkspur ferry terminal, with half a dozen tasty ales—

try the malty *Albion Amber* or the creamy *St Brendan's Irish Red*—all brewed on the premises.

Pelican Inn, Hwy-1, Muir Beach (☎383-6000). Good selection of traditional English and modern Californian ales, plus fish and chips (and rooms if you overdo it).

Sam's Anchor Cafe, 27 Main St., Tiburon (☎435-2676). Slightly posey hang-out for folk off the yachts and wharf rats right on the water, it's packed on weekend afternoons but better after the sun goes down or during the week. They also do a good range of food.

Sweetwater, 153 Throckmorton Ave., Mill Valley (☎388-3820). Large open room full of beer-drinking locals that after dark evolves into Marin's prime live music venue (see below).

Nightlife

Amadeus, 20 Main St., Tiburon (☎435-3966). Stylish small café and dance club, with jazz/fusion weeknights and funk at the weekend. Open nightly 9pm–1am, cover $3–5.

Fourth Street Tavern, 711 4th St., San Rafael (☎ 454-4044). Gutsy, no-frills beer bar with free, bluesy music most nights.

New George's, 842 4th St., San Rafael (☎457-1515). Large dance floor and wide range of music in a friendly, good-time place that doubles as a charcoal grill restaurant. Performers range from local cover bands to Leon Redbone to Robyn Hitchcock, and cover varies from nothing to $15.

Sweetwater, 153 Throckmorton Ave., Mill Valley (☎388-3820). Small, comfortable saloon that brings in some of the biggest names in music, from jazz and blues all-stars to Jefferson Airplane survivors.

CHAPTER TWELVE

THE WINE COUNTRY

San Francisco during the summer can be a shock—persistent fog and cool temperatures dog the city from May to September—but you only have to travel an hour north to find a warm and sunny climate among the rolling hills of the Napa and Sonoma valleys, known collectively as the **Wine Country**. With its cool, oak-tree shaded ravines climbing up along creeks and mineral springs to chapparal-covered ridges, it would be a lovely place to visit even without the vineyards, but as it is, the "wine country" tag dominates almost everything here, including many often overlooked points of historical and literary interest. The Wine Country area doesn't actually account for all that much wine—production is something like five percent of the California total, most of which is of the Gallo and Paul Masson jug-wine variety and comes from the Central Valley. But far and away the best wines in the country come from here. The region has been producing wines since the days of the Spanish missions, and though most of the vines withered during Prohibition, the growers have struggled back and these days manage to turn out premium vintages that satisfy enophiles around the world. Not surprisingly, it's a wealthy region, and rather a smug one, thriving as much on its role as a vacation land for upper-crust San Franciscans as on the wine trade: designer eateries (all with massive wine lists) and luxury inns line the narrow roads that, on summer weekends especially, are bumper-to-bumper with wine-tasting tourists.

By and large the **Napa Valley** is home to the bigger concerns, but even here the emphasis is on quality rather than quantity, and the high-brow tones of the winery tour guides-cum-wine merchants can get maddeningly pretentious. However, wineries are everywhere, and while the town of **Napa** is sprawling and quickly done with, the many small towns farther up the valley, particularly **St Helena**, have retained enough of their turn-of-the-century homestead character to be a welcome relief. **Calistoga**, at the top of the valley, offers the best range of non-wine-related distractions—mostly various methods of soaking your bones in tubfuls of hot spring water.

On the western side of the dividing Mayacamas mountains, the small, backroads wineries of the **Sonoma Valley** reflect the more down-to-earth nature of the place, which is both more beautiful and less crowded than its neighbor to the east. The town of **Sonoma** itself is by far the most attractive of the Wine Country communities, retaining a number of fine Mission-era structures around its gracious central plaza. **Santa Rosa**, at the north end of the valley, is the region's sole urban center, handy for budget accommodation but otherwise unremarkable.

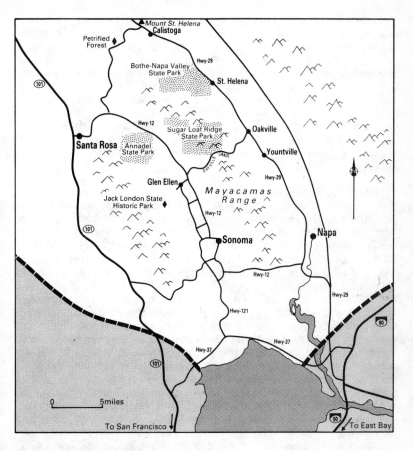

Arrival and Getting Around

The Wine Country region spreads north from the top of San Francisco Bay in two parallel, thirty-mile-long valleys, Napa and Sonoma, divided by the oak-covered Mayacamas mountains. As long as you avoid the rush hour traffic, it takes about an hour to reach along either of two main routes: from Marin County, via the Golden Gate Bridge and US-101, and from the East Bay, via the Bay Bridge and I-80. Since its attractions are spread out over a fairly broad area, a **car** is all but essential, particularly if you're pressed for time.

Greyhound buses from San Francisco and the East Bay head up through the Napa Valley twice a day, along Hwy-29, stopping at Napa, St Helena, Calistoga, and Santa Rosa. *Greyhound* also has direct buses five times a day from San Francisco to Santa Rosa. From Santa Rosa, *Sonoma County Transit* (☎707/576-RIDE) bus #30 serves the Sonoma Valley once an hour, through Glen Ellen to Sonoma and back again—tickets to Sonoma cost $1.70.

Another less satisfying but easier option is to sign up for one of the guided **bus tours** offered by *Gray Line* (☎558-9400) from San Francisco. These cost $37.50, and leave from Union Square at 9am, visiting a winery in each valley, stopping for lunch in Yountville and returning to the city at about 6:30pm. Much more exciting, but a definite indulgence, are the widely hyped **hot-air balloon rides** over the Napa Valley. These usually lift off at dawn (hot air rises more strongly in the cold morning air) and last a fairly magical ninety minutes, winding up with a champagne brunch. The first and still the best of the operators is *Napa Valley Balloons* (☎707/253-2224), which flies out of Yountville. Others include *Ballooons Above The Valley* (☎707/253-2222) and *Once in a Lifetime* (☎707/942-6541). The crunch comes when you realize the price—around $120 a head.

Cycling in the Wine Country

If you don't have a car, it's possible to get around under your own steam, using the fairly limited bus services and **cycling** the rest of the time. You can bring your own bike on *Greyhound*, or rent one locally for around $20 a day from a number of places, including *Bryan's Napa Valley Cyclery*, 4080 Byway East, Napa (☎707/255-3377); *St Helena Cyclery*, 1156 Main Street, St Helena (☎707/963-7736); and *Sonoma Wheels*, 523 Broadway, Sonoma (☎707/935-1366).

Both valleys are generally flat, although the peaks in between are steep enough to challenge the hardest of hill-climbers. If the main roads through the valleys are packed out, as they are most summer weekends, try the smaller parallel routes: the **Silverado Trail** in Napa Valley and the less evocatively named but nonetheless pretty **Arnold Drive** in Sonoma Valley. For would-be Kings of the Mountains, the **Oakville Grade** between Oakville in the Napa Valley and Glen Ellen in the Sonoma Valley has tested the world's finest riders: you can still make out traces of "Go Hinault!" and "C'mon LeMond!" daubed on the roadway for the *Coors Classic* tours some years ago.

If you feel like some company, or just want to be sure everything goes smoothly, a few local firms organize **tours**, providing bikes, helmets, food, and sag wagons in case you get worn out. In Calistoga, *Cruisin' Jules* (☎707/942-0421) specializes in mountain bike downhill runs, and *Rob Mondavi's Napa Valley Biking Picnics* (☎707/252-1067) set up more leisurely tours—highlighted by gourmet lunches—all over the Napa area. Ambitious, multi-day tours are put together by *Backroads Bicycle Tours*, 1516 5th Street, Berkeley (☎527-1555).

Information

Not surprisingly for such a tourist-dependent area, the Wine Country has a well-developed network of **tourist information** outlets, though the keen rivalry that exists between the two valleys means that it's next to impossible to find out anything about Sonoma when you're in Napa, and vice versa. While the various small town **Chambers of Commerce** rarely do more than hand out useless brochures, both the **Napa Chamber of Commerce**, 1556 First Street, Napa (Mon–Fri 10am–5pm, Sat & Sun 11am–3pm; ☎707/226-

7455), and the **Sonoma Valley Visitor's Bureau**, 453 First Street East (Mon–Sat 9am–4pm, Sun 9am–3pm; ☎707/996-1090), in Sonoma's central plaza, should be able to tell you all you need to know about their respective areas. If you're keen on **touring the wineries**, both the above places sell handy **maps** ($1) that give the lowdown on the hundreds of producers.

Accommodation

As it's only an hour from Union Square to the Wine Country, most people are content to come for a long day, visiting a few of the wineries and maybe having a picnic or a meal before heading back to the city. This is fine if you have a car and are happy to spend most of the day in it, but if you really want to absorb properly what the region has to offer, plan to spend at least one night here, either **camping** out in the heavily wooded state parks or pampering yourself in one of the many (generally pricey) **hotels** and **bed and breakfast inns** that provide the bulk of the area's accommodation options. If you're not into roughing it, or having a romantic getaway, there are a few medium-priced **motels** along the main roads, much like anywhere.

At peak times rooms of all descriptions can seem to be booked up, and if you have a hard time finding a place, avail yourself of one of the many **accommodation services** here—*Accommodation Referrals* (☎707/963-8466); *Inns of Sonoma Valley* (☎707/996-INNS); *Reservations Unlimited* (☎707/252-1985); or the *Napa Valley Tourist Bureau* (☎707/944-1557). If all else fails, head into Santa Rosa, the region's biggest town, where you'll always be able to find a room.

Motels and Hotels

Calistoga Inn, 1250 Lincoln Ave., Calistoga (☎707/942-4101). Comfortable rooms in a landmark building; doubles from $55.

The Comfort Inn, 1865 Lincoln Ave., Calistoga (☎707/942-9400). Quiet, modern motel on the edge of town, with double rooms from $60 per night.

El Bonita Motel, 195 Main St., St Helena (☎707/963-3216). Old roadside motel recently done up in Art-Deco style; doubles $50.

El Pueblo Motel, 896 W. Napa St., Sonoma (☎707/996-3651). Basic highway motel with doubles for $55 per night.

Hillside Inn, 2901 4th St., Santa Rosa (☎707/546-9353). Clean, attractive motel with swimming pool; doubles $45.

Hotel St Helena, 1309 Main St., St Helena (☎707/963-4388). Opulently redecorated 1881 inn, with doubles from $85.

Jack London Lodge, 13740 Arnold Drive, Glen Ellen (☎707/938-8510). Modern motel near the Jack London State Park, with a good restaurant and swimming pool. Doubles from $55 a night.

Magliulo's Pensione, 691 Broadway, Sonoma (☎707/996-1031). Cosy accommodation with excellent Italian restaurant attached. Doubles from $55.

Motel 6, 3380 Solano Ave., Napa (☎707/226-1811). Basic rooms, no frills. Doubles $38 per night.

Mount View Hotel, 1457 Lincoln Ave., Calistoga (☎707/942-6877). Lively Art-Deco-style hotel with nightly jazz and an excellent restaurant. Doubles from $65.

Sonoma Hotel, 110 W Spain St., Sonoma (☎707/996-2996). Antique-filled rooms in an 1870 hotel just off Sonoma Plaza. Doubles from $65.

Vintage Inn, 6541 Washington St., Yountville (☎707/944-1112). Huge luxury rooms—all with fireplaces—plus swimming pool and free bike rental. Handy for Yountville's many fine restaurants, and great for a romantic getaway. Doubles $120.

White Sulphur Springs, 3100 White Sulphur Springs Rd., west of St Helena (☎707/963-8588). A relaxing retreat from the hyper-tourism of the Napa Valley, unpretentious rooms in a ramshackle old 300-acre hillside resort; double rooms from $45 a night.

Bed and Breakfast

Gaige House Inn, 13540 Arnold Drive, Glen Ellen (☎707/935-0237). Restored Victorian farmhouse in country setting. Doubles from $75; no children under 12.

Thistle Dew Inn, 171 W. Spain St., Sonoma (☎707/938-2909). Newly restored rooms near Sonoma Plaza, plus full breakfast and free bike rental. Doubles from $80.

The Cinnamon Bear, 1407 Kearney St., St Helena (☎707/963-4388). Quirky, sumptuously furnished inn. Doubles from $65.

Camping

Bothe-Napa Valley State Park (☎707/942-4575). Four miles south of Calistoga on Hwy-29. Good hiking along shaded creek plus a somewhat incongruous swimming pool; plots with showers for $10 per night. Book by credit card (☎800/444-7275).

Calistoga Fairgrounds, 1435 Oak St., Calistoga (☎707/942-5111). More for campervans and motor homes, though tent plots are available for $12 per night.

Sugarloaf Ridge State Park, east of Hwy-12 near Kenwood (☎707/833-5712). Uncrowded site overlooking the Sonoma Valley, with plots for $10 a night. Book by credit card (☎800/444-7275).

The Napa Valley

A thirty-mile strip of gently landscaped corridors and lush hillsides, the **Napa Valley** looks more like southern France than a near-neighbor of the Pacific Ocean. In spring the valley floor is covered with brilliant wild flowers which mellow into mulled autumnal shades by grape-harvest time. The Native Americans who lived here named the fish-rich river which flows through the valley "Napa," meaning "plenty," and although the name was adopted by the Spanish missionaries who arrived in the early 1800s, the Indians themselves were soon wiped out. The few ranchos the Spanish and Mexicans managed to establish in the valley were in turn taken over by Yankee traders, and by the 1850s California was part of the US and the town of Napa had become a thriving river port, sending agricultural goods to San Francisco and serving as a supply point for the local farmers and ranchers. Before long Napa was bypassed by the railroads and unable to compete with other, deep-water Bay Area ports, but the area's fine climate saved it from oblivion, encouraging a variety of crops including the grape, which spawned the now super-lucrative wine industry.

The town of **NAPA**, at the southern end of the valley, is still the area's economic lynchpin, and the highway sprawl that greets travelers is fair warning of what the rest of the town has to offer. But for a proud courthouse, and some intriguingly decrepit old warehouses (ripe for gentrification) along the river, there's not much to see, though it's not bad for food, and the **tourist office** is the most helpful in the whole valley. **YOUNTVILLE**, the next town north, similarly has little to see, though it boasts the highest proportion of **places to eat** in the whole region.

St Helena

The first town really worth a stop is **ST HELENA**, 22 miles north of Napa, not much more than a large village really, and one of the prettiest Napa Valley settlements. Its main street, Hwy-29, is lined by some of the Wine Country's finest old buildings, most of which have been restored to—or maintained in—prime condition. The town is also at the heart of the greatest concentration of wineries (see below), although the best reason to spend time here is to check out its unlikely collection of literary attractions.

The best of these is the **Silverado Museum** (Tues–Sun noon–4pm; free), housed in the old St Helena Public Library building just off Main Street in the center of town, which has a collection of over 8000 articles relating to Robert Louis Stevenson, who spent just under a year in the surrounding area, honeymooning and recovering from an illness. It's claimed to be the second most extensive collection of Stevenson artifacts in the US, though the only thing of interest to any but the most obsessed fan is a scribbled-on manuscript of *Dr Jekyll and Mr Hyde*. The other half of the building is taken up by the **Napa Valley Wine Library** (same hours), a briefly entertaining barrage of photos and clippings relating to the development of local viniculture. Another, more bizarre collection is on display on the north side of town at 1515 Main Street, where the **Ambrose Bierce House** bed and breakfast inn is packed with memorabilia of the misanthropic ghost-story writer, who lived here for some fifteen years before heading off to die for Pancho Villa in the Mexican Revolution.

Calistoga

Beyond St Helena, toward the far northern end of the valley, the wineries become prettier and the traffic a little thinner. At the very tip of the valley, nestling at the foot of Mount St Helena, **CALISTOGA** is far and away the most enjoyable of the Napa towns, with a few good wineries but really better known for its mud baths and hot springs—and the mineral water bearing its

NAPA VALLEY WINERIES

There are over a hundred **wineries** in the Napa Valley, almost all of which offer tastings, though comparatively few have tours. Since all produce wines of a very high standard, it's entirely a question of taste which ones you visit: you may have sampled or heard of certain wineries that you want to search out, or you may simply prefer to make a casual tour, stopping off in places you like the look of. The following selections, listed from south to north, are some long-standing favorites, plus a few lesser-known hopefuls. Keep in mind that the intention is for you to get a sense of a winery's product, and perhaps buy some, rather than get drunk on the stuff, so don't expect more than a sip or two of any one sort—though some wineries do sell wines by the glass. If you want to buy a bottle, particularly from the larger producers, you can in fact usually get it cheaper in supermarkets than at the wineries themselves.

Stag's Leap, 5766 Silverado Trail, east of Yountville (☎707/944-2020) (tasting daily 10am–4pm; tours by appointment). The winery that put Napa Valley on the international map by beating a bottle of Chateau Lafitte-Rothschild at a prestigious Paris tasting way back in 1976. Still quite highly rated.

Robert Mondavi, 7801 St Helena Highway, Oakville (☎707/963-9611). Long the standard-bearer for Napa Valley wines ("Bob Red" and "Bob White" are house wines at many a fine California restaurant), they also have far and away the most informative and least hard-sell tours. Tours and tasting daily 9am–5pm, book ahead in summer. For true aficionados, free half-day tours are also available.

Berringer Brothers, 2000 Main St., St Helena (☎707/963-7115). Known as the Rhine House, this is the Napa Valley's most famous piece of architecture, gracing the cover of many a wine magazine and modeled on an ancestral Gothic mansion in the brothers' native Germany. Expansive lawns and a grand tasting room, heavy on the dark wood, make for quite a regal experience. Tours and tasting daily 10am–4pm; closed in August.

Christian Brothers, 2555 Main St., St Helena (☎707/963-0765). This was the world's largest winery when erected in 1889, but was a bit of a white elephant that kept changing hands until its present owners—oddly enough a Catholic teaching order—bought it in 1950, and it now turns out extremely popular sparkling wines. Tours and tasting daily 10am–4pm.

Conn Creek Winery, 8711 Silverado Trail, St Helena (☎707/963-9100) (tasting 10am–4pm daily; tours by appointment). A truly modern organization whose lightweight stone and steel building is worlds away from the cutesy old-stone image that's the norm in the rest of the valley.

Clos Pegase, 1060 Dunaweal Rd., Calistoga (☎707/942-4981). A flamboyant upstart at the north end of the valley, this high-profile winery emphasizes the links between fine wine and fine art, with a sculpture garden around buildings designed by the noted post-modern architect Michael Graves. No tours, tastings daily 10:30am–4:30pm.

name which adorns every Californian supermarket shelf. Sam Brannan, the young Mormon entrepreneur who made a mint out of the Gold Rush, established a resort community here in 1860. In his groundbreaking speech he attempted to assert his desire to create the "Saratoga of California," modeled upon the Adirondack gem, but in the event committed a spoonerism and coined the town's unique name.

Calistoga's main attraction, then as now, has nothing to do with wines, but rather with another pleasurable activity: soaking in the soothingly hot water that bubbles up here from deep inside the earth. Suiting its all-natural source, the town has evolved into a homey, health-conscious kind of place, with many spas and volcanic mud baths that draw jaded urban dwellers up here for the weekend. The extravagant might enjoy checking out *Dr. Wilkinson's Hot Springs*, 1507 Lincoln Avenue (rooms and treatment from $100 per night; ☎707/942-4102): a legendary health spa and hotel whose heated mineral water and volcanic ash tension-relieving treatments have been featured on the TV show, *Lifestyles of the Rich & Famous*. If swaddled luxury is not what you're after, there are a number of other, more down-to-earth establishments spread along the mile-long main drag, Lincoln Avenue. *Nance's Hot Springs*, 1614 Lincoln Avenue (☎707/942-6211), for example, which offers a full mineral rub-down, blanket sweat, steam bath, and massage for around $30.

Another sign of Calistoga's lively underground activity is the **Old Faithful Geyser** (daily 9am–5pm; $3), two miles north of town on Tubbs Lane, off Hwy-128, which spurts boiling water sixty feet into the air at fifty-minute intervals. The water source was discovered while drilling for oil here in the 1920s, when search equipment struck a force estimated to be up to a thousand pounds per square foot; the equipment was blown away, and, despite heroic efforts to control it, the geyser has continued to go off like clockwork ever since. Landowners finally realized that they'd never tame it and turned it into a high-yield tourist magnet.

A further local tourist trap is the **Petrified Forest** (daily 10am–5pm; $3), two miles west of Calistoga on the steep road over the hills to Santa Rosa—a forest that was toppled during an eruption of Mount St Helena some three million years ago. The entire redwood grove was petrified by the silica-laden volcanic ash seeping into the decomposing fibers of the uprooted trees which gradually became a forest of stone trees.

Mount St Helena

The clearest sign of the local volcanic presence is the massive conical mountain that marks the north end of the Napa Valley, **Mount St Helena**. The 4343-foot summit is worth a climb for its great views—on a very clear day you can see Point Reyes and the Pacific coast to the west, San Francisco to the south, the towering Sierra Nevada to the east, and impressive Mount Shasta to the north. It is, however, a long hot climb (five steep miles each way), and you need to set off early in the morning to enjoy it—take plenty of water (and maybe a bottle of wine).

The mountain and most of the surrounding land are protected as the **Robert Louis Stevenson State Park** (daily 8am–sunset; $2), though the connection with him is fairly weak: it was here that in 1880 Stevenson spent his honeymoon in a bunkhouse with Fanny Osborne, recuperating from tuberculosis and exploring the valley. The bunkhouse remains, but there is little else about the park's winding roads and dense shrub-growth to evoke its days of former notoriety, though it's a pretty enough place to take a break from the wineries and have a picnic. Stevenson liked the area and wrote about it copiously. In his novel, *Silverado Squatters*, he describes the highlight of the honeymoon as the day he managed to taste eighteen of local wine baron Jacob Schram's champagnes in one sitting. Quite an extravagance, especially when you consider that Schramsberg champagne is held in such high esteem that Richard Nixon took a few bottles when he went to visit Chairman Mao.

BARS *Ana's Cantina, Compadres, Willett's Brewing Company.*
RESTAURANTS *All Seasons, Bosko's Ristorante, Checkers Pizza, The Diner, Doidge's, La Boucane, Mustards, PJ's Cafe.*

The Sonoma Valley

On looks alone the crescent-shaped Sonoma Valley beats Napa hands down. This smaller and altogether more rustic valley curves between oak-covered mountain ranges from the Spanish colonial town of **Sonoma** a few miles north along Hwy-12 to **Glen Ellen**, before ending up at the region's main city, **Santa Rosa**. The Sonoma Valley is also known as the "Valley of the Moon," after the Native American legend popularized by long-time resident Jack London which tells how, as you move through the valley, the moon seems to rise several times from behind the various peaks. Far smaller than Napa, most of the Sonoma Valley's wineries are informal, family-run businesses, many within walking distance of Sonoma itself, and with far fewer visitors—making it very much the stress-free alternative to the busy Napa Valley.

Sonoma

Behind a layer of somewhat touristy shops and restaurants, the small town of **SONOMA** retains a good deal of its Spanish and Mexican architecture. Set around a spacious plaza, the town has a welcoming feel that's refreshing after brash Napa, although as a popular retirement spot, with a median age of about fifty and a matching pace, it's not exactly bubbling with action. The **visitors' bureau** (Mon–Sat 9am–4pm, Sun 11am–3pm; ☎707/996-1090), in the middle of the leafy central plaza, has walking-tour plans of the town and excellent free maps and guides to the wineries. What there is to see in the town itself will take no more than an hour: Sonoma is a place better known for its history than its sights.

It's hard to believe now that Sonoma was the site of a key event in West Coast history, but the so-called **Bear Flag Revolt** was just that—at least as far as the flag-waving Fourth of July crowds who take over the central square are concerned. In this much-romanticized episode, American settlers in the region, who had long lived in uneasy peace under the Spanish and, later, Mexican rulers, were threatened with expulsion from California, along with all other non-Mexican immigrants. In response, a band of thirty armed settlers—some of whom came from as far away as Sacramento—descended upon the disused and unguarded presidio at Sonoma, taking the retired and much-respected commander Colonel Guadalupe Vallejo as their prisoner. Ironically, Vallejo had long advocated the American annexation of California and supported the aims of his rebel captors, but he was nonetheless bundled off to Sutter's Fort in Sacramento and held there for the next two months while the militant settlers declared California an independent republic. The Bear Flag, which served as the model for the current state flag, was raised on Sonoma Plaza. A month later the US declared war on Mexico, and without firing a shot took possession of the entire Pacific coast.

In memory of all this, there's a monument to the Bear Flag revolutionaries in the middle of the plaza, and across the street to the north, in **Sonoma State Historic Park**, there are some rusty old cannons and the spooky-looking remains of the old Mexican presidio; the ragged flag is on display inside a small **museum** (daily 8am–5pm; $2). Next door, the restored **Mission San Francisco Solano de Sonoma** (daily 10am–5pm; $1) was the northernmost and last of the California missions and the only one established while California was under Mexican rule. Half a mile west of the plaza along Spain Street stands the ornate old home of General Vallejo, dominated by profusely decorated filigreed eaves and slender Gothic-arched windows. There's a chalet-style storehouse next door that's been turned into a **museum** (daily 9am–5pm; free) of artifacts from the general's reign.

SONOMA VALLEY WINERIES

There are fine **wineries** all over the Sonoma Valley, though some of the best are concentrated in a well-marked group a mile east of Sonoma Plaza, down East Napa Street. Some are within walking distance, but often along quirky back roads, so take a winery map from the tourist office and follow the signs closely. If you're tired of chasing around, Sonoma also has the handy *The Wine Exchange of Sonoma*, 452 First Street East (☎707/938-1794), a commercial tasting room where you can sample the best wines from all over California.

Buena Vista Winery, 1800 Old Winery Rd. (☎707/938-1266). Oldest and grandest of the wineries, although the wine itself has a reputation for being pretty mediocre, and the 100-year-old stone champagne cellars—the best thing about the place—are being refashioned into yet another pricey restaurant. Tasting daily 10am–5pm, tours daily at 2pm, Sat and Sun also at 11:30am.

Hacienda Wine Cellars, 1000 Vineyard Lane (by appointment only; ☎707/938-3220). A lavish Spanish colonial building, with some great topiary in the gardens and extensive vineyards. The wines are relatively inexpensive, middle-of-the-range vintages that appeal to the pocket and palate alike; if you're looking to buy a case, this one's a safe bet. Tastings daily 10am–5pm, tours by appointment.

Gundlach-Bundschu, 3775 Thornsberry Rd. (☎707/938-5277). Set back about a mile away from the main cluster, this is more highly regarded for its wine, having stealthily crept up from the lower ranks of the wine league to regularly steal awards from the big names. The plain, functional building is deceptive—this is premium stuff and definitely not to be overlooked. No tours, but tasting daily 10am–5pm.

Glen Ellen and Jack London State Park

While it makes for a soothing drive up the valley there's really very little to see north of Sonoma apart from a few small towns and the **Jack London State Park** (daily 8am–dusk; $3 per car)—just ten minutes from Sonoma on the London Ranch Road which curves sharply off Hwy-12 close to tiny **GLEN ELLEN** village. Jack London lived here with his wife for the last years of his short, unsettled life, on a 140-acre ranch in the hills above what he described as the "most beautiful, primitive land in California." A series of paths and walking trails lead through densely wooded groves to the remains of the Wolf House, where they lived until an arson attack reduced most of it to a pile of rubble in 1913, leaving only the huge stone chimney and fireplaces. London died three years later and is buried on a hill above the trail to the Wolf House. After his death London's wife Charmian built the more formal House of Happy Walls, which today serves as a small **museum** (daily 9am–4pm; free), with many photographs and artifacts—including the desk where he cranked out his 2000 words a day—enlivening the otherwise dry information detailing the writer's life and work.

Santa Rosa

Sixty miles due north of San Francisco on US-101, and about twenty miles from Sonoma, **SANTA ROSA**, the largest town in Sonoma County, sits at the top end of the Sonoma Valley and is more or less the hub of this part of the Wine Country. It's a very different world from the indulgence of other Wine Country towns, however, much of it given over to shopping centers and road-side malls, and signs downtown that ban teenagers from cruising the rarely packed but confusing system of one-way streets.

Probably the most interesting thing about Santa Rosa is that it was the fictional home town of Raymond Chandler's private eye Philip Marlowe; after that it's all downhill. The **Luther Burbank Home and Gardens** at the inter-section of Santa Rosa and Sonoma Avenues (April–Sept only Wed–Sun 10am–3:30pm; $1) may kill an hour or two: California's best-known turn-of-the-century horticulturalist is remembered here in the house where he lived and in the splendid gardens where he created some of his most unusual hybrids. If you're not into gardening, nip across the street to the **Ripley Museum**, 492 Sonoma Avenue (Wed–Sun 11am–4pm, March–Oct only; $1.50), where you might expend twenty minutes or so in one of the cartoonist Ripley's mediocre "Believe It or Not" chain of museums—Santa Rosa was Ripley's home town.

Eating and Drinking

Opportunities for **consuming** are everywhere in the Wine Country, and stan-dards (and prices) are as high as—or higher than—anywhere in San Francisco. California Cuisine has caught on in a big way here, and freshness and innovative presentation are very much in evidence. Many of the eateries are completely dependent upon the tourist trade, and some towns seem to have more restaurants than population. **Yountville**, in particular, is little more than a string of high-style eateries, any of which is up there with the best San Francisco has to offer, with prices to match. **Calistoga** is more low key, but still a gourmet paradise. Other fine places are sprinkled throughout the two valleys if you keep an eye out, though odds are that the great little place you stumble upon will be bringing in the San Francisco crowds before long.

Straight **drinking** spots are more rare, thanks perhaps to the free drinks on offer from the various wineries. There are a couple worth a look, though most are decidedly locals' hang-outs.

Cafés and Takeouts

Bosko's Ristorante, 1403 Lincoln Ave., Calistoga (☎707/942-9088). Standard Italian restaurant doing good-value fresh pasta dishes, cheap and cheerful, and popular with families.

Checkers Pizza, 1414 Lincoln Ave., Calistoga (☎707/942-9300). Range of soups, salads, and sandwiches, plus adventurous pizzas and good pasta dishes.

The Diner, 6476 Washington St., Yountville (☎707/944-2626). Start the day's wine-touring off right, with cups of good strong coffee and brilliant breakfasts. Open until 3pm Tuesday to Friday, until 10pm at weekends for flavorsome Mexican dinners.

Doidge's, 1313 Main St., St Helena (☎707/963-1788). Like the one in San Francisco's Marina District, this small café specializes in Eggs Benedict and other morning treats.

La Casa, 121 East Spain St., Sonoma (☎707/996-3406). Friendly, festive Mexican restaurant across from Sonoma Mission.

PJ's Cafe, 1001 2nd St., Napa (☎707/224-0607). A Napa institution, open 11am–10pm every day for pasta, pizzas, and sandwiches.

Parsley's, 522 Broadway, Sonoma (☎707/935-0803). Home-style diner with good soups and a salad bar. Breakfast and lunch only.

Restaurants

All Seasons, 1400 Lincoln Ave., Calistoga (☎707/942-9111). Friendly bistro serving up good-sized portions of California Cuisine, but best known for its massive wine list, many of which are available by the glass. Main dishes cost $10–20.

Depot Hotel 1870, 241 1st St. West, Sonoma (☎707/938-2980). Reliable American and northern Italian food in a well-restored old hotel.

Grist Mill Restaurant, 14301 Arnold Drive, Glen Ellen (☎707/996-3077). Creekside dining in a spacious converted mill. A large menu plus an extensive list of local wines.

La Boucane, 1778 2nd St., Napa (☎707/253-1177). Mouthwatering chunks of tender meat prepared in imaginative sauces, plus perfect fish (especially shellfish) and vegetables. Dinner only, main dishes cost $12–25.

Mustards, 7399 St Helena Highway (Hwy-29), Yountville (☎707/944-2424). Credited with starting the late 1980s trend toward "grazing" food, emphasizing tapas-like titbits rather than main meals. Reckon on spending $15–20 a head.

Bars

Ana's Cantina, 1205 Main St., St Helena. Long-standing unpretentious saloon and Mexican restaurant.

Compadres, 6539 Washington St., Yountville. Not so much a bar as a margarita factory; buy 'em by the pitcher or supercharged with shots of Cuervo Gold. They also serve a wide range of Mexican food.

Joe Frogger's, 527 4th Ave., Santa Rosa. Lively bar with free live music most nights.

Sonoma Saloon, 110 West Spain St., Sonoma. Funky old saloon that's 100 years old and still going strong; the adjoining dining room focuses on local cheeses and baked goods.

Willett's Brewing Company, 902 Main St., Napa. An anomaly in wine-obsessed Napa, this pub cranks out a range of good beers—all brewed on the premises—best drunk on their outdoor patio overlooking the Napa River.

PART FOUR

THE
CONTEXTS

THE HISTORICAL FRAMEWORK

Though its recorded history doesn't stretch back very far, even by US standards, in its 150 years of existence San Francisco has more than made up for time. The city first came to life during the California Gold Rush of 1849, an adventure which set a tone for the place that it sustains to this day, both in its valuing of individual effort above corporate enterprise and in often nonconformist policies that have given it perhaps the most liberal image of any US city. The following account is intended to give an overall view of the city's development; for a rundown of the figures—both past and present—that have helped shape the city, see the "San Francisco People" glossary at the end of *Contexts*.

NATIVE PEOPLES

For thousands of years prior to the arrival of Europeans, the **aboriginal peoples** of the Bay Area flourished on the naturally abundant land, living healthily and apparently fairly peacefully, one of the first colonists finding them "constant in their good friendship, and gentle in their manners." Numbering around 30,000, they lived mainly by hunting game and fishing, grouped in small, tribal villages of a few

hundred people. Most belonged to the coastal **Miwok** tribe that inhabited most of today's Marin County, as well as the Sonoma and Napa valleys; the rest were **Costanoans**, who lived in smaller villages sprinkled around the bay and down the south coast of the peninsula.

Very few artifacts from the period survive, and most of what anthropologists have deduced is based on the observations of the early explorers, who were by and large impressed by the Indian way of life—if not their "heathen" religion. Indian boats, fashioned from lengths of tule reed, were remarkably agile and seaworthy. Of the buildings, few of which were ever intended to last beyond the change of seasons, the most distinctive was the *temescal* or sweat lodge. Kule Loklo, a replica Miwok village in the Point Reyes National Seashore, gives a good sense of what their settlements might have looked like.

Since there was no political or social organization beyond the immediate tribal level, it was not difficult for the colonizing Spaniards to effectively wipe them out, though this was admittedly more through infectious epidemics than through outright genocide. Nowadays no Bay Area Native American tribes survive on their aboriginal homelands.

EXPLORATION AND CONQUEST

Looking at the Golden Gate from almost any vantage point, it's hard to imagine someone not noticing such a remarkable opening to the Pacific. Nevertheless, dozens of **European explorers**, including some of the most legendary names of the New World conquest—Juan Cabrillo, Sir Francis Drake, Sebastian Vizcaino—managed to sail by for centuries, oblivious of the great harbor it protected. Admittedly, the passage is often obscured by fog, and even on a clear day the Bay's islands, and the East Bay hills which rise up behind, do disguise the entrance to the point of invisibility. However, many of them would doubtless turn in their graves if they knew what they had missed discovering.

The Englishman **Sir Francis Drake** came close to finding the Bay when he arrived in the *Golden Hind* in **1579**, taking a break from plundering Spanish vessels in order to make repairs. His supposed landing spot, now called Drake's Bay, off Point Reyes north of San Francisco, had "white bancks and cliffes" that reminded him of Dover. Upon going ashore, he was met by a band of native Miwok Indians who greeted him with food and drink and placed a feathered crown upon his head; in return, he claimed all of their lands, which he called Nova Albion (New England), for Queen Elizabeth I, apparently leaving behind a brass plaque, a copy of which (once thought to be authentic, though since proved to be a forgery) is now on display in the Bancroft Library at the University of California in Berkeley.

Fifteen years later the Spanish galleon **San Augustín**—loaded to the gunwales with treasure from the Philippines—moored in the same spot but met with a tragically different fate. After renaming Drake's Bay to honor their patron saint, San Francisco de Asis (Francis of Assisi), disaster struck: the ship was dashed against the rocks of Point Reyes and wrecked. The crew were able to salvage some of the cargo and enough of the ship to build a small lifeboat, on which they traveled south all the way to Acapulco, the Spanish base of operations in the Pacific, hugging the coast for the entire voyage and still sailing right past the Golden Gate. Indeed it was not until the end of 1769 that Western eyes set sight on the great body of water now called San Francisco Bay.

COLONIZATION: THE MISSION ERA

The **Spanish occupation** of the West Coast, which they called "Alta California," began in earnest in the late 1760s, following the Seven Years' War, partly due to military expediency (to prevent another power from gaining a foothold), partly to Catholic missionary zeal—they intended to convert the heathen Indians. Early in **1769** a company of 300 soldiers and priests set off from Mexico to establish an outpost at Monterey, half of them by ship, the other half overland. A number stopped to set up the first California mission at San Diego, and an advance party—made up of some sixty soldiers, mule skinners, priests, and Indians, and led by Gaspar de Portola—continued up the coast, blazing an overland route. It was hard going, especially with their inadequate maps, and not surprisingly they overshot their mark, ending up somewhere around Half Moon Bay.

Trying to regain their bearings, Portola sent out two scouting parties, one north along the coast and one east into the mountains, both groups returning with extraordinary descriptions of the Golden Gate and the great bay, which they thought must be the same "Bahia de San Francisco" where the *San Agustín* had come to grief almost two centuries earlier. On November 4, 1769, the entire party gathered together on the ridgetop, overwhelmed by the incredible sight: Father Crespi, their priest, wrote that the bay "could hold not only all the armadas of our Catholic Monarch, but also all those of Europe." Portola's band barely stayed long enough to establish a mission and gather up supplies before turning around and heading back to Monterey. They made little note of the great bay they had found, but the settlement they founded was to become the capital and commercial center of Spanish California.

It took the Spanish another six years to send an expedition 85 miles north to the bay Portola had discovered. In May **1775**, Juan Manuel de Ayala piloted the ship *San Carlos* through the Golden Gate, becoming the first Europeans to sail into San Francisco Bay. The next year Captain **Juan Bautista de Anza** returned with some 200 soldiers and settlers to establish the **Presidio of San Francisco** overlooking the Golden Gate, as well as a mission three miles to the southeast, along a creek he named Nuestra Senora de Dolores—"Our Lady of Pain," referring to the labor-pains of the Virgin Mary. From this came the mission's popular—and still current—name, **Mission Dolores**.

Over the coming years four other Bay Area **missions** were established. Santa Clara de Asis, forty miles south of Mission Dolores, was founded in 1777; San Jose de Guadalupe, established in 1797 near today's Fremont, grew into the most successful Bay Area mission. In 1817 the *asistencia*, or auxiliary mission San Rafael Arcangel was built in sunny Marin County as a convalescent hospital for priests and Indians who had been taken ill at Mission Dolores. The last, San Francisco Solano, was built at Sonoma in 1823, the only mission established under Mexican rule.

The mission complexes were broadly similar, with a church and cloistered residence structure surrounded by irrigated fields, vineyards, and more distant ranchlands, the whole protected by a small contingent of soldiers. Indian neophytes were put to work making soap and candles but were treated as retarded children, often beaten and never educated. Objective facts about the missionaries' treatment of the Indians are rare, though mission registers record twice as many deaths as they do births, and their cemeteries are packed with Indian dead. Many of the missions suffered from Indian raids, the now ubiquitous red-tiled roofs replacing the earlier thatch the better to withstand fire.

To grow food for the missions and the forts or presidios, **towns**—called *pueblos*—were established, part of the ongoing effort to attract settlers to what was still a distant and as yet undesirable territory. The first was laid out in 1777 at San Jose, in a broad, fertile valley south of the Mission Santa Clara. Though it was quite successful at growing crops, it had no more than a hundred inhabitants until well into the 1800s. Meanwhile, a small village—one not sanctioned by the Spanish authorities—was beginning to emerge between Mission Dolores and the presidio, around the one deep-water landing spot, southeast of today's Telegraph Hill. Called **Yerba Buena**, "good grass," after the sweet-smelling minty herb that grew wild over the windswept hills, it was little more than a collection of shacks and ramshackle jetties. Although the name San Francisco was not applied to it until the late 1840s, this tiny outpost formed the basis of today's metropolis.

THE MEXICAN REVOLUTIONS AND COMING OF AMERICANS

The emergence of an independent **Mexican state** in 1821 spelled the end of the mission era, and within a few years the new republic had secularized the missions and handed over their lands to the few, powerful families of the "Californios"—mostly ex-soldiers who'd settled here after being discharged from the army. The Mexican government exerted hardly any control over distant Yerba Buena and was generally much more willing than the Spanish had been to allow foreigners to remain as they were, as long as they behaved themselves. A few trappers and adventurers had passed by in the early 1800s and, beginning in the early 1820s, a number of British and Americans started arriving in the Bay Area, most of them sailors who jumped ship, but also including a few men of property. The most notable of these

immigrants was **William Richardson**, an Englishman who arrived on a whaling ship in 1822 and stayed for the rest of his life, marrying the daughter of the presidio commander and eventually coming to own most of southern Marin County, from where he started a profitable shipping company and ran the sole ferry service across the treacherous bay waters. Following Richardson's lead, dozens more began coming—almost without exception males who, like him, tended to fit in with the existing Mexican culture, often marrying into established families and converting to the Catholic faith.

As late as the mid-1840s, Monterey was still the only town of any size on the whole west coast, and tiny Yerba Buena (population 200 or so) made its livelihood supplying passing ships, mainly Boston-based whaling vessels and the fur traders of English-owned **Hudson's Bay Company**. Though locals lived well, the Bay Area was not obviously rich in resources, and so was by no means a major issue in international relations. However, from the 1830s onward, the **US government** decided that it wanted to buy all of Mexico's lands north of the Rio Grande, California included, in order to fulfil its "Manifest Destiny," to embrace the continent from coast to coast. They were, apparently, open to discussion, but any such negotiations were rendered unnecessary when, in June 1846, the Mexican-American War broke out in Texas, and US naval forces quickly took over the entire West Coast, capturing San Francisco's presidio on **July 9, 1846**.

A revealing—although historically insignificant—episode, one which set the tone for the anarchic growth of the Bay Area over the next fifty years, took place around this time. An ambitious US Army captain, John C. Fremont, had been working to encourage unhappy settlers to declare independence from Mexico and to set himself up as their leader. By assembling an unofficial force of some sixty sharpshooting ex-soldiers, and by spreading rumors that war with Mexico was imminent and unavoidable, he managed to persuade settlers to take action: the **Bear Flag Revolt**. On June 14, some thirty farmers and trappers descended upon the abandoned presidio in Sonoma and took the retired commandant Colonel Guadupe Vallejo captive, raising a makeshift flag over the plaza and declaring California independent. The flag—which featured a roughly drawn grizzly bear above the words "California Republic"—was eventually adopted as the California state flag, but this "California Republic" was short lived. Just three weeks after the disgruntled settlers hoisted their flag in Sonoma, it was replaced by that of the Stars and Stripes, and California remained **US territory**. Ironically, just nine days before the Americans took formal control, **gold** was discovered on January 24, 1848, in the Sierra Nevada foothills a hundred miles east of the city, a fact which was to change the face of San Francisco forever.

THE GOLD RUSH

At the time of **gold discovery**, the Bay Area had a total (non-native) population of some 2000 people, about a quarter of whom lived in tiny **San Francisco**, which had only changed its name from Yerba Buena the year before. By the summer of 1848 rumors of the find attracted a trickle of prospectors, and when news of their subsequent success filtered back to the coast (relayed by a local storekeeper **Sam Brannan**, in Portsmouth Square), soldiers deserted and sailors jumped ship, and most towns were abandoned as would-be settlers dropped everything to head for the gold fields. The first prospectors on the scene made fantastic fortunes—those working the richest "diggings" could extract more than an ounce every hour—but the real money was being made by merchants charging equally exorbitant prices for essentials. Even the most basic supplies were hard to come by, and what little was available was outrageously expensive: a dozen eggs for $50, a shovel or pickaxe twice that. Exuberant miners willingly traded shotglasses of gold dust for an equal amount of whisky—something like $1000 a go. Though it took some time for news of the riches to travel, soon men were flooding in to California from all over the globe to share the wealth, in the most extraordinary migration in history. Within a year some 100,000 men—known collectively as the **Forty-Niners**—had arrived in California. About half of them came overland, after a three-month slog across the continent, and headed straight for the mines. The rest arrived by ship and landed at San Francisco, expecting to find a city where they could recu-

perate before continuing the arduous journey. They must have been disappointed with what they found: hulks of abandoned ships formed the only solidly constructed buildings, rats overran the filthy streets, and drinking water was sparse and often contaminated.

Few of the new arrivals stayed very long in San Francisco, but, if anything, life in the mining camps proved even less hospitable. As thousands of moderately successful but wornout miners returned to San Francisco, especially during the torrential rains of the **winter of 1849–50**, the shanty town began to grow into a proper city. Ex-miners set up foundries and sawmills to provide those starting out with the tools of their trade, and increasing numbers of people arrived to take advantage of the miners' success, selling them clothing, food, drink, and entertainment. It was to the city that successful miners went to blow their hardearned cash, a place of luxury hotels and burlesque theaters which featured the likes of Lola Montez, whose "spider dance," performed semi-clad, enthralled legions. Throughout the early 1850s immigrants continued to pour through the Golden Gate, and although the great majority hurried on to the mines, enough stayed around to bring the city's population up to around 50,000 by the end of 1853. Of these, more than half were from foreign parts—a wide-ranging mix of Mexicans, Germans, Chinese, Italians, and others.

Within five years of the discovery of gold the easy pickings were all but gone, and as the freewheeling mining camps evolved into increasingly large-scale, corporate operations, San Francisco evolved from frontier outpost into a substantial city, with a growing industrial base, a few newspapers, even its own branch of the US Mint. But as revenues from the gold fields ceased expanding in the late 1850s, the speculative base which had made so many fortunes quickly vanished. Lots which had been selling at a premium couldn't be given away, banks went bust, and San Francisco had to declare itself **bankrupt** as a result of years of corrupt dealing. The already volatile city descended into near-anarchy, with vigilante mobs roaming the streets enforcing their particular brand of justice. By the summer of 1856 the "Committee of Vigilance," led by William Coleman and the ever-present Sam Brannan and made up of the city's most successful businessmen, was the **de facto government** of the city, having taken over the state militia and installed themselves inside their "Fort Gunnybags" headquarters, outside which they regularly hanged petty criminals (admittedly after giving them a fair trial), to the amusement of gathered throngs. A few of the most radically minded vigilantes proposed seceding from the Union, but calmer heads prevailed, and the city was soon restored to more legitimate government. The rest of the 1850s were comparatively uneventful, as San Francisco prepared for what was to become the biggest boom in the city's boom-and-bust cycle.

THE BOOM YEARS (1860–1900)

In the 1860s San Francisco enjoyed a bigger boom than that of the Gold Rush, following the discovery of an even more lucrative band of precious **silver ore** in the Great Basin mountains of western Nevada. Discovered just east of Reno in late 1859, and soon known as the **Comstock Lode**, it was one of the most fantastic deposits ever encountered: a single, solid vein of silver, mixed with gold, ranging from ten to over a hundred feet wide and stretching a little over two miles long, most of it buried hundreds of feet underground. Mining here was in complete contrast to the free-lance prospecting of the California gold fields, and required a scale of operations unimagined in the California mines, many of San Francisco's great engineers, including George Hearst, Andrew Hallidie, and Adolph Sutro, putting their minds to the task.

As the mines had to go increasingly deeper to get at the valuable ore, the mining companies needed larger and larger amounts of capital, which they attracted by issuing shares dealt on the burgeoning San Francisco **Stock Exchange**. Speculation was rampant in the Comstock mine stock, and the value of shares could rise or fall by a factor of ten, depending on the day's rumors and forecasts; Mark Twain got his literary start publicizing, for a fee, various new "discoveries" in his employers' mines. Hundreds of thousands of dollars were made and lost in a day's trading, and the cagier players, like James Flood and James Fair, made millions.

While many San Franciscans were enjoying unsurpassed prosperity throughout the 1860s,

thanks to the Comstock silver, few people gave much thought to the decade's other major development, the building of the **transcontinental railroad**, completed in 1869 using imported Chinese laborers. Originally set up in Sacramento to build the western link, the **Central Pacific** and later **Southern Pacific** railroad soon expanded to cover most of the western US, ensnaring San Francisco in its web of control. Wholly owned by the so-called **Big Four**—Charles Crocker, Collis P. Huntington, Mark Hopkins, and Leland Stanford—the Southern Pacific "octopus," as it was caricatured in the popular press, exercised an absolute monopoly over transport services in the Bay Area. Besides controlling the long-distance railroads, they also owned San Francisco's streetcar system, the network of ferry boats that criss-crossed the bay, even the cable car line that lifted them up California Street to their Nob Hill palaces.

However, not everyone reaped the good fortune of the Nob Hill elite. The coming of the railroad usurped San Francisco's primacy as the West Coast's supply point, and products from the East began flooding in at prices well under anything local industry could manage. At the same time the Comstock mines ceased to produce such enormous fortunes, and economic depression began to set in. The lowering of economic confidence was compounded by a series of droughts which wiped out successive harvests, and by the arrival in San Francisco of thousands of now unwanted **Chinese workers**, who had been brought over to build the transcontinental railroad. As unemployment rose throughout the late 1870s frustrated workers took out their aggression in racist assaults on the city's substantial Chinese population, and though there were many instances of violent acts against individual Chinese people, most of the workers' displeasure was channeled into political activity; mass demonstrations were held all over the city, at which thousands rallied behind the slogan "The Chinese must Go!"

Though it seemed to some that San Francisco was powered by ignoble motives and full of self-serving money-grabbers, there were a few exceptions, even among its wealthiest elite, namely **Adolph Sutro**, a German-born engineer who'd made one fortune in the Comstock mines and another buying up land in the city—in 1890 he was said to own ten percent of San Francisco, even more than the Big Four. But Sutro was an unlikely millionaire, as compassionate and public-spirited as the Big Four were ruthlessly single-minded; in fact, when the Southern Pacific tripled fares to a quarter on the trolley line out to Golden Gate Park, Sutro built a parallel line that charged a nickel. He also built the Sutro Baths and the Cliff House and in 1894 was elected mayor of San Francisco on the Populist Party ticket, campaigning on an anti-Southern Pacific manifesto which promised to rid San Francisco of "this horrible monster which is devouring our substance and debauching our people, and by its devilish instincts and criminal methods is every day more firmly grasping us in its tentacles." Sutro died in 1898, with the city still firmly in the grasp of the "octopus."

THE GREAT EARTHQUAKE AND AFTER

San Francisco experienced another period of economic expansion in the **early years of the 1900s**, due in equal part to the Spanish-American War and the Klondike Gold Rush in Alaska. Both of these events increased ship traffic through the port, where dockworkers were beginning to organize themselves into **unions** on an unprecedented scale, getting together to form the mighty longshoremen's association, which in later years was a political force to be reckoned with in the city. It was a hard fight to win recognition and better wages, resulting in fairly constant unrest, the police being brought in to scare off strikers and prevent picket lines from shutting down the waterfront. But this economic instability was nothing compared to the one truly earth-shattering event of the time: the **Great Earthquake of 1906.**

The quake hit San Francisco on the morning of April 18, 1906, and at 8.1 on the Richter scale was the most powerful one ever to hit anywhere in the US, before or since (over ten times the force of the 1989 earthquake). It destroyed hundreds of buildings, but by far the worst destruction was wrought by the conflagration that followed, as ruptured gas pipes exploded and chimneys toppled, starting fires that spread right across the city. The **post-earthquake fire** virtually leveled the entire area from the waterfront, north and south of

Market Street, west to Van Ness Avenue, whose grand mansions were dynamited to form a firebreak. Comparatively few people, around 500 in total, were killed, but about half the city's population—some 100,000 people—was left homeless and fled the city. Many of those who stayed set up camp in the barren reaches of what's now Golden Gate Park, where soldiers from the Presidio undertook the mammoth task of establishing and maintaining a tent city for about 20,000 displaced San Franciscans.

During **the ten years following the earthquake** San Francisco was rebuilt with a vengeance, reconstructing the city as it was and largely ignoring the grand plan drawn up by noted designer Daniel Burnham just a year before the disaster. The city council had given its approval to this plan, which would have replaced the rigid grid of streets with an eminently more graceful system of axial main boulevards filled in with curving avenues skirting the hills and smaller, residential streets climbing their heights. However, such was the power and influence of the city's vested interests that the status quo was quickly reinstated, despite the clear opportunity afforded by the earthquake.

To celebrate its recovery, and the opening of the Panama Canal—a project which had definite implications for San Francisco's trade-based economy—the city fathers undertook what turned out to be perhaps the city's finest moment—the **1915 Panama Pacific International Exhibition**, which lasted throughout the year. Land was reclaimed from the bay for the exhibition, and on it an elaborate complex of exotic buildings, including Bernard Maybeck's exquisite Palace of Fine Arts and centering on the 100-meter-high, gem-encrusted Tower of Jewels, was constructed. Hundreds of thousands visited the fair, but at the end of the year all of the buildings, save the Palace of Fine Arts, were torn down and the land sold off for the houses that now make up the Marina district.

The exhibition was a great success and proved to the world that San Francisco had recovered from the earthquake's destruction. But the newly recovered civic pride was tested the next year by one of the city's more disgraceful episodes when, on the eve of America's involvement in **World War I**, a pro-war parade organized by San Francisco's business community was devastated by a **bomb attack** which killed ten marchers and severely wounded another forty. In their haste to find the culprit, the San Francisco police arrested half a dozen of the city's radical union agitators. With no evidence other than testimony since proven to have been perjured, activist **Tom Mooney** was convicted and sentenced to death, along with his alleged co-conspirator Warren Billings. Though neither, fortunately, was executed, both of them spent most of the rest of their lives in prison; Billings wasn't pardoned until 1961, 45 years after his unsafe conviction.

THE ROARING TWENTIES

The war years had little effect on San Francisco, but the period following the war, the **Roaring Twenties**, when, despite Prohibition, the jazz clubs and speakeasies of the Barbary Coast district were in full swing, was in many ways San Francisco's finest hour. The city was still the premier artistic and cultural center of the West Coast, a role it would relinquish to Los Angeles by the next decade, and its status as an international financial hub (both major international credit card companies, today's Visa and Access had their start here) was as yet unchallenged by the upstart southern metropolis. The strength of San Francisco as a banking power was highlighted by the rise of the Bank of America—founded as the Bank of Italy in 1904 by A.P. Giannini in North Beach—into the largest bank in the world.

The buoyant 1920s quickly gave way to the Depression of the 1930s but, despite the sharp increases in unemployment, there was only one major battle on the industrial relations front. On **"Bloody Thursday,"** July 5, 1934, police protecting strike-breakers from angry picketers fired into the crowd, wounding thirty and killing two longshoremen. The army was sent in to restore order, and in retaliation the unions called a **General Strike** which saw some 125,000 workers halt work, bringing the Bay Area economy to a standstill for four days. Otherwise there was little unrest, and, thanks in part to **WPA sponsorship** of arts schemes, some of the city's finest monuments—Coit Tower, for example, and most importantly the two great bridges—were built during this time. Before the **Bay and Golden Gate bridges** went up, in 1936 and 1937 respectively, links

between the city and the surrounding towns of the Bay Area were provided by an impressive network of **ferry boats**, some of which were among the world's largest. In 1935, the ferries' peak year, some 100,000 commuters a day were crossing the bay by boat, but just five years later the last of the boats was taken out of service, unable to compete with the increasingly popular automobile.

WORLD WAR II

The Japanese attack on Pearl Harbor and US involvement in **World War II** transformed the Bay Area into a massive war machine, its industry mobilizing quickly to provide weaponry and ships for the war. **Shipyards** opened all around the bay—the largest, the Kaiser Shipyards in Richmond, was employing over 100,000 workers on around-the-clock shifts just six months after its inception—and men and women flooded into the region from all over the country to work in the lucrative concerns. Entire cities were constructed to house them, many of which survive—not least Hunter's Point, on the southern edge of the San Francisco waterfront, which was never intended to last beyond the end of hostilities but which still houses some 15,000 of the city's poorest people. A more successful example is Marin City, a workers' housing community just north of Sausalito, which—surprisingly considering its present-day air of leisured affluence—was one of the most successful wartime shipyards, able to crank out entire ships in a single day.

THE FIFTIES

After the war, thousands of GIs returning from the South Pacific came home through San Francisco, and many decided to stay. The city spilled out into new districts, and, especially in suburbs like the Sunset, massive tracts of identical dwellings, subsidized by federal loans and grants, were thrown together to house the returning heroes—many of whom still live here. The accompanying economic prosperity continued unabated well into the 1950s, and in order to accommodate increasing numbers of cars on the roads, huge **freeways** were constructed, cutting through the city. The Embarcadero Freeway in particular formed an imposing barrier, perhaps appropriately dividing the increasingly office-oriented Financial

District from the declining docks and warehouses of the waterfront, which for so long had been the heart of San Francisco's economy.

As the increasingly mobile and prosperous middle classes emigrated from inner city areas, new bands of literate but disenchanted middle-class youth began to move in to the areas left behind, beginning, in the middle part of the decade, in the bars and cafés of North Beach, which began to change fast from a previously staunch Italian neighborhood into the Greenwich Village of the West Coast. The **Beat Generation**, as they became known, reacted against what they saw as the empty material-ism of 1950s America by losing themselves in a bohemian orgy of jazz, drugs, and Buddhism, expressing their disillusionment with the status quo through a new, highly personal and expressive brand of fiction and poetry. The writer **Jack Kerouac**, whose novel, *On the Road*, became widely accepted as the handbook of the Beats, both for the style of writing (fast, passionate, unpunctuated) and the lifestyle it described, was in some ways the movement's main proponent, and is credited with coining the term "Beat"—meaning beatific—to describe the group. Later, San Francisco columnist Herb Caen somewhat derisively turned "beat" into beatnik, after Sputnik. San Francisco, and particularly the **City Lights Bookstore**, at the center of North Beach, became the main meeting point and focus of this diffuse group, though whatever impetus the movement had was gone by the early 1960s.

THE SIXTIES

Though the long-term value of their writing is still debatable, there's no doubt that the Beats opened people's minds, though it was an offshoot of the group, the **hippies**, that really took this task to heart. The term was originally a Beat put-down of the inexperienced but enthu-siastic young people who followed in their hedonistic footsteps, the first hippies appearing in the early 1960s, in cafés and folk music clubs around the fringes of the Bay Area university campuses. In common with their Beat fore-bears, they eschewed the materialism and the nine-to-five consumer world, preferring an escapist fantasy of music and marijuana that became adapted as a half-baked political state-ment about society and where it was going wrong.

The main difference between the Beats and the early hippies, besides the five years that elapsed between them, was that the hippies had discovered—and regularly experimented with—a newly available hallucinogenic drug called LSD, better known as **Acid**. Since its synthesis, LSD had been legally and readily available, mainly through psychologists who were interested in studying its possible thera-peutic benefits. Other, less scientific research was also being done by a variety of people, many of whom, from around 1965 onward, began to settle in the Haight-Ashbury district west of the city center, living communally in huge but low-rent Victorian houses, in which they could take acid and "trip" in safe, controlled circumstances. **Music** was an inte-gral part of the acid experience, and a number of bands—the Charlatans, Jefferson Airplane, and the Grateful Dead—came together in San Francisco during the summer of 1966, playing open-ended dance music at venues like the Fillmore Auditorium and the Avalon Ballroom.

Things remained on a fairly small scale until the spring of **1967**, when a free concert in Golden Gate Park attracted some 20,000 people and, for the first time, media attention. Articles describing the hippies, most of which focused on their prolific appetites for sex and drugs, attracted a stream of newcomers to the Haight from all over the country, and within a few months the **"Summer of Love"** was well under way, with some 100,000 young people descending upon the district.

In contrast to the hippy indulgence of the Haight-Ashbury scene, across the bay in Berkeley and Oakland **revolutionary politics**, rather than drugs, were at the top of the agenda. While many of the hippies opted out of politics, the student radicals threw themselves into political activism, beginning with the Free Speech Movement at the University of California in 1964. The FSM, which started as a protest against the university's banning of on-campus political activity, laid the groundwork for the more passionate **anti-Vietnam War** protests that rocked the entire country for the rest of the decade. The first of what turned out to be dozens of **riots** occurred in June 1968, when students marching down Telegraph Avenue in support of the Paris student uprising were met by a wall of police, leading to rioting that continued for the next few days. Probably the most famous event in Berkeley's radical history took place in **People's Park**, a plot of university-owned land that was taken over as a community open space by local people. Four days later an army of police, under the command of Edwin Meese—who later headed the US Department of Justice in the Reagan years—tear-gassed and stormed the park, accidentally killing a bystander and seriously injuring over 100 others.

Probably the most extreme element of late-1960s San Francisco emerged out of the impoverished flatlands of Oakland—the **Black Panthers**, established by Bobby Seale, Huey Newton, and Eldridge Cleaver in 1966. The Panthers were a heavily armed but numerically small band of militant black activists with an announced goal of securing self-determination for America's blacks. From their Oakland base they set up a nationwide organization, but the threat they posed, and the chances they were willing to take in pursuit of their cause, were too great. Thirty of their members died in gun battles with the police, and the surviving Panthers lost track of their aims: Eldridge Cleaver later became a right-wing Republican, and Huey Newton was killed over a drugs deal in West Oakland in 1989.

CONTEMPORARY SAN FRANCISCO

The unrest of the 1960s continued on into the **early 1970s**, though never again at such a fevered pitch. One last headline-grabber was the kidnapping in 1974 of heiress Patty Hearst from her Berkeley apartment by the *Symbionese Liberation Army*, or **SLA**, a hardcore bunch of revolutionaries who used their wealthy hostage to demand free food for Oakland's poor. Hearst later helped the gang to rob a San Francisco bank, wielding a sub-machine gun. Otherwise, certainly compared to the previous decade, the 1970s were quiet times, which saw the opening of the long-delayed *BART* high-speed transit system, as well as the establishment of the **Golden Gate National Recreation Area** to protect and preserve 75,000 acres of open space on both sides of the Golden Gate Bridge.

Throughout the 1970s, it wasn't so much that San Francisco's rebellious thread had been broken, but rather that the battle lines were being drawn in different places. The most distinctive political voices were those of the

city's large **gay and lesbian communities**. Inspired by the so-called Stonewall Riots in New York City in 1969, San Francisco's homosexuals began to organize themselves politically, demanding equal status with heterosexuals. Most importantly, gays and lesbians stepped out into the open and refused to hide their sexuality behind closed doors, giving rise to the gay liberation movement that has prospered worldwide over the last two decades. One of the leaders of the gay community in San Francisco, **Harvey Milk**, won a seat on the Board of Supervisors, becoming the first openly gay man to take public office. When Milk was **assassinated** in City Hall, along with Mayor George Moscone, by former Supervisor Dan White in 1978, the whole city was shaken. When White was found guilty of manslaughter, not murder, the gay community erupted in riotous frustration, burning police cars and laying siege to City Hall.

The **1980s** have seen the city's gay community in retreat to some extent, with the advent of **AIDS** in the early part of the decade devastating the confidence of activists and toning down what was a very promiscuous scene. There has, inevitably, been something of a moral backlash against gays, though perhaps less so than in the rest of the country, and the gay community—in conjunction with City Hall—is fighting an impressive and dignified rearguard battle to deal with the disease.

Mayor **Diane Feinstein**, who took over after the death of Moscone, oversaw the construction of millions of square feet of office towers in the downtown Financial District, despite angry protests against the **Manhattanization** of the city. Feinstein is among the most prominent female politicians in America and looks set to become the next governor of California, despite her having dumped a tangled mess of financial worries onto the lap of her successor, the present mayor **Art Agnos**.

Many of the problems facing San Francisco—urban poverty, drug abuse, homelessness, and of course the AIDS crisis—are much the same as those encountered by any major Western city right now. On top of this, the city was shaken by a major **earthquake** in October 1989, 7.1 on the Richter scale—an event watched by 100 million people on nationwide TV since it hit during a World Series game between Bay Area rivals, the *San Francisco Giants* and *Oakland A's*. Despite it being a sizable tremor, only a couple of dozen people were killed by the quake, and only isolated parts of the city were badly damaged (Marina took the biggest battering). Clearing up after the earthquake has been disorganized to say the least, and it's debatable how well the city's buildings would withstand a *really* big one. But, these problems aside, San Francisco remains a city that few residents would forsake for anywhere else.

WRITERS ON SAN FRANCISCO

San Francisco has attracted more than its share of purple prose over the years, and writers seem to pull out all the stops trying to capture the city's great beauty and unique energy. However, some of the best San Francisco writing has been in the form of journalism. The pieces below are essentially dispatches from the city at various key points in its history, starting with the pre-earthquake, Gold Rush town, through the heady days of the Sixties, and rounding off with a contemporary view.

ANTHONY TROLLOPE

The immensely popular Victorian novelist **Anthony Trollope** *traveled extensively throughout the United States in the latter part of the 1800s. This letter was apparently written in a fit of pique upon his return from the Sandwich Islands in 1875, though it wasn't published until 1946.*

NOTHING TO SEE IN SAN FRANCISCO

My way home from the Sandwich Islands to London took me to San Francisco, across the American continent, and New York, whence I am now writing to you my last letter of this series. I had made this journey before, but had on that occasion reached California too late to visit the now world famous valley of the Yo Semite, and the big pine trees which we call Wellingtonias. On this occasion I made the excursion, and will presently tell the story of the trip,—but I must first say a few words as to the town of San Francisco.

I do not know that in all my travels I ever visited a city less interesting to the normal tourist, who, as a rule, does not care to investigate the ways of trade or to employ himself in ascertaining how the people around him earn their bread. There is almost nothing to see in San Francisco that is worth seeing. There is a new park in which you may drive for six or seven miles on a well made road, and which, as a park for the use of a city, will, when completed, have many excellencies. There is

also the biggest hotel in the world, so the people of San Francisco say, which has cost a million sterling—5 millions of dollars—and is intended to swallow up all the other hotels. It was just finished but not opened when I was there. There is an inferior menagerie of wild beasts, and a place called the Cliff House to which strangers are taken to hear seals bark. Everything—except hotel prices—is dearer here than at any other large town I know and the ordinary traveler has no peace left him either in public or private by touters who wish to persuade him to take this or the other railroad route into the Eastern States.

There is always a perfectly cloudless sky over head unless when rain is falling in torrents, and perhaps no where in the world is there a more sudden change from heat to cold in the same day. I think I may say that strangers will generally desire to get out of San Francisco as quickly as they can, unless indeed circumstances may have enabled them to enjoy the hospitality of the place. There is little or nothing to see, and life at the hotels is not comfortable. But the trade of the place and the way in which money is won and lost are alike marvelous. I found 10/- [10 shillings] a day to be about the lowest rate of wages paid to a man for any kind of work in the city, and the average wages of a housemaid who is, of course, found in everything but her clothes, to be over £70 per annum. All payments in California are made in coin, whereas in the other states of the union except California, Oregon and Nevada, monies are paid in depreciated notes,—so that the two dollars and a half per day which the laborer earns in San Francisco are as good as three and a quarter in New York. No doubt this high rate of pay is met by an equivalent in the high cost of many articles, such as clothing and rent; but it does not affect the price of food which to the laboring man is the one important item of expenditure. Consequently the laboring man in California has a position which I have not known him to achieve elsewhere.

In trade there is a speculative rashness which ought to ensure ruin according to our old world ideas, but which seems to be rewarded by very general success. The stranger may of course remember if he pleases that the millionaire who builds a mighty palace is seen and heard of and encountered at all corners, while the bankrupt will probably sink unseen into obscurity. But in San Francisco there is not much of bankruptcy; and when it does occur no one seems to be so little impressed as the bankrupt. There is a good nature, a forebearance, and an easy giving of trust which to an old fashioned Englishman like myself seem to be most dangerous, but which I was assured there form the readiest mode of building up a great commercial community. The great commercial community is there, and I am not prepared to deny that it has been built after that fashion. If a young man there can make friends, and can establish a character for honesty to his friends and for smartness to the outside world, he can borrow almost any amount of money without security, for the purpose of establishing himself in business. The lender, if he feel sure that he will not be robbed by his protege, is willing to run the risk of unsuccessful speculation.

As we steamed into the Golden Horn (sic) the news reached us that about a month previously the leading bank in San Francisco, the bank of California, had "burst up" for some enormous amount of dollars, and that the manager, who was well known as one of the richest men and as perhaps the boldest speculator in the State, had been drowned on the day following. But we also heard that payments would be resumed in a few days: and payments were resumed before I left the city: that no one but the shareholders would lose a dollar, and that the shareholders were ready to go on with any amount of new capital; and that not a single bankruptcy in the whole community had been caused by this stoppage of the bank which had been extended for a period over a month! How came it to pass, I asked of course, that the collapse of so great a monetary enterprise as the bank of California should pass on without a general panic, at any rate in the city? Then I was assured that all those concerned were goodnatured, that everybody gave time,—that bills were renewed all round, and that in an hour or two it was understood that no one in San Francisco was to be asked for money just at that crisis. To me all this seemed to be wrong. I have always imagined that severity to bankrupt debtors,—that amount of severity which requires that a bankrupt shall really be a bankrupt,—is the best and indeed the only way of ensuring regularity in commerce and of preventing men from tossing up with other people's money in the confidence that they may win and cannot lose. But such doctrines are altogether out of date in California. The money of depositors was scattered broadcast through the mining speculations of the district, and no one was a bit the worse for it,—except the unfortunate gentleman who had been, perhaps happily, removed from a community which had trusted him long with implicit confidence, which still believed him to be an honest man, but which would hardly have known how to treat him had he survived. To add to the romance of the story it should be said that though this gentleman was drowned while bathing it seems to be certain that his death was accidental. It is stated that he was struck by apoplexy while in the water.

I was taken to visit the stock-brokers' Board in San Francisco, that is the room in which mining shares are bought and sold. The trader should understand that in California, and, still more, in the neighboring State of Nevada, gold and silver mining are now very lively. The stockjobbing created by these mines is carried on in San Francisco and is a business as universally popular as was the buying and selling of railroad shares during our railroad mania. Everybody is at it. The housemaid of whom I have spoken as earning £70 per annum, buys Consolidated Virginia or Ophir stock with that money;—or perhaps she prefers Chollar Potosi, or Best and Belcher, or Yellow Jacket, or Buckeye. She probably consults some gentleman of her acquaintance and no doubt in 19 cases out of 20 loses her money. But it is the thing to do, and she enjoys that charm which is the delectation of all gamblers. Of course in such a condition of things there are men who know how the wind is going to blow, who make the wind blow this way and that, who can raise the price of shares by fictitious purchases, and then sell, or depreciate them by fictitious sales and then buy. The housemaids and others go to the wall, while the knowing men build palaces and seem to be troubled by no seared consciences. In the mean time the brokers drive a roaring trade, whether they purchase legitimately for others or speculate on their own account.

The Stock Exchange in London is I believe closed to strangers. The Bourse in Paris is open to the world and at a certain hour affords a scene to those who choose to go and look at it of wild noise, unintelligible action, and sometimes apparently of demoniac fury. The uninitiated are unable to comprehend that the roaring herd in the pen beneath them are doing business. The Stock Exchange Board in San Francisco is not open to strangers, as it is in Paris, but may be visited with an order, and by the kindness of a friend I was admitted. Paris is more than six times as large as San Francisco; but the fury at San Francisco is even more demoniac than at Paris. I thought that the gentlemen employed were going to hit each other between the eyes, and that the apparent quarrels which I saw already demanded the interference of the police. But the uproarious throng were always obedient, after slight delays, to the ringing hammer of the Chairman and as each five minutes' period of internecine combat was brought to an end, I found that a vast number of mining shares had been bought and sold. Perhaps a visit to this Chamber, when the stockbrokers are at work between the hours of eleven and twelve, is of all sights in San Francisco, the one best worth seeing.

HUNTER S. THOMPSON

*One of the most exciting and controversial of essayists, **Hunter S. Thompson** is a trouble-maker and muck-raker of the first order. Equally wild away from his typewriter, his experiences have included a spell with the Hell's Angels in San Francisco, about whom he wrote his first book. His later fascination with Richard Nixon reached its culmination in his long and consistently unforgiving book* The Great Shark Hunt, *from which the extract below is taken. After lying relatively low for a while at his Colorado ranch, he resurfaced in the 1980s to write a column for the* San Francisco Examiner, *pieces of which have been brought together in his latest collection of essays,* Generation of Swine.

THE "HASHBURY" IS THE CAPITAL OF THE HIPPIES

In 1965 Berkeley was the axis of what was just beginning to be called the "new left." Its leaders were radical, but they were also deeply committed to the society they wanted to change. A prestigious faculty committee said the Berkeley activists were the vanguard of "a moral revolution among the young," and many professors approved.

Now in 1967 there is not much doubt that Berkeley has gone through a revolution of some kind, but the end result is not exactly what the original leaders had in mind. Many one-time activists have forsaken politics entirely and turned to drugs. Others have even forsaken Berkeley. During 1966, the hot center of revolutionary action on the coast began moving across the bay to San Francisco's Haight-Ashbury district, a run down Victorian neighborhood of about forty square blocks between the Negro/Fillmore district and Golden Gate Park.

The "Hashbury" is the new capital of what is rapidly becoming a drug culture. Its denizens are not called radicals or beatniks, but "hippies" and perhaps as many as half are refugees from Berkeley and the old North Beach scene, the cradle and the casket of the so-called beat generation.

The other half of the hippy population is too young to identify with Jack Kerouac, or even with Mario Savio. Their average age is about twenty, and most are native Californians. The North Beach types of the late nineteen-fifties were not nearly as provincial as the Haight-Ashbury types are today. The majority of beatniks who flocked into San Francisco ten years ago were transients of the East and Midwest. The literary artistic nucleus—Kerouac, Ginsberg, et al—was a package deal from New York. San Francisco was only a stop on the big circuit: Tangier, Paris, Greenwich Village, Tokyo and India. The senior Beats had a pretty good idea what was going on in the world; they read newspapers, traveled constantly and had friends all over the globe.

The word "hip" translates roughly as "wise" or "tuned-in." A hippy is somebody who "knows" what's really happening, and who adjusts or grooves with it. Hippies despise phoniness; they want to be open, honest, loving, free. They reject the plastic pretence of twentieth-century America, preferring to go back to the "natural life," like Adam and Eve. They reject any kinship with the Beat Generation on the ground that "those cats were negative but our thing is positive." They also reject politics, which is "just another game." They don't like money, either, or any kind of aggressiveness.

A serious problem in writing about the Haight-Ashbury is that most of the people you have to talk to are involved, one way or another, in the drug traffic. They have good reason to be leery of strangers who ask questions. A twenty-two-year-old student was recently sentenced to two years in prison for telling an undercover narcotics agent where to buy some marijuana. "Love" is the password in the Haight-Ashbury, but paranoia is the style. Nobody wants to go to jail.

At the same time, marijuana is everywhere. People smoke it on the sidewalks, in doughnut shops, sitting in parked cars or lounging on the grass in Golden Gate Park. Nearly everyone on the streets between twenty and thirty is a "head," a user of either marijuana, LSD, or both. To refuse the proffered joint is to risk being labeled a "nark"—a narcotics agent—a threat and a menace to almost everybody.

With a few loud exceptions, it is only the younger hippies who see themselves as a new breed. "A completely new thing in this world, man." The ex-beatniks among them, many of whom are now making money off the new scene, incline to the view that hippies are, in fact, second generation beatniks and that everything genuine in the Haight-Ashbury is about to be swallowed—like North Beach and the Village—in a wave of publicity and commercialism.

Haight Street, the great white way of what the local papers call "hippieland," is already dotted with stores catering mainly to the tourist trade. Few hippies can afford a pair of $20 sandals or a "Mod outfit" for $67:50. Nor can they afford the $3:50 door charge at the Fillmore Auditorium and the Avalon Ballroom, the twin wombs of the "psychedelic, San Francisco, acid-rock sound." Both the Fillmore and the Avalon are jammed every weekend with borderline hippies who don't mind paying for the music and the light shows. There is always a sprinkling of genuine, bare-foot, freaked-out types on the dance floor, but few of them pay to get in. They arrive with the musicians or have other good connections.

Neither of the dance palaces is within walking distance of the Hashbury, especially if you're stoned, and since only a few of the hippies have contacts in the psychedelic power structure, most of them spend their weekend nights either drifting around on Haight Street or loading up on acid—LSD—in somebody's pad. Some of the rock bands play free concerts in Golden Gate Park for the benefit of those brethren who can't afford the dances. But beyond an occasional Happening in the park, the Haight-Ashbury scene is almost devoid of anything "to do"—at least by conventional standards. An at-home entertainment is nude parties at which celebrants paint designs on each other.

There are no hippy bars, for instance, and only one restaurant above the level of a diner or a lunch counter. This is a reflection of the drug culture which has no use for booze and regards food as a necessity to be acquired at the least possible expense. A "family" of hippies will work for hours over an exotic stew or curry in a communal kitchen, but the idea of paying $3 for a meal in a restaurant is out of the question.

Some hippies work, others live on money from home and many are full-time beggars. The post office is a major source of hippy income. Jobs like sorting mail don't require much thought or effort. A hippy named Admiral Love of the Psychedelic Rangers delivers special-delivery letters at night. The admiral is in his mid-twenties and makes enough money to support an apartmentful of younger hippies who depend on him for their daily bread.

There is also a hippy-run employment agency on Haight Street and anyone needing part-time labor or some kind of specialized work can call and order as many freaks as he needs; they might look a bit weird, but many are far more capable than most "temporary help," and vastly more interesting to have around.

Those hippies who don't work can easily pick up a few dollars a day panhandling along Haight Street. The fresh influx of curiosity-seekers has proved a great boon to the legion of psychedelic beggars. During several days of roaming around the area, I was touched so often that I began to keep a supply of quarters in my pocket so I wouldn't have to bargain over change. The panhandlers are usually barefoot, always young and never apologetic. They'll share what they collect anyway, so it seems entirely reasonable that strangers should share with them.

The best show on Haight Street is usually on the sidewalk in front of the Drog Store, a new coffee bar at the corner of Masonic Street. The Drog Store features an all-hippy revue that runs day and night. The acts change sporadically, but nobody cares. There will be at least one man with long hair and sunglasses playing a wooden pipe of some kind. He will be wearing either a Dracula cape, a long Buddhist robe, or a Sioux Indian costume. There will also be a hairy blond fellow wearing a Black Bart cowboy hat and a spangled jacket that originally belonged to a drum major in the 1949 Rose Bowl parade. He will be playing the bongo drums. Next to the drummer will be a dazed-looking girl wearing a blouse (but no bra) and a plastic mini-skirt, slapping her thighs to the rhythm of it all.

These three will be the nucleus of the show. Backing them up will be an all-star cast of freaks, every one of them stoned. They will be stretched out on the sidewalk, twitching and babbling in time to the music. Now and then somebody will fall out of the audience and join the revue; perhaps a Hell's Angel or some grubby, chain-draped impostor who never owned a motorcycle in his life. Or maybe a girl wrapped in gauze or a thin man with wild eyes who took an overdose of acid nine days ago and changed himself into a raven. For those on a quick tour of the Hashbury, the Drog Store revue is a must.

Most of the local action is beyond the reach of anyone without access to drugs. There are four or five bars a nervous square might relax in, but one is a Lesbian place, another is a hangout for brutal-looking leather fetishists and the others are old neighborhood taverns full of brooding middle-aged drunks. Prior to the hippy era there were three good Negro-run jazz bars on Haight Street, but they soon went out of style. Who needs jazz, or even beer, when you can sit down on a public kerbstone, drop a pill on your mouth and hear fantastic music for hours at a time in your own head? A cap of good acid costs $5, and for that you can hear the Universal Symphony, with God singing solo and the Holy Ghost on drums.

Drugs have made formal entertainment obsolete in the Hashbury, but only until somebody comes up with something appropriate to the new style of the neighborhood. This summer will see the opening of the new Straight Theater, formerly the Haight Theater, featuring homosexual movies for the trade, meetings, concerts, dances. "It's going to be a kind of hippy community center," said Brent Dangerfield, a young radio engineer from Salt Lake City who stopped off in San Francisco on his way to a job in Hawaii and is now a partner

in the Straight. When I asked him how old he was he had to think for a minute. "I'm twenty-two," he said finally, "but I used to be much older."

Another new divertissement, maybe, will be a hippy bus line running up and down Haight Street, housed in a 1930 Fagol bus—a huge, lumbering vehicle that might have been the world's first house trailer. I rode in it one afternoon with the driver, a young hippy named Tim Thibeau who proudly displayed a bathtub under one of the rear seats. The bus was a spectacle even on Haight Street: people stopped, stared and cheered as we rumbled by, going nowhere at all. Thibeau honked the horn and waved. He was from Chicago, he said, but when he got out of the Army he stopped in San Francisco and decided to stay. He was living, for the moment, on unemployment insurance, and his plans for the future were hazy. "I'm in no hurry," he said. "Right now I'm just taking it easy, just floating along." He smiled and reached for a beer can in the Fagol's icebox.

Dangerfield and Thibeau reflect the blind optimism of the younger hippy element. They see themselves as the vanguard of a new way of life in America—the psychedelic way— where love abounds and work is fun and people help each other. The young hippies are confident that things are going their way.

The older hippies are not so sure. They've been waiting a long time for the world to go their way, and those most involved in the hip scene are hedging their bets this time. "That back to nature scene is okay when you're twenty," said one. "But when you're looking at thirty-five you want to know something's happening to you."

Ed Denson, at twenty-seven, is an ex-beatnik, ex-Goldwaterite, ex-Berkeley radical and currently the manager of a successful rock band called Country Joe and the Fish. His home and headquarters is a complex of rooms above a liquor store in Berkeley. One room is an art studio, another is an office; there is also a kitchen, a bedroom and several sparsely furnished areas without definition.

Denson is deeply involved in the hippy music scene, but insists he's not a hippy. "I'm very pessimistic about where this thing is going," he said. "Right now it's good for a lot of people. It's still very open. But I have to look back at the Berkeley scene. There was a tremendous optimism there, too, but look where all that went. The beat generation? Where are they now? What about hula-hoops? Maybe this hippy thing is more than a fad; maybe the whole world is turning on but I'm not optimistic. Most of the hippies I know don't really understand what kind of a world they're living in. I get tired of hearing about what beautiful people we all are. If the hippies were more realistic they'd stand a better chance of surviving."

LEWIS LAPHAM

Lewis Lapham comes from a firmly establishment San Francisco family: his grandfather was mayor of the city. Despite these top-notch connections, he grew completely disenchanted with the town and California as a whole, and headed east to become the editor of the highly respected Harpers magazine. The following account describes what irks him about a city that so many people love so unquestioningly.

LOST HORIZON

For the past six or seven weeks I have been answering angry questions about San Francisco. People who know that I was born in that city assume that I have access to confidential information, presumably at the highest levels of psychic consciousness. Their questions sound like accusations, as if they were demanding a statement about the poisoning of the reservoirs. Who were those people that the Reverend Jim Jones murdered in Guyana, and how did they get there? Why would anybody follow such a madman into the wilderness, and how did the Reverend Jones come by those letters from Vice-President Mondale and Mrs. Rosalynn Carter? Why did the fireman kill the mayor of San Francisco and the homosexual city official? What has gone wrong in California, and who brought evil into paradise? Fortunately I don't know the answers to these questions; if I knew them, I would be bound to proclaim myself a god and return to San Francisco in search of followers, a mandala, and a storefront shrine. Anybody who would understand the enigma of San Francisco must first know something about the dreaming narcissism of the city, and rather than try to explain this in so many words, I offer into evidence the story of my last assignment for the *San Francisco Examiner.*

I been employed on the paper for two years when, on a Saturday morning in December of 1959 reported for work to find the editors talking to one another in the hushed and self-important way that usually means that at least fifty people have been killed. I assumed that a ship had sunk or that a building had collapsed. The editors were not in the habit of taking me into their confidence, and I didn't expect to learn the terms of the calamity until I had a chance to read the AP wire. Much to my surprise, the city editor motioned impatiently in my direction, indicating that I should join the circle of people standing around his desk and turning slowing through the pages of the pictorial supplement that the paper was obliged to publish the next day. Aghast at what they saw, unable to stifle small cries of anguished disbelief, they were examining twelve pages of text and photographs arranged under the heading LOS ANGELES—THE ATHENS OF THE WEST. To readers unfamiliar with the ethos of San Francisco, I'm not sure that I can convey the full and terrible effect of this headline. Not only was it wrong, it was monstrous heresy. The residents of San Francisco dote on a romantic image of the city, and they imagine themselves living at a height of civilization accessible only to Erasmus or a nineteenth century British peer. They flatter themselves on their sophistication, their exquisite sensibility, their devotion to the arts. Los Angeles represents the antithesis of these graces; it is the land of the Philistines, lying somewhere to the south in the midst of housing developments that stand as the embodiment of ugliness, vulgarity, and corruptions of the spirit.

Pity, then, the poor editors in San Francisco. In those days there was also a *Los Angeles Examiner,* and the same printing plant supplied supplements to both papers. The text and photographs intended for a Los Angeles audience had been printed in the Sunday pictorial bearing the imprimatur of the *San Francisco Examiner.* It was impossible to correct the mistake, and so the editors in San Francisco had no choice but to publish and give credence to despised anathema.

This so distressed them that they resolved to print a denial. The city editor, knowing that my grandfather had been mayor of San Francisco and that I had been raised in the city, assumed that he could count on my dedication to the parochial truth. He also knew that I had studied at Yale and Cambridge universities, and although on most days he made jokes about the future of a literary education, on this particular occasion he saw a use for it. What was the point of reading all those books if they didn't impart the skills of a sophist? He handed me the damnable pages and said that I had until five o'clock in the afternoon to refute them as false doctrine. The story was marked for page 1 and an eight-column headline. I was to spare no expense of adjectives.

The task was hopeless. Los Angeles at the time could claim the residence of Igor Stravinsky, Aldous Huxley, and Christopher Isherwood. Admittedly they had done their best work before coming west to ripen in the sun, but their names and photographs, together with those of a few well-known painters and a number of established authors temporarily engaged in the writing of screenplays, make for an impressive display in a newspaper. Even before I put through my first telephone call, to a poet in North Beach experimenting with random verse, I knew that cultural enterprise in San Francisco could not sustain the pretension of a comparison to New York or Chicago, much less to Periclean Athens.

Ernest Bloch had died, and Darius Milhaud taught at Mills College only during the odd years; Henry Miller lived 140 miles to the south at Big Sur, which placed him outside the city's penumbra of light. The Beat Generation had disbanded. Allen Ginsberg still could be seen brooding in the cellar of the City Lights Bookshop, but Kerouac had left town, and the tourists were occupying the best tables at Cassandra's, asking the waiters about psychedelic drugs and for connections to the Buddhist underground. Although I admired the work of Evan Connell and Lawrence Ferlinghetti, I doubted that they would say the kinds of things that the city editor wanted to hear. The San Francisco school of painting consisted of watercolor views of Sausalito and Fisherman's Wharf; there was no theater, and the opera was a means of setting wealth to music. The lack of art or energy in the city reflected the lassitude of a citizenry content to believe its own press notices. The circumference of the local interest extended no more than 150 miles in three directions—as far as Sonoma County and Bolinas in the north, to Woodside and

Monterey in the south, and to Yosemite and Tahoe in the east. In a westerly direction the civic imagination didn't reach beyond the Golden Gate Bridge. Within this narrow arc the inhabitants of San Francisco entertained themselves with a passionate exchange of gossip.

At about three o'clock in the afternoon I gave up hope of writing a believable story. Queasy with embarrassment and apology, I informed the city editor that the thing couldn't be done, that if there was such a place as an Athens of the West—which was doubtful — then it probably was to be found on the back lot of a movie studio in Los Angeles. San Francisco might compare to a Greek colony on the coast of Asia Minor in the fourth century B.C., but that was the extent of it. The city editor heard me out, and then after an awful and incredulous silence, he rose from behind his desk and denounced me as a fool and an apostate. I had betrayed the city of my birth and the imperatives of the first edition. Never could I hope to succeed in the newspaper business. Perhaps I might find work in a drugstore chain, preferably somewhere east of St. Louis, but even then he would find himself hardpressed to recommend me as anything but a liar and an assassin. He assigned the story to an older and wiser reporter, who relied on the local authorities (Herb Caen, Barnaby Conrad, the presidents of department stores, the director of the film festival), and who found it easy enough to persuade them to say that San Francisco should be more appropriately compared to Mount Olympus.

I left San Francisco within a matter of weeks, depressed by the dreamlike torpor of the city. Although in the past eighteen years I often have thought of the city with feelings of sadness, as if in mourning for the beauty of the hills and the clarity of the light in September when the wind blows from the north, I have no wish to return. The atmosphere of unreality seems to me more palpable and oppressive in San Francisco than it does in New York. Apparently this has always been so. Few of the writers associated with the city stayed longer than a few seasons. Twain broke camp and moved on; so did Bierce and Bret Harte. In his novel *The Octopus,* Frank Norris describes the way in which the Southern Pacific Railroad in the 1890s forced the farmers of the San

Joaquin Valley to become its serfs. The protagonist of the novel, hoping to stir the farmers to revolt and to an idea of liberty, looks for political allies among the high-minded citizens of San Francisco. He might as well have been looking for the civic conscience in a bordello. A character modeled after Collis Huntington, the most epicurean of the local robber barons, explains to him that San Francisco cannot conceive of such a thing as social justice. The conversation takes place in the bar at the Bohemian Club, and the financier gently says to Norris's hero that "San Francisco is not a city . . . it is a midway plaisance."

The same thing can be said for San Francisco almost a hundred years later, except that in the modern idiom people talk about the city as "carnival." The somnambulism of the past has been joined with the androgynous frenzy of the present, and in the ensuing confusion who knows what's true and not true, or who's doing what to whom and for what reason? The wandering bedouin of the American desert traditionally migrate to California in hope of satisfying their hearts' desire under the palm tree of the national oasis. They seek to set themselves free, to rid themselves of all restraint, to find the Eden or the fountain of eternal youth withheld or concealed from them by the authorities (nurses, teachers, parents, caliphs) in the walled towns of the East. They desire simply to be, and they think of freedom as a banquet. Thus their unhappiness and despair when their journey proves to have been in vain. The miracle fails to take place, and things remain pretty much as they were in Buffalo or Indianapolis. Perhaps this explains the high rate of divorce, alcoholism, and suicide. The *San Francisco Examiner* kept a record of the people who jumped off the Golden Gate Bridge, and the headline always specified the number of the most recent victim as if adding up the expense of the sacrifice to the stone-faced gods of happiness.

BOOKS

TRAVEL/IMPRESSIONS

Martin Amis *The Moronic Inferno and Other Visits to America* (Viking Penguin $16.95). Essays by an English observer that pull no punches in their dealings with US life and culture, including the moral majority, militarism, and high-energy consumerism.

John Miller (ed.) *San Francisco Stories* (Chronicle $10.95). Patchy collection of writings on the city with contributions from Lewis Lapham, Tom Wolfe, Dylan Thomas, and Hunter S. Thompson to name a few.

Czeslaw Milosz *Visions from San Francisco Bay* (Farrar, Straus & Giroux $9.95). Written in Berkeley during the unrest of 1968, these dense and somewhat ponderous essays show a European mind trying to come to grips with California's nascent Aquarian Age.

Mark Twain *Roughing It* (Signet $4.50). Vivid tales of frontier California, particularly evocative of life in the silver mines of the 1860s Comstock Lode, where Twain got his start as a journalist and storyteller. His descriptions of San Francisco include a moment-by-moment description of an earthquake.

Tom Wolfe *The Electric Kool-Aid Acid Test* (Bantam $5.95). Tom Wolfe at his most expansive, riding with the Grateful Dead and Hell's Angels on the magic bus of Ken Kesey and the Merry Pranksters as they travel through the early 1960s, turning California on to LSD.

HISTORY, POLITICS, AND SOCIETY

Walton Bean *California: An Interpretive History* (McGraw-Hill $30.95). Blow-by-blow account of the history of California, including all the shady deals and back-room politicking, presented in accessible, anecdotal form.

Joan Didion *Slouching Towards Bethlehem* (Farrar, Straus & Giroux $7.95). Selected essays from one of California's most renowned journalists, taking a critical look at the West Coast of the Sixties, including San Francisco's acid-culture and a profile of American hero John Wayne. In a similar style, *The White Album* (Farrar, Straus & Giroux $7.95) traces the West Coast characters and events that shaped the Sixties and Seventies, including The Doors, Charles Manson, and the Black Panthers.

Edmund Fawcett and Tony Thomas *America and the Americans* (Harper & Row o/p). A wide-ranging, up-to-the-minute, and engagingly written rundown on the USA in all its aspects from politics to sports and religion.

Frances Fitzgerald *Cities on a Hill* (Touchstone Books $9.95). Intelligent, thorough, and sympathetic exploration of four of the odder corners of American culture, including San Francisco's gay Castro district, the bizarre Rajneeshi community, and TV evangelism.

Jamie Jensen *Built to Last—The Grateful Dead 25th Anniversary Tour Book* (New American Library $8.95). Photo-filled history of San Francisco's psychedelic heroes from their early days in the Haight to their present near-divine stature, by one of the authors of this guide.

Charles Perry *The Haight-Ashbury* (Random House o/p). Curiously distant but detailed account of the Haight during the Flower Power years, written by an editor of *Rolling Stone*, a magazine that got its start there.

Mel Scott *The San Francisco Bay Area: A Metropolis in Perspective* (UC Press $18.95). Though somewhat dry and academic, this massive tome will tell you all you ever wanted to know about the evolution of San Francisco and the Bay Area.

Jay Stevens *Storming Heaven: LSD and the American Dream* (Harper & Row $9.95). Aside from being an engaging account of psychedelic drugs and their effect on American society through the Sixties, the epilogue brings things up to date with "designer drugs"—Venus, Ecstasy, Vitamin K, etc—and the inner space they help some modern Californians to find.

Hunter S. Thompson *The Great Shark Hunt* (Warner Books $4.95). Collection of often barbed and cynical essays on contemporary 1960s American life and politics—thought-provoking and hilarious. *Generation of Swine* (Random $8.95) is Thompson's latest collection of caustic musings on the state of America and those who control it, assembled from his regular column in the *San Francisco Examiner*.

Tom Wolfe *Radical Chic & Mau Mauing the Flak Catchers* (Bantam $5.95). Wolfe's waspish account of Leonard Bernstein's fundraising party for the Black Panthers—a protracted exercise in character assassination—is coupled with his equally sharp analysis of white guilt and radical politics in City Hall, San Francisco. Often ideologically unsound, always very funny.

SPECIFIC GUIDES

Adab Bakalinsky *Stairway Walks in San Francisco* (Lexicos $6.95). Small, nicely illustrated guide detailing pretty back streets and stairways through San Francisco's hills. Excellent for turning up lesser-known spots on a walking tour.

California Coastal Commission *California Coastal Access Guide* (UC Press $10.95). The most useful and comprehensive plant and wildlife guide to the California coast, packed with maps and background information.

Don Herron *The Literary World of San Francisco* (City Lights $9.95). A walk through the San Francisco neighborhoods associated with authors who have lived in and written about the city. Detailed and well presented, it's an essential handbook for anyone interested in San Francisco's literary heritage.

Judith Kahn *Indulge Yourself* (Kahn $7.95). The ideal companion for the café animal, this book covers San Francisco's most famous and beautiful coffee spots, giving hints on when to go, what sort of people you'll see, and what's on offer.

Karen Liberatore *The Complete Guide to the Golden Gate National Recreation Area* (Chronicle $7.95). Easy-to-read book covering San Francisco's extensive waterfront areas and large green spaces, with historical perspective. Lots of photos.

Don and Betty Martin *The Best of San Francisco* (Chronicle $8.95). A lighthearted series of top-ten listings of the best that San Francisco has to offer. Categories range from the "Top Ten Seafood Restaurants" to the "Ten Naughtiest Things to do in San Francisco." More amusing than helpful, but some interesting pointers.

Grant Peterson *Roads to Ride* (Heyday Books $12.95). As its subtitle says, this is a bicyclist's topographic guide to the whole Bay Area, and is particularly good on the back roads of Marin County.

Don Pitcher *Berkeley Inside/Out* (Heyday Books $12.95). This is an extremely well written, fully illustrated, and encyclopedic guidebook to the most dynamic small town in the Bay Area.

Peggy Wayburn *Adventuring in the San Francisco Bay Area* (Sierra Club $10.95). If you are planning to spend any time hiking in the Bay Area's many fine wilderness regions, pick up this fact-filled guide, which also details a number of historic walks through the city's urban areas.

FICTION AND POETRY

Ambrose Bierce *The Enlarged Devil's Dictionary* (Dover $2.95). Spiteful but hilarious compilation of definitions (ie "Bore: a person who talks when you wish him to listen") by turn-of-the-century journalist. Bierce also wrote some great horror stories, including the stream-of-consciousness "An Ocurrence at Owl Creek Bridge," collected in *Can Such Things Be* (Citadel $2.95) and his *Collected Writings* (Citadel $11.95).

Richard Brautigan *Hawkline Monster* (Pocket Books $2.95). Whimsical, surreal tales by noted Bay Area hippy writer.

Philip K. Dick *The Man in the High Castle* (Berkeley Pub. $2.95). In this, his first published novel, long-time Berkeley and Marin County-based science fiction author imagines an alternative San Francisco, after the Japanese won World War II. Of his dozens of other brilliant novels and short stories, *Bladerunner* (Balantine $4.95), and *The Transmigration of Timothy Archer* (Pocket Books $2.95) make good use of Bay Area locales.

John Dos Passos *USA* (Houghton Mifflin $20). Massive, groundbreaking trilogy, combining fiction, poetry, and reportage to tap the various strands of the American Experience. Much of the first part, *The 42nd Parallel*, takes place around Sutro Baths and Golden Gate Park.

Allen Ginsberg *Howl and Other Poems* (City Lights $4.95). The attempted banning of the title poem assured its fame, and while *Howl* is an angry rant that will often make you wince, a Whitmanesque voice does shine through in places.

Dashiell Hammett *Novels of Dashiell Hammett* (Knopf $30). Collection of seminal detective stories including *The Maltese Falcon* (Vintage $7.95) and starring Sam Spade, the private investigator working out of San Francisco. See also Diane Johnson's absorbing *The Life of Dashiell Hammet* (Fawcett $8.95).

Jack Kerouac *On the Road* (Signet $4.95). The book that launched a generation with its "spontaneous bop prosody," it chronicles Beat life in a series of road adventures, featuring some of San Francisco and a lot of the rest of the US. His other books include *Lonesome Traveler* (Grove-Weidenfeld $8.95), *The Dharma Bums* (Signet $3.95), and *Desolation Angels* (Perigee $8.95).

David Lodge *Changing Places* (Penguin $5.95). Thinly-disguised autobiographical tale of an English academic who spends a year teaching at UC Berkeley (renamed in the book) and finds himself bang in the middle of the late 1960s student upheaval.

Jack London *Martin Eden* (Airmont $3.50). Jack Kerouac's favorite book, this semi-autobiographical account tracks the early years of this San Francisco-born, Oakland-bred adventure writer. The lengthy opus tells of his rise from waterfront hoodlum to high-brow intellectual, and of his subsequent disenchantment with the trappings of success.

Armistead Maupin *Tales of the City; Further Tales of the City; More Tales of the City; Babycakes; Significant Others; Sure of You* (Harper & Row $10.95 each). Six lively consecutive soap operas, wittily detailing the sexual and emotional antics of a select group of archetypal San Francisco characters, taking them from the late 1970s to the end of the 1980s.

Seth Morgan *Homeboy* (Random $19.95). Recently published novel charting Morgan's experiences of sleaze, degradation, and prostitution in San Francisco. (Morgan was the former junkie boyfriend of Janis Joplin.)

Frank Norris *McTeague: A Story of San Francisco* (Penguin $5.95). Dramatic, extremely violent but engrossing saga of love and revenge in turn-of-the-century San Francisco; later filmed by Erich von Stroheim as *Greed*. Norris's *Octopus* (Penguin $5.95) tells the bitter tale of the Southern Pacific Railroad's stranglehold over the California economy.

Thomas Pynchon *The Crying of Lot 49* (Harper & Row $7.95). Follows the labyrinthine adventures of techno-freaks and pot-heads in 1960s California, revealing the sexy side of stamp collecting.

Vikram Seth *The Golden Gate* (Random $5.95). Slick novel in verse, tracing the complex social lives of a group of San Francisco yuppies.

Gary Snyder *Left Out in the Rain* (North Point Press $9.95). One of the original Beat writers, and the only one whose work ever matured, Snyder's poetry is direct and spare, yet manages to conjure up a deep, animistic spirituality underlying everyday life.

Amy Tan *The Joy Luck Club* (Ivy Books $5.95). Four Chinese-American women and their daughters gather together to look back over their lives. Moving story of immigrant struggle in the sweatshops of Chinatown.

SAN FRANCISCO ON FILM

San Francisco is a favorite with Californian film-makers, the city's staggering range of settings and chameleon-like geography making an often economical choice for the director who needs sunny beaches, swirling fogs, urban decay, and pastoral elegance all at once. Thrillers, in particular, seem to get good milage out of the city—and the city's ridiculous gradients are almost ideally suited to the car chases that Hollywood loves so much. Below is a list of the obvious and not-so-obvious films made about or in California's most beautiful city.

An Eye for an Eye (Steve Carver 1981). Chuck Norris plays an undercover San Francisco narcotics officer who quits the force when his partner is set up and killed. Typical lone-wolf action flick, with Norris flexing his bulk through a series of violent acts on an Oriental drug ring until he nails the bad guy.

Barbary Coast (Howard Hawks 1935). Set in misty, fog-bound turn-of-the-century San Francisco, Edward G. Robinson finds he has competition when he tries to seduce the exotic dancer played by Mariam Hopkins. A brawling adventure film that captures the spirit of a lawless San Francisco.

Bird Man of Alcatraz (John Frankenheimer 1962). Earnest but overlong study of real-life convicted killer Robert Stroud (Burt Lancaster) who becomes an authority on birds while kept in America's highest security prison.

The Birds (Alfred Hitchcock 1963). Some brilliant set-pieces in this allegory about our hostile feathered friends, set on California's rugged coast, just north of San Francisco.

Bullit (Peter Yates 1968). Steve McQueen gives an assured central performance in this overpraised but entertaining cop thriller, which contains the definitive San Francisco Car Chase.

Chan is Missing (Wayne Wang 1982). Low-budget sleeper hangs a thoroughly unpredictable study of San Francisco's Chinatown and the Chinese-American experience on a mystery-suspense peg. Often satirical, it shows a Chinatown the tourists don't usually see.

Common Threads: Stories from the Quilt (Robert Epstein 1989). The maker of *The Times of Harvey Milk* again focuses on gay San Francisco in his sensitive feature-length documentary about the Names Project Memorial Quilt. Talking to six bereaved partners of AIDS victims, it tackles the political and social impact of the disease as well as concentrating on the sacrifice of those involved.

The Conversation (Francis Ford Coppola 1974). This chilling character study of San Francisco surveillance expert Harry Caul (Gene Hackman at his finest) is one of the best films of the Watergate era. The key, titular sequence is set in San Francisco's Union Square.

The Counselor (Alberto De Martino 1973). Italian Mafia movie, dubbed into English and shot in San Francisco. Basically a take-off of both *Bullit* and *The Godfather* and as such with very little to offer.

Crackers (Louis Malle 1983). Donald Sutherland puts in a saving performance in what is otherwise a limp art film about struggling on the back streets of San Francisco. One of a million films that romanticizes being poor.

Dark Passage (Delmer Davies 1947). Humphrey Bogart and Lauren Bacall star in this classic thriller set in fog-bound San Francisco, where Bogart with Bacall's help tries to clear his name for a murder of which he is wrongly accused. A beautifully shot, if unconvincing, film.

Days of Wine and Roses (Martin Manulis 1962). Jack Lemmon plays a likable drunk who drags his wife into alcoholism, too, only to leave her there once he's on the road to recovery. Smart satirical comedy that occasionally slips into melodrama.

The Dead Pool (Buddy Van Horn 1988). Clint Eastwood maintains his unflinching facial expression through this *Dirty Harry Part Five* as he stalks the streets of San Francisco's Chinatown looking for trouble. Repetitive rubbish.

Dim Sum (Wayne Wang 1985). Appealing little film about a more-or-less Westernized Chinese family in San Franciso. A treat.

Dirty Harry (Don Siegel 1971). Sleek and exciting sequel-spawning thriller casts Clint Eastwood in epitomical role as neo-fascist San Francisco cop. Morally debatable, technically dynamic.

D.O.A. (Rudolph Mate 1949). Surprisingly involving suspense movie in which Edmond O'Brien tries to discover who poisoned him before he dies. Excellent use of LA and San Francisco locales.

The Enforcer (James Fargo 1976). *Dirty Harry Part Three* finds Clint Eastwood in typically aggressive mood, at odds with the liberal supervisors that want to stop him from killing every teenage delinquent on the streets of San Francisco. The predictability is relieved only slightly by the appearance of Tyne Daly, who plays a female police officer against ridiculous odds.

Escape From Alcatraz (Don Siegel 1979). Tense, well-crafted picture, based on a true story about an attempted escape from the famous prison.

Eye of the Cat (David Lowell Rich 1969). Extravagant horror tale of a man with a cat phobia who goes to stay with his aging aunt who has an army of them. *Psycho*-esque thriller.

Family Plot (Alfred Hitchcock 1976). The master's last film is a lark about stolen jewels, kidnapping, and psychic sleuthing in and around San Francisco.

Fillmore (Richard T. Heffron 1972). Bad rock movie about San Francisco's famous music venue in the last week of its existence. Good footage of the Grateful Dead, Jefferson Airplane, and Boz Scaggs, but Bill Graham's egomaniacal ranting between the acts soon becomes wearying.

Flower Drum Song (Ross Hunter 1961). Patronizing, remorselessly cute Rogers and Hammerstein musical about love dilemmas in San Francisco's Chinatown.

Fog over Frisco (William Dieterle 1934). A very young Bette Davis plays a wayward heiress who is kidnapped in this terse thriller.

48 Hours (Walter Hill 1982). Eddie Murphy puts in a slick comic performance as the criminal side-kick to Nick Nolte's tough-talking cop, who has 48 hours to wrap up a homicide case. Fantastic shots of San Francisco and quick-witted dialogue make this fast-paced comedy-thriller immensely entertaining.

Foul Play (Colin Higgins 1978). Big money, big cast movie with Goldie Hawn making a radical departure from previous films by playing a dizzy blonde next to a similarly petite Dudley Moore in this comedy thriller that entertains thoroughly. Chevy Chase plays a great pot head.

Freebie and the Bean (Richard Rush 1974). Another San Francisco cop movie that tries to be at once achingly funny and disturbingly violent. James Caan does a credible job of playing one half of a wise-cracking duo, but overall it's a cheap, manipulative piece of tat.

The Frisco Kid (Samuel Bischoff 1935). James Cagney stars in this rough and tumble tale of a shanghaied sailor who rises to power amid the riff-raff of 1860s Barbary Coast.

The Frisco Kid (Howard Koch Jr. 1979). Implausible but amusing comedy about a rabbi who befriends an outlaw on his way to San Francisco. Silly and sentimental, it nonetheless has good comic performances from Gene Wilder and Harrison Ford.

Gentleman Jim (Raoul Walsh 1942). Rich evocation of 1880s San Francisco with Eroll Flynn playing the charming, social-climbing boxer, Gentleman Jim Corbett.

Gimme Shelter (David & Albert Maysles/ Charlotte Zwerin 1970). Legendary film about the Rolling Stones concert that features some rock-accompanied violence and lots of shots of Mick Jagger looking bemused about the notorious murder that took place.

Greed (Erich von Stroheim 1924). Legendary, lengthy silent masterpiece based on Frank Norris's *McTeague*, about the squalid, ultimately tragic marriage of a blunt ex-miner with a dental practice on San Francisco's Polk Street, and a simple girl from nearby Oakland. Dated but unforgettable, including the classic finale in Death Valley.

Guess Who's Coming to Dinner (Stanley Kramer 1967). Well-meaning but slightly flat interracial comedy with Spencer Tracy and Katharine Hepburn playing the supposedly liberal but bewildered parents of a woman who brings home the black man (Sidney Poitier) she intends to marry.

Hammett (Wim Wenders 1982). The film that broke Coppola's *Zeotrope* production company, this is a rich tribute to Dashiell Hammett's search for fiction material in the back streets of San Francisco's Chinatown.

Harold and Maude (Hal Ashby 1971). Very funny black comedy about a death-obsessed teenager and the eighty-year-old woman he befriends at various funerals. A bizarre love story with kooky twists, it clarifies very little but manages to entertain thoroughly.

High Anxiety (Mel Brooks 1977). Juvenile but amusing spoof of Hitchcock's San Francisco-based thrillers—*Vertigo*, *The Birds*, and *Spellbound*. Silly story based around a psychologist who works at the Institute for the Very Very Nervous.

I Remember Mama (George Stevens 1948). Sentimental, nostalgic tribute to family life circa 1910 for a group of Norwegian immigrants in San Francisco. Told through the memories of a now successful authoress, who dwells on her tough past and credits it with making her the woman she is. Enjoyable, if shamelessly romanticized, vision of poverty.

Invasion of the Body Snatchers (Phillip Kaufman 1978). Good re-make of the 1956 classic tale of extraterrestrial pod people erupting into and replacing humans.

It Came From Beneath the Sea (Charles Schneer 1955). A giant octopus destroys San Francisco. Feeble monster movie with laughable special effects.

Jimi Plays Berkeley (Peter Pilafian 1971). The historic Memorial Day Jimi Hendrix concert in Berkeley, interspersed with lots of shots of rampaging students waving their peace signs. Hendrix ignores the peripheral action and just plays.

The Killer Elite (Sam Peckinpah 1975). Familiar themes of betrayal and trust in this mostly straightforward action flick, built around the internal politics of an underground San Francisco company and a wounded agent (James Caan) who seeks revenge. Excellent set-pieces include a Chinatown shoot-out and siege.

The Lady from Shanghai (Orson Welles 1948). Orson Welles and Rita Hayworth star in this twisted and impossible plot about murder, mystery and sexual unease on board a cruise ship. Compelling, if rambling account of the relationship between a clever young man and beautiful older woman.

The Laughing Policeman (Stuart Rosenberg 1973). Walter Matthau and Bruce Dern pair up in yet another brutal San Francisco cop thriller, triggered off by a busload of people being gunned down in the Mission district. Queasy use of gay characters.

The Lenny Bruce Performance Film (John Magnuson 1967). A historical document of Lenny Bruce's penultimate performance at San Francisco's Basin Street West Club, one of the few places he was still allowed to perform, during his lengthy obscenity trial. The film catches Bruce at his maniacal and scalding best, though the excerpts from his trial, which he reads obsessively, get to be exhausting.

The Lineup (Frank Cooper 1958). Film adaptation of the TV series *San Francisco Beat*, about the SFPD capturing a junkie-gunman. An unconvincing plot, but polished acting and fantastic shots of San Francisco.

Magnum Force (Ted Post 1973). Sequel to *Dirty Harry*, with more shots of Clint Eastwood looking tough and San Francisco looking spectacular, though the storyline detailing Harry's rejection of vigilante policing methods is pathetically unbelievable.

The Maltese Falcon (John Huston 1941). Humphrey Bogart is San Francisco private dick Sam Spade in this candidate for best detective movie ever made. Diamond-hard and near perfection.

Out of the Past (Jacques Tourneur 1947). Definitive flashback *film noir* starring Robert Mitchum who has a rendezvous with death and his own past in the shape of Jane Greer. Beautiful and bewildering.

Pal Joey (Fred Kohlmar 1957). Frank Sinatra, Rita Hayworth and Kim Novak star in this slick musical about a lovable cad and rising night-club entertainer. Begins well, but slides alarmingly into cheap sentiment.

Petulia (Richard Lester 1968). San Francisco surgeon George C. Scott takes up with unhappily married kook Julie Christie in richly detailed, deliberately fragmentary comedy drama set in druggy, decadent society.

Play it Again Sam (Herbert Ross 1972). Woody Allen as (what else?) neurotic San Francisco film critic who has an affair with his best friend's wife, Diane Keaton.

Point Blank (John Boorman 1967). Lee Marvin plays a double-crossed gangster out for revenge on his cheating partner. Stands up well as a violent gang thriller, with good location shots of LA and San Francisco, but occasionally over-reaches itself. Angie Dickinson plays a convincingly faithless wife.

The Presidio (Peter Hyams 1988). Crime thriller about a couple of ill-matched cops investigating the murder of a military police-woman. Sean Connery plays a by-the-book army man with conviction, but the story falls embarrassingly apart with inept handling of romance and father/daughter conflicts.

Psych Out (Richard Rush 1968). Pumped out quickly to capitalize on the "Summer of Love." Good performances from Jack Nicholson and Bruce Dern can't save what is basically a compendium of every hippy cliché in the book. Didn't stop it from quickly becoming a cult movie, though.

San Francisco (W.S. Van Dyke 1936). Elaborate, entertaining hokum about a Barbary Coast love triangle circa 1906. The script is upstaged by the climactic earthquake sequence.

Shoot the Moon (Alan Parker 1981). Albert Finney and Diane Keaton star in this strained tale of self-obsessed Marin County trauma and heartbreak. About as affecting as an episode of *Dallas*.

Star Trek IV — The Voyage Home (Leonard Nimoy, 1986). Morality crusaders Kirk & Co are back in San Francisco to save the whales in what is the best of the *Star Trek* series of films so far.

The Times of Harvey Milk (Robert Epstein 1984). Exemplary feature-length documentary about America's first openly gay politician, chronicles his career in San Francisco and the aftermath of his 1978 assassination.

They Call Me Mister Tibbs (Gordon Douglas 1970). Sidney Poitier plays Virgil Tibbs, the black San Francisco cop who sleuths his way to unraveling a murder mystery. Benign thriller.

Time After Time (Nicholas Meyer 1979). Courtesy of the Time Machine, Malcolm McDowell chases Jack the Ripper into twentieth-century San Francisco accompanied by a lot of cheap jokes and violence.

Towering Inferno (Irwin Allen 1974). Disaster film that opened the door for a whole decade of banal catastrophes, this one telling the tale of how the world's tallest building is destroyed by fire on the night of its inauguration. Verging on the ridiculous but saved by great special effects and a cast of stars that includes Steve McQueen, Paul Newman, Faye Dunaway, and Fred Astaire.

Vertigo (Alfred Hitchcock 1958). A tragedy of obsession, stunningly set in San Francisco, in which detective (and lonely voyeur) James Stewart tracks down the long-dead Madeleine played by Kim Novak. Perhaps Hitchcock's most personal and psychologically revealing work.

What's Up Doc? (Peter Bogdanovich 1972). Wildly likable screwball comedy pastiche, set in San Francisco and starring Barbra Streisand and Ryan O'Neal as a cook and a naive professor.

GLOSSARY OF SAN FRANCISCO PEOPLE

AGNOS Art San Francisco's current mayor, elected on a liberal platform in 1987 when Diane Feinstein stepped down to pursue a state political career.

BIERCE Ambrose Came to San Francisco on an army posting, where he began his literary career as a journalist and went on to become the *San Francisco Examiner*'s most satirical and witty staff writer. Spent his old age writing ghost and detective stories, gathered together in his *Collected Works*.

BRANNAN Sam Founded a Mormon colony in the early years of the city and started San Francisco's first newspaper, *The California Star*. Most famous, however, for being the man who brought the news of the discovery of gold in the Sierras, Brannan made a fortune in real estate before drinking his way into poverty and spending his last years alone and forgotten in Escondido, San Diego.

BRIDGES Harry Inspired by Jack London's fiction to leave his native Australia and come to San Francisco to work on sailing vessels, Bridges went on to become the militant leader of the International Longshoremen's Association, a career which brought him disciples and enemies in equal numbers as he led his union through major battles with the Pacific Coast shipowners in 1934 and again in 1971 when he came out of retirement on behalf of his longshoremen. A genuine working-class hero.

BROWER David California-born conservationist, Brower was long-time Director of the Sierra Club (1952–1969) and went on to help found Friends of the Earth.

BROWN Arthur (1874-1957). Oakland-born architect, he built San Francisco's City Hall and Coit Tower.

BROWN Willy San Francisco's flamboyant and outspoken black Democrat politician, who has climbed the political ladder very quickly and was Jessie Jackson's campaign manager in the 1988 presidential race.

BRUBECK Dave Oakland-born pianist and jazz composer, Brubeck brought attention to so-called West Coast Jazz, achieving international celebrity status for himself as a jazz musician along the way.

BRUNDAGE Avery Michigan-born engineer, Brundage went on to become the president of the International Olympic Committee, but he is most famous for his enormous collection of Oriental art, donated to San Francisco's de Young Musem and now known as the Asian Art Museum.

BURNHAM Daniel Chicago architect who was invited by San Franciso's mayor, James D. Phelan, to plan the city's development in the early twentieth century, giving rise to the Beaux Arts complex of Civic Center—though this was in fact only a small part of his ambitious scheme.

CAEN Herb San Francisco's most prominent columnist, Caen has been writing for the *San Francisco Chronicle* since the year dot. Though a touch overrated, he occasionally digs up good dirt on San Francisco's more prominent society figures. Worth reading for the indiscreet gossip.

COIT Lillie Came to San Francisco as a child and reared in the best social circles, she was known for her unusual behavior. Married briefly to Howard Coit, on her death she left $100,000 to the city in order to build Coit Tower, Telegraph Hill's principal landmark, as a memorial to San Francisco's volunteer firefighters.

COOLBRITH Ina San Francisco poet who introduced Jack London to literature when working for the Oakland Public Library. Her poems are collected in the books *Singer of the Sea*, *A Perfect Day*, and *Songs of the Golden Gate*. In recognition of her organization of the World Congress of Authors for the Panama Pacific Exhibition in 1915, the legislature made her the state's first Poet Laureate.

COPPOLA Francis Ford San Francisco-based filmmaker, whose works include *Apocalypse Now*, *The Conversation*, and *One from the Heart*. He still lives in the city and is the owner of the Columbus Tower in North Beach.

DI MAGGIO Joe Began his baseball career in 1932 with the San Francisco Seals and went on to stardom as centerfielder with the New York Yankees. Married Marilyn Monroe in the 1950s.

FEINSTEIN Diane Ex-San Francisco mayor who stepped in when George Moscone and Harvey Milk were assassinated and is currently tipped to be the next Democratic governor of California. Very much the career politician, rumors abound about her dealings with the big business corporations in the late 1970s that led to massive development in San Francisco's Financial District.

FERLINGHETTI Lawrence Founder and still owner of the *City Lights Bookstore*, America's first paperback bookstore, Ferlinghetti became a prominent figure during the Beat movement of the 1950s and had close links with its major figures.

GARCIA Jerry Lead guitarist and vocalist for psychedelic rock gods, the Grateful Dead.

GINSBERG Allen Though born in New Jersey, Ginsberg is associated with San Francisco because of the controversial Beat poem *Howl*, which he wrote in North Beach.

GRAHAM Bill Rock music impresario Graham can in part be credited with the success of psychedelic music, which he promoted through the concerts he staged at the famous Fillmore Auditorium. Still the biggest concert promoter on the West Coast.

HALLIDIE Andrew English-born engineer who emigrated to California in the nineteenth century to work in the Comstock mines, in 1873 he invented the universally loved cable car, which made traveling over San Francisco's ridiculous gradients possible.

HAMMETT Dashiell Hammett traveled to San Francisco as a young man and worked for the Pinkerton Detective Agency, drawing on his experience of the city and the cases he dealt with to write the hard-boiled detective stories that inspired Raymond Chandler and others. His most famous works include *The Maltese Falcon* and *The Thin Man*. In his later years, Hammett was involved in the Hollywood Ten McCarthy witchhunts concerning allegedly un-American activities, and was sent to prison for refusing to testify.

HEARST William Randolph Publishing magnate who as a young man worked on the *San Francisco Examiner* and went on to acquire a string of successful daily newspapers, motion picture companies, and radio stations; he later served briefly as a congressman in New York. Famous for his lavish lifestyle and the incredi-

ble Hearst Castle at San Simeon, south of the city. Orson Welles was inspired by Hearst to make the classic film loosely based on his life, *Citizen Kane*.

HOBART Lewis P. Missouri-born architect, who came to study at the University of California and went on to design the Bohemian Club, Grace Cathedral, and the Steinhart Aquarium.

JOPLIN Janis Texas-born Joplin came to San Francisco at the age of eighteen, where she began her singing career with *Big Brother and the Holding Company*. A central figure in the psychedelic scene, her problem was not LSD but booze and heroin, an overdose of which finally killed her in 1970.

KEROUAC Jack A leading figure of the Beat movement in New York, Kerouac came out to San Francisco in the 1950s, where he drew on his experiences to write the Beats' bible *On The Road*. Spent much of his life returning to stay with his mother in Massachussetts and eventually drank himself into an early grave at the age of 46.

KESEY Ken Oregon-reared Kesey enrolled in a creative writing program at Stanford University, during which time he became involved with psychiatric experiments with LSD— experiences which inspired him to write *One Flew Over the Cuckoo's Nest*. Important, too, for his involvement in San Francisco's psyche-delic scene, Kesey toured the country with his busload of Merry Pranksters in the late Sixties, a time richly chronicled in Tom Wolfe's *Electric Kool-Aid Acid Test*.

LONDON Jack London was an illegitimate child who grew up largely without any formal education, but read books compulsively, a habit that was later to serve him well when he began his prolific writing career that produced *The Call of the Wild*.

MAYBECK Bernard Early modern architect responsible for some of the most beautiful buildings in the Bay Area, the most famous of which was his magnificent Palace of Fine Arts for the Panama Pacific Exhibition in 1915.

MIEGGS Henry Mieggs came to San Francisco at the beginning of the Gold Rush and made a small fortune, carrying lumber from upstate New York, and going on to become a civic leader and build Mieggs Wharf—today's Fisherman's Wharf. Later in life he was involved in a scandal concerning forged city treasury warrants and fled to South America.

MILK Harvey San Francisco's (and perhaps the world's) first openly gay politician, Milk played a key role in the gay emancipation of the 1970s, only to be assassinated at the height of his career and popularity by political rival, Dan White.

MOONEY Tom Radical Socialist labor leader, charged with planting the bomb that killed ten people during a Preparedness Day Parade on San Francisco's Market Street in 1916. He was sentenced to hang for the killings, but the justice of his conviction became a *cause célèbre* for years and in 1939 he was pardoned.

MONTGOMERY John B. Nineteenth-century naval captain in command of the *Portsmouth* during the Mexican War, who occupied San Francisco in 1846 and raised the American flag on the plaza that was the one-time waterfront.

MOSCONE George San Francisco's liberal mayor who was assassinated along with Harvey Milk in 1978.

NORRIS Frank (1870–1902). Highly respected writer, he studied at the University of California and went on to produce acclaimed works such as *McTeague*, *The Octopus*, and *The Pit*.

NORRIS Joshua Abraham "Emperor" London-born Norton came to be known as Emperor Norton after declaring himself "Norton I, Emperor of the United States"—a claim that was no doubt symptomatic of the insanity provoked by his bankruptcy in the rice market. He comported himself regally around San Francisco wearing a military suit and sword, usually accompanied by his two dogs, Bummer and Lazarus. His "loyal subjects" received him sympathetically and were tolerant of his various proclamations and commands, the most famous of which was a plan to build a bridge across the bay. Upon his death, the city conducted a formal civic funeral in honor of his services to the city.

POLK Willis (1865–1924). An architect, he came to San Francisco as a young man and became involved with a bohemian group known as Les Jeunes. He also headed Daniel Burnham's San Francisco office and worked on his city plan. Known for his elegant brown shingle designs.

SANTANA Carlos San Francisco-based guitar virtuoso renowned for his blending of Latin rhythms into pop music.

STANFORD Leland Made his fortune as one of the Big Four who constructed the Central Pacific Railroad. During a two-year term as governor he was a staunch union supporter, although he is perhaps best known now for the creation of the university in Palo Alto that bears his name.

SUTRO Adolph Prussian-born philanthropist who came to San Francisco and made his fortune in the Comstock silver bonanza. Heavy investment in San Francisco real estate led to him owning almost a twelfth of the entire city, to which he donated many developments, including the Cliff House, Sutro Baths, and the Sutro Library.

TWAIN Mark Spent his early years in native Missouri before embarking on a journalistic career that brought him to San Francisco in 1864. A regular contributor to such publications as *The Golden Era*, *Californian*, and *Territorial Enterprise*, he gained his biggest popularity after writing *Roughing It*, telling exaggerated tales of adventures in the Comstock mining era.

WHITE Dan The murderer of Harvey Milk and George Moscone, White was a disgruntled ex-policeman and city Supervisor whose trial came to be known as the "Twinkie Defense" after his lawyer claimed that White was suffering from temporary insanity caused by harmful additives in fast food. After serving a controversially brief five-year sentence, White was released and committed suicide several months later.

INDEX

HELP US UPDATE

We've gone to a lot of effort to ensure that this first edition of *San Francisco: The Real Guide* is completely up-to-date and accurate. However, things do change—places get "discovered," transportation details alter, restaurants and hotels close down or get renamed—and any suggestions, comments or corrections would be much appreciated.

We'll credit all contributions, and send a copy of the next edition (or any other Real Guide if you prefer) for the best letters. Please write to:

Deborah Bosley and Jamie Jensen, The Real Guides, Prentice Hall Trade Division, 15 Columbus Circle, New York, NY 10023.